59-642   orders 4/28/79

THE UNITED NATIONS

BY LELAND M. GOODRICH

*Charter of the United Nations: Commentary
and Documents* (WITH EDVARD HAMBRO), rev. 1949

*The United Nations and the Maintenance
of International Peace and Security*
(WITH ANNE P. SIMONS), 1955

*Korea: A Study of U.S. Policy in
the United Nations,* 1956

The United Nations, 1959

The
UNITED
NATIONS

Leland M. Goodrich

COLUMBIA UNIVERSITY

THOMAS Y. CROWELL COMPANY

New York · Established 1834

Manufactured in the United States of America
By the Vail-Ballou Press, Inc., Binghamton, N.Y.

Library of Congress Catalog Card Number 59-6442

PREFACE

THIS IS PRIMARILY a book on the United Nations. It is not intended to cover the whole field of international organization and therefore the reader should not expect to find any extended treatment of inter-governmental organizations and agencies, whether global or regional, that are not part of the United Nations system.

I have been prompted to write this book by the belief that there is a place for an analysis and evaluation of the United Nations which will not only meet the needs of undergraduates in courses in international relations but also be of some interest and value to all who wish to gain some understanding of what the United Nations is, what it has done, and what its role is to be in the troubled world in which we live.

There is a tendency on the part of those who write and speak on international relations to fall into two rather extreme attitudes toward the United Nations. On the one hand, there are those who follow in the footsteps of the internationalists and League of Nations advocates of the 'twenties and look upon the United Nations with excessive optimism, failing to see its practical limitations and the magnitude of the difficulties which stand in its way. On the other hand, there are those who go to the other extreme of viewing the United Nations as a factor of little or no constructive usefulness in a world of competing national interests and power rivalries, and who see real danger in taking the organization too seriously.

In this study I have sought to combine realism with idealism. We cannot deny, I think, the significance of the purposes and principles of the United Nations. These are commitments of all its Members which no one of them cares to disavow. It is equally important to examine how the structure, functions, and procedures of the Organization are related to these purposes and principles, and what concessions are made in practice to the requirements of power politics and national interest. It is necessary to understand the limitations of the United Nations, both those resulting from its lack of power and those resulting from the

v

world political situation. Much of the current disillusionment has been the result of over-selling the Organization, leading people to expect results beyond its true capacity. It is necessary to see the future of the United Nations in the right perspective and to realize that its goals can only be realized in substantial measure after long and untiring effort. The practical alternative to the United Nations today is not a stronger and more efficient world organization, but none at all.

There are many acknowledgements of help received that I should make: to the Brookings Institution in Washington for the opportunity to participate in their United Nations studies which has helped me greatly in the preparation of this book; to my students at Columbia who in seminars and lecture courses have helped me to develop my own thinking about the United Nations; to members of the United Nations Secretariat and others who have participated officially in the work of the Organization, who have been helpful in many ways, especially in providing material for tables and charts; to Miss Gabriella Rosner who has ably helped me as research assistant the past two years; to the Rockefeller Foundation for assistance available under a grant to Columbia in support of a research program in international organization; to Schuyler C. Wallace for encouragement and sympathetic interest and more specifically for relieving me of some teaching responsibilities to give me more time to write; and finally to my wife whose constant encouragement and willingness to put up with my preoccupations have made this book possible.

LELAND M. GOODRICH

Columbia University

CONTENTS

Chapter **I**

INTERNATIONAL ORGANIZATION IN THE MODERN WORLD

A VISITOR from Mars might be greatly impressed by the degree of Earth-man's control over nature—on the assumption of course that Martians had not equalled our scientific achievements. But if he were a rational human being, he would be greatly puzzled by the inadequacy of our political and social institutions and concepts for dealing with the problems which have been created by our scientific advances. If we think in terms of our knowledge of the earth, the extent to which we are technically capable of developing and using its resources to meet human needs, the facility and speed with which people can travel and communicate with each other, and the number of our common concerns, Wendell Willkie's "One World" makes a great deal of sense. It seems to describe quite accurately the fact of human involvement and the limits of the common concerns of mankind. But if we look at the political and social arrangements under which people live together and seek to deal with their common affairs, "One World" ceases to be a reality, and becomes a myth, or at best a goal to be realized in the distant future.

How explain this contradiction? There would probably be considerable difficulty in finding any explanation which would be fully satisfactory to everyone who has given the matter serious thought. Nevertheless, one point would seem to be reasonably clear. In dealing with his physical environment, man has shown a capacity for imaginative, logical, and constructive thought and action which he has not dis-

1

played in ordering his relations with his fellow man. This is perhaps not surprising if we stop to realize that man's conduct in his relations with other men is frequently determined by wholly irrational forces, that the relations of man to man are not capable of being determined with the scientific exactitude of those of matter to matter. Since man is, to some extent, he would like to think, the master of his own destiny, he must also pay the price of his follies.

The World of States

Geologists do not agree on the age of the earth nor do anthropologists agree on how long man has been on it. In either case, however, the span of time involved is beyond human comprehension. Archaeologists have succeeded in pushing the record of human culture beyond 3000 B.C., but for the historian the record remains quite incomplete for many centuries. For as long as we have historical records, the story has been that of the rise and fall of civilizations. In the long perspective of recorded history, the social order which we know today is of quite recent origin. There is little reason to believe that it will be more enduring than its predecessors, particularly if it fails to reduce its inner tensions and adapt its social institutions and attitudes to the needs of survival.

From the point of view of social organization, what is perhaps most distinctive of the world of the twentieth century is its excessive fragmentation. We live on a planet which can be encircled in less time than it took, in 1789, to go from New York to Philadelphia. Every part of it is dependent in some respect or other on every other part. The very existence of life itself in any part can be endangered by the explosion of atomic devices anywhere. And yet the people of the world are politically organized into some eighty-odd sovereign states with more to come, each claiming to be treated as the sovereign equal of every other, and each claiming the right to determine its own domestic and foreign policies, often without regard to the wishes or concerns of others.

This kind of political fragmentation—this division of peoples into independent political units—is not the necessary expression of man's political nature. It was not true of the period of the Roman Empire. It was not characteristic of Europe during the Middle Ages when the Roman Catholic Church and the Holy Roman Empire were able between them to keep alive the idea of the essential unity of the world. The break-up of this unity into independent political entities was not a sudden process, nor did it occur simultaneously in all parts of Europe. It acquired momentum in the seventeenth century religious wars. It was associated with the revival of Greek philosophy and Roman law and the Protestant challenge to the Roman Catholic Church. It came with a great upsurge of human curiosity which found expression in the exploration of the physical world as well as the world of ideas and beliefs. It appeared to represent progress at the time, and was probably a necessary condition to the great advances that were subsequently made in man's mastery of nature, and in the improvement of the conditions of human life. Nevertheless, it has left us with a heritage of political institutions and attitudes which have in important respects ceased to be adequate to the needs of the world today.

Beginnings of International Organization

The existence of interests common to the peoples and governments of various states and requiring some concerted action on the part of these governments was recognized from the moment of the emergence of the modern state system. It is, therefore, not surprising that the Thirty Years' War (1618–1648) which marked, according to leading historians, the birth of the modern state system also witnessed the publication of the first systematic treatise on international law. Hugo Grotius' *De Jure Belli et Pacis* was an important landmark in the development of a body of rules and principles which sovereign states would accept as binding upon them in their relations with each other. Before this time, however, the rulers, first of the Italian city states and then of the emerging states of Western Europe, saw both the necessity of sending diplomatic representatives to foreign courts and the advantage of according certain privileges and immunities to such representatives on the basis of mutuality. While philosophers and jurists contributed greatly to the initial development of international law, its acceptance by sovereign rulers was basically due to their recognition of the fact that they could not live together without their relations being regulated to some extent by agreed rules and principles.[1]

In particular, these rules and principles were necessary to the orderly conduct of non-hostile relations. A good example of the inconvenience and chaos resulting from the absence of such rules is provided by the Congress of Westphalia (1642–1648). The settlement of the so-called Thirty Years' War was delayed for years because of

[1] See Arthur Nussbaum, *A Concise History of the Law of Nations,* rev. ed. (New York: The Macmillan Company, 1954).

haggling over procedural details which at later conferences were easily settled on the basis of agreed principles.

During the seventeenth and the greater part of the eighteenth century, European politics were dominated by the concerns of dynastic rulers. Within state frontiers, absolute monarchs, such as Louis XIV of France and Frederick the Great of Prussia, enforced order, administered justice, levied taxes and performed the services which it pleased the rulers to perform. The relations between states were primarily the relations between rulers and were conducted by methods of secret diplomacy. The increase of the wealth and power of the monarch was the chief object of policy; public welfare and opinion were at best of secondary importance. The Industrial and the French Revolutions changed all this. They unleashed forces which on the one hand radically increased both the responsiveness of governments to peoples and the interdependence of states; and on the other, created attitudes and movements which were to make more difficult the adaptation of political institutions and methods to the needs of growing interdependence.

Nationalism and Internationalism

The French Revolution marked the emergence of nationalism as a dominant force in the world. Up until this time, sovereign states had existed and people had been aware of belonging to distinct cultural groups, but now for the first time loyalty to the state and national consciousness were combined in a force which was to revolutionize the world.[2] The emergence of nationalism was coexistent with the emergence of democracy. In a sense nationalism became the cement holding together a people no longer subjected to the rule of an absolute monarch. Loyalty to the ideal or reality of the national state, i.e., the state consisting of a unified cultural group, became the most potent force of the nineteenth and twentieth centuries.[3] Even though communism has within the past few decades seemed a potentially more powerful influence, recent events suggest that even communism must yield to nationalism in the strength and ubiquity of its appeal.

[2] See C. J. H. Hayes, *Essays on Nationalism* (New York: The Macmillan Company, 1926).

[3] On the nature and historical development of nationalism, see Hans Kohn, *The Idea of Nationalism* (New York: The Macmillan Company, 1944); C. J. H. Hayes, *The Historical Evolution of Modern Nationalism* (New York: Richard R. Smith, 1931); and Alfred Cobban, *National Self-Determination* (New York: Oxford University Press, Inc., 1945).

The strength and pervasiveness of the appeal of nationalism are particularly apparent when we look at the changes that have taken place in the political map of the world within the past century and a half. These changes have been particularly significant in Europe. In two instances, Italy and Germany, the effect of nationalism was to reduce substantially the number of independent political entities by merging existing states composed of peoples of common language and culture into larger national states. In the majority of cases, however, the effect of nationalism was to increase the numbers of states by dividing multi-national states into smaller national units. Thus the Netherlands, as territorially defined at Vienna in 1815, became the states of Belgium and the Netherlands as the result of the revolution of 1830 and the recognition of the independence of Belgium by the Great Powers in 1839. Through successive acts of partial liquidation—by revolution, war, and great power decisions—the Ottoman Empire was gradually dismembered and replaced by the independent states of Greece, Bulgaria, Romania, Yugoslavia, Albania, and Turkey. Finally, as the result of war and revolution, the Austro-Hungarian Empire was dissolved and the Russian Empire transformed, with the result that after the First World War the map of Europe showed the new states of Austria, Hungary, Czechoslovakia, Poland, Finland, Estonia, Latvia, and Lithuania, not to mention important changes in the boundaries of existing states.

The Second World War released and encouraged nationalist forces in Asia and Africa, which were shortly to produce changes in the political map as great and as significant in their consequences as those which had taken place in Europe during the earlier period. As the result of the dissolution of the Italian and Japanese Empires, and the transformation and disintegration of the British, French, and Dutch colonial empires, there has occurred not only a substantial increase in the number of independent national states but also a relative increase in the number of Asian and African states.[4]

But while nationalism has accentuated the political fragmentation of the world and in particular has increased the number of independent states, the industrial and technological advances resulting from the Industrial Revolution have increased the interdependence of the various parts of the world and made existing political arrangements and current attitudes increasingly anachronistic. Though governments under the influence of nationalism tended to emphasize independence and national

[4] Whereas only 10 of the 63 states which at one time or another were members of the League of Nations were Asian or African states, of the 82 states that were members of the United Nations at the end of 1957, 31 were Asian or African.

exclusiveness, under the compulsions of day-to-day life they found it necessary to develop systematic and regularized procedures and agencies for dealing with their common concerns. Furthermore, as the consequences of war became more serious to contemplate, the common interest in preserving peace provided a basis for organized cooperation. These developments we will now consider in greater detail.

The inventions and technological advances of the late eighteenth and the nineteenth centuries greatly increased the economic, social, and cultural interdependence of peoples who at the same time were engaged in creating new and more numerous political boundaries. As the result of revolutionary changes in methods of production, e.g., the use of water power and steam to operate improved machines, some countries, notably Great Britain, developed much greater efficiency than others in the production of manufactured goods. These countries came to see an advantage in concentrating on manufacturing while they imported foodstuffs that they had hitherto produced and raw materials of which they had increasing need. As the result of such a division of labor, accompanied by the growth of individual consumption, foreign trade became increasingly important for many states and the conditions under which it was carried on became a matter of common concern to many nations.

Along with improvements in the methods of production came a revolutionary increase in the speed and physical facility of travel, transportation, and communication. The increase in international trade and in the number of people who travelled, and the increased contacts between peoples across national boundary lines, made it difficult for governments to provide needed facilities and to perform necessary regulatory functions by wholly independent action. Thus, for example, it became clear by the 1860's that independently operated national postal services were completely inadequate to meet the needs of the time. At the Berne Conference of 1874, the leading national postal administrations agreed to establish what later came to be known as the Universal Postal Union; a workable basis for international postal service was created. Even before this time, in 1865, governments had discovered that the invention and development of the telegraph created problems which could be satisfactorily handled only through an international organization, the International Telegraphic Union.

The increased facility and speed of travel and transport across national frontiers and water barriers helped to complicate and make more difficult the performance of recognized police functions, particularly the exercise of controls in the interest of safety, health, and good morals. The speeding up of transportation by substituting steam propulsion for sail meant that in many situations the established methods used by governments to protect their citizens against epidemics and diseases brought in from abroad were quite inadequate. Cooperation between governments in providing information and establishing controls became necessary. The effective regulation of traffic in narcotics was not possible so long as individual governments were forced to rely on their own independent action. The safety of life at sea obviously required for maximum effectiveness the cooperation of governments in establishing and enforcing agreed standards.[5]

Striking evidence of the interdependence of the peoples of the world is found in the remarkable flowering during the nineteenth and twentieth centuries of private international organizations formed and operating across national frontiers. Such organizations have become an important part of the world's economic, financial, social, cultural, and intellectual life. They demonstrate that while people are banded together in national states they find it necessary, in order to provide adequate satisfaction for certain needs, to participate in a variety of private, non-governmental, international organizations. These organizations, in addition to helping satisfy individual needs which governments do not meet, have provided strong and effective support for various efforts to develop organized international cooperation at the governmental level.[6]

The growth of economic and social interdependence and recognition that certain common human needs can only be met by organized intergovernmental cooperation have brought some modification or alleviation of the excessive tendency toward world political fragmentation. Still, it must be recognized that (1) the growing belief that war would result from unrestrained competition of nation states, and (2) fear of the economic and social consequences of war, have chiefly motivated efforts to organize international political relations on an orderly and stable basis.

Before the First World War, the need for some limitation of the right of governments to engage in war and for constructive cooperation between governments in the larger interest of peace and stability was recognized. However, the legitimacy of the use of war as an instrument of national policy was admitted in principle. Efforts made to outlaw war

[5] For detailed accounts of the development of international technical cooperation, see Leonard Woolf, *International Government* (London: George Allen & Unwin, Ltd., 1916), pp. 153–265, and Paul S. Reinsch, *Public International Unions,* 2nd ed. (Boston: World Peace Foundation, 1916).

[6] See Lyman C. White, *International Non-Governmental Organizations* (New Brunswick: Rutgers University Press, 1951).

were partial and marginal in character. One of the conventions drafted and approved at the Second Hague Conference of 1907 outlawed the use of armed force in the collection of contract debts. For the most part, however, the international law and practice of the time assumed the legality of war and concentrated rather on reducing the occasions for its use and regulating the manner of its employment. During the nineteenth century, the use of arbitration for the settlement of certain kinds of disputes became increasingly common. In addition, the major powers of Europe, recognizing a common interest in the preservation of peace, cooperated effectively in many instances to keep war from breaking out or spreading as the result of incidents in such sensitive areas as the Balkans.[7] The relative success of the major powers in preventing wars or in localizing conflicts, taken together with the growing costs and destructiveness of war, convinced many people that a general European or World War was impossible, or if possible, must be of short duration.

The First World War and the Establishment of the League

Any belief that recognition of the economic consequences would keep nationalist rivalries from engulfing the world in war was destroyed, however, by the events of the late summer and fall of 1914, and the years that followed. It had to be recognized not only that war was a possibility, but also that it could assume world-wide proportions and be sustained over a comparatively long period of time, regardless of cost and destructiveness. It was recognized that man's capacity for manipulation and planning had to be turned to the task of arranging relations between peoples and states so that war would be less likely to occur in the future, and if it occurred would be suppressed by the joint forces of those committed to the maintenance of peace. This point of view found strong support in the programs of various private organizations such as the League to Enforce Peace. President Wilson was an eloquent and effective exponent of this view and was instrumental in getting it translated into working international arrangements at the end of the First World War.

The League of Nations was founded with the horror and destruction of war still vivid experiences. Had it not been for President Wil-

[7] On the work of the European Concert, see Woolf, *op. cit.,* pp. 24–63; and Robert B. Mowat, *The Concert of Europe* (New York: The Macmillan Company, 1931).

son's insistence that the League Covenant be made an integral part of the peace settlement, that advantage be taken of the willingness of war-weary peoples and governments to accept some limitation of national sovereignties in order to preserve peace, it is quite unlikely that any League of Nations would have been established.

A number of factors influenced the nature of the League. In the first place, though the war constituted a revolutionary situation permitting statesmen to embark on radical courses of action, there was no inclination on the part of the statesmen at Paris, nor was it indeed possible, to break completely with the past. The new organization, revolutionary though it might be in the sweep of its conception and many of its details, was therefore constructed to a large extent along lines dictated by past experience. Many of the concepts, institutions, and practices of the preceding century—the recognition of a body of international law, the international conference, the concert of great powers, arbitration, the public international union, the recognition of a general interest in peace—were taken over and incorporated into the new document. While imaginative thinking and constructive statesmanship made important contributions through the introduction of new ideas, the further development of old practices, and the integration of old and new elements into a world system, it would be entirely erroneous to view the League as something wholly or even largely created out of whole cloth.[8]

Furthermore, the nature of the League was profoundly influenced by the world situation existing at the time it was established. Unfortunately, perhaps, the conditions which were favorable to the establishment of the League were also such as to encourage the creation of a particular kind of League, one well adapted to promoting the interests of the victors. While the association of the League with the peace settlement helped to assure its coming into being, and made certain that it would have important work to do in the years immediately ahead, it also meant that at least initially the League was preeminently a league of victor nations and that its character in practice, would largely be determined by their special interests and concerns. Thus, from the beginning, the League was viewed by France and certain other European states primarily as a means of keeping defeated Germany from again becoming a threat to their security. Consequently, we find in the discussions of the League from the beginning, a constant emphasis on the security function of the League. Its potential creative role in bringing

[8] See Alfred O. Zimmern, *The League of Nations and the Rule of Law, 1918–1935* (London: Macmillan and Company, Ltd., 1936), pp. 1–274.

about adjustments in international relations which would make the established legal order more acceptable, and therefore provide a more substantial basis for peace and security, was neglected.

The Nature of the League

The League of the Covenant was a voluntary association of states that had as its primary purpose the maintenance of international peace and security on the basis of law and justice. But it was also to be a means of promoting international cooperation in dealing with a variety of problems not directly and immediately related to peace. Thus, quite explicitly, though not in as great detail as does the Charter of the United Nations, the Covenant recognized the need for organized international cooperation to create conditions of economic stability and well-being; to combat recognized social evils; to encourage cultural and intellectual exchanges; and to further the development of dependent peoples (at least some of them). In sum, the Covenant recognized that it was not enough to deal with disputes and threatening political situations as they arose or to seek the limitation of national armaments or the strengthening of arrangements for peaceful settlement or collective security; it was also necessary to create world-wide economic, social, and political conditions which would be favorable to peace and which would make it undesirable and unnecessary for governments to embark on policies and courses of action which would create the danger of violent conflict.

To achieve these purposes, the members of the League were required to assume certain obligations toward each other. They undertook to respect and guarantee the territorial integrity and political independence of each member. They agreed to submit their disputes to peaceful procedures of settlement or adjustment. They undertook not to resort to war in violation of their obligations under the Covenant. They agreed to apply sweeping economic and financial measures against any state doing this. They recognized that the maintenance of peace required the reduction of national armaments. They assumed certain broad commitments with respect to their economic and social policies. Generally speaking, however, these commitments left wide discretion in their implementation. The creation of permanent machinery to assist in the implementation of the purposes and principles was desirable, indeed necessary.

Since the League was an organization of states, its membership was from the beginning a matter of the greatest importance; only members were under the obligation to respect its principles and to cooperate in achieving its purposes. While the authors of the Covenant did not intend that the League should be universal initially and established certain conditions that states, applicants for membership, had to satisfy, it was their hope that the organization soon would become universal. This hope, however, was never realized. At one time or another 63 states were members of the League, but at no one time were there more than 58 members. The United States and Hejaz (after 1932, part of Saudi Arabia) never joined. Germany did not become a member until 1926, and the Soviet Union not until 1934. Japan, Germany, and Italy withdrew in the thirties in protest against League acts or failures to act of which they did not approve. Fundamentally, however, it was the failure of the United States to join which brought into question from the beginning the adequacy of the League for achieving the purposes set forth in the Covenant.[9]

To achieve the League's purposes, the Covenant provided for the establishment of permanent organs with defined functions and powers and agreed rules of procedure. These organs, speaking generally, were developments of methods and procedures that had been utilized with considerable frequency and success during the nineteenth century. The Assembly, in the words of the Covenant, was declared competent to "deal at its meetings with any matter within the sphere of action of the League or effecting the peace of the world." In addition, the Assembly was to have a number of more specific functions, including the election of non-permanent members of the Council; the election of judges of the Permanent Court of International Justice, concurrently with the Council; the control of League finances; the review of the activities of the League; the admission of new members; and the initiation of Covenant amendments.

In practice, the Assembly assumed many of the functions of a popular legislative body. Based as it was on the principle that each member should have equal representation and equal voting power, the Assembly was the organ in which both the views of great and small states found expression. It was a forum for debate and discussion where issues could be elucidated, opinions expressed, and general agreements developed, often expressed in the form of resolutions. By virtue of its powers of discussion and recommendation and the control which it had over finances, it was the means for regularly reviewing the League's work and pointing the directions in which the work should develop.

If the Assembly could with a little imagination be viewed as the popular legislative organ of the League, the Council could, with similar

[9] See Denna F. Fleming, *The United States and World Organization, 1920–1933* (New York: Columbia University Press, 1938).

license, be looked upon as the executive organ. Though its general competence was described in language identical with that used to describe what the Assembly could do, it was given certain more specialized functions which emphasized its executive character. For example, it had special responsibilities in connection with the settlement of disputes; it could advise members on collective measures to be taken in case of aggression; it was made responsible for formulating proposals for the reduction of national armaments; it exercised general supervision over the mandate system with the approval of the Assembly; and it appointed the Secretary-General.

In recognition of the special responsibilities of the Council, account was taken in its constitution of the unequal capacities of states to contribute to the maintenance of international peace and security, and generally of the unequal importance of states in the achievement of League purposes. The Principal Allied and Associated Powers [10] were made permanent members of the Council, while four non-permanent members were to be elected by the Assembly from among the remaining members of the Organization for fixed terms. The Covenant initially provided that the number of permanent members should exceed the number of non-permanent members, five to four. Since the United States did not join the League, the permanent members were never in the majority, and beginning in 1922, when the Assembly voted to increase the number of non-permanent members to six, the balance was progressively shifted in favor of the lesser powers.[11] Thus, the concept of a "Concert of Great Powers" which had in part inspired the initial establishment of the Council fell into the background. Without the authority which it would have derived from being the instrument of Great Power cooperation, the Council was unable to compete effectively with the Assembly for power and influence, and its relative importance in the League system tended to decline.[12]

The Council and the Assembly were representative bodies, meeting periodically but with changing personnel. The Presidency of the Council rotated each month. The Assembly elected a new president annually. In a sense, the only permanent high-ranking official of the League, functioning day in and day out, was the Secretary-General, who headed

[10] United States, United Kingdom, France, Italy, and Japan. The United States was an Associated Power; the others Allied Powers.

[11] The Covenant originally provided for four non-permanent members of the Council; by 1939, this number had been increased to eleven.

[12] On the respective roles of the Council and Assembly, see Felix Morley, *The Society of Nations* (Washington: The Brookings Institution, 1932), Chs. 10–15.

the Secretariat. The Covenant did not even define the functions of the Secretary-General and his staff, it being assumed that they would be those of conference secretariats and international bureaux of the nineteenth century. In practice the Secretariat, and particularly the Secretary-General, assumed much greater importance than their names implied. As the highest permanent official of the Organization, the Secretary-General, in addition to supervising the secretarial and technical operations of his staff, came to exercise considerable influence on the conduct of governments as well. Perhaps the chief significance of the League Secretariat was that for the first time an international civil service was developed, composed of skilled persons drawn from different nationalities who were united in loyalty to a world organization.[13]

In addition to these three organs, the Covenant provided for the establishment of a Permanent Court of International Justice. The Court was to perform a two-fold function in so far as the League was concerned. First, it was to be an important, if not the principal means of settling disputes of a legal nature, such as disputes over the interpretation of treaties. Second, it was to be the organ which would advise the Assembly and Council on legal questions that might arise in the performance of their functions. Formally, the Court never became as closely associated with the League organs as was originally intended, largely because hope persisted that the United States, even though it might not join the League, would be willing to become a party to the Court Statute. It was believed that the United States would find it easier to join the Court if the Statute was kept separate from the Covenant, and the relation of the Court to the League was not openly stressed. Since the Statute of the Court was a separate treaty, it was possible for states not members of the League to become parties to it. In actual fact, however, the Court was an important element of the League system and one of its most successful features.[14]

Any complete description of the structure of the League would have to include mention of the technical organizations—economic and financial, communications and transit, and health—and of the numerous committees and commissions through which the League functioned, particularly in the promotion of economic and social cooperation.[15]

[13] See Egon F. Ranshofen-Wertheimer, *The International Secretariat: A Great Experiment in International Administration* (New York: Carnegie Endowment for International Peace, 1945).

[14] On the work of the Court, see Manley O. Hudson, *The Permanent Court of International Justice,* rev. ed. (New York: The Macmillan Co., 1943).

[15] See Harriet E. Davis (ed.), *Pioneers in World Order* (New York: Columbia University Press, 1944); and League of Nations, *Ten Years of World Cooperation* (Geneva, 1930).

Also, mention would have to be made of the International Labour Organization which, though largely autonomous, was closely related to the League both in purpose and in important structural and operational details. The United States joined the ILO in 1933, and played a leading part in its activities subsequently, particularly during the Second World War.

Work of the League

The League actively functioned over a period of about two decades.[16] During the first five years (1920–1925), it dealt often, but not always successfully, with a number of questions resulting from the war, and progressively established itself as an important force in international relations. During the succeeding five years (1925–1930), it enjoyed relative peace and tranquility. It was a period of general prosperity and cooperative relations among the major powers (with the exception of the Soviet Union). No serious challenges were offered to League principles; complicated political problems such as disarmament and the more effective organization of peace were tackled with patience, tolerance, and some expectation of constructive results; and the possibilities of further cooperation in the economic and social field were explored and in some respects implemented. The years 1931–1936 witnessed a series of political and military challenges to League principles and authority which the League and its members, weakened by the world economic and financial collapse, were unable to meet. This was a period of steady retreat under the impact of forces which an organization of the nature of the League seemed incapable of controlling once they had been released. In quick succession, League failure to check Japanese aggression in Manchuria was followed by: the rise of Hitler to power in Germany and German rearmament; the collapse of League disarmament discussions; the failure of League sanctions against Italy following Mussolini's attack on Ethiopia in October, 1935; and German remilitarization of the Rhineland in March, 1936, in clear violation of the Treaty of Versailles and the Locarno pact.

At a time when the United States appeared to be ready for limited cooperation with the League in the maintenance of peace and security, those members whose interest clearly lay in the preservation of international peace and security by collective means, were so obsessed with domestic political, economic, and financial problems, and the short-

[16] For authoritative history of the League see F. P. Walters, *A History of the League of Nations,* 2 vols. (New York: Oxford University Press, Inc., 1952).

range requirements of national security that they were incapable of rising to the new opportunity. From 1936 on, the League as an organization for the maintenance of peace and security, was generally recognized as having little life left. The expulsion of the Soviet Union in 1940 following its attack on Finland was its last dying, feverish gesture. Efforts to salvage the League as an organization for furthering international cooperation in economic and social matters met with some measure of success, and during the War, some of the technical aspects of the League's work were continued.

Why was the League experiment unsuccessful? To put the question more bluntly, why did the League fail? It must be conceded that the League did fail in its principal purpose, namely the maintenance of international peace and security. The outbreak of the Second World War was tragic testimony to this fact. And to all but the most blind, the events from 1935 on were conclusive. Of course it must be recognized that to speak in terms of League failure is in a sense misleading since the League by its very nature was a means which could be used effectively or ineffectively. Responsibility in the last analysis rested on states which under the League system were the repositories of power. Nevertheless, in the eyes of its supporters, the League was a method or a system by which abuses of national power would be made more difficult, if not eliminated, and states would find it in their interest or would be compelled to respect certain rules of conduct and cooperate for common ends. It didn't work out that way. Why?

In the first place, there were undoubtedly some technical deficiencies in the League system. The Covenant prohibited "resort to war." In the practice of the League, governments interpreted this phrase in a narrow technical sense, as in dealing with Japanese military action in Manchuria in 1931, with the result that its purpose was largely nullified. The Covenant required unanimity for most substantive decisions of the Council and Assembly; this enabled a member preparing for or actually engaged in aggression to block effective countermeasures. The Covenant provided that national armaments should be reduced to the lowest point "consistent with national safety." This provided a basis for France's argument that it could not agree to reduce its armaments because of the threat of future German aggression. But while these provisions of the Covenant may have been invoked to justify or make possible policies and acts which were incompatible with the purposes of the League, it would be inaccurate to say that the technical deficiencies provided the explanation or even an important part of the explanation, of League failures.

To some, the close association of the League with the peace settlement at the end of World War I was an important defect of the League system. It is true that the League was established as part of the peace settlement and that at many points the League was associated with carrying out terms of the peace treaties. It is also true that the League was bitterly attacked, particularly in the defeated countries and in the Soviet Union, as the instrument of vindictive and unjust peace settlements. Nevertheless, one must recognize that even if (1) the Covenant had not been made an integral part of the peace treaties; (2) the League had not been set up at the conclusion of the war by the victor nations; and (3) the League had not been given specific duties to perform in connection with the carrying out of the peace treaties, as an organization for the maintenance of international peace and security, it inevitably was concerned with preserving the established order against efforts to change it by unilateral force. A part of this established order, after the War, consisted of the peace treaties which had been imposed by the victors upon the vanquished. Consequently, whether the League had been established during the War, at the close of the War, or after the peace settlements had been concluded, it was bound to have the task of keeping the peace on the basis of these settlements once they had been made. The League discharged its responsibilities in connection with the enforcement of peace treaties in the cause of more rather than less justice. The League's role in settling the Saar question is a case in point. It administered the territory and then supervised the plebiscite in which Saarlanders voted for reunion with Germany. Perhaps the League was not as effective an instrument of revision as it might have been, but that was due to its nature and to the policies of member states, not to its association with unjust peace treaties.

Many would find the principal cause of League failure in the fact that the United States did not join the organization. There is undoubtedly a strong case to be made for the responsibility of the United States. Nevertheless, it is necessary to make some distinctions and introduce some qualifications. It is undoubtedly reasonable to assume that if the United States had joined the League in the beginning and had provided the leadership and had been prepared to assume the responsibilities that it later did during the early years of the United Nations, the League would have been saved from the failure which overtook it. If, on the other hand, the United States had joined, but notwithstanding, had pursued essentially isolationist and short-sighted policies as it did during the inter-war period, membership alone would not have made the difference.

The failure of the United States to join the League, to provide the leadership and assume the responsibilities which other governments and peoples had been led to expect was a crippling blow. It decisively affected the policies of other leading members and the role which the organization would henceforth play. It fatally weakened it as an organization of collective security and of peaceful change, and it limited the scope of its geographical effectiveness to the sphere of influence of the major European powers. It restricted the possibilities of effective action in furthering economic and social cooperation, though this situation was shortly remedied in large measure by the readiness of the United States to cooperate with the League in non-political matters. But while United States non-participation did severely limit the role and effectiveness of the League in the maintenance of international peace and security, with the measure of cooperation that the United States was prepared to offer from the early thirties on, the members of the League, especially the leading European members, had it within their power to make the League effective in the European and Mediterranean areas. What was lacking was the will on their part, and for this, very little blame can justly be placed on the United States.

An attempt at a more fundamental explanation is made by those who find the cause of League failure in the wrongness of its general approach. They argue that international peace and security cannot be maintained by imposing legal restrictions on states and by seeking to organize collective measures to be applied automatically regardless of what may be the national interest in a particular situation. The whole theory that the maintenance of peace and security is a common interest of states, and that when that peace is threatened or violated states can reasonably be expected to take the necessary measures in common to preserve it is called in question. Those who take this view would argue that a necessary condition of peace is a balance of power and that only if the balance is maintained by appropriate military measures, will national policies and international arrangements for the maintenance of international peace and security be effective.[17] Whether the necessary condition of international peace and security is a balance of power or a superiority of power on the part of those desiring peace is perhaps a debatable question. It would seem, nevertheless, that the specific failures of the thirties were not due so much to the absence of, or the failure to maintain a balance of power as to the shortsightedness, the confusion, and the political impotence of the governments of those countries which had the power and a clear interest in using it to keep the peace, but which failed to take advantage of the opportunities presented. It was not the assumptions that were wrong or the system that

[17] See Gerhart Niemeyer, "The Balance-Sheet of the League Experiment," *International Organization,* VI (1952), pp. 537–558.

was defective; rather, it was a human failure, the inability of peoples and governments to develop and carry out those policies which their best interests in the not-so-long run required.

Finally, there is the argument of the world government people that the League was foredoomed because it was based on the principle of cooperation between sovereign states. This argument insists that the effective maintenance of world peace and security requires the establishment of a world authority with adequate power to deal directly with individuals. There is no doubt that history thus far gives a large measure of support to this view. Nevertheless the alternative offered is a quite impractical one for the forseeable future. While the argument calls attention to a fundamental weakness of the League, it would be defeatist in the extreme to allow this line of thought to discourage efforts to achieve desired objectives by less perfect means until the time comes when the more perfect means become practicable.[18]

SUGGESTED READINGS

Brierly, J. L. *The Law of Nations,* 5th ed. New York: Oxford University Press, 1955.

Davis, Harriet E. (ed.) Pioneers in World Order. New York: Columbia University Press, 1944.

Dunn, F. S. *The Practice and Procedure of International Conferences.* Baltimore: Johns Hopkins University Press, 1929.

Hayes, C. J. *The Historical Evolution of Modern Nationalism.* New York: Richard R. Smith, Publisher, Inc., 1931.

Howard-Ellis, C. *The Origin, Structure and Working of the League of Nations.* Boston: Houghton Mifflin Company, 1929.

Hudson, Manley O. *By Pacific Means.* New Haven: Yale University Press, 1935.

Mangone, Gerard J. *A Short History of International Organization.* New York: McGraw-Hill Book Company, Inc., 1954.

Niemeyer, Gerhart, "The Balance-Sheet of the League Experiment," *International Oragnization,* VI (1952), pp. 537–558.

Nussbaum, Arthur. *A Concise History of the Law of Nations,* rev. ed. New York: The Macmillan Company, 1954.

[18] For statements of the case for world government see Frederick L. Schuman, *The Commonwealth of Man* (New York: Alfred A. Knopf, Inc., 1952). For analysis of difficulties, see Gerard J. Mangone, *The Idea and Practice of World Government* (New York: McGraw-Hill Book Company, 1951).

Reinsch, Paul S. *Public International Unions,* 2nd ed. Boston: World Peace Foundation, 1916.

Rothwell, C. E. "International Organization and World Politics," *International Organization,* III (1949), pp. 605–619.

Walters, F. P. *A History of the League of Nations.* 2 vols. New York: Oxford University Press, 1952.

Woolf, Leonard. *International Government.* London: George Allen & Unwin, Ltd., Brentano's, 1916.

Zimmern, A. *The League of Nations and the Rule of Law.* London: Macmillan and Company, Ltd., 1936.

Chapter II

THE ESTABLISHMENT OF
THE UNITED NATIONS

WITH THE LEAGUE'S failure to deal effectively with Italian aggression against Ethiopia, German remilitarization of the Rhineland, and foreign intervention in Spain, no serious thought was given, nor was timely action taken to strengthen the League and make it more effective for the future. The thoughts of peoples and governments of member states became concentrated on saving their own skins. Some centered their efforts on strengthening their own military positions and temporarily appeasing the aggressor in the vain hope that time was on their side. Others sought safety in reducing or withdrawing from League commitments and retreating to isolation and neutrality.

Even with war imminent, no attempt was made to use League machinery and procedures to prevent it. Following Germany's invasion of Poland in September, 1939, events unfolded largely as if the League of Nations did not exist. The only use made of League machinery for keeping the peace was the expulsion of the Soviet Union following its attack on Finland. With the end of "the phony war" in the spring of 1940, the active assistance of the United States to the Western Allies progressively increased and its eventual full participation became increasingly certain. The German military invasion of the Soviet Union in June 1941, and the Japanese attack on Pearl Harbor on December 7, 1941 turned the military conflict into a world-wide struggle. The United States was now involved on an all-out basis. Pearl Harbor was quickly followed by the signing in Washington on January 1, 1942 of the Declaration by United Nations [1] which became the legal basis of a

[1] Executive Agreement Series 236. Text is reproduced in Leland M. Goodrich and Edvard Hambro, *Charter of the United Nations: Commentary and Documents,* rev. ed. (Boston: World Peace Foundation, 1949), p. 570.

powerful military coalition and which was to provide the name for the successor to the League of Nations.

The Second World War and Renewed Interest in a World Organization

Even during the critical early years of the War when it was far from certain that the challenge of the military aggressors would be successfully met, thought was being given in United States and United Kingdom official circles to the question whether some kind of international organization should be established to assist in maintaining peace and security and if so, what form it should take. When President Roosevelt and Prime Minister Churchill met off the coast of Newfoundland for their famous Atlantic meeting in the summer of 1941, Churchill was desirous that in their joint declaration they should give explicit expression to their hope that some form of international organization should be created to provide a greater sense of security after the War. Roosevelt was unwilling at this time to subscribe to such an explicit commitment, chiefly, it would appear, because he was not convinced that congressional and public opinion in the United States was yet prepared for it.[2] The agreed declaration, subsequently known as the Atlantic Charter, did however inferentially recognize the need of some form of permanent international organization by providing for the disarmament of aggressive nations "pending the establishment of a wider and permanent system of general security."[3]

Early in 1942, the Advisory Committee on Post-War Foreign Policy, established by the Department of State with the President's enthusiastic approval, initiated serious consideration within the Department of international problems which would be facing the United States with the conclusion of hostilities. In June, attention was explicitly focussed on the problem of a permanent international organization. While this initially was the assignment of a special subcommittee, it soon became a major part of the Committee's total concern. It was as the result of this initiative, and subsequent discussion within the Department and between Department personnel and the President and Congressional leaders, that proposals were finally drafted which were

[2] For an account of the Roosevelt-Churchill talks, see Sumner Welles, *Where Are We Heading?* (New York: Harper & Brothers, 1946), ch. I, and Robert E. Sherwood, *Roosevelt and Hopkins* (New York: Harper & Brothers, 1948), ch. XVI.

[3] Text of Charter is reproduced in Goodrich and Hambro, *op. cit.*, p. 569.

later presented to the major allies of the United States for consideration during the Dumbarton Oaks Conversations.[4]

While the Governments of the United States and the United Kingdom had by the summer of 1943 reached the point where they were prepared to seek the establishment of a permanent international organization to assist in maintaining international peace and security, the position of the Soviet Union had not been clearly defined. One of the purposes which Secretary Hull had in mind in agreeing to participate in a Conference of Foreign Ministers in Moscow in October, 1943 was to get the agreement of the Soviet Union to the general principle that such an organization should be established. In this he succeeded. In Paragraph 4 of the Declaration of Four Nations on General Security, signed by the foreign ministers of the Soviet Union, the United Kingdom, and the United States and the ambassador of the Republic of China, the signatories declared

> *that they recognize the necessity of establishing at the earliest practicable date a general international organization, based on the principle of sovereign equality of all peace-loving states, and open to membership by all such states, large and small, for the maintenance of international peace and security.*[5]

It was also agreed that informal conversations should take place with a view to achieving agreement on proposals for such an organization. Subsequently at Teheran, Churchill, Roosevelt, and Stalin confirmed this statement of purpose by declaring, in words that seem somewhat empty in the light of subsequent events, their common policy "to seek the cooperation and active participation of all nations, large and small, whose peoples in heart and mind are dedicated, as are our own peoples, to the elimination of tyranny and slavery, oppression and intolerance." [6]

Drafting the Charter of the U.N.

In the late summer and early fall of 1944, conversations were held at Dumbarton Oaks in Washington, first between delegations of the

[4] The story of Department of State action is told in United States Department of State, *Postwar Foreign Policy Preparation, 1939–1945*, Publ. 3580 (Washington: Government Printing Office, 1950).

[5] For text of Moscow Declaration, see Goodrich and Hambro, *op. cit.*, pp. 571–72. See also *The Memoirs of Cordell Hull* (New York: The Macmillan Company, 1948), II, chs. 92–93.

[6] For full text of the declaration, see Department of State, *Bulletin*, IX (1943), p. 409.

United States, the United Kingdom, and the Soviet Union, and then between the first two and a delegation of the Republic of China, to achieve agreement at the technical level on proposals for a "general international organization." The participants accepted as the basis for their discussions a draft proposal which had been prepared in the Department of State and which had received the general approval of important Congressional leaders.[7]

In the course of these conversations, one basic difference of opinion between the major allies was eliminated but a second was left unresolved. It was finally agreed that the proposed organization should not be exclusively limited in its functions to the maintenance of international peace and security. It had been the original Soviet position that the organization should be exclusively devoted to that task, and that it should not be concerned with the promotion of international cooperation in dealing with economic and social problems. The Department of State was insistent that the proposed organization not be so limited. In this it had the full support of the President and of the United Kingdom delegation. The Soviet delegation finally yielded though it did not take the same interest in the economic and social aspects of the new organization's work as in the political. This was certainly understandable in the light of the Communists' view of the nature of capitalism and their conviction of the inevitability of its destruction.

The second difference of opinion which was not completely resolved related to the respective roles of the major and lesser powers in the proposed organization. The Soviet position was that even in an organization with broader functions than they first proposed, the dominant and decisive role of the major powers should be clearly established. Equal participation of the smaller states in an innocuous debating organ was conceded, but little more. Furthermore, the Soviet Union insisted that in the peace and security field all substantive decisions should require major-power unanimity. Under the proposed organizational structure, this meant that in the Security Council the five permanent members would have a veto power on substantive decisions. The Soviet position was based on an allegedly realistic view of the role of military power in international relations, and more particularly upon a desire to safeguard the special interests of the Soviet Union by making it impossible for any important decision to be taken without its consent. The United States and the United Kingdom agreed in principle that the major powers should be accorded special roles more or less proportional to their power and general importance but they were not inclined to press the principle as far as the Soviet Union.

[7] For text see *Postwar Foreign Policy Preparation*, pp. 595–606.

In particular, the United States, at least, was desirous of recognizing the principle of equality in form if not in substance, somewhat in the manner in which the Latin American republics were treated as equals in the Inter-American system of cooperation. As regards the requirement of agreement of the major powers for Security Council decisions, the United States and the United Kingdom were insistent that this should not be applied to the extent of preventing a matter from being discussed or permitting a state to be a judge in its own case. While it was possible to get agreement on the respective roles of the General Assembly and the Security Council, the Dumbarton Oaks conferees were not able to agree on a formula governing the voting procedure of the Security Council. In this and other respects the Dumbarton Oaks Proposals were incomplete, and yet they did represent agreement of the major powers on most of the important questions to be considered in the drafting of a charter for the proposed organization. Without question, the extent of agreement was encouraging, particularly considering the background of hostility and distrust that had featured relations between the Soviet Union and the Western democracies before and during the early years of the War.[8]

The Dumbarton Oaks Proposals called for an international organization which had many of the features of the old League but which had others thought to embody the lessons of the League experience. Thus, while it was, like the League, to be an organization of multifold purpose, the promotion of economic and social cooperation was given more explicit recognition than in the Covenant. The maintenance of international peace and security was not only recognized as being the primary objective of the proposed organization, but implicitly at least, the objective was placed ahead of the advancement of international law and justice. In defining certain basic commitments of members, it was proposed to go beyond the Covenant and prohibit the threat or use of force, not just "resort to war" under specified conditions. While the Proposals envisaged a Security Council of limited membership and a General Assembly including all members, they differentiated the functions of the two bodies more sharply than did the League Covenant, and further, restricted the Security Council to dealing with matters of peace and security. They provided for a new organ, the Economic and Social Council, to deal with economic and social problems under the authority

[8] For the text of the Dumbarton Oaks Proposals, see Department of State, *Bulletin*, XI (1944), pp. 368–76 and Goodrich and Hambro, *op. cit.*, pp. 572–82. No official records of the Dumbarton Oaks Conversations are available. A generally reliable contemporary account was given by James Reston in *The New York Times*, Aug. 15–Oct. 3, 1944.

of the General Assembly. The League Covenant called for automatic sanctions to be applied by all members against any state which resorted to war in violation of the Covenant; the Proposals envisaged a system of progressive enforcement measures to be administered by the Security Council in which the major powers would have a decisive influence. The League Covenant envisaged a system of economic and social co-operation which would be largely if not fully integrated into the League structure; the Dumbarton Oaks Proposals called for a considerably more diffuse arrangement, with the proposed organization exercising very limited control over a variety of autonomous functional organizations.

The Dumbarton Oaks Proposals were in many respects incomplete. They did not contain any provision regarding Security Council voting procedure, a gap which was later filled by agreement of Roosevelt, Churchill, and Stalin at Yalta. They did not contain provisions with respect to non-self-governing territories, largely due to the hostility of Churchill to any arrangement for subjecting parts of the British Empire to any form of international control, and to the lack of agreement within the Administration in Washington on the details of any specific proposals, especially as might be applied to Japanese islands in the Pacific. They left unanswered some basic questions regarding a proposed international court of justice. They did not deal adequately, if at all, with a number of matters of a technical nature, such as the relation of the proposed Charter to other international agreements and the privileges of United Nations officials. They contained no provision for the next step to be taken in establishing the proposed organization, a need that was also met at Yalta when the three heads of states agreed on the time, place, and composition of a United Nations Conference to put into final form the charter of the proposed organization.

On March 5, 1945, the United States, in the name of the four sponsoring Governments (the Republic of China, the Soviet Union, the United Kingdom and the United States) issued invitations to forty-five other signatories of the Declaration by United Nations, in accordance with the Yalta agreement. No invitation was extended to Poland because the Sponsoring Governments had been unable to agree on the government to be recognized. In the invitation it was suggested that the Conference consider the Dumbarton Oaks Proposals, "as affording a basis" for the proposed charter. It was also indicated that if the invited governments desired "in advance of the Conference to present views or comments concerning the proposals," the Government of the United States would "be pleased to transmit such views and comments to the other participating Governments."

The Conference convened at San Francisco on April 25, 1945, with all the sponsoring and invited Governments represented. Subsequently, after rather heated disagreement between the Soviet Union on the one hand and the United States and the United Kingdom on the other, a division that was prophetic of things to come, the Conference voted to invite the Governments of Argentina, the Byelorussian S.S.R., the Ukrainian S.S.R., and Denmark to send representatives, thus bringing the total number of participating states to fifty.

To perform its assigned function, the drafting of the charter of the proposed organization, the Conference organized itself into a number of commissions and committees, and over a period of about two months, the proposals of the Sponsoring Governments and the proposals and comments of other participating governments were given careful consideration.[9] Each delegation had the opportunity to participate in the consideration of all proposals and suggestions, not only once but several times, since before final adoption every proposal had to be considered by the appropriate technical committee, by the appropriate commission and by the Conference in plenary session. Furthermore, every delegation had the right to participate in the final decision on an equal basis since there was no weighting of votes. Furthermore, decisions could be taken by a special majority vote, thus opening up the possibility that the major powers might be overruled by the Conference.

Nevertheless, in the actual work of the Conference, decisions were never allowed to get too far out of line with the wishes of the sponsoring Governments and France. This was true for a very obvious reason. While the commissions and the committees, and the Conference in plenary sessions might approve provisions to which one or more of the major powers objected for inclusion in the Charter, not even the Conference had the authority to bind a participating state to ultimate ratification of the Charter and participation in the work of the Organization. Since it was recognized that a necessary condition of an effective organization was the participation of the major powers, especially the United States and the Soviet Union, each in effect had a veto, the effectiveness of which was roughly proportional to the importance of the participation of the power concerned to the success of the Organization.

Nevertheless, at San Francisco, the smaller states did exercise considerable influence on the nature of the organization to be established. In part this was due to the unwillingness of the major powers to go

[9] For the proceedings of the Conference, see *Documents of the United Nations Conference on International Organization* (London and New York: United Nations Information Organization, 1945–1946). For a description of the organization of the Conference, see Goodrich and Hambro, *op. cit.,* pp. 10–20.

too far in disregarding widely expressed views. In part it was because the major powers did not maintain a fully united front with the result that on some issues the lesser powers got a measure of support from one or more of the big five. Thus, on the question of the powers of the General Assembly the lesser states received considerable support from the willingness of the United States to go further than the Soviet Union in strengthening the position of that organ.

Generally speaking, the smaller states concentrated on trying to limit the discretionary powers of the Security Council and the influence of the major powers in particular, to extend the rule of law, to enlarge the role of the General Assembly vis-à-vis the Security Council, and to extend United Nations functions in the economic and social field. They were in large measure responsible for getting revisions of the Dumbarton Oaks Proposals that made it quite clear that the Security Council should not exercise its powers in a completely arbitrary way and that the Council's power of binding decision did not extend to imposing terms of settlement or adjustment, thereby making possible another "Munich." While the smaller states were able to impose certain checks on the Council in the exercise of its function of peaceful settlement and adjustment, they were unsuccessful in their efforts to limit the right of veto of the major powers or to limit appreciably the discretion of the Council in the exercise of its enforcement function in case of a threat to or breach of the peace. The smaller states were instrumental in getting a substantial revision of the Dumbarton Oaks Proposals regarding the functions and powers of the General Assembly. While the significance of this change does not appear to have been fully appreciated at the time, the basis was thus laid for a subsequent development which was completely to alter the relationship of the General Assembly to the Security Council as envisaged in the Dumbarton Oaks Proposals.

The Charter as finally adopted, partly as the result of pressure exercised by the smaller states, placed much more emphasis than did the Dumbarton Oaks Proposals on the role of the Organization in promoting international cooperation in economic and social matters. The specific areas of United Nations action and the objectives to be achieved were more clearly defined. The functions and powers of the General Assembly and the Economic and Social Council were extended and clarified. Finally, it was largely on the insistence of certain of the smaller states that the amendment provisions of the Dumbarton Oaks Proposals were revised in order to facilitate and make somewhat more certain a later review of the Charter and thus to provide the opportunity to reconsider those provisions which were accepted at San Francisco by some of the smaller states with considerable reluctance.

The Charter of the United Nations, as drafted at San Francisco, was signed on June 26 by the delegations of all fifty states participating in the Conference. Article 110 provided that it would enter into force upon the deposit of ratifications by the Republic of China, France, the Soviet Union, the United Kingdom and the United States, and by a majority of the other signatory states. By October 24, this condition had been fulfilled. The General Assembly met for its first session on January 10, 1946. On April 16, by resolution of its Assembly meeting for the last time in Geneva, the League of Nations ceased to exist.

The Organization for which the Charter of the United Nations provided was not in most respects essentially different from the League of Nations.[10] The question naturally arises: Why was the attempt not made to revise the Covenant and continue the League in modified form? The reasons are fairly clear. First, the League was associated in people's minds with failure, and it was thought wise to start with a clean break with the past, at least in form. But most important of all, the two governments whose active participation was considered essential to the success of the new organization—the United States and the Soviet Union—for different reasons wished to start afresh. Washington was fearful of Senate repercussions if the organization admitted League ancestry. Moscow, having been the only member of the League to be expelled, was not particularly enamoured with the idea of a League connection. The question of whether to revise the Covenant or start anew was not even raised at San Francisco; in fact most delegations made it a point studiously to avoid any reference to the League. The work of the Conference no doubt suffered from the studied avoidance of direct contact with League personnel or experience as if it were a possible source of contamination.

Nature of the United Nations

Like the Covenant of the League, the Charter, though the constitution of an international organization, is in fact a treaty between the states parties to it. The treaty basis of the new organization was emphasized by the provisions for its entrance into force which followed the usual pattern of multipartite agreements. While the Charter contained no express provision for its termination or for the withdrawal of individual Members, it was agreed at San Francisco that the right

[10] See Leland M. Goodrich, "From League of Nations to United Nations," *International Organization,* I (1947), pp. 3–21.

of withdrawal existed.[11] The hope was expressed that this right would be exercised only for important reasons, but it was recognized that each Member would be the sole judge whether the right was to be exercised. The Charter does provide for its revision, and of course the procedures specified can be used to terminate the United Nations or to replace it by an entirely new organization.

The Charter provides for a multipurpose organization. While the maintenance of international peace and security is to be the first and primary purpose of the organization, the development of friendly relations, the achievement of international cooperation in dealing with economic and social matters, and the harmonizing of national actions in the attainment of common ends are explicitly declared to be among the purposes for which the Organization was established. In a sense, of course, it can be argued that these are all related to the maintenance of international peace and security since the attainment of this purpose requires not only that threatening disputes and situations be dealt with as they arise, but also that all relations between nations shall be friendly and conducive to peace. In other words, the maintenance of international peace and security requires preventive as well as curative action. Nevertheless, the Charter emphasizes that human welfare is a purpose to be distinguished from peace and security, and that this purpose stands on its own feet so far as the United Nations is concerned.

For the guidance of the Organization and its Members in the pursuit of these purposes, the Charter prescribes certain principles which for the most part are listed in Article 2. These principles have to do both with the nature and authority of the Organization and the powers and duties of Members. Strictly speaking, they are not legal rules of the kind that you would expect a court to interpret. Rather they are in the nature of political principles laid down for the guidance of the Member states and the organs of the United Nations.

The first of these principles—the first in order of listing and one of the most basic—is that of the "sovereign equality" of all Members. This provides the key to the nature of the Organization in so far as its relations to its Members are concerned. The United Nations is not a world state; the organization for which the Charter provides is in no sense that of a world government. The usual powers of government are left to the Members and the United Nations and its organs have only those functions and powers which are granted to them. Furthermore, in no case, except for the power of the Security Council to direct

[11] See the declaration approved by the Conference, the text of which is given in Goodrich and Hambro, *op. cit.*, pp. 142–45.

Members to apply political, economic, and military measures to maintain international peace and security, is an organ of the United Nations empowered to obligate any Member to take any substantive action in its relations with other states except with its consent. Furthermore, just as every state initially decides whether it wishes to be a Member, so any state can decide that it does not wish to continue membership and can on its own responsibility withdraw. Of course the principle of sovereign equality is even more fully recognized in the case of permanent members of the Security Council since no substantive decision of that organ can be taken without their consent.

Closely related to the principle of sovereign equality is the principle set forth in Article 2, paragraph 7, that the Organization may not intervene in any matter which is essentially within the domestic jurisdiction of a state. This is a further indication of the desire of the authors of the Charter to protect the authority of Member states. It was intended to have a significance similar to that of the tenth amendment of the United States Constitution. The inclusion in the Charter of the domestic jurisdiction principle in its present form was largely the result of United States initiative. It reflected the special concern of members of the United States delegation to the Conference, especially the Congressional members, to make it clear that there would be no United Nations interference in matters considered to be domestic in nature.

While the Charter stresses the associational character of the United Nations and emphasizes the "sovereign equality" of its Members, it imposes important limitations upon their conduct. It places on all Members the duty to settle their international disputes by peaceful means and to refrain in their international relations "from the threat or use of force against the territorial integrity or political independence of any state, or in any other manner inconsistent with the Purposes of the United Nations." Thus, Members are under a more extensive duty to refrain from the use of force than were members of the League. In addition, it is the duty of Members to give every assistance to the United Nations in any action taken in accordance with the Charter, and to refrain from giving assistance to any state against which the United Nations is taking preventive or enforcement action. Furthermore, the Organization shall take necessary action to insure that non-Members act in accordance with United Nations principles in so far as necessary to the maintenance of international peace and security.

With a view to creating the conditions of stability and well-being which are considered necessary to peaceful and friendly relations among nations, the responsibility is placed on the United Nations to promote:

(a) *higher standards of living, full employment, and conditions of economic and social progress and development;*

(b) *solutions of international economic, social, health, and related problems; and international cultural and educational cooperation; and*

(c) *universal respect for, and observance of human rights and fundamental freedoms for all without distinction as to race, sex, language, or religion.*

To achieve these purposes, Members pledge themselves ". . . to take joint and separate action in cooperation with the Organization." [12]

Members having responsibilities for the administration of non-self-governing territories recognize the principle that the interests of the inhabitants of these territories are paramount and accept ". . . as a sacred trust the obligation to promote to the utmost, within the system of international peace and security established by the present Charter, the well-being of the inhabitants of these territories." [13] In the case of territories placed under trusteeship, the obligations of the administering states are defined in greater detail, and detailed provision is made for United Nations supervision.

The Charter provides for two categories of Members: first, those states that became Members by signing the Charter at San Francisco and subsequently ratifying it or that, having been among the signatories of the Declaration by United Nations, subsequently signed and ratified the Charter; and second, those states that subsequently satisfy the qualifications for membership and are admitted in accordance with the procedure prescribed by Article 4 of the Charter. With few exceptions the original Members of the United Nations were states that had joined the anti-Axis coalition. Thus, the United Nations at the time of its establishment was associated with the cause of the victor nations in a world war as had been the League. Furthermore, the provisions regarding the qualifications and admission of new Members were written under the influence of wartime psychology and purpose. While some delegations at the San Francisco Conference wished to achieve universal membership at the earliest opportunity, the Charter as finally adopted emphasized that membership was something to be earned by the right kind of conduct and, furthermore, that under certain conditions membership or at least the privileges of membership could be taken away if Charter principles were openly and flagrantly violated.

[12] Articles 55 and 56.   [13] Article 73.

Structure, Functions and Powers

To facilitate the achievement of the declared purposes of the United Nations, the Charter provides for the establishment of six principal organs and such subsidiary organs as may be found necessary. The six principal organs are: the General Assembly; the Security Council; the Economic and Social Council; the Trusteeship Council; the International Court of Justice; and the Secretariat. Except for the Councils, the pattern follows closely that of the League of Nations. However, the authors of the Charter did undertake a more detailed definition of the functions and powers of these organs and their relationship to each other than was to be found in the Covenant.

The General Assembly was conceived as the organ which could be most closely assimilated, in function and in structure, to a representative legislative body. It consists of all Members of the United Nations; each Member has one vote. Decisions on important questions are taken by a two-thirds vote; on other matters a majority is sufficient. It has a wide range of functions which may be conveniently grouped under the following six heads: discussion and recommendation, supervision, control of finances, election, admission of new members, and the initiation of proposals for Charter review and amendment.

The power of the General Assembly to discuss and recommend is very broad indeed. In fact, by the terms of Article 10 of the Charter, it extends to "any questions or any matters within the scope of the present Charter or relating to the powers and functions of any organs provided for in the present Charter." The Charter imposes two important limitations, however, on this power, In the first place, the Assembly must refer to the Security Council any question on which action is necessary, understood to mean enforcement action, either before or after discussion, but in any case before making a recommendation. And second, the General Assembly must refrain from making any recommendation on any dispute or situation in respect to which the Security Council is engaged in exercising its functions under the Charter. These limitations are consistent with the Charter principle that the primary responsibility for the maintenance of international peace and security is vested in the Security Council, and that, normally, disputes and situations affecting international peace and security will be dealt with by that organ. The General Assembly, however, is explicitly empowered, subject to the provisions of Article 12, to recommend measures for ". . . the peaceful adjustment of any situation, regardless of origin, which it deems likely

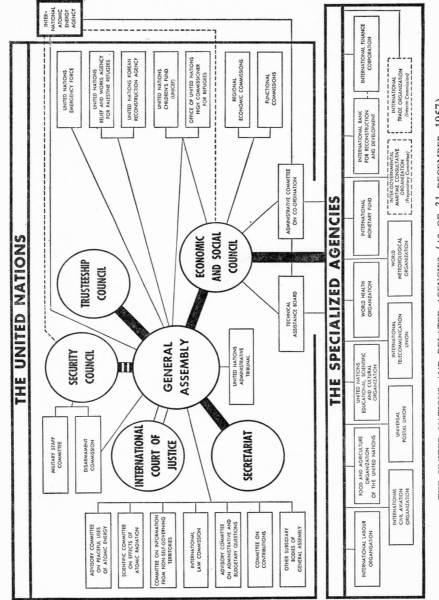

THE UNITED NATIONS

INTERNATIONAL ATOMIC ENERGY AGENCY

UNITED NATIONS EMERGENCY FORCE

UNITED NATIONS RELIEF AND WORKS AGENCY FOR PALESTINE REFUGEES

UNITED NATIONS KOREAN RECONSTRUCTION AGENCY

UNITED NATIONS CHILDREN'S FUND (UNICEF)

OFFICE OF UNITED NATIONS HIGH COMMISSIONER FOR REFUGEES

REGIONAL ECONOMIC COMMISSIONS

FUNCTIONAL COMMISSIONS

TRUSTEESHIP COUNCIL

ECONOMIC AND SOCIAL COUNCIL

SECURITY COUNCIL

GENERAL ASSEMBLY

UNITED NATIONS ADMINISTRATIVE TRIBUNAL

ADMINISTRATIVE COMMITTEE ON CO-ORDINATION

MILITARY STAFF COMMITTEE

DISARMAMENT COMMISSION

INTERNATIONAL COURT OF JUSTICE

SECRETARIAT

TECHNICAL ASSISTANCE BOARD

ADVISORY COMMITTEE ON PEACEFUL USES OF ATOMIC ENERGY

SCIENTIFIC COMMITTEE ON EFFECTS OF ATOMIC RADIATION

COMMITTEE ON INFORMATION FROM NON-SELF-GOVERNING TERRITORIES

INTERNATIONAL LAW COMMISSION

ADVISORY COMMITTEE ON ADMINISTRATIVE AND BUDGETARY QUESTIONS

COMMITTEE ON CONTRIBUTIONS

OTHER SUBSIDIARY BODIES OF GENERAL ASSEMBLY

THE SPECIALIZED AGENCIES

INTERNATIONAL FINANCE CORPORATION

INTERNATIONAL TRADE ORGANIZATION (Interim Commission)

INTERNATIONAL BANK FOR RECONSTRUCTION AND DEVELOPMENT

INTER-GOVERNMENTAL MARITIME CONSULTATIVE ORGANIZATION (Preparatory Committee)

INTERNATIONAL MONETARY FUND

WORLD METEOROLOGICAL ORGANIZATION

WORLD HEALTH ORGANIZATION

INTERNATIONAL TELECOMMUNICATION UNION

UNITED NATIONS EDUCATIONAL, SCIENTIFIC AND CULTURAL ORGANIZATION

UNIVERSAL POSTAL UNION

FOOD AND AGRICULTURE ORGANIZATION OF THE UNITED NATIONS

INTERNATIONAL CIVIL AVIATION ORGANIZATION

INTERNATIONAL LABOUR ORGANISATION

THE UNITED NATIONS AND RELATED AGENCIES (AS OF 31 DECEMBER 1957)

to impair the general welfare or friendly relations among nations." [14] With this exception, however, it was the sense of the Charter as drafted at San Francisco that the General Assembly should deal with questions of a general nature and, in its discussions and recommendations, should be chiefly concerned with developing general policies and agreements. If an analogy to the organs of state government is permissible, the General Assembly was viewed as a legislative body rather than as a court or an executive organ.

The second principal organ is the Security Council. The Security Council is a small body of eleven members with the Republic of China, France, the Soviet Union, the United Kingdom, and the United States having permanent membership. The six non-permanent members are elected for two-year terms by the Assembly, with special attention being given to their contribution to the maintenance of international peace and security and to equitable geographical distribution. While each member of the Council has one vote, these votes do not have equal weight, since on substantive questions it is necessary that the majority of seven include the affirmative votes of the permanent members. On the Security Council thus constituted, the Members of the United Nations confer "primary responsibility for the maintenance of international peace and security" and they agree that the Council in carrying out its duties under this responsibility acts on their behalf. In addition, the Charter expressly authorizes the Council to deal with disputes and situations with a view to the settlement or adjustment of those whose continuance endangers international peace and security; to adopt provisional measures or take enforcement action, with a view to maintaining or restoring international peace and security, in case of any threat to the peace, breach of the peace or act of aggression; and to formulate plans for the regulation of national armaments.

To give substance to the Council's enforcement action, the Charter provides that Members shall undertake to place armed forces and facilities at the disposal of the Council and that the Council may order Members to take such political, economic, or military measures as it deems necessary to the discharge of its responsibility. In effect the Charter places upon the major powers—the powers who would be the principal contributors of armed forces and whose cooperation would be essential to effective collective measures of whatever nature—the primary responsibility for the maintenance of international peace and security. By requiring their agreement, the framers of the Charter assumed that each permanent member would find it in its national interest to cooperate loyally and effectively to this end.

[14] Article 14.

The third principal organ of the United Nations—the Economic and Social Council—had no counterpart in the League of Nations. In a sense, however, it was anticipated when the Bruce Committee in 1939 recommended that the Assembly establish a special committee, responsible to that organ, to perform the functions of the Council in the economic and social field.[15] Many at the time felt that the Council—essentially a political organ—was ill-suited to deal with economic and social problems. Furthermore, it was thought that this particular part of the League's work should be brought more directly under the direction and supervision of the Assembly. This way of thinking was accepted by those who wrote the Charter. The Economic and Social Council for which the Charter provides is composed of eighteen members elected by the General Assembly for three-year terms. The Assembly is left free in making its choices though the authors of the Charter assumed that it would be guided by the contributions which Members made to the work of the Organization in the social and political fields. The Charter gives the Council a variety of powers, including the power to initiate studies, to make recommendations, to prepare draft conventions, and to negotiate agreements with the specialized agencies, but it states that the Council shall perform its functions "under the authority of the General Assembly."

The Trusteeship Council is also an organ without counterpart in the League system. Its primary function is the exercise of supervision over the working of the trusteeship system, the successor to the League mandates system. The authors of the Charter appear to have concluded that international supervision could be more effectively exercised by an organ containing the official representatives of governments, acting under the authority of the General Assembly, than by an organ such as the League Council primarily concerned with questions of peace and security, and acting with the advice of a group of technical experts, such as the Permanent Mandates Commission. The provisions of the Charter governing composition of the Trusteeship Council were a compromise between the demands of the administering and non-administering states. The Council consists of three categories of members: all members administering trust territories, all permanent members of the Security Council, and a number of members elected by the General Assembly sufficient to create an even balance between members of the Trusteeship Council administering trust territories and non-administering members. The Charter gives the Council authority to receive and review reports from the administering authorities, to receive petitions, to send visiting missions, and to make recommendations. It states, how-

[15] See Walters, *op. cit.*, II, pp. 756–62.

ever, that these functions are to be performed "under the authority of the General Assembly."

The fifth principal organ is the International Court of Justice. Unlike the Permanent Court of International Justice which had been set up as an independent organ, largely to attract United States adherence, the International Court is declared to be "the principal judicial organ of the United Nations" [16] and its Statute an integral part of the Charter. Except for these formal differences, the International Court of Justice is essentially the same Court as functioned during the League period. It is composed of fifteen judges chosen by the General Assembly and the Security Council voting concurrently. It is the tribunal to which Members are encouraged by the Charter to submit their legal disputes. It acts in an advisory capacity to the General Assembly and the Security Council on legal questions which may be referred to it, and to other organs and specialized agencies which may be authorized by the Assembly to request opinions.

The sixth principal organ is the Secretariat. Under the League excellent progress had been made in developing an international secretariat which came to be recognized as indispensable to the effective functioning of the organization. The authors of the Charter largely built on League experience. Partly on the basis of that experience but partly also on the basis of a somewhat different conception of the role of the Secretary-General, they decided to give to him a more important political role than had been formally enjoyed by his League predecessor. Thus, he is given the power on his own responsibility to bring any matter threatening international peace and security to the attention of the Security Council.

Unlike the League Covenant, the Charter of the United Nations defines in considerable detail the methods and procedures to be used in achieving the purposes of the United Nations. Thus, in chapters VI, VII and VIII, dealing with the maintenance of international peace and security, it is expressly stated (1) that Members shall, in the first instance, seek to settle their disputes by peaceful means of their own choice; (2) that the Security Council is the United Nations organ to which disputes not so settled and situations likely to lead to friction should normally be submitted; and (3) that the Council shall make recommendations with respect to methods or terms of settlement only in case of those disputes or situations the continuance of which is likely to endanger international peace and security. Thus, the Council is not to be used to deal with every dispute and source of friction but only

[16] Article 92.

those of a fairly serious nature. Furthermore, the Charter makes it clear that in case of a threat to the peace, a breach of the peace, or an act of aggression, the Council is the organ to take action and that it is expected to act promptly. In dealing with such a situation, the Council must itself decide whether it should try peaceful means of settlement, call upon the parties to adopt provisional measure, or immediately order enforcement action. If the Council decides to take enforcement measures, Members of the United Nations are required to give it full support. It cannot order a particular Member to take military action unless that Member has previously undertaken by agreement to place military forces and facilities at the disposal of the Council and then only to the extent of the undertaking. The authors of the Charter assumed, however, that Members would shortly conclude such agreements and that once they had become active participants in collective measures, they would be willing to do what was necessary to bring them to a successful conclusion.

Furthermore, the Charter provides for formulation by the Council and acceptance by Members of a system of international regulation of armaments. It is to be noted, however, that the Charter does not stress disarmament as an independent approach to peace and security but, rather, emphasizes that a minimum level of armaments should be available for United Nations purposes. By emphasizing the primary responsibility of the Security Council and making agreement among its permanent members a precondition of any Security Council decision, the Charter makes the effectiveness of the United Nations in the maintenance of international peace and security dependent, in the first instance, upon the willingness and ability of the major powers to work together. In a sense, this is a return to the "Concert of Europe" idea which had been a dominant factor in world politics during the century between the Napoleonic Wars and the First World War. Thus, the League system of mutual guarantees, legal undertakings, and automatic sanctions was largely discarded in favor of a more flexible system based on great power cooperation.

However, the authors of the Charter did not put all their eggs in one basket. At San Francisco, in particular, there were those who were doubtful about the effectiveness of a peace and security system that was wholly dependent on the willingness of the Great Powers, especially the Soviet Union, to cooperate, once the war was over. There were also, as we have seen, those who believed that the smaller states should be given a larger role to play. Under the influence of such doubts and desires, provisions were put into the Charter which provided the basis for alternative developments in case the system centered on the Security Council failed to function effectively.[17] For one thing, the powers of the General Assembly were defined in terms broad and comprehensive enough to allow that organ to play a more important role than was initially envisaged—at least by the major powers. In the second place, Article 51 was inserted expressly to safeguard the right of individual and collective self-defense in case of armed attack pending effective action by the Security Council. This laid the basis for mutual assistance agreements which states facing a common danger might consider necessary to provide for their security in the absence of an effective United Nations security system.

To achieve international cooperation in the solution of economic and social problems, the Charter follows, in general, the same approach as the League of Nations. Only in respect to the structure of cooperation are there significant differences. Mention has already been made of the creation of a new organ—the Economic and Social Council—concerned exclusively with problems in this field. Of even more fundamental importance is the emphasis placed on a more decentralized approach. The authors of the Charter openly recognized that there were and would be a variety of intergovernmental organizations dealing with economic, social, and cultural problems. Not only the inevitability, but even the desirability of this highly diversified approach was recognized. Instead of trying to bring all activity under the aegis of the United Nations, it was frankly recognized that the United Nations would be only one of many efforts in this field and that the most it could hope to achieve, through discussion, recommendation, and negotiation, was to bring the more important of the autonomous organizations into a satisfactory working relationship with the United Nations and with each other. Thus, the United Nations was intended to become a coordinating rather than an operating agency in many fields of activity.

With respect to non-self-governing territories, the Charter has registered one very important advance for all, while providing what was hoped would be a more effective system of control for those territories placed under formal international trusteeship. The great advance of the Charter is in establishing the duty of all states administering non-self-governing territories to regard as paramount the interests of the inhabitants, to carry out defined policy objectives, and to transmit to the Secretariat statistical and other information on economic, social, and educational conditions in these territories. Thus the basis is laid for a measure of international accountability in the administration of all non-

[17] See John Foster Dulles, *War or Peace* (New York: The Macmillan Company, 1950).

self-governing territories. As regards those territories placed under trusteeship, the great advance over the League system is in making provision for visiting missions to be sent to the territories and in placing the supervision of the administration of these territories under the ultimate responsibility of the General Assembly.

While the San Francisco Charter fell considerably short of the hopes and aspirations of many at the time, in important respects it did represent improvement over the Covenant and seemed to provide a reasonably promising basis for a more secure peace in the postwar era. That these modest hopes have to a considerable degree been disappointed is largely due to political developments in the period since the War that do not seem to have been fully anticipated at the time the Charter was written.

SUGGESTED READINGS

Feis, Herbert. *Churchill, Roosevelt, Stalin.* Princeton: Princeton University Press, 1957.

Goodrich, Leland M. "From League of Nations to United Nations," *International Organization,* I (1947), pp. 3–21.

Goodrich, Leland M., and Hambro, Edvard. *Charter of the United Nations: Commentary and Documents,* 2nd ed. Boston: World Peace Foundation, 1949.

Hull, Cordell. *The Memoirs of Cordell Hull.* 2 vols. New York: The MacMillan Company, 1948.

Levi, Werner. *Fundamentals of World Organization.* Minneapolis: University of Minnesota Press, 1950.

Russell, Ruth B. *A History of the United Nations Charter.* Washington: The Brookings Institution, 1958.

Shotwell, James T. *The Great Decision.* New York: The Macmillan Company, 1945.

Stettinius, Edward R., Jr. *Roosevelt and the Russians: The Yalta Conference.* New York, Doubleday & Company, Inc., 1949.

"Symposium on World Organization," *Yale Law Journal,* LV, No. 5 (August, 1946).

United Nations Information Organization. *Documents of the United Nations Conference on International Organization, 1945.* London and New York, 1945–1946.

United States Department of State. *Postwar Foreign Policy Preparation, 1939–1945.* Publication 3580. Washington: Government Printing Office, 1949.

United States Department of State. *Charter of the United Nations, Report to the President on the Results of the San Francisco Conference, by the Chairman of the United States Delegation, the Secretary of State, June 26, 1945.* Publication 2349. Washington: Government Printing Office, 1945.

Webster, Sir Charles. *The Making of the Charter of the United Nations.* Creighton Lecture, University of London, November, 1946.

Wolfers, Arnold. *Conflict and Compromise at San Francisco.* New Haven: Yale Institute of International Studies, 1945.

Chapter III

DREAM AND REALITY: THE POSTWAR WORLD

THOUGH THE United Nations was initially conceived as an organization with a number of purposes, all who participated in its establishment were agreed that its primary purpose—the purpose which must be achieved if other purposes were to be attained—was the maintenance of international peace and security. For the achievement of this purpose, it was taken as axiomatic, by the Sponsoring Governments at least, that the necessary basis was "the unity of those nations which formed the core of the grand alliance against the Axis." [1] It was the absence of this unity in the postwar years, in fact the progressive deterioration of relations between the Soviet Union and the Western Powers after the signing of the Charter, which was the factor chiefly reponsible for the failure of the San Francisco dream to be more fully realized in postwar reality.

There was another assumption, also important to recognize, which underlay much of the planning that went into the establishment of the United Nations. This assumption was never so explicitly stated and was never so widely accepted, but it was implicit in much that was said and done. Its failure to materialize also had a profound effect on the subsequent development of the United Nations. This was the assumption that the world after the Second World War would be essentially a continuation of the world of the League period, a world dominated by the values, interests, and power of the West. It was recognized of course that the emergence of Communist Russia as a great military power and a necessary participant in the world politics of the future

[1] *Charter of the United Nations, Report to the President on the Results of the San Francisco Conference by the Chairman of the United Nations Delegation, The Secretary of State, June 26, 1945.* Dept. of State Publ. 2349, p. 68.

41

would require that some accommodation to new values and interests would have to be made. It was also recognized that the peoples of Asia and Africa were emerging to an awareness of their own cultures and their own national futures, but it was assumed that this development would be guided by the West and that it would not in the forseeable future radically alter the balance of power and influence between the Western World and the East, between those nations heirs of Judaic-Greek-Roman culture and the world of Islam, Buddhism, and Confucianism. This assumption, too, proved to be somewhat overoptimistic from the West's point of view.

The Ideological Conflict

One of the basic causes of the failure of unity among the major powers and a contributing cause to the weakening of Western influence in the new organization was the emergence of communism as an ideology challenging the basic assumptions and values of Western liberal democracy. The challenge was all the more effective because, after the war the Soviet Union was one of the truly great military powers.

The Bolshevik Revolution of 1917 had brought into power in Russia a revolutionary government committed to the overthrow of capitalism throughout the world and the victory of communism. During the initial period of revolutionary ardor until 1921, Russian Communist leaders vigorously sought to stimulate world-wide revolutionary activity through the Communist International, or Comintern. After 1921, and particularly after Stalin's assumption of undisputed power in the middle twenties, the emphasis was placed on the development of Socialism within the country and on making the Soviet Union strong, rather than on revolutionary activity. Nevertheless, the Comintern continued to function, and its activities were viewed with strong suspicion in non-Communist countries.

United States recognition in 1933, the entrance of the Soviet Union into the League in 1934, and its vigorous espousal of the cause of collective security against Italy and Germany resulted in some softening of Western attitudes toward Moscow. In fact, 1939 saw efforts on the part of the British and French Governments, after the Munich debacle, to bring the Soviet Union into a system of European collective security to take the place of the League system which they had permitted to disintegrate. Munich, however, was apparently interpreted by Stalin as a play by the Western Powers to turn Hitler toward the East and he retaliated by concluding a treaty with Hitler in August, 1939, which gave the Nazi leader assurance that the Soviet Union would not join the West against him. Thus, relations between Moscow and the Western democracies were thrown back to their earlier state of distrust and hostility.

With Hitler's attack on the Soviet Union in June, 1941, relations between Moscow and the Western democracies entered a new phase. Partly, no doubt, to attract the support of the Western democracies and also to help in the mobilization of popular support at home, Stalin and other Soviet leaders emphasized the patriotic nature of the war and the identity of the "democratic purposes" of the Soviet Union and other countries fighting the Axis powers. On January 1, 1942, the Soviet Union became a party to the Declaration by United Nations, after having earlier accepted with some qualification the principles of the Atlantic Charter. In May, 1943, the Praesidium of the Executive Committee of the Communist International, meeting in Moscow, adopted a resolution pronouncing the dissolution of the organization. This action was viewed with wide approval, particularly in the United States, and accounted in part for the considerable improvement in the relations between the United States and the Soviet Union during the War.

There still was evidence, however, that national Communist parties were taking their cue from Moscow and were being used to serve its purposes. Furthermore, even the men in the Kremlin and the party theoreticians were not prepared to deny the existence of a fundamental conflict between Communism and capitalism. Although Stalin and others did argue for peaceful co-existence, there were enough authoritative assertions of the inevitability of armed conflict to cause many in the West to believe that the basic ideological conflict between Moscow and the West was incapable of peaceful adjustment.

However, once the Soviet Union was in the war against Germany, the importance of its contribution to ultimate victory and the overriding appeal of the possibility of its cooperation in the organization of peace and security after the war caused many to discount overmuch, if not overlook the considerations which might lead Soviet Communism to return to its earlier revolutionary and noncooperative ways. There is little doubt that there was a widespread tendency in the West, particularly in Washington, to be overoptimistic regarding the possibilities of Soviet cooperation, even after the failure of Stalin to honor his Yalta promises. On the other hand, it must be admitted that the Soviet leaders had some valid reasons for distrusting the West. There was therefore a situation in which any evidence of lack of good faith or aggressive purpose on the part of one side was likely to be magnified by the other and made the occasion for defensive measures which inevitably worsened rather than alleviated the strained relations.[2]

While fighting continued and a common interest in military victory existed, the form, at least, of cooperation was maintained. At San Francisco, the deep-seated conflicts which existed were largely subordinated, if only on the surface, to common efforts to establish an organization which all desired, or at least from which no one cared to be excluded. But after the Charter was written and came into force, disagreements between Moscow and the West became more open and numerous. Mutual suspicion and distrust were obviously on the increase. Still, the note of ideological conflict was being lightly struck. Even during the debates in the first session of the General Assembly on disarmament, there was an absence of the vituperative and propagandistic speeches which were to characterize later discussion of disarmament and other subjects.

It was in the course of 1947 that the ideological conflict became open and unrestrained and that the incompatibility of Communism and Western democratic values and principles came to be the dominant note. The deadlock over Germany and the announcement of the Marshall program of economic aid were followed in October, 1947 by the establishment of the Communist Information Bureau, or Cominform. This led to renewed emphasis by Moscow on the revolutionary subversive mission of Communist parties throughout the world. It also signalized the intensification of Soviet propaganda emphasizing the alleged abuses of the Western capitalist system, its exploitation of the masses, its denial of basic social and economic rights, its war-mongering proclivities, and its exploitation of the subject colonial peoples. In response, the Western democracies, especially the United States, stepped up their efforts to show that in practice communism was the instrument of Soviet imperialism and meant the denial of basic human rights, the complete subordination of the individual to the state, and the complete subjection of millions of people to a totalitarian system based on exploitation of the many by the few and, of necessity, committed to efforts to maintain and extend its power by brute force.

As the experience of the past has shown, ideological conflicts do not easily lend themselves to peaceful adjustment. Differences become sharpened and accentuated, logical incompatibilities are stressed, and positions are taken on moral grounds. Little room is left for compromise and accommodation. The problems connected with the making

[2] For a detailed account of relations between the three war leaders, see Herbert Feis, *Churchill, Roosevelt, Stalin* (Princeton: Princeton University Press, 1957).

and maintenance of peace after the Second World War would have been difficult and hard to resolve in any case as the experience of past wars and efforts at peace-making had conclusively shown. There can be little doubt, however, that the ideological conflict, which has become interwoven with conflicts of a more traditional nature, has made infinitely more difficult the accommodation and adjustment of divergent national interests and policies.

Bipolarity and the Atomic Bomb

Another consideration which helped to divide the major powers after the War was the nature of their power relations, and, in particular, the development of a condition of bipolarity which was encouraged by the ideological conflict already discussed, the traditional attitudes of the two superpowers, and recent technological developments. Of these developments, that of the atomic weapon has been the most important since it has meant that the availability and use of weapons of maximum destructiveness have been largely restricted to the two superpowers.

During the nineteenth century and until 1914, international politics had been largely dominated by a small, but varying, number of "Great Powers." Their number and their approximation to each other in strength and influence made it impossible for any one to achieve an unchallenged supremacy. Furthermore, under certain circumstances it was to the interest of each to concert with the others to prevent situations from deteriorating into open conflict and to prevent any one of these states from so extending its power and influence as to become a threat to international peace and security. Even allowing for the trend toward alliances to achieve greater security and increased power—the Triple Alliance and the Triple Entente, for example—effective power never became completely polarized into two dominant, mutually exclusive groups. Great Britain never formally relinquished its right to independent action. The United States, rapidly forging to the front as one of the greatest of the "Great Powers," deliberately abstained from any commitments. Japan, though bound to Great Britain by a treaty of alliance after 1902, did not consider this an obstacle to the pursuit of an independent foreign policy.

The First World War resulted in a profound change of these power relations and during the interwar period they were never adequately redefined and integrated into a working system of peace and security. The League of Nations, which was an effort to substitute for the concert of great powers an association of all peace-desiring nations legally committed to use their collective strength to keep the peace, was weakened from the beginning by the refusal of the United States to join and the actively hostile attitude of the Soviet Union. Its loyal members were never able to achieve strength proportionate to their obligations.

The conditions of imbalance and political instability which resulted from the First World War were never satisfactorily remedied in the inter-War period either by the development of an effective system of collective security or by the creation of a stable power equilibrium. This failure was an important cause of the Second World War, which in turn introduced additional elements of uncertainty and instability.

Germany, which in the thirties again assumed the role of a leading European power, was destroyed for the time being as an independent political entity and its territory was placed under the military occupation of the principal victor nations. Neighboring countries that had been brought under German control before or during the War were liberated, but in many cases their political status was left uncertain. In the Far East, the defeat of Japan meant the collapse of its "New Order" and made necessary the determination of the political future of liberated peoples, many of whom before the War had been under a European colonial rule which was now discredited. Since native aspirations for independence were greatly stimulated and strengthened by the war experience, the problems of reconstruction in this part of the world were in some respects more difficult than in Europe.

The effects of the Second World War were not limited, however, to the defeated Axis powers. Some of those that shared in the final military victory and who gained acceptance as permanent members of the United Nations Security Council were gravely weakened by the war ordeal. France, which suffered the ignominy of military defeat and German occupation, emerged from the War militarily weak and politically divided, its economy dislocated, and its national spirit confused and enfeebled. Furthermore, the War had temporarily destroyed or weakened the control of metropolitan France over its colonial empire, and efforts to restore this control, as in Indochina, encountered the strong resistance of nationalist forces. Thus, France found itself less capable than after the First World War of playing an independent and influential role in world politics, even in Europe, and to a large extent dependent upon economic and military assistance from the United States.

While the United Kingdom came out of the war with a record of heroic achievement and with national spirit intact, victory had been won at a high cost. Its economic resources were largely exhausted; only financial aid on a large scale from the United States made possible the achievement of a viable economy without further cruel sacrifices. The development of new instruments of mass destruction, capable of being delivered over great distances, destroyed the last vestiges of its insular security and made the United Kingdom more dependent than ever on the friendship and support of the United States. Because of the exhaustion of national resources and the strength of native nationalist movements, the British government after the War granted independence to a number of its Asian colonies and stepped up the development of self-government in other parts of the Empire. In the Middle East and Eastern Asia, where before the War the British had laid claim to vital interests, and had assumed definite responsibilities, retrenchment and withdrawal became the order of the day.

Although the Republic of China was included, on the insistence of the United States, in the exclusive group of powers that were to have primary responsibility for the maintenance of international peace and security, its internal disunity and its exhaustion as the result of the prolonged war with Japan raised real doubts regarding its ability to play that role. The war with Japan, which had been going on continuously since 1937, the internal struggles between the Communists and the Nationalists, and the rapidly deteriorating internal economic situation left China with little capacity to put its own house in order or to resist such pressures as might be exercised from the outside. Although the Yalta agreement [3] between Churchill, Roosevelt, and Stalin regarding the terms of the Soviet Union's entrance into the war against Japan, and the Sino-Soviet agreement of August 14, 1945,[4] appeared to hold out some hope that the Nationalist Government would be allowed to develop internal strength and stability without outside interference, it soon became apparent that this government did not have the inherent strength or popular support to achieve these results. By the end of 1946, it was clear that China instead of becoming a stabilizing influence in Eastern Asia, as United States policy had desired, would become a major area of contention between the United States and the Soviet Union and an important factor in the power relations between these two countries.

At the end of the Second World War, two powers, and two powers only—the United States and the Soviet Union—appeared to have the actual strength and potential capabilities for effectively defending their interests, and for pursuing policies of their own choice in their rela-

[3] For the text, see "The Conferences of Malta and Yalta, 1945," *Foreign Relations of the United States* (Washington: Government Printing Office, 1955).

[4] For the text, see Department of State, *Bulletin,* XIV (1946), p. 201.

tions with other states and with each other. Though they had been allies in the war against the Axis powers, differences with respect to historical backgrounds, geographical situation, particular national attitudes and interests, ideologies, economic and political systems, and the purposes and principles of their national policies prevented their collaboration from ever becoming very intimate. There was never the same intimacy of contact as between the United States and the United Kingdom. Whenever collaboration was undertaken, it became obvious that there were serious obstacles of distrust and suspicion to be overcome.[5] When, in the closing days of the war, it became known that the United States alone was in possession of an entirely new weapon capable of being a decisive factor in future wars, a new difficulty appeared in the way of this collaboration. From the Soviet point of view, the fact that this weapon had been secretly developed and used without previous consultation to bring Japan quickly to her knees may have seemed an added reason for dealing with the United States as a suspected and potential enemy instead of a trusted ally and collaborator.

Henry L. Stimson, who as Secretary of War had had a major responsibility for the development and use of the atomic bomb, clearly recognized the possible importance of the bomb to future relations between the United States and the Soviet Union. He believed that these relations might be "irretrievably embittered" by the way in which an approach was made to the Soviet leaders on the subject of international control. "If we fail to approach them now with a direct proposal of an arrangement to control and limit the use of the bomb," he wrote in September 1945, "and merely continue to negotiate with them, having this weapon rather ostentatiously on our hip, their suspicions and their distrust of our purposes and motives will increase." [6] Mr. Stimson had in mind a direct proposal by the United States to the Soviet Union of an arrangement to control and limit the use of the bomb and to encourage the development of atomic power for peaceful purposes.

It is impossible to say whether the subsequent course of relations between the United States and the Soviet Union would have been different if such a direct and immediate approach had been made. There is little in the record of these critical years to suggest that it would have been. In any case, Soviet leaders appear not to have been impressed by President Truman's assurance in his Navy Day address of October 27, 1945, that ". . . in our possession of this weapon, as in our possession

[5] See Feis, *op. cit.*

[6] See the "Memorandum for the President, 11 September 1945," in Henry L. Stimson and McGeorge Bundy, *On Active Service in Peace and War* (New York: Harper & Brothers, 1948), pp. 642–46.

of other new weapons, there is no threat to any nation." [7] Though the Soviet leaders raised no objection to referring the question of international control of atomic energy to the United Nations, it immediately became clear in the course of discussions in the Atomic Energy Commission that they had no thought of agreeing to any plan which would place the Soviet Union in a position of inequality with respect to the possession of the bomb for longer than was required to develop it.[8]

With the announcement by President Truman in September, 1949 that the Soviet Union had exploded an atomic device and the subsequent development and explosion of infinitely more powerful and destructive thermonuclear devices by the United States in 1952 and the Soviet Union in 1953, it became obvious that the two superpowers were in the midst of a dangerous race in atomic weapons which was an additional factor in intensifying their mutual fear and suspicion. So long as these two powers alone were able to produce and had available these means of mass destruction, and so long as the possibility of their being used existed, each served as a natural point of security attraction in a world of political instability and insecurity. Some states, particularly Asian and African, sought to remain independent and uncommitted to the side of either major power. When the point was reached—some would say in the summer of 1955—where there was a widespread feeling that it had become too dangerous for anyone to use atomic bombs, there were marked indications of a weakening of bipolarity and moves toward greater independence of action on the part of lesser nations. But even then, uncertainties regarding the circumstances and nature of a future war if it should occur, particularly in the light of the development of tactical nuclear weapons, limited any substantial modification of the condition of bipolarity or of United States-Soviet antagonism as the central fact of world politics.

The Failure of Peace Making

The purpose of the San Francisco Conference was not to draft peace settlements—the war had not yet been won—but rather to provide means for the maintenance of international peace and security once the war had been won and peace had been made. It remained the

[7] U.S. Department of State, *Bulletin,* XIII (1945), p. 656.

[8] For a summary of the discussions in the Atomic Energy Commission and the Security Council, see Leland M. Goodrich and Anne P. Simons, *The United Nations and the Maintenance of International Peace and Security* (Washington: The Brookings Institution, 1955), Part V.

task of the powers engaged in war against the Axis, and primarily those powers which had made the major contributions to the winning of the war, to agree on the terms of the various peace treaties and related settlements which would be needed to restore order and stability to a world rent by war. It was recognized at the time that only on the basis of agreement on the terms of the peace settlements did the possibility of cooperation among the major powers in the maintenance of peace and security exist, and it was assumed, or at least hoped, that these powers would find it in their own interest to achieve this initial agreement. In fact, by the time the San Francisco Conference met, there was still substantial ground for believing that such agreement would be possible. The Declaration by United Nations of January 1, 1942, the Moscow and Teheran agreements, and the Yalta agreements were concrete indications of a large measure of consensus regarding the political objectives to be sought and the means of achieving these purposes. In retrospect, one can query whether the statesmen who made these assumptions had read the lessons of history, which seemed to show that coalitions tend to fall apart once victory had been won, or the contemporary indications of unwillingness, at least on the part of the Soviet Union, to implement general principles which had been agreed to.[9]

At the end of the First World War, peace settlements had immediately been made and the League of Nations was established as an integral part of these settlements with specific functions to perform in connection with their completion and execution. While this association of the League with the peace treaties was a cause of complaint, it did at least assure a large area of initial agreement among the major members of the League. This measure of agreement placed the important tasks the League had to perform within its capacity. The delay in the conclusion of peace treaties at the end of the Second World War was not wholly a matter of explicit decision.[10] Delay was in fact made necessary by the decision of the major allies to insist on the unconditional surrender of the German armies and to undertake military occupation of the country with a view to de-Nazification and demilitarization. Since no effective German Government was recognized at the time of surrender, nor, indeed, did one exist, it was impossible to conclude a peace treaty immediately. In Japan, the situation was somewhat analagous though a Japanese Government headed by the Emperor was maintained. Unavoidable delays in peace-making made it all the more necessary,

---

[9] See Feis, *op. cit.,* for a detailed account of disagreements over Poland and other questions.

[10] For the history of efforts at peace-making, see Redvers Opie and Associates, *The Search for Peace Settlements* (Washington: The Brookings Institution, 1951).

however, that the major victors should agree upon programs of political and economic reconstruction in the defeated states and upon provisions to be incorporated into peace treaties once there were established governments with which they might be concluded.

Even before the end of fighting in Europe, there were clear indications of the difficulties that lay ahead. Although agreement had been reached at Yalta in February, 1945 on the general principles to be applied in the political reconstruction of the liberated areas,[11] even before President Roosevelt's death there was evidence that the Soviet Union in its efforts to set up a Communist regime in Poland was not fully carrying out its Yalta promises.[12] With the surrender of Germany and the completion of the work of the San Francisco Conference, it soon became apparent that the major victors would not be able to reach agreement quickly and easily on the terms of a general European settlement. The intention of the Soviet Government to organize Eastern Europe in accordance with its own purposes and security requirements, seemingly with little attention to its promises at Yalta, became increasingly clear. One explanation of this, no doubt, was the failure of the Western allies, and particularly the United States, to maintain their military strength in Europe after the German surrender. The United States Government, in particular, failed to recognize, at least in practice, that the maintenance of a strong military posture was as necessary to the implementation of its peace objectives as to military victory.

At Potsdam, in August, 1945, agreement was reached among the major allied powers on the procedures to be followed in the negotiation of the peace treaties and on additional requirements to be imposed on Germany.[13] However, the first session of the Council of Foreign Ministers, meeting in London in September and October to consider peace treaties with Italy, Rumania, Bulgaria, Hungary, and Finland, ended in a deadlock over what appeared to be a strictly procedural matter. This was regarded by some observers as a turning point in relations between the Western Powers and the Soviet Union. James Byrnes, then Secretary of State, later referred to it as "a test of whether we really believed in what we said about one world and our desire to build collective security." [14] John Foster Dulles, who participated in the meetings as a Republican spokesman, was later to see the incident in a

[11] Department of State, *Bulletin,* XII (1945), pp. 213–16; and "The Conferences of Malta and Yalta," *op. cit.,* pp. 971–73.

[12] See Feis, *op. cit.,* pp. 571–76.

[13] Department of State, *Bulletin,* XII (1945), pp. 153–60.

[14] James F. Byrnes, *Speaking Frankly* (New York: Harper & Brothers, 1947), p. 105.

more momentous light. To him, it marked the end of an epoch, the epoch of Teheran, Yalta, and Potsdam. It marked the end of any pretense by the "Soviet Communists" that they were friends of the Western Powers. "It began the period when their hostility to us was openly proclaimed throughout the world." [15]

At Moscow, in December, 1945, the Foreign Ministers were able to resolve their differences on procedures to be followed in making the peace treaties. The Conference had little more than adjourned, however, when open disagreement broke out between the Soviet Union and the Anglo-American powers over the situation in Iran. Anglo-American pressure, including use of the United Nations Security Council to induce the Soviet Union to withdraw its forces from Northern Iran, was countered by retaliatory complaints by the Soviet Union and its satellites against the presence of British forces in Greece and Indonesia.

Some ground for optimism, however, was afforded by the success of the major victor nations in finally reaching agreement on the terms of peace treaties with Italy, Bulgaria, Hungary, Rumania, and Finland. These negotiations saw concessions on both sides. In negotiating the Italian treaty the Soviet Union finally conceded that, except for Trieste, Italy and its colonies fell within the sphere of dominant Western influence. On the other hand, the Western powers recognized the dominant position and special interest of the Soviet Union in Eastern Europe and accepted with minor changes the Soviet proposals for peace treaties with Bulgaria, Hungary, Rumania, and Finland. With respect to Germany, however, it was clear that agreement would be difficult to reach as neither Moscow nor the West was willing to accept the views of the other with respect to the treatment of that country. The Western Powers resisted in particular the Soviet reparation claims and the Soviet economic program which would have involved indirectly the payment of Soviet reparation claims by the West.

But the struggle for dominance in Central Europe did not assume "cold war" proportions as the direct result of any development there. This occurred only after the "cold war" had been declared in another but closely related area, the Balkans. During the war, Stalin had recognized that Greece fell within the British sphere for purposes of political reconstruction, and the British had played a leading role in installing a Greek Government in Athens after liberation. By late 1946, however, it had become clear that the Communists, with the support of the Soviet Union and the satellite states, were challenging the authority of this government. When the British Government found it necessary early in

[15] John Foster Dulles, *War or Peace* (New York: The Macmillan Co., 1950), p. 30.

1947, because of its precarious economic position, to discontinue financial and military support to the Greek Government, President Truman on March 12 made his historic statement to the United States Congress—the "Truman Doctrine"—in which he expressed his belief that "it must be the foreign policy of the United States to support free peoples who are resisting attempted subjugation by armed minorities or by outside pressures." [16]

This reaction to Communist pressure in the Eastern Mediterranean came at a time when the United States Government was reconsidering its whole policy toward the Soviet Union. It was the view of the Truman administration that the limits of concession had been reached and that effective means must now be found to check what was thought to be aggressive Soviet expansionism. The economic crisis of western Europe, which had been responsible for British withdrawal from Greece, seemed to require a comprehensive program of economic aid to create conditions of economic and political stability and strength in the area. In June, 1947, Secretary of State Marshall called attention to the need of such a program and declared the willingness of the United States to participate.[17] In the months that followed, the details were worked out and the program was put into effect. The refusal of the Soviet Union to participate and its insistence that other Eastern European countries should likewise refuse to take part, were indicative of the serious view which the Soviet leaders took of the program as a threat to Soviet security and policy objectives. In a real sense, the Truman Doctrine and the Marshall Plan of economic aid marked the beginning of the "cold war" between Moscow and the West.

From this time on, any possibility of agreement that may have previously existed between the Soviet Union and the Western powers on any of the unresolved questions resulting from the War was substantially lessened, since each side viewed these questions increasingly in terms of vital advantages to be gained and positions to be held in case the "cold war" should become hot. Thus, negotiations over Germany collapsed. In the Western-occupied zones, a Western-orientated German Government was established, while in the Soviet zone, a Communist-dominated German Government was set up. In the Far East, the division of Korea, initially undertaken for the purpose of arranging for the surrender of Japanese forces, continued, since the United States and the Soviet Union were unable to agree on the conditions of unification. Division was further hardened by the establishment of two rival

[16] *Documents on American Foreign Relations, 1947* (Princeton: Princeton University Press, 1948), p. 649.

[17] Department of State, *Bulletin*, XVI (1947), pp. 1159–60.

Korean governments, a further result of Great Power rivalry. While a peace treaty was concluded with Japan by the United States and the great majority of the co-belligerents in 1951, the Soviet Union refused to accept this treaty and concluded a separate peace treaty later.

With respect to China, the initial agreement between the Soviet Union and the United States gave way to open rivalry for dominant influence. When the Communists finally took over control of mainland China in 1949, the Soviet Union immediately recognized the Government which the Communists had established in Peking, while the United States continued to recognize the Nationalist Government which had withdrawn from the mainland and established itself on the island of Taiwan (Formosa).

Thus, over ten years after the conclusion of hostilities, the peace settlement which it was assumed would be the manifestation and the basis of great power cooperation is largely incomplete. The problems yet unresolved are not only evidence of deep-seated division and conflict between the Soviet Union and the Western democracies, but also by themselves serious obstacles to the functioning of the United Nations as initially intended.

Nationalism in Africa and Asia

Although the tensions and conflicts associated with the "cold war" have taken the headlines and undoubtedly have been of major importance in shaping the course of world politics and the functioning and role of the United Nations, the emergence of organized nationalist movements in Asia and Africa is a phenomenon which in the long run may have equal, or even greater significance. Before the war, the world was largely dominated by the culture and political influence of the West—western Europe and the countries of the Western Hemisphere. With a few important exceptions, the peoples of Asia and Africa were either subordinate parts of empires or states theoretically independent but still subject to important practical limitations on their sovereignty. Thus, China was subject to the regime of exterritoriality and to limitations on its customs autonomy which seriously restricted its actual independence. India was part of the British Empire though allowed a considerable measure of self-government by London. Egypt, theoretically independent, was, in fact, under British protection.

Particularly in Asia, but to a considerable extent in Africa as well, the war served as a powerful stimulant to nationalism and to demands for independence. This was due in part to demands that were made upon the peoples of the dependencies to assist in the war effort. Perhaps to an even greater extent it was due to Japanese military occupation of areas hitherto under Western colonial rule, and to encouragement that was deliberately given to nationalist movements by the Japanese occupation authorities when they saw that the tide of battle was turning against them. In Indonesia, for example, nationalist demands for independence were undoubtedly encouraged by the Japanese when they saw that sooner or later they must relinquish control.[18] When the time came for the victor nations to consider the conditions of a peaceful and stable world after the war, it became necessary to take cognizance of these nationalist demands and to relax substantially the imperial, chiefly European, rule that existed before the war.

It is significant that of the fifty states that signed the Charter of the United Nations at San Francisco, twelve were Asian or African states,[19] and of these, eight had only recently achieved or were in the process of achieving their full independence. Of the original members of the League, including the neutral states invited to adhere, only six were Asian and African states, and India was far from being independent at the time. It is also significant that of the thirty-one states that have been admitted to the United Nations up to the end of 1958, nineteen have been Asian or African. And more, presumably, will be seeking admission in the not-too-distant future.

This increase, both absolute and relative, in the number of Asian and African states in the United Nations, as compared with the League, does not by itself necessarily mean a corresponding increase in the influence of these areas in world affairs. It must, of course, be recognized that many of them are small, poor, and politically immature. Nevertheless, particularly in the General Assembly, where each member has the same vote as any other, their influence is bound to be considerable. Furthermore, in a world divided between Communism and Western Democracy, and in an organization where this same division exists and powerfully affects its role and functioning, this group of states, in spite of the weakness of its individual members, can exercise an influence disproportionate even to its numerical strength by holding and controlling the balance of power on important issues.

Having in most cases been recently subject to foreign rule, chiefly by western European countries, the peoples and governments of the Asian and African states are inclined to be distrustful of the West and susceptible to many of the claims of Communist propaganda. They have

[18] See George M. Kahin, *Nationalism and Revolution in Indonesia* (Ithaca: Cornell University Press, 1952), ch. IV.

[19] Excluding the Union of South Africa which is treated as European.

been primarily concerned with making their own independence secure and improving their own conditions, and with seeking and obtaining for other peoples similarly situated the independence that they themselves so greatly prize. With these interests and attitudes, they have been as a rule unwilling to align themselves closely with either East or West but have insisted on following an independent course, which they are convinced is most likely to further their own interests. For example, when the question of Chinese Communist intervention in Korea was before the General Assembly in 1950 and 1951, an Asian-Arab bloc of thirteen members was largely instrumental in inducing the Assembly to explore possibilities of peaceful settlement before taking the drastic action desired by the United States.

The Asian and African states have emphasized the role of the United Nations as an instrument for assisting non-self-governing and underdeveloped territories in their economic and social development. They have made frequent appeals to the United Nations for this purpose. As a result of their influence, the United Nations has been much concerned with assisting the transition of peoples from dependence to independence, a role which many European states have viewed with less than enthusiasm. The Asian and African states, for the most part, are not as much inclined as the West to stress the role of the United Nations as a guarantor of the *status quo* against violent change or as an enforcer of legal rights. They are much less interested than the West in the military defense of the free world against communism. Their interests, by and large, have inclined them to favor a mediatory role for the United Nations in the "cold war."

Impact of Postwar Developments on the United Nations

The developments of the postwar period have of course greatly affected the functioning and, indeed, the nature of the United Nations. Anyone who now reads the Charter and the discussions which took place and the comments that were written at the time of its adoption might have some difficulty in recognizing the United Nations of today as the organization for which the Charter provided. While the changes that have occurred bear witness to the flexibility of the Charter and the practical approach of Member governments, they more emphatically testify to the contrasts between the postwar period as it has developed in fact and the world that the Charter framers assumed or at least hoped would exist.

When the Charter was being written the common assumption was that the war then in progress would end with the victory of the anti-Axis Powers and that the victors would be able to agree on the conditions of peace; on new territorial boundaries; on the principles to be applied in the economic and political reconstruction of defeated and liberated countries; and on the future international status of the vanquished nations. These arrangements were to be a part, and a very important part, of the legal order which was to be the basis of United Nations activities in the maintenance of international peace and security. The cooperation among the major powers, which was envisaged as necessary to the effective discharge of the new organization's responsibility for the maintenance of international peace and security, was expected, in large part, to be the product of a common interest in enforcing these arrangements and maintaining international peace and security on the basis of them.

Instead of cooperation, however, the termination of hostilities saw a rapid deterioration of relations between the Soviet Union and the Western Allies. Their failure to agree on the terms of the major peace settlements and their inability to harmonize even their views on the application of principles to which they had agreed meant that conflict rather than cooperation became the order of the day, and conflict on fundamental principles, not just details of application. Thus, there emerged a wide range of questions relating to the reconstruction of the war-shattered world, with respect to which, agreement among the major powers was necessary if the United Nations was to function as its framers had intended. In the absence of such agreement, the effectiveness of the United Nations as a modified concert of powers for the maintenance of peace and security was limited to those comparatively few situations where in spite of fundamental differences of motives and ultimate objectives the major powers could achieve a measure of agreement on immediate goals. In those cases where this measure of agreement was not possible, where the Soviet Union and the Western allies were in complete disagreement as to the course to be followed, either the United Nations was not asked to play a part, or if it was, it was used by one side as a means of bringing hostile pressure on the other, not as a device for facilitating and registering a common agreement.

Not only has the role of the United Nations been affected by the conflict among the major powers resulting from the "cold war"; it has also been significantly modified by the other important alignment that has emerged in the postwar period, the alignment of the Asian-African states in support of independence for non-self-governing territories—chiefly on the Asian and African continents—and international assistance in the economic, social, and political development of under-developed territories. The strength of this bloc, at least numerically, and the persistence and vigor with which its members have made known their demands have resulted in the United Nations' assuming an important role as an instrument for the progressive liquidation of colonialism and the mobilization of the resources of the more advanced nations to assist in the development of the backward areas of the world. Instead of being primarily concerned with maintaining international peace and security by supporting the *status quo* against change by force, the United Nations has perhaps made its major political contribution as an agency for bringing about changes in the *status quo,* especially the transition of non-self-governing territories to self-government or complete independence. While Article 14 of the Charter, of which Senator Vandenberg was the principal author, envisioned the General Assembly as an organ of peaceful revision, it is quite clear that neither this article or other articles of the Charter were based on a full conception of the role which the General Assembly and the Security Council have in practice come to play.

Both the "cold war" and the activities of the Asian-African bloc in support of nationalist movements have affected the role of the General Assembly and have given it an importance far beyond the hopes of its strongest supporters at San Francisco. Repeated uses of the veto by the Soviet Union in the Security Council have led the United States and its supporters to make increasing use of the General Assembly to perform those functions which had originally been regarded as the special province of the Security Council. Thus, in 1950, when it became apparent that the Security Council could no longer function effectively in dealing with aggression in Korea, the General Assembly, on United States initiative, assumed for itself a residual responsibility to take necessary measures to maintain or restore international peace and security in case of a threat to or breach of the peace. Not only the Western Powers but also the Soviet Union and its allies have seen an advantage in making use of the General Assembly instead of the Security Council as a forum in the war of words. This tendency to develop and strengthen the role of the Assembly has been further accentuated by the interest of the smaller powers in building up the role and prestige of the organ in which they have equal votes and where the right of veto does not exist. The Asian and African states in particular have seen in the Assembly the means by which they can bring strong pressure to bear on the colonial powers to grant independence to their subject peoples.

Particularly in the maintenance of international peace and security, the operating methods and procedures of the United Nations have been deeply affected by postwar developments. As the result of the failure to conclude military agreements under Article 43 and the frequent use of the veto by the Soviet Union, the Security Council has been unable to use the military powers vested in it by Article 41 of the Charter. Consequently, one of the distinctive features of the United Nations, in comparison with the League of Nations, has not materialized in fact. As a result, the Security Council, no less than the General Assembly, has found itself largely limited to making recommendations, even when dealing with threats to the peace or breaches of the peace. Thus, the manner of applying collective measures in case of any threat to or breach of the peace, in the one case where this has been possible, has resembled more closely the pattern followed by members of the League when applying sanctions against Italy than the model established in the Charter which was hailed initially as a great advance over League practice.

But while the United Nations has in this respect been forced back into the pattern of the League, in another it has as the result of postwar developments assumed a character all its own. While League discussions and recommendations generally had as their purpose the achievement of a broad consensus, United Nations discussions and recommendations, under the influence of the divisions that have emerged in the postwar period, and the acceptance of the majoritarian principle in the Charter, have tended to take on the character of propaganda and political moves. Thus, in the debates in United Nations organs, national positions are often stated in extreme, if not abusive terms. Votes are solicited and attempts are made to influence voting behavior, not so much to achieve general agreement as to embarrass or weaken the position of the opposition. The tone of discussion in the Assembly and the Councils, thus, has often been set by the conflicts and divisions that have existed, not by a common desire to achieve some satisfactory accommodation in the interest of international peace and security and the general welfare.

Finally, the inability of the United Nations to provide acceptable assurance that international peace and security will be maintained, and the use made of United Nations organs to further purely national purposes by subordinating serious debate and the furtherance of agreement to propaganda and the exploitation of differences, have encouraged many states to look to forms of international cooperation other than the United Nations to further their common purposes. The conclusion of collective self-defense agreements under Article 51 has become a common, instead of an exceptional practice. Rather than relying primarily on the United Nations for the international guarantee of their security, Members have come to place their principal reliance on collective self-defense arrangements such as the Rio treaty, NATO, SEATO, the ANZUS treaty, the Bagdad treaty, and the Warsaw treaty. Furthermore, there has been a considerable tendency to by-pass the United Nations so far as economic and social cooperation is concerned, as witness the Marshall program of economic aid to Western Europe, the Organization of European Economic Cooperation, the Coal and Steel Community, the Organization of American States, and the Colombo Plan.

In sum, world developments since 1945 have had a very large, and in some respects one might even say catastrophic effect on the United Nations. These developments have affected its role, substantially lessening it, and subordinating it in certain respects to the forces in contention; they have altered the relations of its organs; they have modified its operating procedures; they have changed its importance in the eyes of Member governments as a means of achieving by cooperation the common goals of national policies.

SUGGESTED READINGS

Albrecht-Carrié, René. *A Diplomatic History of Europe since the Congress of Vienna.* New York: Harper & Brothers, 1958. Chaps. XIV–XV.

Brodie, Bernard, ed. *The Absolute Weapon: Atomic Power and World Order.* New York: Harcourt, Brace & Company, 1946.

Buehrig, Edward H. "The United States, the United Nations and Bi-Polar Politics," *International Organization,* IV (1950), pp. 573–584.

Byrnes, James F. *Speaking Frankly.* New York: Harper Brothers, 1947.

Dennett, Raymond, and Johnson, Joseph E., eds. *Negotiating with the Russians.* Boston: World Peace Foundation, 1951.

Dulles, John Foster. *War or Peace.* New York: The Macmillan Company, 1950.

Emerson, Rupert and Claude, Inis L., Jr. "The Soviet Union and the United Nations: An Essay in Interpretation," *International Organization,* VI (1952), pp. 1–26.

Feis, Herbert. *Churchill, Roosevelt, Stalin.* Princeton: Princeton University Press, 1957.

Fox, W. T. R., "The United Nations in the Era of Total Diplomacy," *International Organization,* V (1951), pp. 265–273.

————. *The Super-Powers.* New York: Harcourt, Brace & Company, 1944.

Goodrich, Leland M., and Simons, Anne P. *The United Nations and the Maintenance of International Peace and Security.* Washington: The Brookings Institution, 1955. Chaps. II and III.

Holborn, Hajo. *The Political Collapse of Europe.* New York: Alfred A. Knopf, Inc., 1951.

Johnson, Joseph E. "The Soviet Union, the United States and International Security," *International Organization,* III (1949), pp. 1–13.

Mosely, Philip E. "Peace-Making, 1946," *International Organization,* I (1947), pp. 22–32.

Opie, Redvers and Assoc. *The Search for Peace Settlements.* Washington: The Brookings Institution, 1951.

Roberts, Henry L. *Russia and America.* New York: Harper & Brothers, 1956.

Sherwood, Robert E. *Roosevelt and Hopkins.* New York: Harper & Brothers, 1948.

Chapter IV

THE UNITED NATIONS
AS LIVING INSTITUTION

THE CHARTER that was approved by the San Francisco Conference and which became effective on October 24, 1945, provided the legal basis for an international organization devoted to important common purposes. The United Nations was brought to life in a rapidly changing world. As we have seen, by the time the Charter entered into force and more particularly, by the time the principal organs began to function, the world political situation had seriously deteriorated and a major assumption on which the effectiveness of the Organization had been based seemed increasingly devoid of reality. If the infant Organization was to survive and become a factor of importance in the life of the world it was necessary from the beginning that it show a capacity to adapt itself to changing conditions and to develop roles and activities which might not even have been envisaged by its founders. To meet the needs of a rapidly changing world and to find a place of importance in this world, adaptation and growth were the alternatives to death and oblivion.

The Legal Basis and Nature of the Organization

The United Nations has a legal basis. The Charter is an agreement between states, though it is at the same time the constitution of a world organization. It is clear that the Organization rests on the consent of its Members. It can not be successfully argued, as was done in the case of the Federal Government under the Constitution of the United States, that it derives its authority from the people of the Member states. While the Charter begins with words which suggest this—"We the peoples of the United Nations . . . have resolved to combine our efforts to accomplish these aims"—, it shortly adopts the more conventional language of international agreements. For it goes on to state that ". . . accordingly, our respective Governments, through representatives assembled in the City of San Francisco . . . have agreed to the present Charter of the United Nations and do hereby establish an international organization to be known as the United Nations." It is clear from this and the remaining provisions of the Charter that the United Nations is the creation of governments and that it is primarily responsive to governments and not to the peoples they represent.

The Charter, furthermore, makes it quite clear that the United Nations is not intended to have the kinds of functions and powers that are commonly vested in states. It has no authority to create rights and duties for individuals, except those persons who may be in its employ. It cannot directly force individuals to serve in its armed forces. It deals generally with the governments of its Members instead of with their citizens. And in dealing with governments, it does not have, generally speaking, the kind of powers that the Federal Government of the United States has in dealing with the states. It cannot at will send its officials and armed forces into the territory of Member states to uphold its authority. It cannot take decisions of substance that are binding upon Members, except for the special authority vested in the Security Council when dealing with threats to and breaches of the peace. And the exercise of this authority requires the unanimity of the Council's permanent members. While the United Nations must rightly be viewed not as a superstate, but rather as a voluntary association of states for certain common purposes, it does have a personality of its own, responsibilities of its own, and the power to take decisions which produce certain legal consequences for its Members.

The Court of International Justice asserted in a very forthright manner the international personality of the United Nations in the advisory opinion which it gave April 11, 1949, on the question of *Reparation for Injuries Suffered in the Service of the United Nations.*[1] In giving its opinion on the rather technical point whether the United Nations had the capacity to bring an international claim against a state, the Court observed that

> *the Organization was intended to exercise and enjoy, and is in fact exercising and enjoying, functions and rights which can only be explained on the basis of the possession of a large measure of international personality and the capacity to operate upon an inter-*

[1] *I.C.J. Reports 1949,* pp. 174–220.

national plane. It is at present the supreme type of international organization, and it could not carry out the intentions of its founders if it was devoid of international personality. It must be acknowledged that its Members, by entrusting certain functions to it, with the attendant duties and responsibilities, have clothed it with the competence required to enable those functions to be effectively discharged.[2]

That the United Nations has an international legal personality and the capacity for performing legal acts is shown by various provisions of the Charter and international agreements and is illustrated amply from the experience of the United Nations. Under the Headquarters Agreement with the United States,[3] the United Nations is recognized as having rights to property within the Headquarters District and to take such measures, including the exercise of police authority, as may be necessary to the performance of its functions. Under Article 100 of the Charter, each Member undertakes to recognize the "exclusively international character" of the responsibilities of the Secretary-General and his staff. Under the Staff Regulations established by the General Assembly, members of the staff are required to take an oath of loyalty to the United Nations. Contracts of employment are between the United Nations and staff members. By the terms of Article 43 of the Charter, the Security Council, one of the principal organs of the United Nations, is directed to conclude agreements with Members specifying the forces and facilities which each Member places at the disposal of the Council. These examples amply demonstrate the possession by the United Nations of an international personality and the capacity for performing a wide variety of legal acts.

In addition, the organs of the United Nations are given the power to take decisions on a wide range of matters which produce a variety of legal consequences for members. The General Assembly, the Councils, and the International Court of Justice can make binding decisions on questions of their internal procedure. The General Assembly has certain powers of decision in the election of members of other organs. Likewise, its decisions regarding the annual budget and the apportionment of expenditures create legal obligations. The Assembly, on the recommendation of the Security Council, can take legally binding decisions on the admission of new members, and it may also, on like recommendation, suspend or expel a Member. Security Council decisions regarding measures to maintain or restore peace in case of a threat to or a breach of the peace are binding upon Members, including those not

[2] *Ibid.*, p. 179.   [3] U.N. Doc. A/427, Oct. 27, 1947, pp. 9–18.

members of the Council. Within the range of their respective compe-
tences, the General Assembly, the Security Council, the Economic and
Social Council and the Trusteeship Council can make recommendations
to Members with respect to matters properly before them. While these
recommendations are not legally binding, they may have important legal
consequences for Members and in any case are not lightly disregarded.
Thus, for example, though the Security Council's recommendation of
June 27, 1950, to Members to give assistance to the Republic of Korea
was not binding, all Members were obligated to recognize the validity of
action taken in accordance with that recommendation. With respect to
disputes submitted to it by agreement of the parties,[4] the International
Court of Justice can give decisions binding on the parties. All these
powers of decision or recommendation vested in the United Nations
organs can be exercised by a majority or special majority vote. Only
in the case of the Security Council is there the possibility that a particular
state will be able, by its sole negative vote, to prevent a decision from
being taken and this "right of veto" is limited to permanent members.

The United Nations as a Commitment to Common Values

The United Nations, however, is something more than a legally
constituted body with defined powers. While the legal structure of the
Organization is important, and determines the legal framework within
which its activities may be carried on, by itself it does not provide the
driving force, the dynamic quality, which has given to the Organization
a unique authority and influence in world affairs. It is because of this
dynamic quality, essentially moral in nature, that the United Nations
must be viewed as being something more than just the sum of its parts.
For this same reason, the United Nations must be viewed as something
more than a bit of machinery which is available to Members, and which
under certain conditions they may use for the furtherance of the
particular national interest which may be considered important at the
particular moment.[5]

It is as the expression of the common values and interests of the
peoples and governments of the Member states that the United Nations

[4] This agreement may take the form of a special agreement relating to the
particular dispute or of the acceptance of the Court's compulsory jurisdiction by
a declaration under Article 36 of the Statute or other act.

[5] On the dynamic quality of the United Nations, see A. H. Feller, *United Nations and World Community* (Boston: Little, Brown & Co., 1952).

has perhaps its chief importance in the world today. Notwithstanding the cultural differences which separate the peoples of the world and which are accentuated by the political division of the world into eighty-odd sovereign states, there are certain common purposes and principles which appeal to people everywhere and which governments profess to accept as being not only morally good but also as conforming to the best interests of their respective peoples. These are purposes and principles that have been the result of an evolutionary development over many decades. They have found expression in the writings of philosophers and publicists, in the programs of private organizations, in the laws and policies of governments, and in international agreements. These purposes and principles, as they have developed and have been generally accepted find expression in the Charter of the United Nations.

What are these common values that find expression in the Charter? In the first place, the Members of the United Nations are in agreement on the desirability of settling disputes peacefully and in conformity with the principles of justice and international law and of thus avoiding the use of force except for Charter purposes. The first purpose of the United Nations is declared to be the maintenance of international peace and security. No government would publicly disassociate itself from the principle that the maintenance of international peace and security is desirable and that to this end individual states should refrain from the use of force. It is significant that even the opposing parties in the "cold war" profess fervently their loyalty to peace, protest that they have no aggressive intentions, and justify their armaments solely on the ground of self-defense. Any government that attempted to justify deliberate use of force to achieve some exclusive national purpose or publicly announced that it was not in favor of the peaceful settlement of an existing dispute would incur such widespread criticism as to weaken critically its international prestige.

But this is not the only commonly accepted value which the Charter embodies. It is also widely accepted by peoples and governments that friendly relations among nations are desirable, and that such relations can best be achieved on the basis of equal rights and self-determination. There may of course be wide differences of opinion as to the circumstances under which this principle is to be applied, and the consequences of such application, but its basic validity is not likely to be openly questioned.

Another generally accepted value which the Charter sets forth is the desirability of improving the economic and social well-being of peoples. The desirability of promoting and encouraging respect for human rights and fundamental freedoms "without distinction as to race, sex, language, or religion" is also generally recognized, though it must be admitted that differences as to what these rights and freedoms are, and the relative importance to be attached to each are so great as largely to vitiate this general acceptance. Also, there is widespread agreement today that the old colonialism is a thing of the past, and that, as the Charter states, the interests of the inhabitants of colonial areas should be a paramount consideration in the administration of these territories, and that a responsibility rests on the administering state to promote their security and well-being.

As the institutional expression of these common values, the United Nations has an authority which would not be possessed by any piece of machinery or any organizational device. Not only in the discussions within the United Nations but also in negotiations and activities carried on outside, Members find it necessary to show devotion to these values and to avoid being placed in the position of appearing openly to violate or disregard them.

Of course it must be admitted that the common values which the Charter sets forth are stated in very general terms and that their generality affords such latitude in their interpretation as to permit their being disregarded to a large degree in practice. Furthermore, it must also be granted that the organs of the United Nations, generally speaking, do not have the authority to interpret and apply these principles in any conclusive manner and that as a result Members are left largely free to decide not only how these purposes and principles are to be interpreted but also whether any serious effort should be made to apply them. Notwithstanding, there is good reason to believe that Members of the United Nations have been substantially influenced in their policies and actions by the purposes and principles set forth in the Charter and by the interpretations given to them by the organs of the United Nations.

Some would argue that these represent values that only the West takes seriously, or that in any case these are not values which have any validity for the Communist world. It is even suggested that the West may place itself at a disadvantage in adhering to them. Nevertheless, if we look at the record, we find that the Soviet Union and other communist states have shown deference to these values, even if not to the same extent as have the countries of the West and of the non-Communist world. In 1946, for example, the Soviet Union withdrew its troops from Iran after it had been publicly accused in the Security Council of violating the territorial integrity and political independence of Iran in violation of the Charter. The final lifting of the Berlin Blockade in 1949 was undoubtedly due in part to the widespread condemnation of Soviet action. In 1956, the General Assembly's disapproval of their military intervention in Egypt was an important factor in inducing France and the United Kingdom to withdraw their forces.

But it is not alone, or primarily, as a system of moral restraints on Members that the purposes and principles of the Charter have helped to make the United Nations a significant force in international relations. In addition, these purposes and principles have provided the conceptual framework within which United Nations discussions have taken place and have defined the ends toward which United Nations activity has been directed. While delegates may seek to exploit technicalities to their advantage, they do not find it advisable to do so in open disregard of basic principles. More often, these principles and purposes set the tone and direction of discussion and set the limits within which an accommodation of national attitudes and interests in terms of a common policy, attitude, or program becomes possible.

When we think of the United Nations as an institution for dealing constructively with the problems of the modern world, we must, therefore, direct our attention to those provisions of the Charter which define the common ends for which Members have agreed to cooperate and the principles which they have accepted as guides to their conduct. Without these the machinery of the United Nations would simply provide additional diplomatic tools; with them, the mechanism acquires driving power and direction. Primarily because of these provisions of the Charter, the United Nations has been able to develop a role of vital importance as the expression of the will of a nascent world community.

The Development of the United Nations

While the provisions of the Charter setting forth purposes and principles define the conceptual framework and direction of world cooperation, and other provisions prescribe the machinery and methods to be used, neither are self-operative. Both require interpretation, adaptation, and even change to meet new situations as they arise and to meet old situations more effectively. The United Nations was conceived to be a permanent international organization, and since it was called upon to function in a highly dynamic and changing world, to be permanent it had to be adaptable. The Charter consequently could not be thought of as providing a rigid, unchangeable legal framework. It must have flexibility and adaptability.

While the Charter provides for formal amendment, this has not been the most important method of Charter development and change. In fact it has been the least important up to now, since it has never been used. The methods that have been used to permit the Organization to develop and adapt itself to new conditions without amendment of the Charter have been interpretation, non-application, and supplementary agreement.[6]

AMENDMENT

The Charter prescribes two methods by which amendments may be proposed. In the first place, they may be proposed by the vote of two-thirds of the members of the General Assembly. Secondly, they may be proposed by two-thirds vote of a General Conference called by vote of the General Assembly and the Security Council.[7] Once the amendment has been proposed and submitted to Member states for consideration according to their constitutional procedures, it becomes effective when ratified by two-thirds of the Members of the Organization, including the permanent members of the Security Council.

The amendment procedure thus makes it possible for any permanent member of the Security Council to prevent a proposed amendment from entering into force. On the other hand, any other Member of the Organization may find itself in the position where it is bound by an amendment which it has refused to ratify. This would appear to constitute a violation of the principle of sovereign equality. It was in part to ease the situation of those Members who, on the one hand, might be frustrated by the failure of a proposed amendment which they favored to become effective because of a veto and, on the other, might find themselves in the position of having to accept an objectionable amendment, that the San Francisco Conference adopted a statement approving the right of withdrawal from the Organization.[8]

While the question of holding a General Conference to review the Charter was placed on the agenda of the tenth session of the General Assembly in 1955, as required by Article 109 of the Charter, there was no substantial support at that time for holding such a conference. Nor has any proposal for an amendment received the amount of support in the General Assembly necessary for submission to Members. One im-

---

[6] On general subject of Charter development, see Francis O. Wilcox and Carl M. Marcy, *Proposals for Changes in the United Nations* (Washington: The Brookings Institution, 1955), ch. I.

[7] The vote required in the Security Council is the affirmative vote of any seven members. In the General Assembly, a two-thirds vote is required, except that when the question of holding such a conference was automatically placed on the agenda of the General Assembly at its tenth session, a majority was sufficient.

[8] See Goodrich and Hambro, *op. cit.,* pp. 142–44.

portant reason for this, apart from the recognition of the futility of such action in the absence of agreement among the permanent members of the Security Council, has been the belief that practically all desirable changes can be achieved by other means. In other words, the methods of interpretation and supplementary agreement have been so successful and are considered so promising that formal amendment has not been considered necessary.

INTERPRETATION

Though interpretation has been the principal method by which the Charter has been adapted to new conditions, there is no specific provision for it in the Charter itself. A number of proposals were made at San Francisco for giving the International Court of Justice or the General Assembly special powers in this connection. None of them was adopted. Instead, the Committee on Legal Problems (IV/2) adopted a statement, subsequently approved by the Conference,[9] which accepted the view that each organ would interpret such parts of the Charter as applied to its own functions and that Members would be free to use the various expedients available to them to achieve the interpretation of Charter provisions of special concern to them. Thus, in effect, the Conference left the organs and Members of the Organization free to determine for themselves and by such procedures as they might choose the meaning of Charter provisions.

This highly decentralized system of Charter interpretation runs counter to widely accepted ideas regarding the requirements of a legal order. For one thing, the principle of judicial review according to which the courts have a special role in constitutional interpretation is accepted in the United States. The principle of judicial review, however, is not generally accepted in other countries and there was little sentiment at San Francisco for giving the Court the authority to pass on all questions of Charter interpretation. In fact, even under the United States Constitution, the legislative and executive departments have important responsibilities for constitutional interpretation so far as their own powers and procedures are concerned, and the power of judicial review is exercised only with respect to those questions that can properly be brought before the Courts in actual litigation.

Under the Charter, there is one possibility of using the Court for Charter interpretation that does not exist under the American constitu-

[9] Goodrich and Hambro, *op. cit.,* pp. 547–51; UNCIO, *Documents,* XIII, pp. 709–10.

tional system. The General Assembly and the Security Council, and the other organs of the United Nations with the Assembly's consent, may ask the Court to give advisory opinions on legal questions, including questions of Charter interpretation. This has been done in a number of cases.[10] Nevertheless, one cannot say that the Court through its advisory function has thus far been an important participant in the work of interpreting the Charter.

The two major objections to the practice that has been followed in the interpretation of the Charter are that it assures no uniformity of interpretation, and that it does not even assure that Members will be guided by the interpretations adopted by particular organs so far as the work of the particular organs is concerned. Thus, the Security Council and the General Assembly can adopt different views regarding the interpretation of the membership provisions of the Charter, and a Member, the Soviet Union for example, can adopt a view of its own.

But in spite of the weaknesses of the United Nations' overly decentralized system of Charter interpretation, and the confusion that can result from it, interpretation has played an important role in the development of the United Nations. Only a few examples need be given here. As we shall see shortly, the domestic jurisdiction provision of the Charter has been interpreted in practice in such a way as to deprive it of much of the limiting effect on United Nations activities which many at San Francisco feared it would have. The provisions of the Charter defining the powers of the General Assembly have been liberally interpreted to permit that organ to assume major responsibilities for the maintenance of international peace and security, even in dealing with threats to the peace and breaches of the peace which were originally regarded as being the very special responsibility of the Security Council. The provision of Article 27, paragraph 3, regarding Security Council voting procedure on substantive questions, has been interpreted to mean that an abstention or an absence in the case of a permanent member does not constitute a veto. The Charter provision authorizing the General Assembly to appoint the Secretary-General upon the recommendation of the Security Council has been interpreted to permit the General Assembly to extend the term of an incumbent without Council approval. These are only examples of the interpretations which the

---

[10] *Conditions of Admission of a State to Membership in the United Nations* (1948); *Reparations for Injuries Suffered in the Service of the United Nations* (1949); *Competence of the General Assembly in the Admission of a State* (1950); *International Status of South-West Africa* (1950); and *Effect of Awards of Compensation made by the United Nations Administrative Tribunal* (1954).

organs of the United Nations and its Members are continuously making in the course of the day-by-day activities of the Organization.[11]

NON-APPLICATION

Unfortunately, perhaps, especially from the point of view of one who attaches importance to the rule of law, important changes in the Charter system have occurred as the result of non-application or neglect. This is a form of nullification, which becomes more common under the Charter than under the United States Constitution because of the requirement of great power agreement for many important decisions.

There can be no question that the United Nations has been given a different character from what was originally intended as the result of the failure or refusal of Members and organs to implement certain provisions of the Charter. The most striking example of this has been the failure of Members to conclude the special agreements under Article 43 by which they would undertake to place armed forces and facilities at the disposal of the Security Council. Failure to conclude these agreements has meant that the Security Council has not had at its disposal the military forces which it would need to exercise to the full its powers to maintain or restore international peace and security. However, it must be admitted that failure to conclude the agreements is not the real cause of the Council's weakness but rather another result of the primary cause, namely, the inability of the permanent members to agree. Another example of non-application was the by-passing of the Charter provision requiring that trust agreements should be concluded in the first instance between "the states directly concerned." [12]

There are a number of instances where it is somewhat uncertain whether the result has been achieved by interpretation or non-application. For example, Article 27 (3) provides that non-procedural decisions in the Security Council shall be taken by the affirmative vote of seven members "including the concurring votes of the permanent members." This has been applied in practice as though it read "permanent members present and voting." Is that fair interpretation or is it non-application? Again, the Charter provides [13] that the non-permanent members of the Council shall be elected by the General Assembly, ". . . due regard being specially paid, in the first instance to the contribution of Members of the United Nations to the maintenance of international peace and

[11] See U.N., *Repertory of Practice of United Nations Organs,* 5 vols. (New York, 1955) and *Repertoire of the Practice of the Security Council, 1946–1951* (New York, 1954), and *Supplement, 1952–1955* (New York, 1957).

[12] Article 79. See below, p. 311.   [13] Article 23, par. 1.

security and to the other purposes of the Organization, and also to equitable geographical distribution." The question arises whether what many believe is excessive attention to geographical distribution should be regarded as an interpretation or a non-application of this particular provision of the Charter. Needless to say, interpretation, particularly when left to political organs, can produce a great variety of results and the line separating interpretation from non-application is not always easy to draw.

SUPPLEMENTARY AGREEMENTS

In much the same way that the provisions of the United States Constitution on the organization and powers of the Federal Government and the rights and duties of citizens have been amplified and further developed by legislation, the Charter has been further developed by supplementary agreements entered into between its Members. There are many examples of such agreements. Article 57, for instance, provides that "various specialized agencies, established by intergovernmental agreement and having wide international responsibilities" shall be brought into relationship with the United Nations; Article 63 describes how these agreements are to be concluded. The provisions of the agreements that have thus been entered into supplement the provisions of the Charter and anyone seeking to understand the exact nature of the relationship of the United Nations to the specialized agencies would need to become familiar with them.

Again, Article 79 states that "the terms of trusteeship for each territory to be placed under the trusteeship system" shall be defined in an agreement approved by the appropriate organ of the United Nations.[14] These agreements supplement the Charter provisions regarding the powers and duties of administering authorities and must be considered an essential part of the Charter system. Finally, Articles 104 and 105 give the United Nations and its officials, and the representatives of Members rights, privileges, and immunities which are considered necessary to the functioning of the Organization. These rights, privileges, and immunities are defined in detail in the Convention on the Privileges and Immunities of the United Nations, approved by the General Assembly on February 13, 1946,[15] and the Agreement between the United Na-

---

[14] The General Assembly or, in the case of strategic areas, the Security Council.

[15] For the text, see Goodrich and Hambro, *op. cit.,* pp. 652–58; and U.N., General Assembly, *Resolutions Adopted . . . During the First Part of its First Session . . .* (Doc. A/64), pp. 25–27.

tions and the United States of America Regarding the Headquarters of the United Nations, signed June 26, 1947.[16]

Whether a particular agreement relating to matters within the purview of the Charter is to be regarded as supplementing the Charter and consequently determining the nature of the Organization's development is not always easy to determine. By the terms of Article 102, no Member can assume an obligation under any international agreement which contravenes its obligations under the Charter. This provides a form of legal assurance that agreements entered into by Members will be consistent with the Charter. It does not necessarily follow, however, that they supplement the Charter in the sense of further defining the nature of the United Nations, its structure, functions, powers, and procedures, and the rights and obligations of its Members. Whether they do depends on their substance. The North Atlantic Treaty, for example, while it imposes upon its members duties additional to those imposed by the Charter, does implement the right of collective self-defense which the Charter recognized in Article 51 and does supplement the Charter in the sense that it provides in some detail how international peace and security are to be maintained in a particular area in case the Security Council is not able to discharge the responsibility which the Charter places upon it. On the other hand, it would be wrong to say that the North Atlantic Treaty Organization constitutes a part of the United Nations. Rather it represents an alternative approach. The same would be true of other collective self-defense arrangements concluded under Article 51.

The United Nations and Domestic Jurisdiction

For the most part, the provisions of the Charter are positive and forward looking in that they envisage the establishment of an international organization which will have positive functions to perform with a view to achieving conditions of peace, security, and human betterment. In this spirit, Charter provisions have been interpreted and applied liberally on the assumption, well stated in the opinion of the International Court of Justice to which reference has already been made,[17] that the Organization must be presumed to have those powers which are conferred upon it by necessary implication as being essential to the performance of its duties. This principle, of course, has not been applied to justify powers

[16] For text, see Goodrich and Hambro, *op. cit.,* pp. 640–52; and U.N., Doc. A/427, Oct. 27, 1947, pp. 9–18.

[17] See above, pp. 63–64.

of binding decision when only the power of recommendation is given, but it has been used in a number of instances to expand the powers of United Nations organs into areas hitherto reserved to state action. Thus, it has provided the basis for expanding the authority of the United Nations, both in breadth and in depth.

Two principles, which are found explicitly stated in the Charter, have provided the chief bases for contesting such a development. One is the principle of sovereign equality which has been invoked not only to support the claims of small states to equality with the large states, but also, and more particularly by the Soviet Union, to support the claims of states, large and small, that their independence be respected and that no one, even the Organization, interfere in matters which are subject to the sovereign determination of the state. More particularly, the principle of sovereign equality has been invoked by the Soviet Union to support its insistence that the so-called "right of veto" of the permanent members of the Security Council be left intact. In so arguing, the Soviet Union is, of course, not so much interested in protecting the sovereignty of the smaller states as in safeguarding its own interests as a major power which, since the United Nations was established, has found itself very frequently in a minority position in Security Council voting.

But though the principle of sovereign equality has been frequently invoked to limit the United Nations, the principle that has most commonly been used for this purpose is that of domestic jurisdiction. The domestic jurisdiction principle was introduced into the Charter, as we have seen, in a more inclusive form than was given to the same principle by the Covenant. By the terms of the Charter provision,[18] the principle applies to all activities of the United Nations. The language is very sweeping:

> *Nothing contained in the present Charter shall authorize the United Nations to intervene in matters which are essentially within the domestic jurisdiction of any state or shall require the Members to submit such matters to settlement under the present Charter; but this principle shall not prejudice the application of enforcement measures under Chapter VII.*

It is reasonably clear from the discussions at San Francisco that the domestic jurisdiction principle was given this form, and listed as one of the basic principles of the Organization, because of the fear of the United States Government that under the expanded powers given the United Nations in the economic and social fields, the United Nations

[18] Article 2, par. 7.

might interfere in matters that had traditionally been regarded as within the exclusive jurisdiction of states. This attitude no doubt reflected uncertainty over what might be the Senate attitude toward the Charter, in view of earlier Senate opposition to the League Covenant, if United States domestic jurisdiction in such matters as immigration, tariffs, and civil rights was not protected. In the course of the discussions at San Francisco, considerable apprehension was expressed concerning the possible effect of this provision on the activities of the United Nations. Many feared that it would have a damaging influence.

In actual practice, the domestic jurisdiction principle has not had the restrictive effect which was feared, though it has undoubtedly provided a peg on which to hang many an argument against the United Nations taking any action or taking a particular action. It would be difficult to establish that in any instance the domestic jurisdiction principle has been the decisive factor in causing an organ of the United Nations to refuse to take action. The protests that have been made have been against the failure of the United Nations to take the domestic jurisdiction principle more seriously, instead of the reverse. The complaints have come from governments which maintain that for all practical purposes the domestic jurisdiction principle has been disregarded, rather than that it has been applied too vigorously or too often. The experience with the application of the domestic jurisdiction principle provides many examples of the liberal interpretation of the powers of United Nations organs, and the strict interpretation of the limitations placed upon them.

The domestic jurisdiction principle has been invoked most frequently in the General Assembly, which is not surprising considering the broad terms in which the competence of the Assembly is defined in the Charter and the tendency which the Assembly has shown to expand its functions and powers. Though the proposal has been made that the International Court of Justice be requested to give an advisory opinion on the interpretation of the domestic jurisdiction principle in particular circumstances, in no instance has this been done. The political organs of the United Nations have insisted on making their own interpretations. This position has been defended on a number of grounds. First, it has been pointed out that under the San Francisco statement,[19] the right of each organ to interpret its functions and powers was recognized. Second, any obligation to request the Court for an opinion has been denied on the ground that this would for all practical purposes amount to acceptance of the Court's compulsory jurisdiction. Third, it has been argued that the domestic jurisdiction principle is a political

[19] See above, p. 70.

principle—as stated by Mr. Dulles at San Francisco—and that consequently it should be interpreted and applied by the political organ in which the question is raised and which alone is in the position to properly evaluate the political factors. To ask the Court for an opinion would put the political organ in a legal straight jacket and would deprive it of the discretion needed to discharge its responsibilities. Finally, it has been pointed out that requesting an opinion would mean delay when prompt action is desirable, and that this delay might be endless, considering that the question of competence involves not alone the nature of the subject matter, but also the nature of the action which it is proposed to take. If a number of proposals were made, a separate opinion would have to be requested on each.

The fact that the political organs have taken the responsibility for interpreting and applying the domestic jurisdiction principle in so far as their own particular actions are concerned has had important consequences. First, it has undoubtedly resulted in a more liberal, and some would say more confused, interpretation of the powers of United Nations organs and consequently a more narrow interpretation of the domestic jurisdiction limitation than would have been given by a court of law. Second, there has been a tendency on the part of individual Members to play down the domestic jurisdiction principle in those instances where they want United Nations action and to stress its importance and inviolability when it is to their interest not to have the United Nations take any action. As a result, decisions of United Nations organs on the application of the domestic jurisdiction principle, particularly those of the General Assembly, are likely to be decided more by bloc alignments and considerations of advantage and expediency than by any reasoned attempt to apply objective standards to the situation in question. The net result, as we have seen, has been to reduce the importance of the domestic jurisdiction principle as a limitation and to enlarge the possibilities of United Nations action. Nevertheless, since the political organs of the United Nations are for the most part limited to advice and recommendation, and therefore depend upon the willing cooperation of Members to achieve practical results, the enlargement of United Nations activity in the form of discussion and recommendation does not necessarily mean that the United Nations is more effective as an agency for getting things done.

While the practice of United Nations organs in the interpretation of the domestic jurisdiction principle has not been conducive to the creation of a consistent body of precedents, particularly since it is not always clear whether or how the principle is being interpreted and applied, there are, nevertheless, two basic questions that must be answered, implicitly or explicitly, whenever and wherever the domestic jurisdiction principle is invoked. Is the matter under consideration essentially within the domestic jurisdiction of the State? Does the proposed action constitute intervention? So far as the Charter is concerned, a matter may be of an essentially domestic nature, and yet the United Nations organ may take action with respect to it so long as it does not "intervene." Similarly, in order for intervention to be unlawful under Article 2 (7), it is necessary that the intervention be in a matter which is "essentially within the domestic jurisdiction" of a state.

The organs of the United Nations have certainly not been very consistent or clear as to what they regard as matters essentially within the domestic jurisdiction of a state. It would appear, however, that they have accepted in substance the opinion of the Permanent Court of International Justice in the Tunis-Morocco Nationality Decrees case that the question whether a certain matter is domestic or not is essentially relative, and depends upon the development of international relations.[20] Where a state is obligated by international customary law or treaty to act in a certain way, it can hardly be said that a matter with respect to which that obligation is asserted is essentially within the state's domestic jurisdiction. Where on the other hand a state has undertaken only to cooperate with other states to attain certain objectives such as the furtherance of respect for human rights, or the promotion of certain broad objectives such as the social and political development of non-self-governing peoples under its administrative authority, the question arises whether these undertakings have the effect of removing unilateral acts of a government in these fields from the protection of the domestic jurisdiction principle. The political organs of the United Nations have not been clear as to how they answer this question, but their inclination would seem to be to assert the right to exercise substantial pressure on the party that is the object of complaint. But whether the pressure exercised is such as to constitute "intervention," thus making it necessary to treat the subject matter as non-domestic if Article 2 (7) is to be respected, the political organs of the United Nations do not say. Thus, they leave the boundary between domestic and international matters a gray and indefinite zone, where the action of the United Nations appears to be determined more by considerations of political expediency than logical or legal determination.

The United Nations' political organs, and particularly the General Assembly, have been equally inconclusive regarding the meaning of intervention. It would appear that certain actions do not constitute intervention. Putting a question on the agenda does not constitute interven-

[20] P.C.I.J., Series B, no. 4, pp. 23–24.

tion since it is a necessary preliminary to discussion and to any decision as to whether the matter is within the competence of the organ. Likewise, discussion is not generally regarded as intervention though under certain circumstances public debate may have a coercive effect. But when we consider possible courses of action beyond discussion the answer is not so clear. There have been assertions to the effect that intervention must be defined along traditional lines as "dictatorial interference . . . in the affairs of [a] state for the purpose of maintaining or altering the actual condition of things." [21] Such a narrow definition, however, implying as it does the use of force, certainly could not have been intended, since Article 2 (7) specifically excludes from the operation of the principle enforcement action under Chapter VII of the Charter. Furthermore, the organs responsible for dealing with matters in the economic and social field, where the danger of intervention was chiefly feared at San Francisco, can only recommend. It would therefore appear that if the domestic jurisdiction prohibition has any substance and, more particularly, if it is going to serve at all the purpose of its authors, it must apply to recommendations. That has been the view generally accepted by Members of the United Nations.

There would seem to be some basis in United Nations practice for believing that a recommendation addressed to all Members, though it is intended to apply to only one or two, does not constitute intervention. Nor does a recommendation addressed to the states directly involved in a dispute or situation so long as it is limited to calling upon them to settle their differences in accordance with Charter principles and offering the services of the United Nations as a friendly intermediary. If, however, the recommendation calls upon the parties to take specific action or seeks to allocate blame, the recommendation takes on a different character.[22] But the final conclusion must be that with respect to the definition of intervention, as well as essentially domestic matters, the political organs of the United Nations have been evasive and have tended to favor a practical solution which leaves many legal loose ends dangling, much to the annoyance of those who would like to see a little more attention given to legal order and rationality.

[21] L. Oppenheim, *International Law*, 8th ed. by H. Lauterpacht (London: Longmans, Green and Co., Ltd., 1955), I, p. 305.

[22] For further discussion of the interpretation of the domestic jurisdiction principle, see Goodrich and Hambro, *op. cit.*, pp. 110–21; Quincy Wright, "Domestic Jurisdiction and the Competence of United Nations Organs," Commission to Study the Organization of Peace, *Ninth Report* (1955), pp. 42–61; and M. S. Rajan, *United Nations and Domestic Jurisdiction* (Calcutta: Orient Longmans, 1958).

Conclusion

From this brief review of the nature of the United Nations and its process of development, it is clear that the Organization, though being much less than a world government, is much more than a piece of machinery available to diplomats when they want to make use of it. It is an organization with a continuing life, a recognized legal personality, and the capacity to take decisions and engage in actions which, while they may not create legal duties for its Members and have effective coercive force, do nevertheless constitute means of influence which Members regard as important and which do have an effect upon their conduct.

Furthermore, the United Nations is not a static but a dynamic organization. Though it must in principle function within the limits of a Charter in many respects quite detailed in its provisions and difficult to amend, the possibilities of growth and adaptation without formal amendment have proven to be very great indeed. By interpretation, principally, but also by failure to implement certain provisions of the Charter and by supplementary agreement, the United Nations has come to have a quite different character in many respects than was planned by its original architects. Probably the most important change has been the enlargement of the role of the General Assembly, especially at the expense of the Security Council, and the decline in the importance of the collective security function, largely because of the "cold war."

The possibility of growth through interpretation has been greater because of the relatively liberal view which the principal organs of the United Nations have taken regarding their own powers. This has been due in part to the fact that each organ has insisted on being the judge of its own competence, and has not been willing to accept the principle of judicial review or the superiority of court interpretation. And yet the Court of International Justice itself, in more than one instance, has asserted the principle of liberal interpretation with respect to the powers of United Nations organs. Not only has the growth and adaptation of the United Nations been facilitated by the liberal interpretation of the positive grants of powers to United Nations organs, but also, the organs of the United Nations have been unwilling generally to interpret the limitations of the Charter—more particularly the domestic jurisdiction principle—as constituting serious restrictions upon United Nations activities.

However, it must be recognized that in spite of the liberal interpretation of United Nations powers by the organs themselves, there is a limitation of fundamental importance which the United Nations has not been able to escape, and which is inherent in the nature of the Organization as a voluntary association of states. Though the United Nations can exercise great influence through the moral and legal force of its purposes and principles and through the persuasive action of its organs, the fact remains that Members are left free to determine the specific course of conduct they will follow and the extent to which they will be guided by these purposes and principles or influenced by the action of United Nations organs. They can refuse to participate in discussion, and to carry out recommendations. If they refuse to carry out orders of the Security Council or judgments of the Court there are serious limits to what the United Nations can do to enforce its decisions. It remains undeniable that the authority of the United Nations is largely moral and must so remain. Its effectiveness is largely dependent on the responsiveness of its Members to the purposes and principles set forth in the Charter and to the considered views of other Members expressed in United Nations discussions as to how these purposes and principles should be interpreted and carried out.

SUGGESTED READINGS

Claude, Inis, Jr. *Swords into Plowshares.* New York: Random House, Inc. 1956. Chap. 9.

Feller, A. H. *United Nations and World Community.* Boston: Little, Brown and Company, 1952.

Goodrich, Leland M. "The United Nations and Domestic Jurisdiction," *International Organization,* III (1949), pp. 14–28.

Goodrich, Leland M. and Hambro, Edvard. *Charter of the United Nations: Commentary and Documents,* 2nd and rev. ed. Boston: World Peace Foundation, 1949.

Jenks, C. Wilfred. "The Legal Personality of International Organizations," *British Yearbook of International Law,* XXII (1945), pp. 267–75.

Morgenthau, H. J. "The New United Nations and the Revision of the Charter," *Review of Politics,* XVI (1954), pp. 3–21.

"Pollux." "The Interpretation of the Charter," *British Yearbook of International Law, 1946,* XXIII (1946), pp. 54–82.

Rajan, M. S. *United Nations and Domestic Jurisdiction.* Calcutta: Orient Longmans, 1958.

Robinson, Jacob. "The General Review Conference," *International Organization,* VIII (1954), pp. 316–30.

U.S. Senate Committee on Foreign Relations, Subcommittee on the United Nations Charter. *How the United Nations Charter Has Developed.* Staff Study No. 2. Washington: Government Printing Office, 1954.

Wilcox, Francis O. and Marcy, Carl M., *Proposals for Changes in the United Nations.* Washington: The Brookings Institution, 1955. Chaps. I–II.

Wright, Quincy. "Domestic Jurisdiction and the Competence of United Nations Organs," in Commission to Study the Organization of Peace, *Ninth Report* (1955), pp. 42–61.

Chapter V

THE UNITED NATIONS
AND ITS MEMBERS

THE UNITED NATIONS is an organization of states, based on the principle of the "sovereign equality" of its Members. It is only through the cooperation of its Members that its purposes can in full measure be achieved. While the organs of the United Nations may by their discussions and recommendations exert influence on the attitudes and conducts of Member states, their power to take and enforce binding decisions is limited indeed. Furthermore, even decisions to recommend require the cooperation of governments since the political organs of the United Nations, being composed of Member states—except for the Secretariat and the International Court of Justice—can only take decisions to the extent that Member governments, or at least a substantial part of them, are in accord. The membership of the Organization, therefore, is a matter of the greatest importance. It may be a decisive factor in determining the role of the United Nations in international affairs and its effectiveness in achieving its declared purposes.

Membership being a matter of much fundamental importance, it is not surprising that questions of membership have received a great deal of attention during the dozen-odd years of the Organization's existence. Nor is it perhaps surprising that the consideration of these questions has been deeply influenced by political considerations, particularly by the calculations and strategies of the parties to the "cold war." In an organization based in part at least upon the principle that ballots should be substituted for bullets as a method of decision and influence, it could not long escape the architects and directors of national policies that the voting lineup in the organs of the United Nations, particularly the General Assembly, was a matter of considerable importance.

The Conditions of Membership

The Charter follows the example of the League Covenant in providing that certain states are original Members of the United Nations and that others may be admitted to membership by decision of the Organization if they satisfy certain conditions.[1] In following this example, the Charter subscribes to the proposition that membership in an international organization for the maintenance of international peace and security and the promotion of international cooperation in economic and social matters should be limited on a qualitative basis to those states that provide some evidence of worthy conduct and intention.

Like the League, the United Nations had its beginnings in a victorious military coalition the members of which appeared convinced of the justice of their cause, and of their duty to use their power as victors to create a world order which would give assurance that peace and security on a just and acceptable basis would be maintained in the future. The proposal which the United States submitted to the other major allies for consideration at Dumbarton Oaks in August and September 1944 provided that the initial members of the new organization should be the states that were allied in war against the Axis powers and those associated with them, together with such other states as the allies might determine.[2] The only agreement reached at Dumbarton Oaks was that membership should be open to "peace-loving states." At Yalta the three Heads of Governments agreed that a conference should be held at San Francisco to draft the Charter and that the United States should invite to this conference all states which became signatories of the Declaration by United Nations by March 1, 1945. This meant that the only states initially invited to attend the San Francisco Conference were those which by March 1 had declared war against one of the Axis powers, and presumably these would be original members of any organization they might agree to establish. The Conference subsequently decided, after an open clash between the Soviet Union and the United States, to invite Argentina, Denmark, and the two Soviet Republics of Byelorussia and the Ukraine to take part in the Conference. These states became signatories of the Charter as finally approved and original Members of the United Nations.[3] Thus the original Mem-

[1] See Art. 1 of the Covenant and Art. 4 of the Charter.
[2] See U.S. Department of State, *Postwar Foreign Policy Preparation, 1939– 1945*, Publ. 3580 (Washington: Government Printing Office, 1949), p. 596.
[3] Poland was not represented at the Conference because of inability of the Big

bers of the United Nations were almost without exception the members of the wartime coalition, now victorious over Germany and about to become victorious over the other major Axis partner, Japan.

Not only did the United Nations have its origin as a war coalition, but the peacetime organization was also conceived as having for its principal purpose the maintenance of international peace and security, by joint force if necessary, and on the basis of the existing order, including terms imposed by the victor nations. Consequently Members were expected to be in general sympathy with the purposes of the United Nations as a war coalition, and to be willing to accept and join in guaranteeing against change by force the new postwar order, a large part of which would consist of the arrangements decided upon by the victors. A primary duty of membership would thus be to participate loyally in such measures as might be found necessary by the Security Council to the maintenance or restoration of international peace and security. No state could fully perform this duty, it was argued, unless it was prepared to accept the specific obligations of the Charter, and unless its record was such as to justify the belief that it not only subscribed to Charter purposes but was prepared in fact to discharge the obligations of membership.

Though in the course of preliminary discussions in the Department of State there had been considerable support for the idea of universality and though this idea received a good deal of support at San Francisco, particularly from some of the Latin American republics, there were certain practical difficulties in the way of achieving the objective immediately as well as serious objections in principle. How, for example, could a state which did not at the time desire to participate or which because of war conditions had no effective or generally recognized government be made a member of the new organization? What authority did the states represented at the San Francisco Conference, for example, have to declare other states members of the proposed organization against their will or in the absence of an explicit statement of their desires? Faced with practical difficulties of this kind, the exponents of universalism limited their efforts to defining the conditions of membership in such a way as to facilitate rather than delay the achievement of universality.

It was agreed from the beginning of any official consideration of the matter that membership in the proposed organization should be limited to states, though there was an inclination not to insist on the requirement of full independence. The Covenant had used the phrase

Three to agree on the Polish Government to be recognized, but subsequently signed the Charter and became an original member.

"any fully self-governing State, Dominion or Colony," obviously to cover such categories as dominions of the British Commonwealth, and colonies possessing a substantial measure of self-government such as India. It was taken for granted at the time the Charter was being written that India and the Philippines would be original members, even though not fully independent at the time and at the Yalta Conference it had been agreed that at least two of the Soviet republics—certainly not independent—would be accepted as original members. Thus, the principle that states alone would be members of the Organization was never applied in any narrow sense. In fact it would be difficult to justify the inclusion of the Ukraine and Byelorussia under any generally accepted definition of a state in international law.

As we have seen, the four governments that were parties to the Moscow Declaration of October, 1943, and that were represented in the Dumbarton Oaks Conversations of August–October, 1944, were in agreement that membership in the organization should be limited to "peace-loving" states. Presumably this word of description had overtones derived from war experience and thinking. States that were engaged in the war on the Axis side or that gave support to or showed sympathy with the Axis cause were clearly not "peace-loving" and required reformation before they could qualify. Since there could be no satisfactory objective test of the "peace-loving" quality other than war participation—which could not be accepted for long—and since each state applying for membership of course declared itself to be "peace-loving," this condition of membership was widely recognized from the beginning as being open to highly subjective interpretation and application. At the San Francisco Conference, where there was a majority demand that states not among the original membership should prove their qualifications, there was insistence on some test more specific and tangible than peace-loving character. Thus, the Dumbarton Oaks text, making "peace-loving" character the only qualification, was revised to read

> *Membership in the United Nations is open to all other peace-loving states which accept the obligations contained in the present Charter and, in the judgment of the Organization, are able and willing to carry out these obligations.*[4]

It is to be noted that this phraseology expressly reserved to the Organization the right to determine whether in its judgment—and that of course meant the judgment of the responsible organs—the applicant was "able and willing" to carry out the obligations contained in the Charter. This was not left to the decision of the applicant himself. In

[4] Article 4, par. 1.

other words the requirement was not to be satisfied by any formality. Furthermore, the technical committee dealing with this matter, in its report accepted by the Conference, stated that its failure to recommend various elements that should be taken into account in making this decision, did not imply that ". . . in passing upon the admission of a new member, considerations of all kinds cannot be brought into account." [5]

Both in the formulation of United States proposals and in the discussions at Dumbarton Oaks there appears to have been general agreement that new members should not be admitted without the consent of the major powers. This was a departure from the provisions of the League Covenant which provided for the admission of new members by two-thirds vote of the Assembly alone. There were several reasons for this insistence on the special role of the major powers in the admissions process. The general reason was that the Organization was viewed as having the primary function of maintaining international peace and security and it was therefore reasoned that the major powers which were to have a special responsibility in this area should also have a special part in determining whether applicants for membership were able and willing to discharge their responsibilities.

There were special reasons why particular governments insisted on the rule of concurrence. The State Department, for example, appears to have come to the conclusion that the United States should have a veto in order to be in the position to head off any attempt to give separate membership to the Soviet Republics. At Dumbarton Oaks, there was agreement that while new members should be admitted by decision of the General Assembly, the Assembly should take its decision only on recommendation of the Security Council. While proposals were made at San Francisco to give the power exclusively to the General Assembly, and thus follow the League precedent, the Sponsoring Governments and France stood firmly by their agreed position that the Security Council should first consider an application and decide whether or not to recommend the applicant for admission. It was clearly understood that the General Assembly need not follow the recommendation but it was equally well understood that admission could not take place without a favorable recommendation. Nor was there any real doubt that a decision to recommend was a decision on a non-procedural question requiring the concurrence of the permanent members.

In addition to the matter of admission of new members, the San Francisco Conference considered the questions of withdrawal, suspension, and expulsion. Whereas during the drafting of the League Covenant

[5] UNCIO, *Documents,* VII, p. 326.

President Wilson reluctantly came to the conclusion that it was necessary to have a provision permitting withdrawal in order to get Senate approval, the position of the United States Government during the drafting of the Charter was that no such provision should be introduced, though the right of withdrawal was to be assumed. In the end, largely to satisfy those states which were not at all happy over certain provisions of the Charter that the sponsoring Governments insisted must be accepted, notably the provisions regarding Security Council voting procedure, a declaration was approved by the Conference which admitted the right of withdrawal.[6]

The discussions at San Francisco on suspension and withdrawal re-emphasized the importance that was attached to the peace and security function of the Organization. Though some states argued strongly against any provision for expulsion on the ground that universality should be the goal and a recalcitrant state could better be controlled as a Member than as a non-Member, the Conference finally decided to make provision for expulsion as well as suspension. The Soviet Union was particularly insistent that a Member which persistently violated the principles of the Charter should be treated as "a cancerous growth" and removed from the Organization.

Membership and the "Cold War"

No substantive issue that has come before the United Nations has afforded more striking evidence of the impact of the "cold war" than has the membership issue. From the time that the Security Council's Committee on the Admission of New Members first met at the end of July, 1946, down to December, 1955, when the membership deadlock was finally broken, no discussion occurred and no decision was taken with respect to the admission of a new Member which was not to some extent affected by the strategy of the participants in the "cold war." Under the leadership of the United States, the non-Communist Members of the United Nations, particularly those most closely associated in efforts to contain Communism, were generally inclined to insist on the strict fulfillment of membership qualifications under the Charter in the context of Western non-Communist values. If the Security Council had followed this course in making its recommendations, the result, certainly not unwelcome to the West, would have been to strengthen numerically and relatively the bloc of Members prepared to join in collective efforts to restrain Communist expansion.

[6] UNCIO, *Documents,* I, pp. 616–17; Goodrich and Hambro, *op. cit.,* pp. 143–144.

The Soviet Union, on the other hand, was generally inclined to use the veto as a means of obtaining the admission of its candidates, and sought to interpret Charter terms and the terms of other pertinent international agreements in such a way as to disqualify applicants that might be expected to line up against the Communist bloc in the "cold war." The increasing importance of the political role of the General Assembly and the importance attached to the results of General Assembly voting, led the leading protagonists in the "cold war" increasingly to be influenced by the likely effect on Assembly voting of the admission of particular states. With considerations of this nature playing an important, if not decisive role, it is not surprising that up to the time of the Tenth General Assembly, the great majority of states applying for admission were turned down and those that were admitted were viewed as being uncommitted in their attitudes toward "cold war" issues.

In 1946, nine applications for admission to the United Nations were received: Albania, People's Republic of Mongolia, Afghanistan, Jordan, Ireland, Portugal, Iceland, Thailand, and Sweden. When the Security Council began its consideration of the report of its Committee on the Admission of the New Members, the United States representative proposed that the Council recommend to the General Assembly the admission of all applicants to "seek as great universality as may be possible." [7] This proposal, made in spite of some reservations regarding the qualifications of particular applicants, received considerable support and was implicitly based on the assumptions that universality of membership was desirable and that the Charter provisions regarding qualifications should not be so rigorously interpreted and applied as to delay the achievement of this goal. The Soviet representative took the view, however, that each application must be studied separately and that the Council should reach a decision on the merits of each case. As a result of this Soviet stand, the United States representative withdrew his proposal and henceforth insisted that the Council follow the course on which the Soviet Union had initially insisted. The result was that only four of the nine applicants were recommended by the Council and admitted by decision of the General Assembly—Afghanistan, Iceland, Sweden, and Thailand.[8] Albania and Mongolia failed to receive the necessary seven affirmative votes in the Council, and Ireland, Jordan, and Portugal were vetoed by the Soviet Union.[9]

[7] U.N. Security Council, *Official Records,* First Year, 54th Meeting (28 Aug. 1946), p. 42.

[8] The admission of Thailand was delayed by the insistence of France that a treaty settling outstanding boundary issues should be first concluded.

[9] For report of the Council's Committee on the Admission of New Members giving reasons advanced for member positions, see U.N. Document S/133, Aug. 21, 1946.

The following year, 1947, eight more states applied—Hungary, Italy, Austria, Romania, Yemen, Bulgaria, Pakistan, and Finland. Of these five were "enemy" states during the war with which peace treaties had been concluded which had entered into force. At Potsdam, the Governments of the United States, the United Kingdom, and the Soviet Union had agreed that the conclusion of peace treaties would enable them to support applications from these states for membership in the United Nations.[10] Nevertheless, the United States and the United Kingdom took the view that Bulgaria, Hungary, and Romania had by their disregard of certain provisions of the peace treaties disqualified themselves for membership while the Soviet Union refused to join in the recommendation of either Finland or Italy except on condition that the three communist states be recommended, thus reviving the idea of treating applications in one package which it had earlier considered improper. Austria was vetoed by the Soviet Union because of the continued military occupation of its territory by American, British, and Soviet forces. Only Yemen and Pakistan succeeded in running the gauntlet of "cold war" maneuvering, and in the case of Pakistan, action was little more than a formality since India, of which it had been a part, was an original Member.

The following year, 1948, Burma, Ceylon, and Israel applied. Burma, which had acquired independence outside the Commonwealth was admitted, as was Israel the following year. It is interesting to note that the Soviet Union did not object to the admission of Israel at this time even though the Arab states were opposed. The Soviet representative in the Council vetoed Ceylon, even though an Asian state and newly independent, professedly because of doubts regarding Ceylon's independence and sovereignty.

Except for the admission of Indonesia in 1950, the deadlock on the admission of new Members was complete for all applications from 1949 to 1955. Following the recognition by the General Assembly of the Republic of Korea in December, 1948, the Republic applied for membership in 1949, but its application was vetoed by the Soviet Union. The application of its Communist counterpart in North Korea, the Democratic People's Republic, was not even referred to the Security Council's Committee on the Admission of New Members for consideration. Nepal's application for admission was vetoed by the Soviet Union. In 1951, applications were received from Libya, Viet-Nam and its Communist counterpart, the Democratic Republic of Viet-Nam (under Ho Chi Minh). Libya, which had become an independent state under a

[10] *Documents on American Foreign Relations,* 1948, p. 934; Department of State, *Bulletin,* XIII (1945), p. 159.

program adopted by and carried out under the supervision of the United Nations, was vetoed by the Soviet Union. This was indicative of the completeness of the deadlock that had developed, since Soviet policy before 1950 would probably have supported the admission of Libya as an Arab state. Now, Soviet policy apparently was to insist on the admission of Communist sponsored states or none at all. The Soviet veto of Viet-Nam was not surprising, nor the failure of the application of the Communist counterpart even to be referred to the Council's Committee, considering the Korean precedent. In 1952, Cambodia, Japan, and Laos applied, and their applications encountered Soviet vetoes in the Security Council.[11]

Efforts to Break the Deadlock

The deadlock on membership applications became a source of growing concern to Members of the United Nations in the years following 1950, particularly to those who believed that the effectiveness of the Organization would be increased by the achievement of universality. There was widespread resentment over Soviet use of the veto to prevent states from being admitted that were regarded by the great majority of Members as being fully qualified. From 1946 to 1955, the matter was a perennial subject of General Assembly consideration with a view to finding some means of breaking the deadlock.

The efforts that were made fell roughly into two categories: legal and political. When the Security Council initially considered its procedure in dealing with membership questions, the Australian representative took the view that applications should be first considered by the General Assembly, that the Security Council should only consider and make recommendations with respect to matters relating to peace and security, and that decisions on membership should be taken by the Assembly alone. This view was not accepted by other members of the Council as being consistent with Charter provisions.[12]

Several Members, especially Latin American states, have argued at various times that the General Assembly should consider an application as having been favorably recommended if it received seven affirmative votes in the Security Council, that members of the Security Council

---

[11] For a summary of action on membership applications, 1946–53, see U.S. Senate Committee on Foreign Relations, Subcommittee on the United Nations Charter, *The Problem of Membership in the United Nations,* Staff Study No. 3 (Washington: Government Printing Office, 1954), p. 5.

[12] U.N. Security Council, *Official Records,* First Year, Fifty-Fifth Meeting (Aug. 28, 1946), pp. 47–60.

should be counted as having supported an application if in the course of discussion they had admitted that the applicant met the qualifications of the Charter, or that the General Assembly could assume the responsibility of admitting new Members if the Council was prevented from acting by the abuse of the veto. These views have never received general support. The suggestion that the General Assembly might admit a state to membership in the absence of a favorable Council recommendation led to a request to the International Court of Justice to give an opinion on the question whether this was permissible under the Charter. The Court had no difficulty in reaching a negative answer.[13]

The principal legal argument in the General Assembly was that the Soviet Union was making improper use of its veto power by opposing applicants for reasons unrelated to Charter requirements. In 1947, this contention assumed greater concreteness since in the course of Council consideration of the applications of Finland and Italy the Soviet representative admitted that they were qualified but stated that since Bulgaria, Hungary, and Romania were also qualified in the opinion of his government he would insist on "all or none." [14] Thus, he made the admission of Finland and Italy dependent on a condition not explicitly stated in the Charter. The General Assembly subsequently asked the Court, in spite of the Soviet contention that such a request was improper, to give an opinion on the question whether a member of the Council was "juridically entitled to make its consent to admission dependent on conditions not expressly provided" by Article 4 of the Charter. The majority of the Court answered in the negative.[15] Some of the judges, a minority, were of the opinion, however, that the decision of the Council to recommend, like that of the General Assembly to admit, was a political decision and that members could properly base their individual positions on considerations other than the conditions listed in Article 4, paragraph 2, of the Charter. Subsequently the Assembly asked the Council to reconsider the applications that had been vetoed on grounds not enumerated in the Charter, but the Soviet Union refused to alter its stand.

Political efforts to break the deadlock centered on proposals that the permanent members of the Security Council reconsider their positions, that they consult with a view to reaching agreement on the admission

[13] *Competence of Assembly Regarding Admission to the United Nations, Advisory Opinion: I.C.J. Reports 1950,* p. 4.

[14] U.N. Security Council, *Official Records,* Second Year, 204th Meeting (Sept. 25, 1947), p. 2414–15.

[15] *Admission of a State to the United Nations (Charter, Art. 4), Advisory Opinion: I.C.J. Reports 1948,* p. 57.

of certain states, or that they agree to refrain from the use of the veto on membership questions. In 1947, the General Assembly recommended that the permanent members of the Security Council

> *consult with a view to reaching agreement on the admission to membership of the applicants which have not been recommended hitherto, and to submit their conclusions to the Security Council.*[16]

In April, 1949, the Assembly adopted a resolution recommending that the permanent members agree among themselves upon what possible questions they might forbear to exercise the veto, giving attention particularly to a list prepared by the Interim Committee which included recommendations for the admission of new Members.[17]

In the course of Security Council consideration of the membership deadlock in September, 1949, the Soviet delegation proposed the admission of all thirteen states, not including the Republic of Korea, which had applied up to that time. This proposal was defeated in the fourth session of the General Assembly in late 1949. It received some support outside the Soviet-controlled bloc but was opposed by the great majority of members. They argued that, though universality might be a desirable goal, applicants that were not qualified should not be admitted and therefore the qualifications of each applicant should be judged on its merits. The opinion of the Court was cited in suport of this position.

During the Assembly's seventh session in 1952, there was increasing evidence of support for a political solution, though members were not yet ready to agree to a package deal. It was argued that each applicant should be given the benefit of the doubt and should be denied admission only on the basis of clear evidence, going beyond mere suspicion and accusation. A Special Committee was set up to make a detailed study of various proposals. It reported in June, 1953, that after a detailed study of various proposals and suggestions, it had come to the conclusion that none of them were likely to find general acceptance among Members.

The conclusion of the Korean armistice in July, 1953, and the resultant lessening of international tension appear to have been in part responsible for the unwillingness of the Eighth Assembly to accept the continuing deadlock. There were indications of growing support for an effort to find some acceptable arrangement which would permit the deadlock to be broken. It was clear that members of the Assembly were becoming restless over failure to move toward a more inclusive member-

[16] General Assembly Resolution 113 (II), Nov. 17, 1947.
[17] General Assembly Resolution 267 (III), April 14, 1949.

	UN	IAEA	ILO	FAO	UNESCO[1]	WHO[2]	BANK	IFC	FUND	ICAO	UPU[3]	ITU[4]	WMO[5]
AFGHANISTAN													
ALBANIA													
ARGENTINA													
AUSTRALIA													
AUSTRIA													
BELGIUM													
BOLIVIA													
BRAZIL													
BULGARIA													
BURMA													
BYELORUSSIAN SSR													
CAMBODIA													
CANADA													
CEYLON													
CHILE													
CHINA													
COLOMBIA													
COSTA RICA													
CUBA													
CZECHOSLOVAKIA													
DENMARK													
DOMINICAN REPUBLIC													
ECUADOR													
EGYPT*													
EL SALVADOR													
ETHIOPIA													
FINLAND													
FRANCE													
GERMANY, Fed. Rep. of													
GHANA													
GREECE													
GUATEMALA													
HAITI													
HONDURAS													
HUNGARY													
ICELAND													
INDIA													
INDONESIA													
IRAN													
IRAQ													
IRELAND													
ISRAEL													

MEMBERSHIP OF THE UNITED NATIONS, THE INTERNATIONAL ATOMIC ENERGY AGENCY AND THE SPECIALIZED AGENCIES (AS OF 31 DECEMBER 1957)

ship for the United Nations and that opposition to the Soviet package proposal was weakening. The Assembly decided to appoint a Committee of Good Offices

> to consult with members of the Security Council with the object of exploring the possibilities of reaching an understanding which would facilitate the admission of new Members in accordance with Article 4 of the Charter.[18]

The Committee of Good Offices was forced to report to the ninth session of the Assembly that it had failed in its efforts to find the basis for an agreed solution. Nevertheless, it was clear in the course of the Assembly's discussions, partly no doubt due to the further lessening in international tension as a result of the ending of fighting in Indochina

[18] General Assembly Resolution 718 (VIII), Oct. 23, 1953.

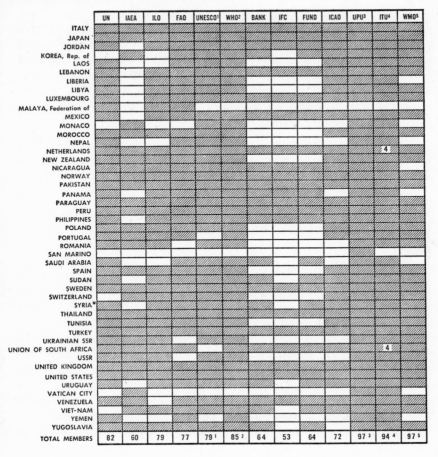

	UN	IAEA	ILO	FAO	UNESCO[1]	WHO[2]	BANK	IFC	FUND	ICAO	UPU[3]	ITU[4]	WMO[5]
ITALY													
JAPAN													
JORDAN													
KOREA, Rep. of													
LAOS													
LEBANON													
LIBERIA													
LIBYA													
LUXEMBOURG													
MALAYA, Federation of													
MEXICO													
MONACO													
MOROCCO													
NEPAL													
NETHERLANDS												4	
NEW ZEALAND													
NICARAGUA													
NORWAY													
PAKISTAN													
PANAMA													
PARAGUAY													
PERU													
PHILIPPINES													
POLAND													
PORTUGAL													
ROMANIA													
SAN MARINO													
SAUDI ARABIA													
SPAIN													
SUDAN													
SWEDEN													
SWITZERLAND													
SYRIA*													
THAILAND													
TUNISIA													
TURKEY													
UKRAINIAN SSR													
UNION OF SOUTH AFRICA												4	
USSR													
UNITED KINGDOM													
UNITED STATES													
URUGUAY													
VATICAN CITY													
VENEZUELA													
VIET-NAM													
YEMEN													
YUGOSLAVIA													
TOTAL MEMBERS	82	60	79	77	79[1]	85[2]	64	53	64	72	97[3]	94[4]	97[5]

* By plebiscite on February 21, 1958, Egypt and Syria were united to form the United Arab Republic. The Secretary-General was informed on March 1 that the new state would be a single Member of the United Nations.

and the Geneva agreements, that the majority of members were now more seriously than ever looking to a negotiated package arrangement as a way out. Even though some doubts might be held regarding the legal compatibility of such an approach with the provision of the Charter, particularly as interpreted by the Court in its advisory opinion, these doubts were increasingly subordinated to the desire to make the Organization more representative and, therefore, many believed, more effective, by substantially enlarging its membership.

By the time the tenth session of the Assembly convened in September, 1955, the Geneva Conference of heads of governments had met and the tensions of the "cold war" seemed to be at a new low. Those seeking to maintain effective opposition against the Soviet package proposal found their position fatally weakened. The Committee of Good Offices, which had been continued by the Ninth Assembly, reported encouragingly that there were indications that the positions of the permanent members of the Security Council were not immutable. On December 8, the Assembly by a vote of 52 to 2 with 5 abstentions requested the Security Council

> to consider, in the light of the general opinion in favor of the widest possible membership of the United Nations, the pending applications for membership of all those eighteen countries about which no problem of unification arises.[19]

In the Security Council, the full implementation of this suggested program was blocked by the Chinese veto of Outer Mongolia and the subsequent Soviet veto of those applications which it had not supported in the past. Nevertheless a new compromise, suggested by the Soviet Union, that excluded Outer Mongolia and Japan from the package was accepted, and on December 14, sixteen new Members were admitted by the General Assembly on recommendation of the Council. Thus, the long deadlock was broken by a political arrangement which some Members found difficult to harmonize with the provisions of Article 4 of the Charter. However, the overwhelming sentiment of the Assembly was favorable to the result since it brought the United Nations substantially nearer to universality of membership, a goal widely accepted as desirable. The following year the Eleventh Assembly, on the recommendation of the Council, admitted Japan, Tunisia, Morocco, and Sudan. And in 1957, Ghana and Malaya were admitted to bring the total to 82, as compared with the 51 members with which the Organization started. When Egypt and Syria became the United Arab Republic on February 21, 1958, the membership was reduced to 81.

Significance of Increased Membership

The expansion of the United Nations' membership entails possible consequences of great importance for the Organization, both for its future role and for the manner in which it discharges that role.[20]

[19] General Assembly Resolution 918 (X). The eighteen countries were Albania, Mongolian People's Republic, Hungary, Romania, Bulgaria, Jordan, Ireland, Portugal, Italy, Austria, Finland, Ceylon, Nepal, Libya, Cambodia, Japan, Laos, and Spain.

[20] See Eric Stein, *Some Implications of Expanding United Nations Membership* (New York: Carnegie Endowment, 1956).

Perhaps the most important and obvious result of this increase in membership is that the regional balance and the balance of political forces have been substantially altered. While the number of western European Members has been increased, from 10 to 16 if we include Austria and Finland, the number of avowedly Communist Members has been increased from 6 to 10, and the number of Afro-Asian states, inclined to "neutralism" in most cases, has increased from 19 to 30. On the other hand, the number of Members from the Western Hemisphere and the old British Commonwealth has remained constant.

While the various regional and political groups do not, for the most part, represent solid and consistent voting blocs,[21] it is nevertheless true that in so far as "cold war" issues have been involved, the American republics, the members of the old British Commonwealth and the western European states have generally acted together in opposing the Communist bloc. The Asian and African states, on the other hand, have been more inclined to follow a neutralist or middle-of-the-road course. With the increase in the size of the Communist and Afro-Asian blocs, it will no longer be as easy as formerly to mobilize a two-thirds vote in favor of an anti-Soviet "cold war" proposal. Nor for that matter will it be easy, if at all possible, for the Communists to get the necessary majorities. The likely consequence is that the United Nations, and more particularly the General Assembly, will become less useful to the Western powers as a means of waging an anti-Soviet campaign. More emphasis is likely to be placed on the mediating role of the United Nations, on its function of harmonizing the conflicting views and actions of its Members, in so far as the "cold war" is concerned. In other words, the expansion of membership is likely to result in more emphasis being placed upon the peaceful settlement and adjustment of disputes and less upon collective measures to resist aggression.[22]

While expanded membership is likely to alter the nature of the role of the United Nations in the "cold war," it may well accentuate the role of the United Nations as a means of achieving self-determination for subject peoples, and of promoting the economic and social development of under-developed countries. In this respect, the substantial increase in the relative strength of the Afro-Asian bloc can be a decisive factor. With the increase in the number of Asian and African Members, it will be considerably easier than before to organize the necessary majorities in support of political self-determination and economic,

[21] For an earlier study of bloc voting, see Margaret Ball, "Bloc Voting in the General Assembly," *International Organization,* V (1951), pp. 3–31.

[22] General Assembly action in dealing with the Hungarian and Middle East situations would tend to support this conclusion. The United Nations Emergency Force was not established as an instrument of enforcement, but rather to assist in restoring and maintaining peace by agreement.

social, and political development. In the past, the Communist states and many of the Latin-American republics have quite consistently given their support to these causes, even if for much different reasons. This same support can presumably be relied on in the future, and the enlarged size of the Afro-Asian bloc gives assurance that the role of the United Nations will be pushed with increasing vigor. It also becomes unlikely that the Charter will be revised to restrict the role of the Organization in these matters, either directly or by a more explicit and restrictive formulation of the domestic jurisdiction principle.

Already, it has become clear that one consequence of expanded membership is pressure to increase the number of elected members of United Nations organs in order to give broader representation and more opportunity for participation to the smaller states. It is doubtful whether, broadly conceived, adequate representation of regional or other group interests requires any enlargement of the elective segments of the United Nations Councils, except perhaps in the case of the Economic and Social Council. However, the simple desire of states to increase their chances of being elected is sufficient to produce substantial pressure for an increase in the number of elected members. The fact, however, that such changes require Charter amendment and that any amendment requires the approval of all the permanent members of the Security Council makes it reasonably certain that this pressure will fail to have much effect.

With 81 Members instead of 60, there will obviously be increased demands of various kinds—upon financial resources, upon physical facilities, upon the staff of the Secretariat, and upon the time of organs and of personnel. Especially since the new Members are to a large extent relatively small states without extensive resources, the increase in membership will mean an increase in work to be done without a corresponding increase in financial contributions from these states. This, in effect, may mean heavier burdens on older Members, unless substantial economies are found possible, but considering the size of the United Nations' budget, these burdens should not be excessive. The increase in membership can be especially serious in its consequences so far as the General Assembly is concerned. It can mean that even more time will be required for the consideration of additional items, an increase not necessarily proportional to the number of new items and their importance; more Member delegates will want the opportunity to talk on each item. If an overburdened General Assembly is not to be overwhelmed by such demands upon it, the development of more efficient procedures—less duplication, more effective limitation of debate, etc.— may be necessary. Furthermore, the definition of more satisfactory relations between the General Assembly and the Councils may at last be recognized as a necessity.

But perhaps the most important consequence of the enlargement of the United Nations—overshadowing all else—is the fact that now the United Nations, to a greater extent than ever before, corresponds with the political world in which it is called upon to operate. There are still important gaps. Germany is outside and presumably will continue to be, so long as it is divided. So is Communist China. Strategically important areas such as Korea and Viet-Nam are excluded. Still, the United Nations has moved much nearer to being the universal organization that it was intended eventually to be than the League of Nations was ever able to become. And to the extent that it has made progress in that direction, it should be able more effectively to achieve the purposes and perform the functions set forth in the Charter, provided of course that its Members are prepared to cooperate. That willingness cannot be assured by any organizational device but at least conditions can be established most conducive to its existence and to the development of the consequences that are desired to flow from it.

The Problem of Representation

Distinct from the problem of admitting new Members is that of determining the representation of states that are already Members. In so far as effective participation in the United Nations is concerned, the decision of an organ denying the right of a delegation to represent a state may have the same practical consequences as a decision not to admit a state to membership. In the case of China, for example, the Chinese people who inhabit mainland China and who are under the effective control of the Peking Government are just as effectively debarred from any participation through their representatives in the United Nations as if the Republic of China were not a Member, unless of course one accepts the thesis that the National Government on Taiwan represents the real interests of these people.

Normally, the problem of representation creates no particular difficulties since the representative appointed by the effective government of the Member state is usually accepted by each organ without question. When, however, there are two authorities which claim to be the government of a state, there arises the necessity of making a choice. This problem arose at the time of the San Francisco Conference when Poland, though a signatory of the Declaration by United Nations of January 1, 1942, was not invited to participate in the San Francisco Conference called to draft the Charter because the Sponsoring Governments were unable to agree on the government which they would recognize as representing Poland. After the conference had adjourned, agreement was reached, however, and through the action of the recognized government Poland became an original Member by signature and ratification of the Charter.

The problem did not arise in the United Nations until November, 1949 when in a cablegram to the President of the General Assembly the Foreign Minister of the Government of the People's Republic of China, the Communist regime which had succeeded in driving the Nationalist Government from the mainland, stated that his government repudiated the legal status of the delegation headed by T. F. Tsiang, appointed by the National Government seated on Taiwan, and held that it could not represent China and had no right to speak on behalf of the Chinese people in the United Nations. This stand was repeated in a cablegram to the governments of members of the Security Council on January 8, 1950. It was supported by the Soviet Union and when the Council refused to accept it, the Soviet representative withdrew.[23] At this time, the great majority of Members of the United Nations, including the United States, France, and the Latin American republics, recognized the National Government as the Government of the Republic of China. The Communist Members, the United Kingdom, and India were among the number that recognized the Peking Government.[24]

After the initial consideration of the question by the Security Council, the Secretary-General requested the preparation of a confidential memorandum on legal aspects of the problem and subsequently made it public.[25] This memorandum argued that the question of representation had been improperly linked with the question of recognition by Member governments. It argued that the proper principle could be derived, however, by analogy from Article 4 of the Charter relating to membership. The obligations of membership could be carried out only by Governments which in fact possessed the power to do so. When a revolutionary government presented itself as representing a state, in rivalry to an existing government, the question at issue should be: Which of these two governments in fact is in a position to employ the resources and direct the people of the state in fulfillment of the obligations of membership? In essence, this required an inquiry as to whether the new

[23] Security Council, *Official Records,* Fifth Year, 459th Meeting (Jan. 10, 1950), pp. 1–4.

[24] The Nationalist Government was recognized by 43 Members and the Communist Government by 16.

[25] U.N. Doc. S/1466, March 9, 1950.

government exercised effective authority within the territory of the state and was habitually obeyed by the bulk of the population. If these facts were established, United Nations organs should accord to the new government the right of representation even though individual Members might refuse to accord recognition for political reasons which they considered valid.

During the fifth session of the General Assembly the question was discussed at some length. The United Kingdom, supported by a number of other members, took a position similar to that of the Secretary-General's memorandum, that for purposes of representation in the United Nations, that government should be recognized which was in effective control of all, or nearly all, the state's territory and which had the allegiance of the overwhelming majority of the population.

The majority, however, under United States leadership, took a position more or less similar to that outlined by Cuba, namely that a revolutionary government to be recognized for purposes of representation must exercise effective authority, be based on the consent of the population, be able and willing to achieve the purposes of the Charter and fulfill its obligations under the Charter and international law, and respect human rights and fundamental freedoms. In effect this argument adopted as conditions of recognition for purposes of representation, the conditions which Article 4 of the Charter requires that an applicant for admission must satisfy.

The General Assembly finally adopted a resolution which really evaded the main issue.[26] It recommended that the question of representation, wherever it arises, should be considered "in the light of the Purposes and Principles of the Charter and the circumstances of each case," that the question should first be considered by the General Assembly, and that the attitude adopted by the General Assembly should be taken into account by other organs and by the specialized agencies.

During the following six years there was no change in the position of the United Nations organs and the specialized agencies on the question of Chinese representation. Two factors were important in producing this result: (1) the attitude of the United States Government, reflecting the bitter opposition to the Communist regime in China which pervaded the country and Congress; and (2) the military intervention of Communist China in Korea which strengthened United States opposition as well as the opposition of other Members to the seating of Chinese Communist representatives. It had become reasonably clear by the Tenth Assembly in 1955, however, that the opposition of the United States was all that stood in the way of the reversal of the Assembly's position.

[26] General Assembly Resolution 396 (V), Dec. 14, 1950.

Since this opposition was largely based on domestic political attitudes, any lessening of it was not likely to result from arguments such as had been adduced in the Secretary General's memorandum or in the Assembly debates. A change in opinion in the United States was necessary. Conceivably a factor in producing this change might be the danger of United States isolation on the issue and some evidence that world communism had dropped its aggressive purposes.

Failure to seat the representatives of the Peking government means that the government which is in effective control of China, representing a substantial part of the world's population and an important sector of the world's surface, does not participate in the work of the United Nations, even though the Republic of China is a Member. Since it has become increasingly obvious that Communist China is not just a temporary phase of China's development but, rather, represents an increasingly important force in international relations, particularly those of the Pacific area, failure to seat representatives of Communist China in the United Nations means that many important questions such as Korea, the limitation of armaments, and security in eastern Asia and the western Pacific cannot be usefully discussed nor realistic solutions sought through the United Nations. Whether one approves of the Communist regime in China or not, there can be no denying that it represents a factor of increasing importance in world politics, and the question may well be asked whether the purposes and principles of the United Nations can more effectively be furthered by bringing this force within the operations of the United Nations or by keeping it outside. If universality is a cause worthy of espousal in so far as membership is concerned, does not the same principle have application in the matter of representation? [27]

SUGGESTED READINGS

Ball, Margaret. "Bloc Voting in the General Assembly," *International Organization,* V (1951), pp. 3–31.

Briggs, Herbert W. "Chinese Representation in the United Nations," *International Organization,* VI (1952), pp. 192–209.

Brown, Benjamin H., and Greene, Fred. *Chinese Representation: A Case Study in United Nations Political Affairs.* New York: Woodrow Wilson Foundation, 1955.

[27] For an excellent discussion of the subject, see Herbert W. Briggs, "Chinese Representation in the United Nations," *International Organization,* VI (1952), pp. 192–209.

Claude, Inis, Jr. *Swords into Plowshares.* New York: Random House, Inc., 1956. Chap. 5.

Goodrich, Leland M. "American National Interests and the Responsibility of United Nations Members," *International Organization,* VI (1952), pp. 369–80.

Gross, Leo. "Progress Towards Universality of Membership in the United Nations," *American Journal of International Law,* L (1956), pp. 791–827.

Jenks, C. Wilfred. "Some Constitutional Problems of International Organizations," *British Yearbook of International Law,* XXII (1945), pp. 11–72.

Liang, Yuen-li. "Recognition by the United Nations of the Representation of a Member State: Criteria and Procedure," *American Journal of International Law,* XLV (1951), pp. 689–707.

Rudzinski, Alexander W. "Admission of New Members: the United Nations and the League of Nations," *International Conciliation,* No. 480 (April 1952), pp. 143–96.

Stein, Eric. *Some Implications of Expanding United Nations Membership.* New York: Carnegie Endowment for International Peace, 1956.

U.S. Senate Committee on Foreign Relations, Subcommittee on the United Nations Charter. *The Problem of Membership in the United Nations.* Staff Study No. 3. Washington: Government Printing Office, 1954.

Chapter VI

THE STRUCTURE OF
POWER AND INFLUENCE

WRITERS ON international relations are in general agreement
on the importance of power in the relations between states. Power as a
factor in international relations is not to be thought of solely in terms
of military strength. It includes economic, political, and psychological
elements as well.[1] The importance of power in international affairs
derives in large measure from the nature of international relations.
Under a political system where authority is centered in separate states,
subject to no such controls as exist under a federal system of government, the relative power of each state inevitably becomes an important
and often decisive influence in determining relations between that state
and other states. The exercise of this power in a given situation may
take such forms as largely to conceal it, as, for example, in the relations
of the United States to Canada. Regardless, however, of the form of its
exercise, states are not likely to relinquish voluntarily the advantages
which superior power give them in furthering national purposes. Though
they may be willing to give up the right to exercise this power in certain
ways, they are likely to insist on compensatory arrangements.

Power in International Organization

When states possessing substantial power consider the establishment of and participation in international organizations to facilitate
the achievement of common purposes, they are generally reluctant to
relinquish all advantages which they have enjoyed as the result of

[1] See E. H. Carr, *The Twenty-Years' Crisis, 1919–1939* (New York: The Macmillan Company, 1940), pp. 131 ff.

superior power and seek to have the organization so constituted that they will be able within this framework to continue to exercise the measure of influence they previously have enjoyed. On the other hand, relatively weak states, which in the absence of special arrangements are at the mercy of more powerful states, naturally seek to take advantage of every opportunity offered by international organization to increase their relative power and influence. Consequently, whenever an international organization is established, one of the major concerns of governments in the course of preliminary discussions and negotiations is to see to it that the arrangements made are as favorable as possible to their power position. Those states that have the reputation of being "major powers" seek to retain that status at least in so far as all questions involving their vital national interests are concerned, and those states that are among the "lesser powers" seek to improve their position either by placing limitations on the great or by obtaining institutionalized arrangements by which their influence can be exercised more effectively than hitherto. The same basic concerns are present when it is a matter of determining how the organization, once created, is going to function.

When the League Covenant was being written this problem of the organization of power relations was very much to the fore, particularly in respect to the manner in which the principal purpose of the League, the prevention of war, was to be achieved. The Anglo-American plan proposed that the five Principal Allied and Associated Powers comprise the Council, the organ which would be chiefly concerned with handling particular disputes and situations in which peace might be threatened, and with drafting proposals for the limitation of armaments.[2] This was recognition not only of the fact that the League was in a real sense to be a continuation of the coalition of victor nations, but also of the special interest of the major powers in matters of peace and war and the special contributions they were expected to make to the preservation of peace. Though the Covenant provided that the Council was to include four non-permanent members elected by the Assembly, there still was substantial recognition of the greater importance of the major powers in the provision for their permanent membership. The importance of power even in dealing with social and economic questions and problems of backward areas was recognized in the role assigned to the Council in dealing with these matters. Thus, it was the Council that was made responsible for supervising the administration of mandated territories.

On the other hand, the Covenant defined in very inclusive terms the role of the Assembly and provided for its organization and functioning on much the same lines as previous international conferences of

[2] The United States, United Kingdom, France, Italy, and Japan.

inclusive membership.[3] In principle, each member state, regardless of its relative power, had the same opportunity to participate in its discussions, the same voting power, and the same ability to prevent a decision from being taken. While this equalitarianism seemed to be inconsistent with power politics as it had been practiced, and seemed to mark a departure from the hierarchy of power relationships which had previously prevailed, this was more apparent than real.

The governments of the major powers anticipated that through the Council they would in fact assume a role in the work of the League reflecting their power status. In other words, the Council was viewed in principle as a continuation of the European Concert idea, modified to give representation as a right to selected smaller states. Furthermore, the major powers expected to be able to exercise an influence on General Assembly decisions more nearly proportionate to their actual power status than their formal voting strength might indicate, since in matters of concern to the major powers the lesser powers could be expected to be greatly influenced by major power desires. If necessary, a decision could always be prevented by a negative vote. The practice that developed in the Assembly of adopting *voeux,* i.e., recommendations or expressions of desire, by majority vote did to some extent impinge upon this strictly legal protection of the Great Power position, but it still left informal influence free to operate.

In the actual functioning of the League, the organization of power for which the Covenant originally provided underwent substantial modification. For one thing, the failure of the United States to join upset the relationship between major and minor powers in the Council and successive increases in the number of non-permanent members further modified it. As a result, the major powers tended more and more to deal with important problems of vital concern to themselves through negotiations conducted outside the League so they would not be subject to the limitations of League organization and procedure. Also, for a variety of reasons, the Assembly expanded its role and influence. Though the major powers were protected by the unanimity requirement and the greater influence they could exercise on Assembly discussions and voting, the development of the Assembly's role did tend to emphasize those non-material elements of power with respect to which the smaller states were in the most favorable position to compete with the larger.

In the planning and constructing of the United Nations there was on the part of the major powers,[4] a firm insistence on recognition of

---

[3] E.g., the two Hague Conferences of 1899 and 1907.

[4] In connection with the United Nations, the term is used to describe the Sponsoring Governments and France at the San Francisco Conference.

their special role. In Department of State planning during the early years of the War there was frank recognition of the desirability of so constructing the organization that the major victor nations would have the primary responsibility and necessary power for maintaining international peace and security. In President Roosevelt's early thinking what amounted to a three-power directorate of the victor nations was envisaged, at least for the transitional period. Furthermore, both President Roosevelt and Prime Minister Churchill initially favored the organization of international security on a regional basis, with regional arrangements organized around the dominant major powers in the areas. Official thinking in the United States, the United Kingdom, and the Soviet Union seemed to envisage something closely akin to the European Concert of the nineteenth century.

The Dumbarton Oaks Proposals, representing the views of the Governments of the United States, the United Kingdom, the Soviet Union, and China went far in institutionalizing the dominant power position of these nations. The Security Council, dominated by these powers and France, was to be primarily responsible for dealing with threats to international peace. The General Assembly was envisaged as a conference of Member states which would be responsible for developing general principles of cooperation in the political field and for initiating and developing cooperation in economic and social matters. Special provisions were written into the Charter to prevent the Assembly's encroaching upon the field of the Council's special responsibility. It would be limited to discussion and recommendation in any case, not having the power given to the Council to take binding decisions.

This proposal to give the major victor nations something approaching the same authority in maintaining international peace after the War that they had in prosecuting the War then in progress aroused serious criticism in many quarters. In the United States, some Republican leaders let it be known that this smacked too much of great-power dictatorship, that it did not sufficiently take into account the interests and possible contributions of the smaller nations, and that, besides, it assumed a cooperative spirit on the part of the Soviet Union which might not be forthcoming. Many of the smaller countries, though allies in the War, made it quite clear that they objected to this kind of great-power dictation and in particular feared that it might lead to another Munich-type settlement, if the Great Powers should find this to their interest. In the course of the San Francisco Conference numerous efforts were made to restrict the discretionary powers of the Security Council and more particularly to reduce the influence of the major powers. For the most part these efforts were not successful. However, the effort to broaden the scope of the General Assembly's powers of discussion and recommendation was more successful; this provided the basis for the later development of the General Assembly's role, either as competitor to the Security Council, or as an alternative to the Council in case the latter was incapable of discharging its responsibilities. Articles 10 and 14 of the Charter have become particularly significant in this connection.

Composition and Powers of United Nations Organs

In the Charter as finally written the major powers were generally successful in getting their power positions translated into institutional form in matters relating to the maintenance of international peace and security. While they were forced to make some concessions, none of these would have been fatal to the realization of their purposes had it not been for their failure subsequently to cooperate among themselves. In the economic and social field, they made no serious attempt to achieve this result, being prepared to rely upon the influence which their greater wealth and economic importance gave them and upon the right of each Member to decide for itself how far it would go in accepting proposals made by the United Nations organs. In dealing with problems of non-self-governing territories, the same was generally true though some features of the organization of the trusteeship system gave special assurances to the administering states. For a detailed understanding of the extent to which power relations were actually respected in the establishment of the Organization it is necessary to consider first, the powers of the Organization in relation to its Members, and the powers of the various organs in relation to the structure and voting procedure of these organs.

It is important to remember that the United Nations by its very nature does not infringe upon the independence and sovereign powers of its Members. It is based upon the principle of sovereign equality. It is prohibited from intervening in matters essentially within the domestic jurisdiction of states. In dealing with problems that come within the normal purview of international relations, it does not have governmental power except to a very limited extent. For the most part, organs are limited to inquiry, discussion, and recommendation. Consequently, the fact that in the over-all structure of the Organization more recognition is given to the equalitarian principle than the actual inequalities of states would justify does not necessarily mean that individual states by becoming Members have yielded their special power advantages. Furthermore, while it is not explicitly stated in the Charter, it was clearly understood and agreed at the time the Charter was adopted at San Francisco, that each organ is the judge of its own powers under the Charter and that Members have the usual rights of parties to a multilateral agreement to interpret its provisions for themselves. However, states by becoming Members do undertake not to use force or the threat of force against other states except under certain specified conditions. This means, of course, that in so far as Members respect their obligations they may lose some of the advantages derived from the possession of superior military power. But it can be argued that international law had already seen to that.

Of the various organs of the United Nations the Security Council is the one that was originally intended most closely to reflect existing power relations. The Council was to be composed of five permanent members and six non- permanent members chosen by the General Assembly for two-year terms, ". . . due regard being especially paid, in the first instance to the contribution of Members of the United Nations to the maintenance of international peace and security and to the other purposes of the Organization, and also to equitable geographical distribution." [5] Of the five permanent members, three—the United States, the Soviet Union, and the United Kingdom—were members of the wartime coalition that made the major contributions to the defeat of the Axis Powers. Their continuing cooperation in the Security Council was obviously desirable, if not necessary, if the Council was to discharge its responsibilities effectively. France and China were perhaps less qualified on the basis of power alone to be permanent members. Churchill, in particular, was insistent that France be given that status to assure her cooperation in the maintenance of European peace and security. China, though its internal political condition was uncertain and its military strength problematic, had, nevertheless, hung on doggedly in the war against Japan. From the point of view of United States policy, the development of a strong, democratic China was considered important to the maintenance of peace and security in the Far East, and her inclusion in the Security Council as a permanent member was thought to contribute to the achievement of this purpose.

While the Charter provisions gave no absolute guarantee that the middle-range powers would be more frequently chosen as non-permanent members than the lesser ones, the principal criterion which the Assembly was supposed to take into account was definitely intended to produce that result. So far as the voting procedure of the Security Council was concerned, the requirement of concurrence of the permanent members for all decisions on non-procedural questions gave to

[5] Article 23, par. 1.

the principal possessors of power effective control over the important decisions of the United Nations, including some relating to internal organization.

With the Security Council thus constituted and its voting procedure thus defined, the major powers were willing to vest it with powers which went beyond any that had been given to international organs in the past. It was given not only the power to deal with disputes and situations affecting the peace, like the League Council before it, but also the power to order Members to take a wide variety of measures— diplomatic, economic, financial, and military—to maintain or restore international peace and security, in case of a threat to the peace, breach of the peace or, act of aggression. Giving the Council this kind of authority was only possible because those who would be called upon to make the major contributions to enforcement action were also given decisive influence over decisions. It should also be noted that as the result of pressure by some of the "middle powers" at San Francisco, any Member, before being called upon to take military measures was assured the opportunity to participate in the Council's decisions, but not to the extent of exercising a veto.[6]

In contrast to the Security Council, the General Assembly was originally viewed as the organ most fully expressing the equalitarian principle. As was true of the League Assembly and of earlier meetings such as the Hague Conferences of 1899 and 1907, in the General Assembly all Members have the right to equal representation, equal opportunity to participate in discussions, and equal voting power. However, unlike its predecessor, the General Assembly is able to take decisions on substantive matters by a majority or two-thirds vote, depending upon the importance of the question. In addition, the General Assembly is competent to deal under the Charter with a very wide range of matters—"any questions or any matters within the scope of the present Charter or relating to the powers and functions of any organs provided for in the present Charter." [7] More specifically, the Assembly can consider the general principles of cooperation in the maintenance of international peace and security as well as specific questions relating to the maintenance of peace and security; it can deal with a wide range of matters in the field of economic, social, and cultural cooperation; and it can concern itself with the administration of non-self-governing territories, human rights, and self-determination. /

How explain the fact that the major powers were willing at San Francisco to agree to a Charter that vested competence to deal with such a wide range of important matters in an organ such as the General

[6] Article 44.   [7] Article 10.

Assembly? Did they not thereby relinquish to others control over important matters which in the absence of such an organization they would have had by virtue of their superior power? The answer is to be found in the nature of the powers vested in the General Assembly. Unlike the Security Council, it has no power to take decisions binding on Members with respect to their policies and conduct in their international relations. While the Charter authorizes the Assembly to take binding procedural decisions, to perform certain elective functions, to admit new members, and to approve the budget and allocate expenses, the Charter otherwise limits it to initiating studies, discussing matters brought before it, and making recommendations to Members and to other organs.

As a matter of fact, the Soviet Union was strongly averse at San Francisco to expanding unduly the Assembly's power to discuss and recommend, presumably anticipating the possibility that even these limited powers might be used on some future occasion to embarrass it. The other Sponsoring Governments—particularly the United States—appear to have believed that the influence which they would be able to exercise over other members in the course of discussions and preliminary to voting would compensate for the lack of formal safeguards, and would give them reasonable assurance of being able to get favorable decisions. Besides, the Western democracies could not deny this opportunity for discussion and registering formal conclusions in the General Assembly without appearing to be unfaithful to their own political principles, and without jeopardizing friendships and good will upon which the success of their foreign policies depended.

There is surprisingly little regard shown by the provisions of the Charter for power considerations in the organization of the economic and social work of the United Nations. The major powers appear to have been willing in principle to accept the equalitarian principle. The Charter provides for an Economic and Social Council composed of eighteen members, six elected each year by a two-thirds vote of the General Assembly for three year terms. When the Charter was being drafted, it was proposed that the chief industrial nations should be given some assurance of permanent membership, preferably by including some suitable criteria which the Assembly would be required to follow or at least take into account. This practice had been provided in the Constitution of the International Labour Organization with respect to the Governing Body.[8] The final decision, however, was to leave the

[8] Article 7 of the original ILO Constitution provided that eight of the sixteen government representatives on the Governing Body should be appointed by the members of chief industrial importance as determined by the Governing Body.

Assembly complete discretion, on the assumption that it would recognize the necessity, if the Council was to be effective, of including in it United Nations Members of chief industrial importance. In the matter of voting procedure, it was decided at San Francisco that all Council decisions should be taken by majority vote.

While on the surface the provisions regarding the composition and voting procedure of ECOSOC seemed like a great concession on the part of the larger states, much the same considerations that applied to General Assembly voting applied here. Since ECOSOC could only discuss and make recommendations, there was always the possibility of not carrying out the recommendations made. In addition, since the Council was to perform its functions under the authority of the General Assembly, the Council could in a sense be regarded as a subsidiary organ of the Assembly. That being the case, even if the Council reflected more completely the particular interests and influence of the major powers, there was always the possibility of its being overruled. Finally, there was always the need of cooperation on the part of the major powers, or at least some of them, to give effect to any decisions that the Council and Assembly might take in this area, and this provided a built-in assurance that the major powers would have great, if not decisive, influence over decisions taken.

In the case of the Trusteeship Council, the problem of structure and voting procedure was somewhat complicated by considerations not applicable to ECOSOC. First, the Council was given functions and powers under the trusteeship system which involved substantial inter-vention in the administration of certain non-self-governing territories by the administering states. Though the functions of the United Nations with respect to trusteeship were to be exercised by the General Assembly with the assistance of the Trusteeship Council, except in the case of strategic areas, it was clear that the detailed supervision would be exercised in the first instance by the Council. Moreover, it was con-sidered likely that General Assembly action would be guided to a large extent by the decisions of the Trusteeship Council. Furthermore, the Trusteeship Council was not to assist the General Assembly exclusively. In the case of strategic areas under trusteeship, the Security Council was to perform United Nations functions and the Trusteeship Council was to assist it.

These considerations help to explain why it was not possible to constitute the Trusteeship Council in the same way as the Economic and Social Council. In the end, the composition of the Council was deter-mined by competing demands of various groups interested in achieving a favorable power position with respect to the particular functions to be performed. First, there was the conflict between the colonial powers, or more accurately the states in possession of territories likely to be placed under trusteeship on the one hand, and the newly independent states and those sympathetic with the goal of rapid economic, social and political development on the other. Second, there was, to a lesser extent than in the case of the Security Council, the conflict between the interests of the larger and the lesser powers. In the end, a compromise was reached which provided for an equal balance between administering and non-administering states, and at the same time assured membership to all permanent members of the Security Council.

But while certain states were guaranteed permanent membership, they were accorded no special voting privileges. Here again, the consideration that the Council discharged its functions under the authority of the General Assembly and therefore was in a sense a subsidiary organ of the Assembly was probably a determining consideration. Certainly, the major powers and the administering states were willing to accept much less in the way of constitutional protection of their interests than they enjoyed under the Covenant which, first, made the Council responsible for exercising League functions, and second, required the consent of all members of the Council, including the League member invited to sit as a member of the Council while its report as a mandatory was being considered.

While the Secretariat was to have the most pronounced international character of any organ of the United Nations, with the exception of the Court, there was considerable evidence at San Francisco that Governments were aware of the political importance of this organ and of the influence it might have in determining the course of action of the Organization. One important decision at San Francisco was to give the Secretary-General a larger political role than his League counterpart. This, of course, meant that so far as his choice was concerned, political considerations would inevitably play a part. With the possibility that he might use his power and prestige to influence United Nations action in political matters, it was inevitable that the major powers should demand a decisive role in his choice, as they had indeed done in the case of the League Secretary-General even though his role was then conceived in less political terms. It is significant that at San Francisco the major powers stood in united opposition to any proposal to eliminate the requirement of Security Council recommendation in the choice of the Secretary-General, or the requirement of concurrence of the permanent members in making such recommendation. An attempt on the part of the Soviet Union to extend this political control to the Secretary-General's chief assistants was defeated; on this issue, the major powers were not united. Even in laying down the qualifications for staff employment, the Charter makes a concession to the political

factor. It specifies that "due regard shall be paid to the importance of
recruiting the staff on as wide a geographical basis as possible."

The International Court of Justice, alone of the principal organs of
the United Nations, has the power to take substantive decisions binding
upon states while not reflecting to any substantial extent in its formal
structure, the power relations of Member states. The Statute of the
Court does not specify that any of the judges must be nationals or appointees of the major powers. Judges must be persons of "high moral
character, who possess the qualifications required in their respective
countries for appointment to the highest judicial offices, or are jurisconsults of recognized competence on international law." [9] They are
chosen for nine-year terms by the General Assembly and the Security
Council voting concurrently and by majority vote. While this procedure
means that the permanent members of the Security Council are assured
greater influence than the non-permanent members, it does not permit
a permanent member to veto any candidate nor does it make it possible
for the permanent members acting together to dictate the results. There
are, however, provisions which reflect a concern that the Court should
have a broadly representative character. The Security Council and the
General Assembly are required to bear in mind the desirability of
representation of the main forms of civilization and the principal legal
systems of the world, as well as individual qualifications.[10] If there is
on the Court at a particular time a judge of the nationality of one party
to a dispute and not of the other, the second can appoint a national judge
to serve in the particular case.[11] Not more than one national of a state
can serve as a judge at any one time.

The willingness of states, even major powers, to accept the possibility of not being represented on the Court, except in cases to which
they are parties, and in any case of having the Court hand down decisions adverse to them without the possibility of veto can be explained
on a number of grounds. First, the Court does not have the same range
of discretion in taking its decisions as do the political organs. Its
judgments and advisory opinions must be based on international law,
except where the parties agree to a decision *ex aequo et bono*. Second,
the matters submitted to the Court are generally not of such a nature as
to involve considerations affecting highly important national interests,
and, furthermore, if submitted, are submitted with the consent of the
parties,[12] with the full realization that the decision may go against them.

[9] Article 2 of the Statute.   [10] Article 9 of the Statute.
[11] Article 31 of the Statute.
[12] Expressed either by a special agreement for the particular dispute or by
acceptance of the Court's compulsory jurisdiction.

Finally, while the Court may give advisory opinions without the consent of the states directly concerned, neither they nor the organs requesting the opinions are strictly speaking bound to accept them.

Development of the Structure of Power and Influence in U.N. Practice

In actual practice, the structure of power and influence in the United Nations has been quite different from what was initially envisaged. The Charter itself has not been amended. The composition, functions, and powers of organs have remained the same on paper. But in the course of the day-to-day interpretation and application of these provisions, a quite different system of power relationships has emerged from that which was anticipated at the time the Charter was approved in San Francisco. Within limits this was inevitable. It is never possible of course to foresee in detail the course of future institutional development. The United Nations being a living thing, it was bound to happen that in the course of the interpretation and application of its Charter to changing circumstances some things would emerge that were different from what had been planned. The radical nature of these changes has been due, however, to the fact that the Charter and the organs for which it provides have been subjected to political pressures and influences in the postwar world which were different in kind and degree from the assumptions of the Charter-makers.

CHOICE OF COUNCIL MEMBERS

In the exercise of its elective functions the General Assembly has generally been guided by the principle of equitable geographic representation. In the case of the Security Council this principle has tended to take precedence over the principle that due regard should be paid to the ability of Members to contribute to the maintenance of international peace and security and to the other purposes of the Organization. Consistently, from the beginning two elected members have been Latin American republics; one has been a western European state; one has been a Middle Eastern state; one a member of the Commonwealth of Nations; [13] and until 1957, one was an eastern European state.[14] In

[13] The Commonwealth seat has in fact been quite commonly so filled as to give representation to Asia or Oceania.

[14] By the compromise agreement under which the Assembly elected Yugoslavia for a 1956–1958 term it was understood that Yugoslavia would resign at the

making regional selections, some attention has been given to the principle of ability to contribute, but clearly this has been a subordinate consideration. This pattern of selection has not however greatly influenced the action of the Council because of the special voting privilege of the permanent members, which in the context of the "cold war," has on most issues been decisive.

In the election of the members of the Economic and Social Council, the Assembly has likewise been guided to a large degree by the principle of geographic representation. Nevertheless, it appears to have given due regard to the industrial importance of Members and to their ability to contribute to the achievement of United Nations goals. Though the Charter contains no provision assuring or even encouraging the re-election of particular Members to ECOSOC, the permanent members of the Security Council have been consistently re-elected, thus for practical purposes acquiring the status of permanent members. Until 1957, seven Members had served three terms, having been re-elected at least once. These were Members of middle industrial importance or large population.[15] An even larger number had served for two terms. This emphasis on relative importance in terms of productivity and population is realized, however, within a basic pattern of geographic representation which is more refined than in the case of the Security Council due to the large number of places to be filled, even excluding the five seats occupied by the permanent members of the Security Council. Under the pattern that has thus far evolved, the membership of ECOSOC includes four Latin American republics, one western European state, one Scandinavian state, two or three from eastern Europe (both Communist and non Communist), one or two from the Middle East, one from the Commonwealth, and one from eastern Asia. This pattern however is likely to be changed under the impact of the increase in membership from 60 to 81 and the unequal effect this has had on the size and voting strength of the different geographic or political groups.

In the case of the Trusteeship Council, since the Charter provides for an even balance between members administering trust territories and non-administering members, the fair assumption is that members elected by the Assembly will be particularly concerned to make the trusteeship system as effective as possible in promoting the welfare of the native peoples and in protecting the larger international interests.

---

end of one year to be succeeded by the Philippines. In 1957, Japan was elected to succeed the Philippines and, thus, the eastern European seat was given for the time being to eastern Asia.

[15] Belgium, Canada, Czechoslovakia, India, Pakistan, Poland, and Yugoslavia.

It is not surprising, therefore, that only those Members of the United Nations who can be expected to take a critical attitude toward colonialism have been elected to the Council. Thus, of the five elected members at the beginning of 1957, two were Latin American republics, one was a Middle Eastern state and two were from south and southeastern Asia. Since the two members who hold their seats by virtue of permanent membership on the Security Council (China and the Soviet Union) are also highly critical of colonialism, there is an even balance between the critics and the defenders of modern colonial administration, though the position of the United States, an administering state, has tended to be somewhat ambivalent.

DECLINING ROLE OF SECURITY COUNCIL

The principal changes in the structure of power and influence have come about as the result of developments that have taken place in the actual functioning of United Nations organs and in the relations between them under the impact of political developments since the war.

The Security Council, which was expected to play the primary role in the maintenance of international peace and security, has, in fact, proved to be relatively much less important. Because of their inability to agree, the major powers have not been able through that organ to exercise the positive influence over the course of international political affairs which their permanent membership and their special voting privileges were expected to assure them. The mechanism has been available; what has been lacking has been a willingness and ability to make use of it.

It has been commonly said that the relative impotence of the Security Council, and its failure to exercise effectively its Charter powers have been due to the abuse of the veto by the Soviet Union. There is a substantial amount of truth to this charge. Nevertheless, it oversimplifies and distorts the actual situation. It is true that as of May 2, 1958, 89 vetoes were cast, and that of these the Soviet Union was responsible for 82. There are, however, a number of considerations to be kept in mind in analyzing the causes of, and the responsibility for, Council ineffectiveness. In the first place, a substantial number of the Soviet vetoes —over half—were exercised on membership applications, and this number was substantially inflated by the repeated practice of the non-Communist members of pressing for Security Council votes on individual membership applications, when it was obvious that a Soviet veto would be exercised. This practice helped to build up the list of Soviet vetoes and provided evidence of Soviet obstructionism. Of the remaining vetoes, four were used to defeat proposals relating to the regulation of armaments and two to prevent the recommendation by the Council of particular persons for appointment as Secretary-General. The rest, about 40 in number, were used to defeat proposals made to carry out the peaceful settlement and enforcement functions of the Security Council.[16]

Whether the veto has been abused is a question which cannot be decided solely on the basis of the number of times it has been used. A veto in itself is not wrong since it is the exercise of the right to dissent recognized in the Charter. Nevertheless, the representatives of the major powers at San Francisco in defending the so-called Yalta voting formula took great pains to explain that it was not to be assumed that the veto would be used "willfully to obstruct the operation of the Council." [17] Consequently it is fair to argue that a permanent member of the Council should not exercise the veto for a small or inconsequential reason. But certainly the fact that the vetoing state is obstructing the will of the majority is not necessarily evidence of abuse.

Have the reasons of the Soviet Union for its use of the veto been such as to establish that its motive is to obstruct the work of the Organization rather than to defend its important interests? This is a difficult judgment to make because it must take into account legitimate Soviet purposes and interests. It would seem that when in 1946 the Soviet Union vetoed a United States proposal on the complaint of Syria and Lebanon on the ground that it did not go far enough in condemning the United Kingdom and France, it certainly was not making a reasonable effort to achieve the consensus necessary to a decision. Likewise, in exercising the veto in a number of membership applications, the Soviet Union appeared to be more interested in establishing a bargaining position than in judging fairly the qualifications of applicants.

While the veto has been many times used, undoubtedly excessively by any fair standard of judgment, the requirement of great power concurrence, with the possibility of a great power veto, has not wholly prevented the Security Council from performing its functions under the Charter in an effective manner. Though the veto was responsible for a serious deadlock over membership and a delay of several years in the admission of some states that were considered by the great majority of

[16] For a list of Security Council vetoes, see Arlette Moldaver, "Repertoire of the Veto in the Security Council," *International Organization,* XI (1957), pp. 261–74. See, also, U.S. Senate Committee on Foreign Relations, Subcommittee on the United Nations Charter (Washington, D.C.: Government Printing Office, 1954); and Aleksander W. Rudzinski, "Majority Rule and Great Power Agreement in the United Nations," *International Organization,* IX (1955), pp. 366–75.

[17] For the text of the statement, see UNCIO, *Documents,* XI, pp. 710–14; and Goodrich and Hambro, *op. cit.,* pp. 216–18.

Members to be fully qualified, the deadlock was subsequently broken. In 1958, the only applications outstanding were those of the Republic of Korea (South), the Democratic People's Republic of Korea (North), the Republic of Viet-Nam (South), the Democratic Republic of Viet-Nam (North) and Outer Mongolia. Four of these represented divided states, where the rival claims of communist and non-communist regimes prevented the achievement of national unification. In the case of Outer Mongolia, the Soviet Union's support had weakened to the extent that it has ceased to insist on its inclusion in a package deal in the face of strongly expressed doubts regarding its independent statehood. Though the Soviet Union used the veto to defeat the reappointment of Trygve Lie as Secretary-General, it subsequently—three years later—proved possible for the permanent members to agree on the name of a successor. In the meantime, Mr. Lie continued to serve under a General Assembly resolution extending his term. In the field of limitation of armaments, the veto simply reflected the inability of the great powers to agree on the principles and details of proposals which when approved by the Council might be submitted to Members for their consideration. If there had been no possibility of a veto, the solution of the problem would be no nearer.

It is primarily with respect to the discharge of its functions of peaceful settlement and enforcement action under Chapters VI and VII that the claim is made that the Security Council, because of the veto, has been ineffective. There is no question that in a sense and to a certain extent this is true. The claim assumes that effectiveness requires positive action in every case, and furthermore the assumption seems implicit in most instances that the Council is not effective if used to defeat a proposal which, though it has the support of all except one or two members of the Council, is not adopted. It is difficult to harmonize these tests of effectiveness with the provisions of the Charter and statements made in the San Francisco Conference and before. Under the Charter as drafted, the possibility of a failure on the part of the permanent members to reach agreement on a particular proposal was certainly envisaged. Furthermore, there is nothing to indicate that the Security Council was expected in every case to take positive action. It was assumed, however, that there would be a willingness on the part of the permanent members to adjust their positions and harmonize their views in order to achieve an agreement. In practice what has happened is that permanent members, and especially the Soviet Union, have taken positions, not with a view to reaching an agreement but rather to accentuate differences and wage propaganda battles.

As a result, the Security Council has been largely ineffective as an organ of mediation in dealing with those problems where the direct power relations of the United States and the Western powers, on the one hand, and the Soviet Union and its satellites, on the other, are concerned. In dealing with the Greek question, for example, the Council was unable to take a decision on the report of its Committee of Investigation. The Council was blocked by Soviet vetoes when it attempted to deal, in 1948, with the complaint of Soviet intervention in Czechoslovakia. It is not clear that the final result in these cases would have been much different if the right of veto had not existed; the agreement of the permanent members was necessary to achieve an easing of the tension in these "cold war" situations.

On the other hand, the Security Council, in spite of the veto possibility, has handled some questions with considerable success. Generally speaking, these have been questions involving relations between states other than the major powers themselves, and not directly affecting the vital interests of these powers. In Palestine, for example, during 1948 and 1949, the Council was successful in bringing fighting to an end. All the permanent members wanted peace, though for different reasons. Later, when this agreement on aims came to an end, when the Soviet Union saw an advantage to be gained from support of the Arab cause, the Security Council ceased to be effective. Likewise, in Indonesia from the middle of 1947 on, the Council was successful first in achieving a cease-fire and the acceptance by the parties of the principles on which a political settlement was to be based, and then, following the second Dutch police action, in bringing an end to hostilities and assisting the parties to reach a political settlement.

Though the Council has had limited success in discharging its responsibilities and though the veto has not proven to be an absolute barrier to effective action, the limited possibilities of the Council for exercising the kind of pressure which the opposing sides in postwar conflicts have demanded have contributed to the progressive decline of its role.

GROWING IMPORTANCE OF THE GENERAL ASSEMBLY

Two considerations have operated powerfully to restrict the use made of the Security Council and to build up the importance of the role of the General Assembly. In the first place, the Security Council has not seemed as effective an instrument for waging the "cold war" as the General Assembly. Though the Council was used to considerable advantage by the West in the opening year of the struggle—1946—in the Iranian case, it became apparent by 1947 that the veto was a real handicap to the use of the Council as a "cold war" instrument, and that in any case the Assembly provided a better platform for lining up broad support for national policies and for seeking to influence world opinion. Though the General Assembly can only recommend, this was not viewed as a particularly important consideration since the Security Council also can only recommend when exercising its function of peaceful settlement. Moreover, in ordering collective measures, it is handicapped not only by the veto but also by the fact that it has no armed forces at its disposal.

During the second session of the General Assembly in 1947, the United States took the lead in bringing before it the Greek and Korean questions, and in proposing the establishment of an Interim Committee better to equip the Assembly for its new role. It was felt that the Committee would be a means of overcoming, in part, the handicap which the Assembly possessed of not being in continuous session. This proposal in substance was to set up a committee of all the Members of the United Nations which during the period when the Assembly was not in session would perform certain of the functions of that body. The Soviet Union objected strongly to the proposal and after its adoption by the Assembly,[18] refused to participate in the Interim Committee on the ground that it was illegally constituted. Partly because of the absence of the Soviet bloc, it was not effective in serving its purpose.

Until the middle of 1948, though increasing use was being made of the General Assembly, the Security Council was still recognized as the organ primarily responsible for dealing with specific disputes and situations of a political character. But by late 1948, there was a marked reduction in the number of meetings of the Security Council, and a decline in the number of political questions considered by that organ in comparison with the General Assembly. The statistics on page 122 are extremely illuminating.[19]

It is obvious that since 1948 the General Assembly has largely supplanted the Security Council as the organ to which Members have chosen to submit political questions for consideration and action.

In view of the specific requirement of the Charter (Article 11, par. 2) that the General Assembly, either before or after discussion but in any case before making a recommendation, must refer any question on which action is necessary to the Security Council, it might be as-

[18] General Assembly Resolution 111 (II), Nov. 13, 1947.

[19] Substantive political questions are those designated "Political and Security Questions" in the Annual Reports of the Secretary-General on the Work of the Organization and which do not relate to constitutional, organizational, and procedural matters, including the admission of new Members or the representation of Members. For detailed information, see the Secretary-General's Annual Reports and the Reports of the Security Council to the General Assembly.

Period	Meetings of the S.C.	Substantive Political Issues Considered by the	
		S.C.	G.A.
Jan. 17, 1946–July 15, 1946	50	5	2
July 16, 1946–July 15, 1947	108	8	4
1947–1948	180	8	5
1948–1949	92	8	11
1949–1950	46	6	10
1950–1951	72	7	19
1951–1952	43	6	12
1952–1953	26	1	14
1953–1954	59	4	11
1954–1955	22	3	15
1955–1956	32	1	11
1956–1957	52	6	13

sumed that the shift that has occurred would apply only to questions where there is no necessity or expectation of collective measures being taken. As a matter of fact, the General Assembly has equally encroached upon this sphere of Security Council activity while respecting in form the Charter provisions. Since the Assembly's powers of discussion and recommendation are defined in general terms, the Assembly has found no difficulty in recommending to Members that collective political measures be taken, as it did against Spain in 1946,[20] or in recommending that direct military assistance be withheld, as it did in 1949 in dealing with the assistance being given to guerrilla forces in Greece by her northern neighbors.[21] In 1950, however, when it became clear that the return of the Soviet representative to the Security Council would prevent that organ from discharging its responsibilities in connection with collective measures in Korea, the United States proposed that the General Assembly explicitly assume the responsibility for dealing with threats to the peace, breaches of the peace, and acts of aggression in case the Council was prevented by the use of the veto from acting. In modified form the United States proposal was adopted by the General Assembly as the "Uniting for Peace" resolution of November 3, 1950.[22] By the terms of this resolution, the Assembly asserted its right to exercise a residual responsibility in any threat to or breach of the peace. In case the Security Council is prevented from exercising its

[20] General Assembly Resolution 39 (I), Dec. 12, 1946.
[21] General Assembly Resolution 288 (IV), Dec. 5, 1949.
[22] General Assembly Resolution 377 (V).

primary responsibility by failure of the permanent members to agree, the General Assembly shall consider the matter with a view to making appropriate recommendations for collective measures, including the use of armed forces in the case of any breach of the peace or act of aggression. Acting under the terms of this resolution, the Assembly has dealt with the Communist Chinese military intervention in Korea beginning in 1950, the Israeli attack on Egypt and the subsequent Anglo-French military intervention in 1956, the Soviet intervention in Hungary, and the situation in Lebanon resulting from alleged infiltration from the United Arab Republic and the landing of American marines at the request of President Chamoun in 1958.

Thus, under the impact of the cold war and because of the failure of the Security Council to meet demands resulting from this conflict, the Security Council has been largely supplanted by the General Assembly as the organ which actually takes responsibility for the maintenance of international peace and security. But the cold war has not been the only political development which has contributed to this result. In addition, the emergence of strong nationalist movements in Asia and Africa and the belief of supporters of these movements that they can achieve more through the General Assembly than through the Security Council have contributed greatly to the enlargement of the Assembly's role.

Generally speaking, these nationalist demands have been directed against western European powers who either have permanent seats in the Security Council or who are supported by permanent members. Consequently, even though the Security Council was useful in getting independence for Indonesia, its value in other instances has been, or would have been had it been used, very limited indeed. The greater value of the General Assembly as a forum for appeal to public opinion and bringing pressure to bear on governments, and the greater likelihood of getting resolutions supporting the claims for self-determination and independence adopted in the Assembly have been decisive reasons for using the Assembly in place of the Council. In fact, in most cases these matters have been brought directly to the General Assembly in the first instance. Only when the Assembly has not been in session and immediate consideration by the United Nations has been considered necessary has appeal been made to the Security Council.

The assumption by the General Assembly of a substantial part of the responsibilities of the Security Council has been the most striking aspect of the growing importance of the General Assembly. It should also be noted, however, that both the Economic and Social Council and the Trusteeship Council have also declined in importance in favor of the Assembly. This is perhaps not so surprising since the Charter states that they shall perform their functions under the authority of the General Assembly. Nevertheless, it was assumed by the authors of the Charter that the relation would somewhat resemble that of executive to responsible legislature under a parliamentary form of government and that the General Assembly would limit itself to formulating general principles and directives and to reviewing the work of the Councils. In actual practice, the recommendations of the Councils are considered in detail by the Assembly, the same arguments advanced in the Council are repeated in the Assembly, and often Council recommendations are reversed or substantially modified. This, of course, places heavy demands upon the time of the Assembly, but more than that, it limits the value and importance of the Councils' work. It means, in the last analysis, that it is frequently in the Assembly that the important debates occur and the real decisions are taken. In the case of the Trusteeship Council, this is particularly significant since the protection which the administering states sought to achieve through the provision for the balanced membership of the Trusteeship Council has largely been lost. In the General Assembly, the voting balance is definitely unfavorable to them. And in view of the importance that self-determination, respect for social and economic rights, and the economic development of underdeveloped areas have acquired in the work of the Economic and Social Council, the new relationship between Assembly and Council has had parallel consequences there.

CONSEQUENCES OF THE GENERAL ASSEMBLY'S NEW ROLE

The fact that the General Assembly has come to have a dominant position in the United Nations does not mean, of course, that differences between Members in respect to power are no longer of any consequence. The Members with superior military and economic resources are capable of exercising greater influence in the General Assembly on most questions than the smaller and weaker states. But this greater influence is not translated into mathematical and legal terms by constitutional provisions. It is dependent upon the ability of the greater power to persuade the lesser state to go along with it.

The methods by which influence can be exercised and the effectiveness of these methods vary greatly. In the case of the Soviet Union, for example, almost dictatorial control is exercised over the conduct, including voting behavior, of the satellite states. In part this is due to the power of the Soviet army. To some degree it is due to the dependence of the satellites on the Soviet Union for protection and economic support. Certainly to a large extent it is due to control through the Communist Party. In the case of the United States, influence takes a variety of forms and is due to a variety of considerations. For those countries that are fearful of Communist aggression, whether from the Soviet Union or Communist China, the fact that the United States is the most powerful champion of non-Communist principles, that it alone has the military power to stop Communist aggression, and that it is prepared to give economic and military support to countries willing to help themselves, are powerful arguments for going along with the United States on any issue arising from the "cold war." Furthermore, those countries which regard the "cold war" issue as the dominant one are willing to follow the United States lead on other issues to assure themselves of United States good will and support.

But when it comes to questions bearing on national self-determination, the political development or liberties of non-self-governing territories, and the economic development of underdeveloped areas, the United States is in a less favorable position to exercise influence because on these issues the smaller and weaker Members do not feel the same compulsions to follow the American lead unless it is one which they approve on its merits. Here the United States does not have the same leverage as on "cold war" issues, and, along with the United Kingdom and France, often finds itself in danger of being outvoted. The fact that the Soviet Union is more often on the winning side in these issues is due not to its superior power but rather to the fact that it is able to take positions on these issues that correspond to the interests of the less developed and less powerful states, particularly the Asian and African.

A study of voting behaviour in the General Assembly shows quite conclusively the influence of the major powers, particularly the United States.[23] On relatively few occasions has the United States been in the minority in General Assembly voting. On political questions, i.e., questions bearing upon peace and security, the United States has with few exceptions been able to get the necessary, and usually overwhelming, majority support for its proposals and positions. Of course, it may find it necessary to make some concessions to other Members, as it did in order to get Assembly approval of its proposal to find Communist China guilty of aggression in 1951. Usually these concessions relate to subsidiary points and not to the main issue. In August 1958, however,

[23] For studies covering the first five years, see John Furey, "Voting Alignments in the General Assembly" (unpublished doctoral dissertation at Columbia University); and Margaret Ball, "Bloc Voting in the General Assembly," *International Organization,* V (1951), pp. 3–31.

following the landing of American marines in Lebanon at the request of President Chamoun, the United States found the task of getting the necessary two-thirds majority for its proposals so difficult that it was willing to settle for a resolution of a stop-gap nature which in effect denied it much of what it had wanted.

The majorities which go along with the United States on these issues usually consist of the Latin American republics, the members of the North Atlantic Treaty Organization, the older Dominions, and a scattering of Asian states that are particularly dependent on United States military assistance. There is no evidence, to date, that this situation has been materially altered by the change that has occurred in Assembly membership since 1955. In the eleventh and twelfth sessions of the General Assembly, for example, the United States was able to get substantial majorities for the draft resolutions which it favored on controversial political issues involving the "cold war" relationship, such as Korea, Hungary, and disarmament.[24] To be sure, there were more abstentions on these votes than had previously occurred, and these abstentions almost without exception were by members of the Asian-African group. Consequently, it can be said that while the United States as leader of the West in the "cold war" is still able fairly consistently to get its majorities, and substantial ones at that, the psychological and political effects of these votes are somewhat lessened by the growing number of abstentions, particularly by members of the Asian-African group. Another evidence of the success of the Western powers in exercising controlling influence over the General Assembly has been their ability to keep key positions in the General Assembly, in so far as the consideration of political questions is concerned, in the hands of states friendly to the West.[25]

On questions that have to do more particularly with human rights, self-determination for peoples and economic and political developments, issues that are of special concern to the Asian and Arab peoples and to the Latin American republics as well, the increased importance of the General Assembly at the expense of all the Councils has had more serious consequences for the major powers of the West. On these questions, the United States, the United Kingdom, and France, in particular,

[24] As regards votes covering all of the major issues confronting the General Assembly at its twelfth session and not only those dealing with "cold war" matters, statistical surveys indicate, however, that 61 per cent of Member states voted less often with the United States in 1957 than in 1956. See text and tables from the *Chronicle of United Nations Activities* reprinted in the *Congressional Record,* 85th Congress, 2nd Sess., Vol. 104, no. 29 (Feb. 25, 1958), pp. 2340–42.

[25] Such positions are those of president of the Assembly and chairman and rapporteur of the First Committee and the Special Political Committee.

generally are not in the position to exercise decisive influence. They have considerable bargaining power, particularly because in many of these matters no effective action can be taken without their approval. Nevertheless, they must face the possibility and even likelihood of adverse votes in the Assembly and of being subjected to organized political pressure which in the absence of the United Nations would be more diffuse and less effective. Certainly, in this area, the growth of the General Assembly's influence has altered adversely their power and influence in world politics, though it has provided the opportunities for imaginative leadership that are far from being exhausted.

The Soviet Union, on the other hand, has had greater cause to be concerned over the shift of emphasis to the General Assembly in so far as political issues directly resulting from the "cold war" conflict are involved since it has no equivalent of the veto in that organ to protect its position. There, the Soviet runs the risk of being consistently outvoted by large majorities on most political questions which are of chief concern to it. It can only depend on the consistent support of its satellites. It can expect some support from the Asian and African members, at least in the form of abstentions. But in the last analysis its only protection is in the fact that technically General Assembly recommendations are not binding. Still, not even the Soviet Government enjoys being placed too often in the position of refusing to carry out or respect a recommendation adopted by a large majority. It would much rather be able by its negative vote to prevent a decision from being taken which is favored by a majority.

But while the Soviet Union has lost negative influence within the United Nations because of the enlarged role of the General Assembly in handling political questions, it has itself seen in the shift some advantage which compensates in part for this loss. The Assembly undoubtedly provides a better forum for directing Soviet propaganda to the world outside, and even within the Organization itself, and some small gain can be found in the tendency of many of the so-called "neutral" or "uncommitted" states to support the Soviet position or at least abstain. Furthermore, on questions where it is able with some apparent justification to accuse the Western Powers of engaging in imperialistic practices and aggressive action, as in the case of the Anglo-French military intervention in Egypt and the landing of American and British forces in Lebanon and Jordan respectively, it finds the Assembly a valuable means of mobilizing strong political pressure against the West. When problems of the non-self-governing territories are under consideration, the Soviet Union welcomes the expanded role of the Assembly because this gives it the opportunity publicly to proclaim its support of the "oppressed peoples" and to join in exercising psychological and political pressure on the Western powers and thus weaken them in their common opposition to Soviet Communism.

The expansion of the General Assembly's role has raised some questions in the minds of many outside of the Soviet Union as to whether this development is desirable with the Assembly organized as it is at present. Is it wise to place in an organ so constituted responsibility for taking decisions on a wide range of political, economic, and social problems, even if these decisions are only recommendations? Can one reasonably expect the United States, the Soviet Union, and other major powers to accept decisions reached by an organ in which each member regardless of size and importance has one vote? Is it reasonable that a member with a population of 150 million should have the same vote as one with a population of 500 thousand? Or that a member with a modern military establishment, great productive capacity, and technological competence should have the same vote as a member without an effective military establishment, modern industry, or a literate population? Should a member which contributes one-third of the revenue of the Organization have no more votes than one which contributes one-two-hundreth of the revenue?

Considerations of this kind have encouraged many to explore the possibilities of some system of weighted voting which would bring voting power more closely into line with real power and importance.[26] But the formulas proposed have generally been complicated and have raised more problems than they resolve. Secretary of State Dulles has proposed an ingenious method by which there would be two votes in the General Assembly, one on the present form and one on a weighted basis, on every important issue. There has been no evidence of enthusiastic support for this proposal. It would seem that for the foreseeable future major powers must rely on their superior ability to persuade and influence other members to go along with them, and if they fail in this, as a last resort refuse to accept the General Assembly's recommendation if it does too much violence to a vital interest.

SUGGESTED READINGS

Claude, Inis, Jr. *Swords into Plowshares*. New York: Random House, Inc., 1956. Chaps 7 and 8.

[26] For a discussion of these possibilities, see Francis O. Wilcox and Carl M. Marcy, *Proposals for Changes in the United Nations* (Washington: The Brookings Institution, 1955), ch. XI.

Goodrich, Leland M. "Development of the General Assembly," *International Conciliation,* No. 471 (May 1951), pp. 229–81.

————. "The U.N. Security Council," *International Organization,* Summer 1958.

Hasluck, Paul. *Workshop of Security.* Melbourne: F. W. Cheshire Pty., Ltd., 1948.

Haviland, H. Field, Jr. *The Political Role of the General Assembly.* New York: Carnegie Endowment for International Peace, 1951.

Jiminez de Arechaga, Eduardo. *Voting and the Handling of Disputes in the Security Council.* New York: Carnegie Endowment for International Peace, 1950.

Koo, Wellington, Jr. *Voting Procedure in International Political Organizations.* New York: Columbia University Press, 1948.

Lee, Dwight E. "The Genesis of the Veto," *International Organization,* I (1947), pp. 33–42.

Liska, George. *International Equilibrium.* Cambridge: Harvard University Press, 1957.

McIntyre, Elizabeth. "Weighted Voting in International Organizations," *International Organization,* VIII (1954), pp. 484–97.

Padelford, Norman J. "The Use of the Veto," *International Organization,* II (1948), pp. 227–46.

Rudzinski, Alexander W., "Majority Rule and Great Power Agreement in the United Nations," *International Organization,* IX (1955), pp. 227–46.

U.S. Senate Committee on Foreign Relations, Subcommittee on the United States Charter. *Representation and Voting in the United Nations General Assembly.* Staff Study No. 4. Washington: Government Printing Office, 1954.

————, *The Problem of the Veto in the United Nations Security Council.* Staff Study No. 1. Washington: Government Printing Office, 1954.

Wilcox, Francis O., and Marcy, Carl M. *Proposals for Changes in the United Nations.* Washington; The Brookings Institution, 1955. Chaps. X and XI.

Chapter VII

THE SECRETARY-GENERAL

AND THE SECRETARIAT

THE GENERAL ASSEMBLY and the three Councils—the Security Council, the Economic and Social Council, and the Trusteeship Council—are organs through which the governments of Member states seek to achieve certain common purposes by establishing areas of agreement either in respect to general principles of action, or in respect to specific courses to follow in actual situations. In these organs, the representatives of Members think, talk, and vote in furtherance of some conception of national interest, though membership in the Organization makes it important that this be clothed in the garment of United Nations purposes and principles. Since these are recognized as being organs of policy-making and political action, Members of the United Nations desire to be in the position to influence discussions and decisions to their advantage.

The Secretariat and the International Court, on the other hand, are not generally regarded as having this political coloration. Their activities are generally viewed as being influenced more predominantly by considerations of an international character. In the case of the Court, opinions and judgments are based on the principles of international law which are presumably accepted by all nations. The law which the Court administers is thought of as having an existence apart from the detailed compromises and adjustments worked out by nationally-oriented diplomats. The process by which this law is discovered is not primarily that of negotiation but rather that of scientific analysis and evaluation of the sources. The judges who are to engage in this work are expected to have qualities of expertness, good judgment, independence of mind, and practical experience. While recognizing their human qualities and possible national sympathies, we expect them to stand apart from national political conflicts and generally are satisfied that they are able to do this.

Likewise, in the case of the United Nations Secretariat, those who are engaged in carrying on its work are expected to subordinate their national feelings and sympathies to the needs of the Organization, and to be guided in their activities by standards of conduct dictated by the Organization which they serve rather than by the states to which they owe allegiance. The Secretariat, like the Court, therefore, requires of its members an international, or United Nations, point of view. It is not enough that its members, by bringing their respective national attitudes and convictions to bear on each other, should be able to produce an acceptable compromise representing an international solution.

The Developing Concept of an International Civil Service

Neither the concept of an international approach to questions nor the reality of a body of officials devoted to the international service is new. What is new in the United Nations experiment and the League of Nations which preceded it, is the extent to which the concept has been accepted, in terms of the number of people involved and the scope and variety of the tasks they are called upon to perform.

Before the establishment of the League of Nations, international secretariats—groups of officials organized to perform international functions of a continuing or temporary nature—were not uncommon. Whenever an international conference was held it was necessary to organize a secretariat to perform essential duties such as making physical arrangements for meetings, preparing conference documents, and keeping records. These secretariats were relatively small by modern standards and were usually provided by the host state from among its own diplomatic staff. The Second Hague Conference of 1907 had a secretariat of about twenty-five members composed of officials appointed by the participating governments. This was something of a new departure. Since these conferences were called to perform specific functions and ended once their purposes had been served or failure had become certain, the secretariats likewise were temporary in character.

With the establishment of permanent technical organizations such as the International Telegraphic Union (1865) and the Universal Postal Union (1874), it became necessary to set up permanent bureaux or secretariats with a wider variety of functions. These organs were made responsible not only for organizing and servicing conferences, but also for doing many things in the periods between conferences, such as making studies, publishing statistical and other information, maintaining registries, and performing certain services in connection with disputes between national administrations. Generally speaking, however, they were composed of national officials lent for the purpose.

Until the time of the establishment of the League of Nations, nothing that could truly be regarded as an international civil service had ever existed. Even when plans were being considered for the organization of the League Secretariat, the proposal was made—by Sir Maurice Hankey—that the work should be assigned to nine national secretaries, one from each Council member, each with his own national staff, who would perform their functions under the supervision of the Secretary-General. Sir Eric Drummond, designated in the Covenant as the first Secretary-General, was responsible for the decision to organize an international secretariat. As Mr. Frank P. Walters has written:

> *The creation of a Secretariat international alike in its structure, its spirit, and in personnel, was without doubt one of the most important events in the history of international politics—important not only in itself, but as the indisputable proof of possibilities which had hitherto been confidently denied.*[1]

At the same time, under the electric leadership of Mr. Albert Thomas, the International Labour Office was being organized as the administrative organ of the International Labour Organization[2] to provide a second example of the rich possibilities of a truly international civil service.

Though the League Secretariat was originally planned and organized to perform a modest role in the work of the organization, various factors combined to increase its importance and make it in fact an indispensable part of the League machine.[3] Among these were the fact that the Secretariat provided the only continuing element in the Organization, the amount of expertise which was developed in the Secretariat, the dependence of the changing representatives of member governments in the Council and Assembly on expert guidance, and the need of the political organs for a vast amount of detailed expert documentation which the Secretariat, of all the League organs, was alone equipped to provide. To a large degree, such successes as the League

[1] *A History of the League of Nations* (New York: Oxford University Press, Inc., 1952), I, p. 76.

[2] On the nature of the International Labour Organization (ILO), see below, pp. 273–274.

[3] On the work of the League Secretariat, see E. F. Ranshofen-Wertheimer, *The International Secretariat: A Great Experiment in International Administration* (Washington: Carnegie Endowment for International Peace, 1945).

enjoyed, particularly in the areas of economic and social cooperation and the development of non-self-governing territories, were due to the existence and effective functioning of an international civil service. This was perhaps even more true in the case of the International Labour Organization. With this background of experience, it was not surprising that in the drafting of the Charter of the United Nations, the desirability, in fact the necessity, of having a strong secretariat organized as an international civil service was taken for granted. The only open question was the extent of its political powers, and not surprisingly, the enlargement of its political role brought some support to proposals to bring the Secretariat under some added degree of national control, at least so far as the top positions were concerned.

It is clear from an examination of the provisions of the Charter, in the light of the discussions that took place in its drafting, that the Secretariat, i.e., the Secretary-General and his staff, were viewed from the beginning as having a role of great importance in the work of the Organization. The Charter states that the Secretariat is one of the principal organs of the United Nations. The Secretary-General is given important executive, administrative, financial, political, and representational functions to perform.[4] He and his staff are protected against improper influence by national governments and are expected to refrain from any action which "might reflect on their position as international officials responsible only to the Organization." The full implications of the Secretariat's position as the only organ other than the Court comprising expert personnel continuously on the job were not spelled out by the authors of the Charter. While it was recognized that an international secretariat serving an organization which depends for its effectiveness upon the free consent of governments cannot have the powers or exercise the influence of a national civil service, it was also clear from League experience that the absence of any permanent central political authority created certain needs that only the Secretary-General and his staff could fulfill.

The Secretary-General

Any international secretariat is the secretary-general—or the director or whatever his title may be—and his staff. One measure of the importance of the secretariat is the size of the staff, although as with all human institutions, there may be a tendency to self-inflation. Ideally, of course, the importance of the office and the size of the staff

[4] Ch. IX of the Charter.

alike are determined by the duties which the secretary-general is called upon to perform.

Before the establishment of the League and the International Labour Organization, the heads of international secretariats—whether temporary or permanent—had limited responsibilities and little discretion in the exercise of the limited powers that were given them. Those who wrote the Covenant of the League were much under the influence of this concept. It is to be noted that the Covenant had little to say about the duties of the Secretary-General other than that he "shall act in that capacity at all meetings of the Assembly and of the Council." [5] Other provisions of the Covenant gave him specific duties which, however, left little opportunity for discretion or did little to provide the basis for the important role which he developed. For the most part, the important role which the Secretary-General came to have and which his staff acquired was built up outside the specific provisions of the Covenant, though within its spirit and operational necessities.

When during the Second World War, the shape of a new international organization was being considered, much attention was given to the role of the Secretary-General. From the experience of the League and the ILO some drew the conclusion that what was needed was an executive head who would provide the leadership which Albert Thomas had given the ILO in its early years.[6] In discussing the question of leadership in 1943, Mr. C. Wilfred Jenks of the International Labour Office expressed the following view:

> *Effective leadership from within by world officers, who are relieved of all national responsibilities and hold their posts for substantial periods, is an indispensable condition of the effective functioning of future world institutions. It is essential to recognize that the duties of the senior officers of world institutions are not those of the traditional civil servant but call for high qualities of constructive statesmanship. . . . Final responsibility for policy will necessarily rest with representative bodies consisting primarily, no doubt, of responsible representatives of governments. . . . The chief executive of a world institution, must, however, assume the duty of systematically presenting the challenge of a world outlook to policy-making bodies consisting of members whose responsibilities are likely to be primarily national, and it will fall to him to defend the decisions of these bodies if they are questioned and to imple-*

[5] Article 7, par. 4.

[6] For an interpretation of Thomas' leadership, see E. J. Phelan, *Yes and Albert Thomas* (London: Cresset Press Ltd., 1936).

ment them in so far as their execution is a matter of primary rather than national action.[7]

In the planning-discussion in the Department of State there was general agreement that the chief administrative officer of the proposed international organization [8] should have a more important political role than his League predecessor had had. Furthermore, it was generally agreed that he should be a man of recognized competence and international reputation. President Roosevelt apparently favored making provision for a permanent political head of the organization who would have an important role in mediating international differences. Presumably under this proposal there would also be a chief administrative officer whose role would be nearer that originally conceived for the League Secretary-General. When the idea of a President or political head of the organization was dropped as not being feasible, the United States planners returned to the earlier emphasis on strengthening the political role of the permanent administrative head.

In the Dumbarton Oaks Conversations, the four participating governments readily reached agreement on provisions regarding the functions, powers, and method of selection of the Secretary-General. In the Proposals he was described as the "chief administrative officer of the organization" and was to be given the right to bring to the attention of the Security Council "any matter which in his opinion may threaten international peace and security." At San Francisco the desirability of giving the Secretary-General an important political role was not challenged. There was some discussion of whether the Secretary-General should be expressly authorized to bring matters to the attention of the General Assembly as well as the Security Council, but the decision not to do this in no way reflected a desire to limit his powers.

The discussions at San Francisco centered on the manner of choosing the Secretary-General, the selection of his principal deputies, and his term of office. While there was much resistance on the part of the smaller powers to giving the permanent members of the Security Council a veto over the choice of Secretary-General, once agreement was reached on Security Council voting procedure, there was reluctant acceptance of the fact that the recommendation of a candidate by the Council was not a simple procedural question. However, having yielded to the major powers on the veto, the smaller states were unwilling to accept any provision specifying a short term since this would make the

[7] "Some Problems of an International Civil Service," *Public Administration Review*, III (1943), p. 94.

[8] Initially "General Secretary" was the preferred title and later "Director General."

Secretary-General too dependent on the permanent members of the Council. It was therefore decided to omit any reference in the Charter to term of office or possibility of re-election.

The proposal which the major powers initially sponsored and which was strongly supported by the Soviet Union that four deputies to the Secretary-General should also be elected by the General Assembly on recommendation of the Security Council was the direct result of the strengthening of the office of Secretary-General and the desire of the major powers in varying degrees, to safeguard their influence. It was finally defeated because to most states represented at the Conference, including some of the major powers, it seemed more important to safeguard the authority and responsibility of the Secretary-General in the choice of his subordinates than to provide guarantees to the permanent members of the Security Council that persons acceptable to them would be appointed to these important positions.

The role of the Secretariat in the work of the United Nations and more particularly the special responsibilities of the Secretary-General under the Charter were carefully explored by the Preparatory Commission and its Executive Committee following the signing of the Charter and before the convening of the General Assembly in London in January, 1946. The conclusions of the Preparatory Commission were of great significance as an expression of the views of the Member governments regarding the functions and responsibilities of the Secretary-General and the importance to be attached to the office.

In its Report,[9] the Preparatory Commission listed under the following six headings the functions which the Charter explicitly assigned to the Secretary-General: general administrative and executive functions, technical functions, financial functions, the organization and administration of the Secretariat, political functions, and representational functions. While recognizing that many of his specific duties under the Charter would naturally be delegated in greater or less degree to members of his staff, the Report emphasized that the execution of these duties "must be subject to his supervision and control" and that "the ultimate responsibility remains his alone." The office, thus, was presented as one demanding qualifications of a high order, political as well as technical. The Commission recommended that the first Secretary-General be appointed for five years and that the appointment be open to renewal at the end of that time "for a further five-year term." Emphasizing the importance of the task of choosing the first Secretary-General and its political sensitivity, considering the relationship which

[9] *Report of the Preparatory Commission of the United Nations* (PC/20, Dec. 23, 1945), pp. 81–103.

he was expected to have to governments, the Commission recommended that the Security Council offer one candidate only for the consideration of the General Assembly, that debate on the nomination in the General Assembly should be avoided, that both nomination and appointment should be discussed at private meetings, and that the voting should be by secret ballot.

When the General Assembly and the Security Council first met in London in January, 1946, one of their most pressing tasks was the appointment of the Secretary-General. In effect, as was fully anticipated by the authors of the Charter, the choice was made by the representatives of the major powers, particularly the Soviet Union, the United Kingdom, and the United States. Neither was successful in getting the candidate of its first choice appointed to the post. After Paul Spaak, the Belgian foreign minister, had been elected President of the General Assembly, Trygve Lie, the Foreign Minister of Norway who had been Spaak's principal rival for the presidency, seemed the logical person to be appointed Secretary-General. He was a prominant political personality, having been active in Norwegian politics and the resistance movement and being at the time Foreign Minister of his country. He was from a country which had played an active role in the war, which was outside the American continent,[10] and which had not committed itself to the cause of any one major power. He was from a relatively small country. While he was not regarded as being unduly under the influence of any one major power, he commanded the confidence of all. He thus seemed well qualified to perform in a satisfactory manner the duties of the Secretary-General, taking into account the new emphasis on the desirability of political initiative and influence. It is significant that in the discussions leading up to Council and Assembly decisions, no candidate was seriously considered or strongly supported on the ground that his personal characteristics and experience would warrant the expectation that he would refrain from undue political initiatives. It was taken for granted that the Secretary-General would play an important political role.

Space does not permit a detailed analysis of the manner in which Mr. Lie performed his various functions. In view of his background, it was not surprising that he should have consistently stressed his political responsibilities. His administrative, technical, and financial responsibilities he recognized and accepted, but these he could in varying degree delegate. His political responsibilities could not so easily be delegated nor, for that matter, in view of his previous experience and in-

[10] Lester Pearson had been opposed by the Soviet Union because of the geographical factor.

terest, was there a desire on his part to delegate them. Furthermore, it was in this area that he was called upon to take initiatives and exercise influence which above all distinguished his office under the Charter from that of the Secretary-General under the League Covenant. There is, therefore, some justification for giving particular attention to this aspect of the Secretary-General's work.

There are a variety of ways by which the Secretary-General can exercise his political influence. His annual report to the General Assembly offers one important means of making known his views and proposing general or specific courses of action. In his public statements—to the press and in talks before private groups—he can make known his views and seek directly and indirectly to influence governments. In his relations with Member governments, whether at headquarters or in visits to national capitals or in official correspondence, he can seek to influence the attitudes and conduct of Members. Under the Charter and the rules of procedure of the Assembly and the Council, he can take the initiative in bringing matters to the attention of these organs. In his secretarial capacity he can influence the course of discussion in and the decisions taken by the various organs.

All of these methods Mr. Lie used vigorously and with some success. No one can deny his boldness in taking initiatives or the vigor with which he sought to influence the action of governments and United Nations organs along the lines he thought desirable.[11]

Consider, for example, some of the efforts which he made. In his annual reports to the General Assembly, particularly after the first two years, he was outspoken in condemning or approving courses of action on the basis of their contribution to achieving the purposes of the United Nations. In his fourth report in 1949, he expressed the view that ". . . it is impossible to obtain lasting security from war by any arrangement that leaves out any of the Great Powers." [12] The year before, he expressed the view that the European Recovery Program held great promise for the restoration of western Europe to political and economic stability. During the Security Council consideration of the Iranian complaint that the Soviet Union was keeping troops in Iran in violation of its international obligations, the Secretary-General on his own initiative submitted a memorandum on the question of the power

[11] See Stephen M. Schwebel, *The Secretary-General of the United Nations: His Powers and Practice* (Cambridge: Harvard University Press, 1952); and Trygve Lie, *In the Cause of Peace* (New York: The Macmillan Company, 1954).

[12] This and the following sentence of his report were an obvious reference to the North Atlantic Treaty. *Annual Report of the Secretary-General on the Work of the Organization, 1 July 1948–30 June 1949* (Doc. A/930), Introduction, p. ix.

of the Council to keep the question on its agenda after the Iranian government had withdrawn its complaint.[13] While the Security Council was considering the Palestine question in 1948, the Secretary-General's staff prepared a memorandum on the power of the Council relative to the implementation of the General Assembly's resolution of the previous November, which was circulated among Members. At the time of the North Korean attack on the Republic of Korea, though the United States requested a meeting of the Security Council to consider the matter, the Secretary-General in reporting on the situation took the occasion to define it as "a threat to international peace." [14] Perhaps his most ambitious initiative was the preparation of a ten-point program for achieving peace through the United Nations which he presented to the governments of the chief Members in the course of visits to their capitals, and which he later asked the General Assembly to consider.[15]

As the result of his political initiatives, Trygve Lie found himself at various times during his years of service in the position of not enjoying the full confidence of one or more of the permanent members of the Security Council. His intervention in the Iranian case (1946), while recognized as being within his powers, was not received with favor by the United States and the United Kingdom, who maintained an opposite point of view to his regarding the Council's powers. His advocacy of the seating of representatives of the Peking Government in the United Nations was regarded by the United States Government with extreme disfavor. While his stand on the Korean question won the support of the United States, it produced a hostile reaction in the Soviet Union which prevented his reappointment in 1950 and made his continuance in office under a General Assembly resolution extending his term a most unsatisfactory experience both for himself and for the United Nations.

In taking the various political initiatives that he did, Trygve Lie did not violate the Charter, in letter or in spirit, nor did he do anything for which he could not have found justification in the discussions which preceded the signing of the Charter or in the expectations that prevailed at that time. It is clear, nevertheless, that his experience demonstrated that the Secretary-General of an organization like the United Nations is subject to certain practical limitations, which prevent him from successfully undertaking the kind of political leadership which we are accustomed to expect from the chief executive of a parliamentary

[13] U.N. Doc. S/39, April 16, 1946.
[14] U.N. Security Council, *Official Records,* Fifth Year, 473rd Meeting (June 25, 1950), p. 3.
[15] See Lie, *op. cit.,* pp. 275–322.

or presidential democracy. For one thing, in dealing with Member governments, the true repositories of governmental authority, he has only powers of persuasion, except as he may be given additional powers by explicit agreement. Second, he represents no independent constituency. Those who elect him are themselves jealous of their powers and apart from their wishes he has no independent source of authority. Finally, unlike Albert Thomas, who was able as the first Director of the ILO to achieve a role of real leadership, the Secretary-General cannot depend upon the backing of powerful pressure groups either in United Nations organs or in the Member states who in the last analysis determine the decisions of these organs. It would appear that Trygve Lie in attempting to provide political leadership did not always take sufficient care to have the support of those whose approval was necessary to the success of his initiatives. Or perhaps it might be better said that he sought to provide leadership too openly and independently, thus putting governments in the position where they could not follow him without serious loss of face.

In November, 1952, Trygve Lie informed the General Assembly of his intention to resign and asked the Assembly to place on its agenda the question of a choice of a successor. During March, 1953, the deadlock in the Security Council was finally broken and on April 7, the General Assembly appointed Dag Hammarskjöld, as recommended by the Security Council. The choice of Hammarskjöld—a man with a background of service as a professional diplomat and economist—marked a return to something more closely approaching the Sir Eric Drummond model of the civil servant working quietly behind the scenes. It soon became clear that while Hammarskjöld fully recognized the political responsibilities of his office, his methods were more traditional than those of his predecessor. While he has undertaken important United Nations missions: negotiating with the Peking Government for the release of United States nationals; his efforts to achieve a settlement of the Suez Canal question; proposing a plan for an international force to secure and supervise the cessation of hostilities in Egypt; establishing and directing the operations of the United Nations Emergency Force which the Assembly voted to create; supervising the clearing of the Suez Canal; and upholding the purposes and principles of the charter in Lebanon and Jordan, he has done these things on the basis of resolutions of the Security Council or the General Assembly, agreements among the major powers, or with the consent, tacit or express, of the power or powers directly concerned.

He has sought to exercise his influence on governments primarily in confidential discussions with their representatives. His annual reports have been restrained in tone though not avoiding positive stands and proposals. In his relations with organs, he has generally been careful to avoid any intervention likely to arouse strong opposition. In implementing resolutions, as in the Egyptian-Israeli crisis, he has been circumspect in the interpretation of his powers. His record to date has demonstrated the possibilities of substantially developing the political role of the Secretary-General in an effective manner, so long as there is full awareness of the fact that in an international organization such as the United Nations the real powers of decision rest with the Member governments, particularly the governments of the major powers, and that, consequently, there are limits to what an international official can do in matters of peace, security, and general welfare without the support of these governments.

While Dag Hammarskjöld has been more circumspect in the exercise of his powers than his predecessor, he has not been unwilling to affirm his duties as a United Nations official committed to the purposes and principles set forth in the Charter. Thus, when the Security Council met to consider the military intervention of France and the United Kingdom in Egypt, he made the following declaration in the Council:

> *The Principles of the Charter are, by far, greater than the Organization in which they are embodied, and the aims which they are to safeguard are holier than the policies of any single nation or people. As a servant of the Organization, the Secretary-General has the duty to maintain his usefulness by avoiding public stands on conflicts between Member Nations unless and until such an action might help to resolve the conflict. However, the discretion and impartiality thus imposed on the Secretary-General by the character of his immediate task may not degenerate into a policy of expediency. He must also be a servant of the principles of the Charter, and its aims must ultimately determine what for him is right and wrong. For that he must stand. A Secretary-General cannot serve on any other assumption than that—within the necessary limits of human frailty and honest differences of opinion—all Member Nations honour their pledge to observe all Articles of the Charter. He should also be able to assume that those organs which are charged with the task of upholding the Charter will be in the position to fulfill their task.*
>
> *The bearing of what I have just said must be obvious to all without any elaboration from my side. Were the Members to consider that another view of the duties of the Secretary-General than the one here stated would better serve the interests of the Organization it is their obvious right to act accordingly.*[16]

[16] U.N. Security Council, *Official Records,* Eleventh Year, 751st Meeting (Oct. 31, 1956), pp. 1–2.

It is significant that this declaration by the Secretary-General was followed by an expression of full confidence in him by the members of the Council.

But while the nature of the United Nations and the powers of Member governments place serious limitations on what the Secretary-General can do, particularly in the political sphere, there are factors present which make it almost inevitable that the office of Secretary-General will continue to be important in the future and which, if discreetly and wisely used, will contribute to the continuing growth of the role of the Secretary-General and his staff. In the first place, the Secretary-General is the only leading personality who is in a position to represent the United Nations continuously. The President of the Security Council changes from month to month. The President of the General Assembly changes from year to year and, besides, is not ordinarily at Headquarters except when the Assembly is in session. The Economic and Social Council and the Trusteeship Council are not continuously in session and in addition are for all practical purposes subsidiary organs of the Assembly. Second, except possibly for the President of the Assembly and this exception is only valid in part, the Secretary-General is the only top-line official who represents all the interests and activities of the United Nations, and who is, therefore, in the position to represent the United Nations before the world. Finally, the Secretary-General has at his command a trained and experienced staff which is familiar with the structure, procedures, and functioning of the Organization. Member representatives and governments find it useful and convenient to rely on the Secretary-General for counsel and guidance, and their policies and actions are influenced thereby. If one envisages an expanding role for the United Nations in the business of world affairs and more particularly for the General Assembly, the Secretary-General and his staff are inevitably going to be an increasingly important factor in this growing influence. And in all likelihood, to the extent that opposing groups within the United Nations tend to balance and neutralize each other, the importance of the Secretary-General's position will increase.[17]

Organization of the Secretariat

An international secretariat, like a national administration, must be organized along certain lines defining functions and responsibilities

[17] See Elmore Jackson, "The Developing Role of the Secretary-General," *International Organization,* XI (1957), pp. 431–45.

to be an efficient working instrument. It was recognized from the beginning that the size of the United Nations' Secretariat and the varied nature of its work would necessitate giving great care to administrative structure. It was taken for granted that the United Nations' Secretariat would be considerably larger than that of the League, and in fact it turned out that the headquarters staff alone became approximately four times as large as the League Secretariat in Geneva.

One of the first questions that the Preparatory Commission had to consider was whether the Secretariat should be organized on a functional basis or in relation to the organs which it had to serve. The Charter specified that appropriate staffs should be permanently assigned to the Economic and Social Council, the Trusteeship Council ". . . and, as required, to the other organs of the United Nations." [18] Clearly, however, it would be redundant and inadequate to organize the Secretariat exclusively on this basis, since some of the work of the Secretariat, like the registration of treaties, did not relate to the work of any other particular organ and many of the services to be provided were by their nature common to all organs.

The Preparatory Commission in its Report did not fully accept either view though its recommendations were for the most part based on the functional principle. "Because the organs of the United Nations have both distinctive and common functions," it concluded, "the staff or secretariat, which serves them at all times, should be so organized as to meet this situation. Every organ, therefore, has at its disposal the services of the whole of the Secretariat, and each Department of the Secretariat serves all the organs as required, subject to one qualification, the proposed Department of Security Council Affairs." Owing to the fact that the Security Council was given ". . . exclusive powers to deal with military and enforcement measures . . . ," the Commission deemed it necessary ". . . that the special units of the Department of Security Council Affairs concerned with these measures should serve the Security Council exclusively." [19]

The General Assembly, when it met in early 1946, in London, accepted the Commission's recommendation, though in somewhat modified form. The eight departments for which it provided were Security Council Affairs, Economic Affairs, Social Affairs, Trusteeship and Information from the Non-Self-Governing Territories, Public Information, Legal, Conference and General Services, and Administrative and Financial Services. Provision was also made for the Executive Office

[18] Article 101, par. 2.
[19] *Report of the Preparatory Commission of the United Nations* (PC/20, Dec. 23, 1945), pp. 87–88.

of the Secretary-General which would perform certain functions in connection with General Assembly meetings as well as functions of a general coordinating nature. There was considerable difference of opinion in the Assembly as to whether there should be separate departments dealing with economic and social affairs. It was so decided, but the Secretary-General was authorized to take such steps as might be necessary to achieve coordination between these two departments and the Economic and Social Council. Since the eight assistant secretaries-general who were to head the departments were thought of not only as having important administrative responsibilities but also as assisting the Secretary-General in his dealings with governments, they were chosen with an eye to their political acceptability. Five of the positions were filled by nationals of the five permanent members of the Security Council. In addition, the national governments were consulted in connection with appointments that were made. Unfortunately, the Secretary-General did not receive the fullest cooperation from governments in making available the best qualified people.

The basic organization which was adopted in 1946 remained without substantial change until 1953, except for the establishment of a Technical Assistance Administration under a Director-General to assist in the administration of the Expanded Program of Technical Assistance. In the course of budget debates in successive years, there were demands for greater administrative efficiency and, in the course of the debates on the 1952 budget estimates, a number of delegations expressed doubts as to the soundness of the existing administrative structure. As a result, the Fifth Committee included in its report to the General Assembly a request that the Secretary-General prepare a study on the desirability of a general reorganization of the Secretariat for submission to the seventh session in 1952. In an explanatory memorandum, the Secretary-General expressed the belief that the structure of the Secretariat should be simplified and the lines of responsibility more clearly defined.[20] He considered eight secretaries-general and a Director-General as too large a number either to act as a coordinating group or to work with him in the consideration and formulation of policy. The Seventh Assembly requested the Secretary-General to prepare a more detailed report,[21] which was submitted to the eighth Assembly in 1953 and approved by it.

In line with these proposals some important changes were made in the organization of the Secretariat. In general these provided a streamlining of the Secretariat and greater flexibility in the use of staff. Three

[20] U.N. Doc. A/2214, Oct. 7, 1952.
[21] U.N. Doc. A/2554, Nov. 12, 1953.

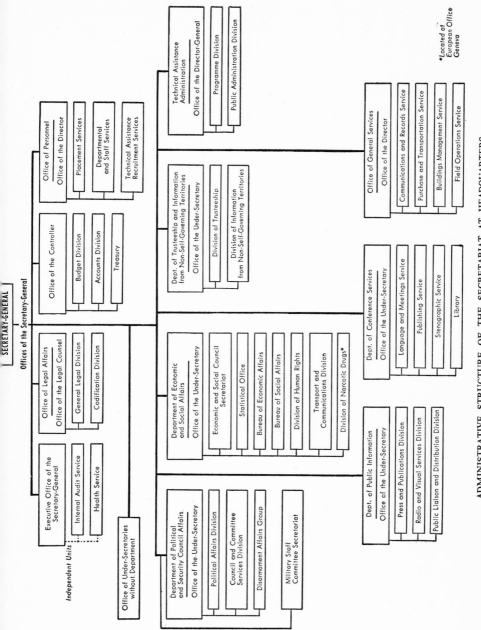

SECRETARY-GENERAL

Offices of the Secretary-General

Independent Units

Executive Office of the Secretary-General
— Internal Audit Service
— Health Service

Office of Legal Affairs
— Office of the Legal Counsel
— General Legal Division
— Codification Division

Office of the Controller
— Budget Division
— Accounts Division
— Treasury

Office of Personnel
— Office of the Director
— Placement Services
— Departmental and Staff Services
— Technical Assistance Recruitment Services

Technical Assistance Administration
— Office of the Director-General
— Programme Division
— Public Administration Division

Office of Under-Secretaries without Department

Department of Political and Security Council Affairs
— Office of the Under-Secretary
— Political Affairs Division
— Council and Committee Services Division
— Disarmament Affairs Group
— Military Staff Committee Secretariat

Department of Economic and Social Affairs
— Office of the Under-Secretary
— Economic and Social Council Secretariat
— Statistical Office
— Bureau of Economic Affairs
— Bureau of Social Affairs
— Division of Human Rights
— Transport and Communications Division
— Division of Narcotic Drugs*

Dept. of Trusteeship and Information from Non-Self-Governing Territories
— Office of the Under-Secretary
— Division of Trusteeship
— Division of Information from Non-Self-Governing Territories

Dept. of Public Information
— Office of the Under-Secretary
— Press and Publications Division
— Radio and Visual Services Division
— Public Liaison and Distribution Division

Dept. of Conference Services
— Office of the Under-Secretary
— Language and Meetings Service
— Publishing Service
— Stenographic Service
— Library

Office of General Services
— Office of the Director
— Communications and Records Service
— Purchase and Transportation Service
— Buildings Management Service
— Field Operations Service

*Located at European Office Geneva

ADMINISTRATIVE STRUCTURE OF THE SECRETARIAT AT HEADQUARTERS

additional offices were placed in the same relation to the Secretary-General as his Executive Office: the Personnel Office and the Finance Office, the duties of the two having hitherto been performed by the Department of Administrative and Financial Affairs, and the Legal Office, replacing the Legal Department. The Departments of Economic and Social Affairs were combined. The Department of Conference and General Services was divided into a Department of Conference Services and an Office of General Services. The Technical Assistance Administration was maintained as a separate unit but its close coordination with the Department of Economic and Social Affairs was placed under the direct supervision of the Secretary-General. Instead of the two top echelons of Assistant Secretaries-General and principal Directors, one echelon of officials was established, namely undersecretaries whose responsibilities would be essentially administrative. Provision was made for two undersecretaries without portfolio to serve as advisers to the Secretary-General on special questions and to undertake special assignments on his behalf. The completed organization of the Secretariat under these proposals is shown on the accompanying chart.

Conditions of an International Civil Service

The provisions of the Charter reflect the view generally accepted at San Francisco that the Secretariat should constitute a truly international civil service. The experience of the League of Nations had provided conclusive proof that an international civil service could be created comparing favorably with the best civil services of the world, and that it was possible to establish ". . . an integrated body of international officials, loyal to the international agency and ready to discharge faithfully the international obligations incumbent upon them." [22]

As the result of League experience, and the experience of the International Labour Office in particular, there was general agreement at San Francisco and in the Preparatory Commission that the Secretariat should be organized and should function in accordance with certain definite principles which would insure its efficiency, its independence, and its international character. These principles which are either specifically enunciated or clearly implied in the provisions of the Charter may be briefly stated as follows: (1) Members of the staff should be chosen on the basis of their qualifications to do the work required of them, efficiently and satisfactorily. (2) Members of the staff thus recruited should loyally serve the United Nations, should refrain from

[22] E. F. Ranshofen-Wertheimer, *op. cit.,* p. 428.

any action inconsistent with their status as international officials, and should be protected against political pressures by their governments. (3) Service in the Secretariat should be viewed as a career, with security, compensation, opportunities for advancement, and other benefits adequate to attract and keep highly qualified personnel. We shall now consider how and to what extent these principles have been applied in practice.

RECRUITMENT OF PERSONNEL

Article 101 of the Charter states explicitly that the paramount consideration in the employment of the staff shall be ". . . the necessity of securing the highest standard of efficiency, competence, and integrity." Taken by themselves, these words would suggest that the positions in the Secretariat are to be filled solely on the basis of personal qualifications. However, in international organizations, even more than in national governments, it has been impossible to keep the selection of administrative personnel free from the application of other criteria. In the League Secretariat, it was recognized from the beginning that the personnel should be representative of the major cultures of the world. For this reason and because of pressures exercised to this end by governments, account was taken of the principle of geographic distribution in the appointment of personnel. This principle was explicitly incorporated into the Charter of the United Nations, thereby making it mandatory upon the Secretary-General to take account of this consideration, though the exact degree could hardly be specified.

The Preparatory Commission in its report stressed the importance of suitable procedures of recruitment which would give reasonable assurance of obtaining persons with the desired qualifications for the positions to be filled. Nevertheless it recognized that deference to the principle of wide geographic distribution would entail the appointment of some officials not so qualified. To alleviate the situation thus created, the Commission recommended a program of in-service training which would assist in bringing the possibly less-qualified "geographic" appointees up to the desired level of competence. The Commission, furthermore, recognized that the Secretary-General would have a tremendous task within an initial period of a few weeks of recruiting a staff three or four times the size of the League Secretariat and that he would not be able under these conditions either to develop the best recruitment procedures or to take into account to any great degree the principle of geographic distribution.

In the initial staffing of the Secretariat, carried out under the emergency conditions that then existed, the Secretary-General drew heavily upon readily available personnel which tended to be concentrated in western Europe, the United Kingdom and the Commonwealth countries, and the United States. The location of United Nations headquarters in the United States and the extensive use of persons employed in the Secretariat of the San Francisco Conference resulted in the initial disproportionate recruitment of citizens of the United States. The result was a staff which did not meet the requirements of wide geographical distribution.

Responding to a General Assembly request, the Secretary-General, in 1948, set forth his understanding of the principle of geographic distribution and the criteria which he proposed to adopt in applying it.[23] He interpreted the principle as not meaning that the nationals of a particular state should have a specified number of posts at a particular grade or grades, or that they should receive a particular percentage of the total outlay in salaries. Rather, he interpreted it as meaning that:

> *in the first place, the administration should be satisfied that the Secretariat is enriched by the experience and culture which each Member nation can furnish and that each Member nation should, in its turn, be satisfied that its own culture and philosophy make a full contribution to the Secretariat.*

Reasonably applied, this interpretation could be expected to strengthen the Secretariat in the particular political context in which it was called upon to function.

The Secretary-General made it clear that the principle was not to apply to posts in the lower categories or at similar salary levels. For the higher positions, the principal criterion to be applied in determining the number of positions to be filled by the nationals of a particular Member was to be the Member's financial contribution. This criterion, however, was to be applied flexibly, a variation of 25 per cent upward or downward being permitted, except that for any Member contributing over 10 per cent of the budget, the variation could only be downward. Since the formulation of this policy, the Secretary-General has been directing his efforts toward full implementation of this criterion. Staff commitments and the requirements of orderly and efficient administration have prevented full realization of the principle of geographic distribution, but the progress made has been generally accepted by Members as reasonable.[24]

[23] General Assembly, *Official Records,* Third Session, Plenary, Annexes, A/652, p. 157; U.N., *Repertory of Practice of United Nations Organs,* V, pp. 227–28.

[24] See U.S. Senate, Committee on Foreign Relations, Subcommittee on the

Some observers feel that the Secretary-General has been more successful in applying the principle of geographic distribution to the general satisfaction of Members than he has been in developing methods of recruiting personnel in accordance with the highest standards of "efficiency, competence and integrity." [25] Nevertheless, it must be recognized that there are great difficulties in the way of developing adequate procedures for recruiting personnel on a merit basis for an international secretariat. The usual methods of competitive examinations, interviews, and analysis of personal records employed in those Western countries with more advanced civil service systems are not wholly satisfactory in the different political context of the United Nations. Differences in the educational systems of different countries make competitive written or oral examinations difficult to use, except for positions requiring highly specialized skills such as interpreters and translators. Nor is any test of technical ability alone enough since for positions in the Secretariat, particularly at the professional level, other qualities often are of equal if not greater importance.

LOYALTY OF INTERNATIONAL OFFICIALS

For an international secretariat to be truly international, it is necessary that its loyalty and devotion to the organization should be assured. Beginning in 1932, members of the League Secretariat were required to make a declaration of fidelity. By it, each member undertook "to exercise in all loyalty, discretion and conscience" the functions entrusted to them.[26] Article 100 of the United Nations Charter provides that the Secretary-General and his staff ". . . shall not seek or receive instructions from any government or from any other authority external to the Organization." They shall also ". . . refrain from any action which might reflect on their position as international officials responsible only to the Organization." Under the Staff Regulations each member of the Secretariat is required to subscribe to the following oath or declaration:

> *I solemnly swear (undertake, affirm, promise) to exercise in all loyalty, discretion and conscience the functions entrusted to me as an international civil servant of the United Nations, to discharge*

United Nations Charter, *The Status and Role of the Secretariat of the United Nations,* Staff Study No. 12 (Washington: Government Printing Office, 1954), pp. 22–23.

[25] See, *The United Nations Secretariat,* United Nations Studies 4 (New York: Carnegie Endowment for International Peace, 1950), pp. 69–70.

[26] Ranshofen-Wertheimer, *op. cit.,* p. 245.

those functions and regulate my conduct with the interests of the
United Nations only in view, and not to seek or accept instructions
in regard to the performance of my duties from any government
or other authority external to the Organization.[27]

There are two aspects of the position of the international official
which require special consideration: his duties as international official
per se irrespective of the particular place that he may occupy in the
administrative hierarchy; and his obligations to his own state.

The Staff Regulations make it clear that members of the Secretariat
shall at all times conduct themselves in a manner befitting their status
as international officials. They shall avoid any action and in particular
any kind of public announcement which may reflect adversely on their
status, or on the integrity, independence, and impartiality which are
required by that status. While not expected to give up their national
sentiments or their political and religious convictions, they are required
to ". . . bear in mind the reserve and tact incumbent upon them by
reason of their international status . . ." [28] and specifically not engage
in any political activity inconsistent with or which might reflect on
their independence and impartiality. While membership in a political
party is permitted, provided it does not entail action or the obligation
to action, public support or criticism of party programs or candidates
or public criticism or support of the policies or actions of national
governments are considered to be improper.

A question of perhaps greater difficulty arises in connection with
a possible conflict between the status of a member of the Secretariat and
his loyalty to his state, particularly when his state is the host state, i.e.,
the one within whose territory he is called upon to perform his duties.
This question presented itself in connection with certain United States
nationals, members of the Secretariat, who, during hearings before a
Special Federal Grand Jury and the Internal Sub-Committee of the
Senate Judiciary Committee in 1952, either admitted having been
members of the Communist Party or, when asked whether they had
been members or had engaged in subversive activities, invoked the
Fifth Amendment. The Secretary-General asked the opinion of three
jurists on certain questions relating to these cases. In their opinion [29]
the jurists expressed the view that membership in the Secretariat "in no

[27] Staff Regulation 1.9. See Secretary-General's Bulletin, St/SGB/Rev. 4,
August 15, 1955, p. 6.
[28] Staff Regulation 1.4.
[29] *Report of the Secretary-General on Personnel Policy* (A/2364, Jan. 30,
1953), pp. 21–33.

way abrogates, limits or qualifies the loyalty a person owes to the state of which he is a citizen." Said the jurists:

> *We can find nothing in the constitution of the United Nations or the provisions governing the employment of its staff which give the least ground for supposing that there is or should be any conflict whatever between the loyalty owed by every citizen by virtue of his allegiance to his own state and the responsibility of such a citizen to the United Nations in respect to work done by him as an officer or employee of the United Nations.*[30]

The jurists' advice to the Secretary-General was that he should regard conviction for a crime involving disloyalty by the national courts, or invocation of the Fifth Amendment, which could only be done on the ground of self-incrimination, as grounds for removal. Thus, they would seem to have sought to avoid the conflict of loyalties by saying in effect that any act of a Secretariat official, national of the host state, which is found by the authorities of that state to involve disloyalty to it should be treated by the Secretary-General as incompatible with the international status of the official, and therefore constituting improper conduct.

It is understandable that under the circumstances prevailing at the time, considerations of political expediency should have influenced the Secretary-General and his advisers to avoid giving offense to public opinion and in particular Congressional opinion in the United States. Nevertheless, it is clear that even a national of the host state may indeed have obligations as a member of the Secretariat which may require action of him in conflict with that which his own government may require. Furthermore, his status as an international civil servant legally assures him protection against certain acts of his government inconsistent with that status. This is not because the United Nations is a superstate, but rather because every Member by virtue of acceptance of the Charter has agreed in advance to recognize Secretariat officials as having an international status entitling them to certain rights, privileges and immunities, including protection in the faithful discharge of official duties.

To emphasize to this extent the primacy of the loyalty of the official to the Organization is not of course to suggest that in the recruitment of officials, in the exercise of judgment as to what kind of persons should be employed at a time when some discretion can be used without violating acquired rights, national loyalty should not be recognized as a desirable personal attitude. On this issue, the proper view would

[30] *Ibid.,* p. 25.

seem to be that in an international organization of sovereign states, persons who have national attachments and loyalties but who, in addition, recognize common interests and purposes to be served beyond the purely national, are best qualified for international service.

Mr. C. Wilfred Jenks, against the background of extensive international experience as an international official, puts it very well:

> *The international outlook required of the international civil servant is an awareness made instinctive by habit of the needs, emotions, and prejudices of the peoples of differently circumstanced countries, as they are felt and expressed by the peoples concerned, accompanied by a capacity for weighing these frequently imponderable elements in a judicial manner before reaching any decision to which they are relevant. It is no part of the duty of an international official to protect in advance the interests of his country of origin; that is the duty of the responsible representatives of that country on policy-making bodies, and of its permanent representatives accredited to the international institution in question.*[31]

CONDITIONS OF SERVICE

In the organization and development of the League Secretariat it was clearly recognized that its efficiency required conditions of service which would attract and encourage persons of the highest qualifications. This was generally accepted when the United Nations was being created. The Preparatory Commission gave a great deal of thought to this matter and in its report to the General Assembly made a number of specific proposals including Draft Provisional Staff Regulations and Staff Rules which in substance were subsequently put into effect.

A first question to be considered was that of salary scale. The establishment of a salary scale also involved the classification of positions within the Secretariat, thus establishing the basis for selective promotions. The Preparatory Commission recommended that salary and allowance scales "should compare favorably with those of the most highly paid home and foreign services, due account being taken of the special factors affecting service in the Secretariat." [32] In practice the scales that have been adopted have met this test. A relatively high level of salaries and allowance has been made necessary by the fact of the

[31] C. Wilfred Jenks, "Some Problems of an International Civil Service," *Public Administration Review*, II (1943), pp. 95–96.

[32] *Report of the Preparatory Commission of the United Nations*, pp. 93–94.

location of the United Nations headquarters in the United States where living costs have been comparatively high.[33]

The classification of positions within the Secretariat has proved to be a problem of some difficulty. In the League Secretariat, what might be called the European tradition was followed. All positions were classified into three main divisions: directors, administrative and secretarial, and manual services. This type of classification resulted in a kind of "caste" system, since movement from one division to a higher division was extremely difficult. The United Nations Preparatory Commission, while recommending that the system of classification and salary grading should be uniform and, especially at the start, broad and simple, did not consider it feasible to develop and recommend a detailed system. Nevertheless, it did state that while the number of categories should not be larger than necessary, there should be established within each category grades marking the different levels of responsibility. The General Assembly authorized the Secretary-General, after discussion with the Advisory Committee of Experts, to develop a plan of classification which would conform to the Commission's recommendations. The plan which was developed differed substantially from that of the League and followed much more closely United States practice. Under it, positions were classified according to duties, responsibilities, and authority.

The scheme provided for nineteen grades with five to seven salary steps in each grade. It soon came to be regarded as unsatisfactory because of its complexity and inflexibility. It was viewed by many as placing undue emphasis upon special qualifications for particular posts instead of general capacity, and as discouraging the flexible use of personnel. In 1950, on the basis of the report of a committee of experts appointed by the Secretary-General, a new plan of classification was introduced which provided for four broad categories—principal officer and director, professional, general service, and manual worker, with salary gradations in each category. This represented a return in essence to the League system with its advantages of greater simplicity and flexibility within categories, but with its danger of introducing a "caste" system.

The idea that satisfactory service should be rewarded by promotion is accepted in principle but there are special difficulties in the way of its application. The Staff Regulations state that ". . . subject to the provisions of Article 101, paragraph 3, of the Charter, and without

[33] For a comparison of League and United Nations staff salaries, see A. Loveday, "Staff Salaries in the U.N. Family," *International Organization,* XI (1957), pp. 635–48.

prejudice to the recruitment of fresh talent at all levels, the fullest regard shall be had in filling vacancies, to the requisite qualifications and experience of persons already in the service of the United Nations." [34] Here we have stated or clearly implied three qualifying considerations: (1) the principle of geographic distribution may make it desirable in a particular case that the vacancy should be filled by appointment from an under-represented country instead of by promotion; (2) there may not be in the Secretariat at the time anyone with the particular technical qualifications required for the post; and (3) the Secretary-General may find it desirable in the interest of good administration or for political reasons to bring in a technically qualified person from the outside. Furthermore, it must be recognized that the size of the Secretariat, in comparison with national civil services, greatly restricts the possibilities of promotion.

Another factor in determining the efficiency and attractiveness of service in the Secretariat is the tenure of appointment. Generally speaking, the Anglo-American approach to the problem is to make the administrative head responsible for the acts of his subordinates and to give him almost unlimited powers of appointment and removal. The continental European approach, on the other hand, is to recognize that the officeholder has a contractual right to his office and to give him legal protection in the enjoyment of that right. Administrative tribunals are established to help provide this protection. The League of Nations tended to adopt the continental approach and the United Nations has followed suit.

"The letter of appointment granted to every staff member contains expressly or by reference all the terms and conditions of employment." [35] It may be a temporary appointment (probationary, fixed-term, or indefinite) or it may be a permanent or a regular appointment. In any case, the person receiving the appointment is required, so long as he holds it, to conform to the provisions of the Staff Regulations and Rules regarding his obligations and duties. The authority of the Secretary-General to terminate an appointment or to dismiss a member of the staff exists in principle but is subject to certain legal restrictions and procedures. Though Mr. Hammarskjöld has been able to get the General Assembly to agree to some enlargement of his discretionary authority, he is still subject to substantial limitations in the interest of the security of tenure of the staff official.

Furthermore, the interpretation of the provisions of the Staff Regulations and Rules governing the exercise by the Secretary-General of his right to terminate or dismiss is not his exclusive responsibility.

[34] Staff Regulation 4.4.   [35] Staff Rule 104.1.

Special advisory procedures are prescribed for all cases where the Secretary-General proposes to use his powers. In addition, the General Assembly has established an Administrative Tribunal composed of persons elected by that organ to decide all appeals by officials from decisions of the Secretary-General. Decisions of the Tribunal are binding upon the parties and upon the General Assembly as the appropriating organ.[36] However, since 1955, as the result of United States dissatisfaction with decisions handed down in the case of eleven of its nationals, dismissed because of failure to cooperate with United States investigatory bodies, the General Assembly adopted a resolution providing for a limited right of appeal to the International Court of Justice through the medium of a committee of the General Assembly composed of members of the last General Committee. If this political committee decides that the Tribunal has failed to exercise its jurisdiction, has erred on a question of law relating to the Charter, or has committed a fundamental error of procedure occasioning a failure of justice, "it shall request an advisory opinion of the Court" which becomes binding on the parties.[37]

Privileges and Immunities

In order that the Secretary-General and his staff should be able to perform their duties freely and independently of outside interference and obstruction it is necessary that they enjoy certain immunities from the jurisdiction and governmental control of Member states. The need of such immunities for the representatives of states when engaged in the performance of their official duties in the territory of other states has long been recognized by international law. The Covenant of the League of Nations provided that officials of the League ". . . when engaged on the business of the League shall enjoy diplomatic privileges and immunities." [38] It also provided that the buildings and other property occupied by the League or its officials should be inviolable. These guarantees were further implemented in agreements concluded between the League and the Swiss Government.

Those who drafted the Charter decided against assimilating United Nations officials to diplomatic officers and adopted instead the functional approach. Article 105 provides that the Organization shall enjoy in the

[36] *Effects of Awards of Compensation Made by the United Nations Administrative Tribunal, Advisory Opinion of July 13, 1954: I.C.J. Reports 1954*, p. 47.

[37] General Assembly Resolution 957 (X), Nov. 8, 1955.

[38] Article 7, par. 4.

territory of each member ". . . such privileges and immunities as are necessary for the fulfillment of its purposes." Also, officials of the Organization ". . . shall similarly enjoy such privileges and immunities as are necessary for the independent exercise of their functions in connection with the Organization." These privileges and immunities have been defined in international agreements approved by the General Assembly and ratified by Members, and in national legislation.

Of the multilateral agreements that relate to the privileges and immunities of the Organization and the officials of the Secretariat, the most important are the Convention on Privileges and Immunities of the United Nations of February 13, 1946,[39] and the Headquarters Agreement between the United States and the United Nations of October 31, 1947.[40] The United States has not ratified the Convention because of objections raised in the Senate to its provisions for exemption of Secretariat personnel from income taxation and military service. Instead, Congress has enacted the International Organizations Immunities Act of December, 1945,[41] which, with these two exceptions, accords substantially the same privileges and immunities as the Convention.

Under the terms of the Charter, international agreements that have been concluded, and relevant national legislation, the headquarters district, including buildings, is placed under the control and authority of the United Nations and is declared inviolable. Freedom of transit to and from the district is assured to the Secretary-General and his staff, as well as the representatives of Members. Freedom of, and adequate facilities for communications are assured. All officials of the United Nations are declared immune from legal process for words spoken or acts performed by them in their official capacities. Except for nationals of the United States who are denied the enjoyment of these privileges vis-à-vis their own government, they are exempt from taxation on salaries and emoluments paid by the United Nations and they are immune from national service obligations. In principle, the Secretary-General and his chief assistants are accorded full diplomatic privileges and immunities, while other officials enjoy those privileges and immunities necessary to the performance of their functions as determined by the Secretary-General. In addition, provision is made for use by Secretariat officials of a *laissez-passer* to be recognized as a valid travel document by all Members.

[39] U.N. Doc. A/43, Annex 1, pp. 687–93.
[40] U.S. Department of State, Publication 3024, pp. 220–34; and General Assembly Resolution 169 (II).
[41] Public Law 291, 79th Congress, 1st session.

Conclusions

More than any other organ, the Secretariat—the Secretary-General and his staff—is responsible for giving, and has the opportunity to give, to the United Nations a role that places it above the diplomatic machinery of the past. In his discreet way, the first Secretary-General of the League recognized the responsibility placed upon him and discharged his responsibilities in such a manner as to create precedents and expectations which were to be decisive in the writing of the Charter. The present Secretary-General of the United Nations, Dag Hammarskjöld, taking advantage of these precedents and expectations while keeping within the limits established by political realities, has carried further the process of establishing on firm foundations the role of the Secretariat as the chief official exponent of the purposes and principles for which the United Nations stands. The statement which Dag Hammarskjöld made on October 31, 1956, will long stand not only as a courageous action, but also as a sound and forceful exposition of the responsibility of the Secretary-General and his staff.

If the Secretary-General is to perform his duties in the spirit of the Charter, he must be supported by a staff which is competent, independent of the political influence of Member governments, and like its chief loyal to the principles and purposes of the Organization. The Organization provides adequate opportunities for adjustments and accommodations to be worked out between the responsible representatives of Member governments without introducing the representational principle into the Secretariat itself. While it is desirable, the world being what it is, that the Secretary-General and his principal advisers should have the confidence of the major powers, there is no sound reason why even these officials should be viewed in any sense as the representatives of Member governments.

If the staff is to meet the requirements of a truly international civil service, it is necessary that every effort should be made to secure highly qualified personnel, to maintain conditions of employment that are most favorable to devoted and efficient service, and to protect members of the Secretariat against improper influences which will detract in any way from the loyal performance of their duties. The record of the United Nations Secretariat, following upon that of the League Secretariat, encourages one to believe that this goal is attainable. While it has been necessary on occasion and in certain respects to bend to political influences and to be guided by considerations of expediency, the relative success with which the Secretariat has borne up under the pressures of the postwar period and has come through the major crisis of its short career is definitely encouraging.

SUGGESTED READINGS

Carnegie Endowment for International Peace. *The United Nations Secretariat*. New York, 1951.

Claude, Inis, Jr. *Swords into Plowshares*. New York: Random House, Inc., 1956. Chap. 10.

Cohen, Maxwell. "The United Nations Secretariat—Some Constitutional and Administrative Developments," *American Journal of International Law,* XLIX (1955), pp. 295–319.

Friedmann, Wolfgang, and Fatouros, Arghyrios A. "The United Nations Administrative Tribunal," *International Organization,* XI (1957), pp. 13–29.

Jackson, Elmore. "The Developing Role of the Secretary-General," *International Organization,* XI (1957), pp. 431–45.

Jenks, C. Wilfred. "Some Problems of an International Civil Service," *Public Administration Review,* III (1943), pp. 93–105.

Lie, Trygve. *In the Cause of Peace*. New York: The Macmillan Company, 1954.

Phelan, Edward J. *Yes and Albert Thomas*. London: Cresset Press, Ltd., 1936.

Ranshofen-Wertheimer, E. F. *The International Secretariat: A Great Experiment in International Administration*. Washington: Carnegie Endowment for International Peace, 1945.

Schwebel, Stephen M. *The Secretary-General of the United Nations: His Political Powers and Practice*. Cambridge: Harvard University Press, 1952.

————. "The International Character of the Secretariat of the United Nations," *British Yearbook of International Law,* XXX (1953), pp. 71–115.

Scott, Frank R. "The World's Civil Service," *International Conciliation,* No. 496 (January, 1954).

U. S. Senate, Committee on Foreign Relations, Subcommittee on the United Nations Charter. *The Status and Role of the Secretariat of the United Nations*. Staff Study No. 12. Washington: Government Printing Office, 1954.

Chapter VIII

KEEPING THE PEACE

IN ANY ORDERED society, the task of keeping the peace is of primary importance. Only on the basis of peace and security can a legal order be developed. A study of the development of English law and political institutions reveals that the earliest concern of the Anglo-Saxon kings was to enforce "the King's peace." Not until reasonable certainty of peace was assured was there the opportunity to develop institutions and procedures which would provide justice through law.

Keeping the Peace under the Charter

In the international community the maintenance of peace and security is also of first importance. So long as force can be used with impunity to achieve selfish ends, the strong will have little reason to use methods of cooperation and accommodation to achieve common purposes, and the weak will find little protection in such procedures. Furthermore, the experience of two world wars has demonstrated not only that war is immensely destructive for all concerned but also that it solves few problems, creates many more than it solves, and generally leaves nations both great and small in a worse condition than it found them. It was, therefore, not surprising that those who wrote the Charter should have been convinced that the first job of the new organization, both in time and in importance, was to keep the peace. In line with this thought, the United States delegation to the San Francisco Conference reported to the President that "if any single provision of the Charter has more substance than the others, it is surely the first sentence of Article 39, which places upon the Security Council the duty to determine the existence of 'any threat to the peace, breach of the peace or act of aggression' and to make recommendations or decide upon

159

measures to be taken 'to maintain or restore international peace and security.' " [1]

By placing emphasis as they did upon the primacy of this particular Charter provision, the members of the United States delegation recognized that without the effective maintenance of peace, the United Nations would not be in the position to perform its other functions. While it was recognized that the successful discharge of its responsibilities for promoting economic and social cooperation and developing friendly relations between states was of the greatest importance and would in the long run contribute to the maintenance of peace and security on a more acceptable and durable basis, it was rightly believed that for these curative and preventive measures to make their contribution, it was necessary that present peace and security be assured. In other words, pending the development by cooperative means of long-range programs and policies that would make the world a better place to live in, it was necessary to maintain conditions of peace and security without which the necessary cooperation would be impossible.

The Charter approach to the problem of maintaining international peace and security is essentially a two-fold one. On the one hand it requires Members to "refrain in their international relations from the threat or use of force against the territorial integrity or political independence of any state, or in any manner inconsistent with the Purposes of the United Nations." [2] In this respect, it goes considerably further than the League Covenant which required members not to "resort to war" under certain defined conditions, but not all.[3] The ambiguity of the term "resort to war" made the League commitment even less restrictive in its legal effect than the corresponding provision of the Charter. On the other hand, the Charter requires that "all Members shall settle their international disputes by peaceful means in such a manner that international peace and security, and justice, are not endangered." [4] This, too, is a more sweeping commitment than was contained in the corresponding provisions of the Covenant. These two commitments are, in effect, the two complementary aspects of one central commitment, not to use force for the achievement of purely national purposes.

But while the Charter of the United Nations goes beyond the

[1] United States Department of State, *Charter of the United Nations, Report to the President on the Results of the San Francisco Conference by the Chairman of the United Nations Delegation, the Secretary of State, June 26, 1945*. Dept. of State Publ. 2349, pp. 90–91.

[2] Article 2, par. 4.   [3] See Articles 12, 13 and 15.

[4] Article 2, par. 3.

Covenant in the duty that it places on Members to abstain from the use of force in the achievement of national purposes, it does not go as far as the Covenant in obligating Members to use collective measures to restrain or suppress any improper use of force by a state. The Covenant contained quite revolutionary provisions in this respect. In addition to the collective guarantee contained in Article 10, which to President Wilson was the heart of the Covenant, Article 16 required members to apply "immediately" sweeping economic and financial sanctions against any state resorting to war in violation of its obligations. Though the application of military sanctions was not made mandatory, the Covenant thus did go far in creating a system of collective security under which each member would be required to assist any other member that might be the victim of aggression. The failure of League sanctions against Italy in 1935–1936 convinced many of the basic weakness of the League system of collective security and was in large measure responsible for the decision of the authors of the Charter to adopt a different approach to the problem of implementation, and to place primary responsibility on the major powers acting in concert instead of relying on the individual actions of all Members responding to a common legal commitment.

The Charter places upon the Security Council the primary responsibility for the maintenance of international peace and security. This responsibility is made particularly clear with respect to measures to be taken in case of a threat to the peace, breach of the peace, or act of aggression. The Security Council alone is expressly directed to determine the existence of such a condition, and to recommend or decide measures to be taken to restore international peace and security.

Furthermore, the Charter defines in considerable detail what particular measures the Council may take and how it is to take them, although it gives the Council very wide discretion in the evaluation of circumstances, the choice of means, and the timing of its actions. Acting under Article 39 and Chapter VI of the Charter, it may exercise its powers of peaceful settlement and adjustment, i.e., it may investigate the dispute or situation and make recommendations to the parties regarding the procedures and methods of settlement and adjustment. Under Article 40 it may call upon the parties to comply with provisional measures intended to prevent an aggravation of the situation, without prejudice, however, "to the rights, claims or position of the parties concerned." Under Articles 41 and 42 it may require Members to take such political, economic and military measures as may be necessary to restore international peace and security.

However, before Members can be required to take military

measures, they must agree to make available on call and "in accordance with a special agreement or agreements . . . armed forces, assistance, and facilities, including rights of passage." These agreements are to govern "the number and types of forces, their degree of readiness and general location, and the nature of the facilities and assistance to be provided." [5] To enable the Council to take urgent military measures, Members undertake under the terms of Article 45 to "hold immediately available national airforce contingents for combined international enforcement action." Until military agreements are concluded placing at the Council's disposal sufficient military forces to enable it to exercise its responsibilities under Article 42, the permanent members of the Security Council are to consult with each other with a view to taking such joint action on behalf of the United Nations as may be necessary to maintain international peace and security.[6]

To assist the Security Council in the performance of its military responsibilities, provision is made for a Military Staff Committee, composed of the Chiefs of Staff of the permanent members or their representatives. The Committee is made responsible under the Security Council for the strategic direction of armed forces placed at the disposal of the Council. The Security Council is authorized to decide whether measures which it orders shall be taken by all Members of the United Nations or by some. Furthermore, Members are required to afford mutual assistance in carrying out these measures.

The Charter system for keeping the peace by enforcement action as constructed at San Francisco was, therefore, one which vested great responsibility and power in the Security Council, along with wide discretion in the discharge of this responsibility and the use of this power. Clearly, since the Security Council could only take action by agreement of all the permanent members, the system could be operative only against a non-permanent member of the Council, and not against a permanent member or for that matter a non-permanent member backed by a permanent member. It clearly depended for its effectiveness on recognition by the permanent members that they had a common interest in keeping the peace and that they should compromise their differences in order that they might cooperate in furthering this common interest.

In addition to emphasizing the primary responsibility of the Security Council for taking enforcement action, the San Francisco Charter also lays down the general principle that enforcement action is a monopoly of the United Nations, that no such action can be taken under any regional arrangement or by any regional agency without the consent of the United Nations given through the Security Council.[7]

[5] Article 43.   [6] Article 106.   [7] Article 53, par. 1.

This principle had been stated without qualification in the Dumbarton Oaks Proposals. In the course of the San Francisco deliberations, however, it was found necessary to introduce two exceptions. One was to the effect that "nothing in the present Charter shall impair the inherent right of individual or collective self-defense if an armed attack occurs against a Member of the United Nations, until the Security Council has taken measures necessary to maintain international peace and security." [8] This exception was introduced to meet two objections to the absolute requirement of Security Council authorization.

First, the Latin-American Republics argued that this requirement made it possible for a non-American permanent member of the Council to veto any collective action that might be taken by the American republics under an Inter-American system of collective security such as was envisaged by the Act of Chapultepec, adopted by the Mexico City Conference of February–March 1945. The other objection was that since the requirement of Security Council authorization made it possible for a permanent member to prevent any action from being taken by the Council, this might lead to a situation in which a state would be deprived of any protection against an attack directed or supported by a permanent member. Clearly, the second objection was based on some skepticism as to whether relations between the Soviet Union and the Western powers would be such as to permit the close cooperation which the effective functioning of the Security Council required. To meet these two objections, and to permit collective action to be taken under certain conditions without the requirement of Security Council authorization, Article 51 was adopted. Significantly, it was placed at the end of Chapter VII and not in Chapter VIII, thus stressing its function of introducing an exception to the total responsibility of the Security Council as well as to the special responsibility of the Council in authorizing enforcement action under regional arrangements.

The second exception that was introduced at San Francisco related explicitly to the requirement of Council authorization of enforcement action under regional arrangements or by regional agencies. It provided that the requirement should not apply in the case of "measures against an enemy state, as defined in paragraph 2 of [Article 53], provided for pursuant to Article 107 or in regional arrangements directed against renewal of aggressive policy on the part of any such state." This exception was introduced to meet the demands of certain of the allies in the Second World War, notably the Soviet Union and France, that Members should be able, without waiting for Security Council authorization, to take such measures as might be necessary to

[8] Article 51.

prevent the "renewal of aggressive policy" on the part of defeated enemy states.

At the time these exceptions were introduced into the Charter, their inclusion was defended on the ground that they were necessary precautions. The emphasis was placed on the importance of the central principle that the United Nations alone and more particularly the Security Council, should be responsible for deciding where, when, and what collective measures should be taken. With the revival of earlier fears, distrusts, and antagonisms between the Soviet Union and the West, these exceptions, particularly that contained in Article 51, have acquired major importance as providing alternative bases for collective measures to keep the peace.

Failure of the Security Council

The full effectiveness of the Security Council as the primary instrument of peace enforcement was premised on two conditions neither of which materialized: (1) the availability to the Security Council of military forces and facilities under the terms of agreements concluded between the Council and Members; and (2) the effective cooperation of the permanent members of the Council in dealing with threats to the peace, breaches of the peace, and acts of aggression.

One of the first acts of the Security Council after its organization in 1946 was to request the Military Staff Committee to examine and report on the question of military agreements under Article 43. Following the Assembly's recommendation in December, 1946, that the placing of armed forces at the disposal of the Council be accelerated, the Council on February 13, 1947, directed the Military Staff Committee to make its report not later than April 30. The Report which the Committee submitted on that date [9] contained forty-one articles. Of these, twenty-five were agreed to by all members of the Committee; agreement on the other sixteen was not possible. Unfortunately, the sixteen articles were the important ones since they dealt with matters, not adequately covered by the Charter, which had to be decided if agreements under Article 43 were to be concluded.

The chief disagreements were between the Soviet Union and the other permanent members, though this division did not hold on all issues. The Soviet Union held fundamentally different views from the

[9] U.N. Security Council, *Official Records,* Second Year, Special Suppl. No. 1, "Report of the Military Staff Committee."

United States and to a somewhat less extent from other permanent members on the all-important questions of the size and composition of the armed forces to be contributed by permanent members; the provision of bases; the location of the forces when not in action; the time of withdrawal of forces; and the manner of logistical support. Generally speaking, the United States favored a large force with great striking power, flexibly composed, organized, and directed, and so stationed as to be readily available. The Soviet Union saw no need of a large force if it was not to be used against a major power; insisted that the principle of equality should govern the contributions of the permanent members; and demanded clear definition of the conditions under which the force could be used. It was obvious from the discussions in the Committee and subsequently in the Security Council that the disagreements resulted primarily from lack of confidence between the Soviet Union and the United States in each other's good faith and intentions. The differences, therefore, were political and not technical in origin, and could only be eliminated at the political level.[10]

Since the governments were not able to resolve their political differences, the deadlock over principles governing the military agreements continued and the Security Council has never been provided with the armed forces and facilities necessary to the full discharge of its responsibilities under the Charter. And since it was the inability of the permanent members to agree that made it impossible to conclude these agreements, it was unlikely that these same permanent members would be able to agree on joint action on behalf of the Organization under Article 106, pending the conclusion of the necessary military agreements. In the one case where this was proposed, when the failure to implement the Assembly's recommendations on Palestine was before the Security Council in February, 1948, the proposal was subsequently withdrawn when it was obvious that the rapidly deteriorating relations between the Soviet Union and the Western Powers made joint action quite out of the question.

Though military forces and facilities were not made available to the Security Council, it was still legally possible for the Council to take measures short of the use of armed force to keep the peace in case of threat or actual violation. There was even the possibility that the Council members might agree to use their own forces or forces voluntarily contributed by other members to achieve this result. But the likelihood

[10] For more detailed consideration of the differences, see Leland M. Goodrich and Anne P. Simons, *The United Nations and the Maintenance of International Peace and Security* (Washington: The Brookings Institution, 1955), pp. 398–405.

of such action being taken was greatly reduced, if not for all practical purposes eliminated by the conflicting purposes of the policies and actions of the Soviet Union and the Western Powers in the postwar period, and by the distrust and hostility that came to characterize their relations.

When Greece complained in December, 1946, that her northern neighbors were threatening the peace by giving aid to guerrillas in northern Greece and later requested that the Council take action under Chapter VII of the Charter, the Soviet Union vetoed proposals that were made. When the Security Council was considering the situation in Indonesia resulting from fighting between Netherlands and Indonesian forces, no decision to take enforcement action was possible, in part because the United States and the United Kingdom were opposed to having Soviet forces introduced into Indonesia, even for international police purposes. Likewise, when the Security Council was asked in 1948 to consider the implementation of the General Assembly's recommendation on Palestine and the situation resulting from fighting between Arabs and Jews, distrust and rivalry between the Soviet Union and the Western Powers and unwillingness on the part of each side to see armed forces of the other introduced into the area, even under Council auspices, seriously delayed any effective action to stop hostilities and were in fact in large measure responsible for failure to implement the Assembly's proposals.

Only under the very special circumstances resulting from the withdrawal of the Soviet representative from the Council in January, 1950, in protest against the seating of the representative of the Chinese National Government was it possible for the Security Council to initiate collective measures in Korea.[11] The possibility of the Council's continuing to carry on the task it had undertaken disappeared with the return of the Soviet representative on August 1, and it is reasonable to surmise that circumstances permitting the Council to act in a situation where the permanent members are in basic conflict will not again occur.

But while the Security Council has been unable, except in one instance, to initiate collective measures of the kind described in Articles 41 and 42 of the Charter, it has in a number of instances been able to exercise sufficient influence on the situation, acting under the provisions of Chapter VI and Articles 39 and 40 of the Charter, to prevent hostilities from breaking out or to bring them to an end. Thus, in dealing with the Dutch "police action" in Indonesia in 1947, the Security Council was able first to get the parties to agree on a cease-fire and the principles of a political settlement, and then to terminate the second Dutch "police

[11] See Leland M. Goodrich, *Korea; A Study of U.S. Policy in the United Nations* (New York: Council on Foreign Relations, 1956), ch. V and Appendix.

action" on terms that gave no profit to violence.[12] The success of the Council in this instance was due primarily to the fact that the principal major powers, for different reasons, were anxious to bring hostilities to an end and to eliminate any excuse that any one of them might have for introducing its national forces into the area. In this particular case, the exercise of economic pressure on the Netherlands by the United States, together with the threat of economic measures by certain Asian countries, contributed greatly to the Dutch decision to yield.[13]

In Palestine, during the period 1947 to 1949, the Security Council was successful in finally bringing Israel and the Arab States to accept a cease-fire and to conclude armistice agreements putting an end to hostilities.[14] To achieve this result, the Council found it necessary to invoke Chapter VII explicitly and threaten action under it. Here again the decisions of the Council were made possible by the fact that the permanent members had a common desire, though for different reasons, to bring an end to the fighting. The Soviet Union was anxious that fighting should end so that the United Kingdom and the United States would have no excuse for sending their armed forces into the area, and the Western Powers were equally anxious to prevent any situation from arising which would provide an excuse for the dispatch of Soviet forces. In the Palestine case, the threat of the United Kingdom to take action under the Anglo-Egyptian Treaty of 1936 which Egypt was anxious to terminate helped persuade the latter to agree to the Council's request for a cease-fire. From 1949 on, and particularly after the North Korean attack and the United Nations counteraction, the Council became a less effective instrument for keeping the peace in the Middle East, specifically, by supervising the enforcement of armistice agreements. Once the "cold war" spread to that area, the Security Council became largely impotent to take any effective action.

The conclusion to be drawn from these and other instances is that while the Security Council has not been able to act as the armed policeman, as the framers of the Charter had intended, it has nevertheless, within those areas where the permanent members have a common interest in preserving or restoring peace, been able to perform its police function with considerable success. This it has done by various forms of persuasion—short of the use of the collective measures authorized

[12] See J. Foster Collins, "The United Nations and Indonesia," *International Conciliation*, No. 459 (March 1950).

[13] On the importance of opinion in The Netherlands, see Whitney T. Perkins, "Sanctions for Political Change—The Indonesian Case," *International Organization*, XII (1958), pp. 26–42.

[14] See L. L. Leonard, "The United Nations and Palestine," *International Conciliation*, No. 454 (Oct., 1949).

in the Charter—persuasion that is usually cloaked in the language of Article 40, providing for provisional measures to be taken "without prejudice to the rights, claims and position" of the parties. Thus, in the resolutions which it adopted in dealing with hostilities in Palestine, it most commonly put its decisions in the form of requests addressed to the parties to cease hostilities or to withdraw their forces from certain areas without prejudice, and in making these requests, the verb "calls upon" was commonly used.

Alternatives to Security Council Action

The worsening relations between the Soviet Union and the Western Powers, resulting in failure to provide the Security Council with the military means to support its decisions and in the frequent inability of that organ to take decisions with respect to serious matters before it because of the Soviet veto, convinced many governments that it was necessary to find alternative methods, within the permissive limits of the Charter, for dealing with threats to the peace, breaches of the peace, and acts of aggression. Two alternatives in particular have received wide support. They have been justified by their proponents as efforts to supplement the limited role which the Security Council can be expected to perform under present conditions and thus to strengthen the United Nations in the achievement of its major objectives.

First, advantage has been widely taken of the provisions of Article 51 which reserves "the inherent right of individual or collective self-defense if an armed attack occurs against a Member of the United Nations," and of Article 53 which permits action to be taken under "regional arrangements" to prevent a renewal of aggressive policy by an "enemy state." Article 51 has been interpreted to mean that Members of the United Nations—and non-members, since the right is inherent—may enter into collective self-defense arrangements under which they may take individual or joint military measures in defense against an armed attack without first being authorized to do so by the Security Council. Secondly, by a liberal interpretation of the provisions of the Charter, particularly Articles 10, 11, and 12, the role of the General Assembly in dealing with threats to the peace, breaches of the peace, and acts of aggression has been substantially developed. This has been done under an interpretation of the Charter provisions which accords to the Assembly a "residual responsibility" for maintaining international peace and security in case the Security Council is prevented from acting by the veto.

COLLECTIVE SELF-DEFENSE ARRANGEMENTS

Taking advantage of the exception to the Council's responsibility introduced by Article 51, a large number of Members and non-Members, following the leadership of the United States, have concluded collective self-defense agreements under the terms of which they give assurance that they will come to each other's assistance in case of military attack. These agreements include the following: the Inter-American Treaty of Mutual Assistance of September 2, 1947, to which the twenty-one American republics are parties; [15] the North Atlantic Treaty of April 4, 1949, to which fifteen states bordering on the Atlantic and the Mediterranean are at present parties; [16] the Mutual Defense Treaty of August 20, 1951, between the United States and the Philippines; [17] the Security Treaty of September 1, 1951, between Australia, New Zealand, and the United States; [18] the Security Treaty of September 8, 1951, between the United States and Japan; [19] the Mutual Defense Treaty of October 1, 1953, between the United States and Korea; [20] the Mutual Defense Treaty of December 2, 1954, between the United States and the Republic of China; [21] the South-East Asia Collective Defense Treaty of September 8, 1954, to which the United States, the United Kingdom, France, Australia, New Zealand, the Philippines, Thailand, and Pakistan are parties; [22] and the Baghdad Pact of February 24, 1955 between Turkey and Iraq to which the United Kingdom, Iran, and Pakistan subsequently adhered, and which the United States supports.[23] This network of agreements finds its unity, apart from common reliance on the provisions of Article 51, in the support or active participation of the United States. The United States, forty-two other Members and two non-Members (the West German Republic and the Republic of Korea) are thus associated in collective self-defense undertakings.

Of these agreements, the Inter-American Treaty of Mutual Assistance of 1947 (popularly called the Rio Pact) is the oldest. It is the expression of a long-recognized common interest of the republics of the Western Hemisphere in the maintenance of peace within the hemisphere and their protection against any attacks from the outside. Beginning in 1823 it was the declared policy of the United States (the

---

[15] U.S. Treaties and other International Acts Series, 1838.

[16] *Ibid.*, 1964.   [17] *Ibid.*, 2529.   [18] *Ibid.*, 2493.

[19] *Ibid.*, 2491.   [20] *Ibid.*, 3097.   [21] *Ibid.*, 3178.

[22] *Ibid.*, 3170.

[23] Great Britain, Treaty Series No. 39 (1956). While Iraq remains for the time being a party to this treaty, its continued participation became doubtful after the overthrow of the Western-oriented government in July, 1958.

Monroe Doctrine) to oppose any attempt by a European power force-fully to colonize or impose its system by force upon any Latin American republic. With the formation of the Union of American Republics in 1889, the principle of cooperation was applied to many non-political aspects of their international relations and in the nineteen-thirties steps were taken to make the principles of the Monroe Doctrine principles of cooperation among the American republics. At the Mexico City Confer-ence of 1945, the participating republics signed the Act of Chapultepec which provided for collective measures in case of any attack upon one of them for the duration of the war, and for the conclusion of a treaty following the establishment of peace, providing for the use of collective measures in case of attack.[24] It was this policy commitment which moved the American republics to demand some qualification of the Dumbarton Oaks requirement that enforcement action under regional arrangements must be authorized by the Security Council, a demand to which Article 51 was a direct response. It was in accordance with this provision that the Inter-American Treaty of Mutual Assistance was concluded.

By the terms of the Inter-American Treaty, "the High Contracting Parties agree that an armed attack by any State against an American State shall be construed as an armed attack against all the American States," each party undertakes "to assist in meeting the attack," and the Organ of Consultation may by a two-thirds vote decide what measures are to be taken, except that no state can be obligated to take military measures without its consent. While this treaty in some respects pro-vided the model for the North Atlantic Treaty of 1949, it has not had the impact of that treaty on international political relations or more spe-cifically upon the role of the United Nations. For one thing, the con-clusion of such a treaty was taken for granted at the time the Charter was written, and was generally accepted as being consistent with the purposes and provisions of the Charter. Furthermore, the existence of the treaty did not add materially to the power of the West vis-à-vis the Soviet Union and was not regarded by the Soviet Union as being directed especially against it. Only very modest steps have been taken to develop and organize military strength in support of the treaty commitments. Tacitly, the power of the United States has been regarded as available in any case for the defense of the parties to it.

The North Atlantic Treaty of April 4, 1949, however, had a quite different history and produced a quite different impact. It was concluded to provide strength in meeting the threat of Soviet expansionism, which,

[24] For text, see *Documents in American Foreign Relations, 1944–1945* (Bos-ton: World Peace Foundation, 1947), pp. 717–20. Argentina did not participate in the Conference but signed the Act later.

in the minds of the parties to the treaty, the United Nations itself was relatively powerless to counter. The idea of an "alliance" of like-minded nations within the framework of the United Nations to meet the Soviet threat first received concrete application in the Treaty of Brussels of March 17, 1948, to which the United Kingdom, France, Belgium, the Netherlands, and Luxembourg were parties.[25] Under this treaty, steps were taken to create a joint military agency under the name of the Western Union Defence Organization for the more effective defense of the parties. Recognition of the need of wider support, particularly in view of the increased tempo of the "cold war" in 1948, led to the conclusion of the North Atlantic Treaty which initially included, in addition to the Brussels Treaty parties, the United States, Canada, Italy, Portugal, Norway, Denmark, and Iceland. Later the Federal Republic of Germany, Greece, and Turkey were included.

Under the terms of this treaty

The Parties agree that an armed attack against one or more of them in Europe or North America shall be considered an attack against them all; and consequently they agree that, if such an armed attack occurs, each of them, in the exercise of the right of individual or collective self-defense recognized by Article 51 of the Charter of the United Nations, will assist the Party or Parties so attacked by taking forthwith, individually and in concert with the other Parties, such action as it deems necessary, including the use of armed force, to restore and maintain the security of the North Atlantic area.[26]

Article 3 provides that

In order more effectively to achieve the purposes of this Treaty, the Parties, separately and jointly, by means of continuous and effective self-help and mutual aid, will maintain and develop their individual and collective capacity to resist armed attack.

The Treaty also provides for political, economic, and cultural cooperation, and establishes a Council to consider matters concerning the implementation of the Treaty.

While the parties to the treaty purport to act within the provisions of the Charter and declare their full loyalty to the purposes and principles of the Charter, the conclusion of the treaty was not only a judgment that the United Nations was ineffective as a peace and security organization but also a declaration of purpose by the parties to place primary

[25] United Nations, *Treaty Series,* XIX (1948), p. 51.
[26] Article 5.

reliance on the new arrangement for such security as might be provided by international means. The history of NATO has borne out this intention. In the years since the treaty was signed, an elaborate organization, consisting of the North Atlantic Council, an international secretariat, a network of working committees, and a substantial military force under a unified command, has been developed.[27] Though based on the principle of sovereign equality, NATO has been able to develop unusual authority and capacity for taking and implementing decisions on matters of peace and security. Many of its members would appear to attach greater importance to its work than to that of the United Nations. More particularly, they consider it to be necessary to their security in a world made insecure by political and technological revolutions. The strength of NATO comes of course from the support of its members, and this in turn can be explained by the fact that to a large extent these members are bound together by ties of common culture, common purposes and values, common interests and common fears.

When we turn to consider the other collective self-defense arrangements that have been concluded under Article 51 of the Charter, with the United States as principal member or promoter, we find that generally speaking they are less firmly rooted in the common interests and traditional attitudes of the parties than the Inter-American treaty and less developed institutionally and in terms of common policies and programs than NATO. The Mutual Defense Treaty between the United States and the Philippines was intended to give the latter some of the assurance of United States support against external attack, from whatever direction, which it had enjoyed as a dependency. The commitment of the parties, as stated in Article IV of the treaty, differs from the NATO formula in that it recognizes more explicitly the fact that each party must take its decisions in accordance with its constitutional procedures. The phrasing is as follows:

> *Each Party recognizes that an armed attack in the Pacific Area on either of the Parties would be dangerous to its own peace and safety and declares that it would act to meet the common danger in accordance with its constitutional processes.*

The Security Treaty between the United States, Australia, and New Zealand was intended to provide security for the latter two countries in particular against possible Japanese as well as Communist aggression. The treaties with Japan, the Republic of Korea, and the Republic of

---

[27] See Lord Ismay, *NATO: The First Five Years, 1949–1954* (Utrecht, 1955) and *Atlantic Alliance,* A Report by a Study Group of the Royal Institute of International Affairs (London, 1952).

China were intended to assure these countries of United States support in case of Communist attack, whether from the Soviet Union or the mainland of China, and thus prevent further expansion of Communism in the Far East.

The South East Asia Treaty was concluded on September 8, 1954, following the agreement reached at Geneva in July to end hostilities in Indochina. It was intended to be a sort of counterpart to NATO, providing for the countries of this region the advantages of mutual assistance in maintaining their independence and security which NATO provided for the nations of the North Atlantic region. It was clear from the beginning, however, that SEATO did not have the support from within the area that NATO received from the countries of the North Atlantic area, and, furthermore, that to make up for this deficiency it was necessary to rely even more heavily on the United States. A basic cause of this weakness was the refusal of many of the countries in the area to recognize that the Communist threat was a major danger to be reckoned with, and the insistence of many that the principal threat to their independence and security did in fact come from other directions.[28] Thus, India professed to be more fearful of attack by Pakistan than of Communist aggression, and Indonesia gave first priority to distrust of Western imperialism, principally Dutch.

Of the eight parties to the Treaty, only three—Pakistan, the Philippines, and Thailand—would normally be thought of as south east Asian countries. Two—Australia and New Zealand—have strategic interests in south east Asia but are themselves well outside the area. One—the United Kingdom—has possessions within the area, and one—France—did have possessions there until their final liquidation by the Geneva agreements of 1954. The major party—the United States—has no territory in the area but is firmly committed to the policy of containing Communist expansion because of the threat that this would carry to its own national interests. Under the terms of Article IV of the Treaty,

> *Each Party recognizes that aggression by means of armed attack in the treaty area against any of the Parties or against any State or territory which the Parties by unanimous agreement may hereafter designate, would endanger its own peace and safety, and agree that it will in that event act to meet the common danger in accordance with its constitutional processes.*

The treaty area is defined as "the general area of South-East Asia, including also the entire territories of the Asian parties, and the general

[28] See W. MacMahon Ball, "A Political Re-examination of SEATO," *International Organization*, XII (1958), pp. 17–25.

area of the South-West Pacific not including the Pacific area north of 21 degrees 30 minutes north latitude." [29] It is further provided that no action can be taken on the territory of a state designated by unanimous agreement under Article IV "except at the invitation or with the consent of the Government concerned." [30] In signing the treaty the United States registered the express understanding that its commitment under Article IV of the treaty applied "only to Communist aggression" but it affirmed its willingness "in the event of other aggression or armed attack" to consult with the other parties to the treaty. While the treaty provides for a Council to consider matters relating to the implementation of the treaty, neither machinery of cooperation nor common policies and programs have been developed in any way comparable to those of NATO. It remains an essentially artificial organization kept alive by United States support and adding little to the strength of the United States in the area.

The Baghdad Pact was the final outcome of efforts to construct a Middle East security organization which would protect the eastern flank of NATO. After efforts to center such a system on Egypt and the Suez Canal had failed, Turkey and Iraq were induced to conclude the Pact of Mutual Cooperation of February 24, 1955. The United Kingdom adhered on April 5, Pakistan on September 23, and Iran on November 3. Though the construction of this collective self-defense arrangement was undertaken principally on the initiative of the United States, that country has not thus far seen its way clear to adhere formally. It has, however, given economic, political, and military support. Under Article 1 of the Pact, the contracting parties undertake to "co-operate for their security and defense . . . consistent with Article 51 of the United Nations Charter." [31] Special agreements to give effect to the cooperation are envisaged. Provision is made for a "Permanent Council at Ministerial level" to function within the purposes of the Pact. Like SEATO, the Baghdad security arrangement is weakened by the fact that the countries of the area are divided on the need of the Pact and the nature of the danger that they face. Though initially it had more effective support from within the area than SEATO, its members were dependent upon outside assistance, especially from the United States. With the overthrow of the pro-Western government of Iraq in July, 1958, it entered a period of crisis.

This development of collective self-defense arrangements by the

[29] Article VIII.

[30] For the text of the treaty and analysis of its provisions and their implications, see Royal Institute of International Affairs, *Collective Defense in South East Asia* (London, 1956).

[31] United Kingdom, *Treaty Series,* No. 39 (1956).

non-Communist countries for meeting a possible Communist attack has been paralleled by comparable action on the part of the Communist countries. Initially, the treaties concluded by the Soviet Union and other Communist countries made use of the exception found in Article 53 by which the requirement of Security Council authorization for the use of armed force did not apply in case of measures taken against an enemy state or under "arrangements directed against renewal of aggressive policy on the part of any such state." [32] Thus, the treaty of March 18, 1948, between the Soviet Union and Bulgaria provided that, in the event of one party being drawn into military action "against a Germany trying to resume her aggressive policy, or with any other State which directly or in any other form would be united with Germany in a policy of aggression," the other party would "at once give military and other aid, in accordance with the means at her disposal." [33] In May, 1955, professedly in answer to the ratification of the Paris Agreements providing for the participation of a remilitarized Germany in the Western European Union, the Soviet Union and seven other East European States—Albania, Bulgaria, Czechoslovakia, the German Democratic Republic, Hungary, Poland, and Romania—concluded a twenty-year treaty of friendship, cooperation, and mutual assistance,[34] the provisions of which with respect to mutual military aid were based on Article 51 of the Charter. The treaty also provided for the creation of a "Joint Command" of all treaty forces, thus nominally, at least, following the NATO example.

Except for the Joint Defense and Economic Cooperation Treaty between the States of the Arab League of June 15, 1950 [35] all the agreements that have been entered into in the exercise of the inherent right of collective self-defense have been the product in part, at least, of the "cold war." While these agreements have been widely viewed as filling a gap in the United Nations system, it does not necessarily follow that they have strengthened the United Nations. To the extent

[32] See for example the treaties of friendship, mutual assistance, and cooperation between the U.S.S.R. and Czechoslovakia, the U.S.S.R. and Yugoslavia, the U.S.S.R. and Poland, the U.S.S.R. and Finland, etc., texts of which are reprinted in U.S. Dept. of State, *Documents and State Papers,* I, No. 4 (July 1948).

[33] See W. W. Kulski, "The Soviet System of Collective Security Compared with the Western System," *American Journal of International Law,* XLIV (1950), pp. 453–476. See also text of the Treaty of Friendship, Alliance and Mutual Assistance, concluded Feb. 10, 1950, between the U.S.S.R. and the People's Republic of China, in *ibid.,* Suppl., pp. 84–86.

[34] For text of treaty, see *ibid.,* XLIX (1955), Suppl., pp. 194–99.

[35] For text, see Arab Information Center, *Document Collection,* No. 1, pp. 21–25.

that they have created a greater sense of peace and security and have helped to establish an equilibrium in power relations which discourages any resort to armed force, they have perhaps strengthened the United Nations by creating conditions favorable to the achievement of its other purposes. To the extent that they instill fear and distrust and harden relations at the "cold war" level, they may in fact weaken the United Nations by creating conditions which make the performance of its tasks more difficult. In any case, it must be recognized that reliance upon these means of achieving national security demonstrates that Members of the United Nations at present are not prepared to rely very heavily on a system of collective security administered through the organs and procedures of the Charter.

DEVELOPMENT OF THE ROLE OF THE GENERAL ASSEMBLY

The second course that has been followed in an effort to fill the gap in the United Nations system of peace and security caused by the impotence of the Council has been to develop the General Assembly as a substitute for the Council and thus create a modified United Nations system which would be more effective under the conditions that have existed since the War than that spelled out in the Charter. As we have seen, this alternative has been based on a liberal interpretation of the Charter provisions relating to the functions and powers of the General Assembly. Some have argued that it is contrary to the Charter plan of collective security as originally envisaged, and to the intentions of those who had the major responsibility for the writing of the Charter. Others have taken the view that such a possible development was anticipated at San Francisco in case the major powers did not cooperate, and that Article 10 was adopted with this end in view.[36]

The Charter does not expressly give the General Assembly the responsibility for dealing with threats to the peace, breaches of the peace, and acts of aggression. It does provide that the General Assembly "may discuss any questions relating to the maintenance of international peace and security" properly brought before it, and may make recommendations with regard to such matters "to the state or states concerned or to the Security Council or to both." [37] It also authorizes the General Assembly to "discuss any questions or any matters within the scope of the present Charter or relating to the powers and functions

[36] See John Foster Dulles, *War or Peace* (New York: The Macmillan Company, 1950), pp. 37–38.
[37] Article 11, par. 2.

of any organs provided for in the present Charter" and to make recommendations as above.[38] These two grants of power to discuss and recommend are subject to the qualification, however, that the Assembly shall not make any recommendation on a dispute or situation with respect to which the Security Council is exercising its Charter functions.[39] However, even with this qualification, these two grants of powers are sufficiently broad to give support to the view that even though the Security Council has the primary responsibility for the maintenance of international peace and security, the Assembly has at least a "residual responsibility" of its own.

There is, however, another provision which, taken together with the specific grants of power to the Security Council, raises some doubt as to how far the General Assembly can go in the discharge of such a "residual responsibility." Article 11, paragraph 2, states that the General Assembly shall, "either before or after discussion," refer any question on which "action is necessary" to the Security Council. Now "action" has been understood to mean "enforcement action" under Chapter VII. If it is further understood to mean only the binding decisions which the Council can take under that Chapter, then of course the Council is the only organ that can take such measures, since the General Assembly can only recommend. This interpretation would not necessarily exclude recommendations by the General Assembly after the Security Council has failed to take action and has removed the matter from its agenda. If, on the other hand, "action" is interpreted to include all decisions regarding collective measures for dealing with threats to the peace, breaches of the peace, and acts of aggression, whether in the form of binding decisions or recommendations, it becomes a little more difficult to justify the possession of any competence by the General Assembly other than the right to discuss and make recommendations at the Council's request. However, the requirement that a matter must be referred to the Council for "action" can be interpreted as still permitting the Assembly to discuss and make recommendations with respect to the matter if, after such a reference has been made, the Council fails to take any decision on the matter.

The development of the General Assembly's role in actual practice began in the first year of the United Nations. After the Security Council had failed to agree on any course of action with respect to the Franco regime in Spain, the question was brought to the attention of the General Assembly which recommended the withdrawal of the heads of diplomatic missions and the exclusion of the Franco Government from mem-

[38] Article 10.   [39] Article 12, par. 1.

bership in the specialized agencies and from participation in conferences held under the auspices of the United Nations.[40] In 1947, Greece's complaint against her northern neighbors for giving aid to guerilla bands was brought to the General Assembly after the Security Council had become deadlocked and had removed the matter from its agenda. The Assembly first established a Special Committee on the Balkans to investigate, observe, and mediate, but when this Committee reported that aid given to the guerrillas threatened the political independence and integrity of Greece and endangered the peace, the Assembly recommended that Members refrain from action which might assist any armed group fighting against the Greek Government.[41] A year later, in 1949, the Assembly recommended that Members refrain from providing arms and other materials of war to Albania and Bulgaria until the Special Committee or another competent United Nations organ had determined that "the unlawful assistance of these States to the Greek guerrillas had ceased." [42]

The major step in the development of the Assembly's role in police action came with the adoption of the "Uniting for Peace" resolution on November 3, 1950. With the return of the Soviet representative to the Security Council on August 1 of that year, it became clear that the Council could no longer perform its functions of directing and coordinating the collective measures that were being taken to repel the North Korean armed attack and restore international peace and security in the area. The United States therefore proposed that the General Assembly assume the responsibility of dealing with such situations when the Security Council was prevented by the veto from acting. The United States proposal, with some minor changes, was adopted by the General Assembly by a large majority.[43] The Soviet Union and its satellites opposed it strongly. Under the terms of the resolution, the General Assembly asserted its competence, in case the Security Council because of the veto failed to discharge its responsibility for the maintenance of peace and security in any case of alleged threat to or breach of the peace, to consider the matter immediately with a view to making "appropriate recommendations to Members for collective measures, including in the case of a breach of the peace or act of aggression the use of armed force when necessary." Provision was made for an emergency

[40] General Assembly Resolution 39 (I), Dec. 12, 1946.

[41] General Assembly Resolution 193 (III), Nov. 27, 1948.

[42] General Assembly Resolution 288 (IV), Nov. 18, 1949. For a detailed discussion of United Nations handling of the Greek question, see the series of articles by Harry N. Howard, Department of State Publications 2986, 3785, 3906, and 4568.

[43] General Assembly Resolution 377 (V), Nov. 3, 1950.

special session within twenty-four hours of the failure of the Council to act. The resolution requested Members to survey their resources to determine the nature and scope of the assistance they might render and to maintain units in their national armed forces so trained, organized, and equipped as to be capable of being promptly made available to either the Security Council or the General Assembly. Furthermore, the resolution provided for a Collective Measures Committee to study and make reports on methods to be used to maintain and strengthen international peace and security.

The General Assembly acted under the terms of this resolution—except that it did not have to meet in emergency session, being in regular session—when it dealt with the Chinese Communist intervention in Korea in late 1950. By its resolution of February 1, 1951,[44] it declared Communist China guilty of aggression and later, on May 18,[45] it recommended the application of enumerated collective economic measures. It did not recommend the initiation of additional military measures, though in its February 1 resolution it had affirmed "the determination of the United Nations to continue its action in Korea to meet the aggression" and called upon "all States and authorities to continue to lend every assistance to the United Nations action in Korea."

Attempts to implement the provisions of the "Uniting for Peace" resolution regarding stand-by forces have not been successful. In response to inquiries from the Collective Measures Committee as to what forces they were prepared to maintain in a state of readiness for United Nations action, Members generally answered vaguely and evasively.[46] Even the United States, while referring to its commitment in Korea and under the North Atlantic Treaty, was unwilling to make any firm promise as to what it was prepared to do in the future.

The substantial increase in, and change in the character of, General Assembly membership as the result of the recent admission of twenty-two new Members has produced increasing doubt as to whether the organ will be any more effective than the Security Council in its new role. When the General Assembly was dealing with Chinese Communist intervention in Korea, most Asian and African Members displayed a special reluctance to take collective measures against China. Furthermore, these Members have generally shown a desire to be "neutral" in the "cold war" and not to participate in collective measures against one side or the other. Since the United States had envisaged the use of the

[44] General Assembly Resolution 498 (V), Feb. 1, 1951.
[45] General Assembly Resolution 500 (V), May 18, 1951.
[46] See General Assembly, *Official Records,* Sixth Session, Suppl. No. 13 (A/1891), "Report of the Collective Measures Committee" (1951).

General Assembly under the "Uniting for Peace" resolution primarily in a "cold war" situation, and since it recognized then that the effectiveness of Assembly action depended upon general support, it is obvious that the growing Asian-African bloc presents a serious difficulty for those who wish to make the Assembly an effective instrument of collective action against the Communists. Furthermore, the development of atomic weapons, especially hydrogen bombs of unbelievable destructiveness, has caused many Members outside Asia and Africa to have increasing doubts about the wisdom of collective enforcement measures where there is risk of a major war. The General Assembly is increasingly being viewed as an organ for debate and conciliation, not for collective enforcement action.

The Israeli, French, and British attacks on Egypt and Russian military intervention in Hungary in October–November 1956 brought a sudden revival of interest in the Assembly's potentialities as a peace-preserving agency. The two situations developed at about the same time and resulted in the calling of an emergency session of the General Assembly. They occupied much of the time and attention of the Eleventh General Assembly. But the results achieved gave further support to the view that, at best, the Assembly could be expected to have only limited effectiveness in restraining any aggressive action by a major power prepared to act in open and continuing disregard of Assembly appeals.

When the Soviet Union undertook to suppress the attempt of the Hungarian people to gain their independence, and thus safeguard Soviet strategic interest, the Assembly repeatedly condemned the action and demanded the withdrawal of Soviet forces.[47] Nevertheless there was no visible evidence that this had any effect on Soviet conduct. Soviet troops completed their task of restoring order and buttressing the puppet government. The Assembly made provision for aid to the refugees and appointed a special committee to take evidence and report on the facts of Soviet intervention.[48] But the Assembly was not prepared to go beyond publicizing the facts, aiding the refugees, refusing to seat representatives of the Russian-supported government, and making fruitless appeals to the Russians to withdraw their forces. Though the Committee characterized Soviet action as "a massive armed intervention by one Power in the territory of another," neither the Assembly nor its more influential and powerful members, the United States included, were

[47] For an account of action taken, see *Yearbook of the United Nations, 1956,* pp. 67–83.

[48] For a report of Committee, see General Assembly, *Official Records,* 11th session, Suppl. No. 18 (A/3592).

prepared to run the risk of a major world conflict by threatening or using armed force to prevent or restrain Soviet intervention.

In the Middle East, on the other hand, the Assembly was more successful. But its success in dealing with the Israeli invasion of Egypt and the intervention of British and French armed forces in 1956 was not due to the use of collective enforcement measures, but rather to the willingness of the states concerned, for many reasons, to yield to the Assembly's demand that hostilities cease and armed forces be withdrawn. A variety of considerations induced this withdrawal. In the case of Great Britain and France these included the reaction of public opinion in Great Britain and the Commonwealth, the opposition of the United States, the fear of Soviet intervention, and the fact that the Assembly facilitated their withdrawal by establishing a United Nations Emergency Force to do some of the things the British and French claimed to be doing themselves. In the case of Israel, the establishment of the Emergency Force, the expectation or hope that Israeli objectives could be achieved at least in part by this means, the dependence of Israel on aid from the United States, and pressure brought to bear by the United States were among the decisive factors causing Israeli compliance with the Assembly's demands. While the General Assembly did not enforce peace by the use of collective measures, it did play an important role in restoring peace by exercising strong moral and political pressure on the British, French, and Israeli Governments to withdraw their forces, and by providing in the United Nations Emergency Force the means whereby the cessation of hostilities and the withdrawal of forces could be supervised and guarantees could be afforded that some of the incidents leading up to hostilities would not be repeated.

Two years later, in August 1958, the General Assembly was again called upon to discharge its responsibilities under the "United for Peace" resolution in the Middle East. Lebanon had charged large-scale infiltration from Syria—now a part of the United Arab Republic—in support of an attempt to overthrow the pro-Western regime of President Chamoun. The Security Council had by its resolution of June 11 directed the dispatch of United Nations observers to Lebanon.[49] Following the military coup in Iraq on July 14 and at the request of President Chamoun, United States forces were dispatched to Lebanon to protect its independence and territorial integrity and two days later British forces were dispatched to Jordan at the request of King Hussein. The Security Council considered the situation but was prevented by the Soviet veto from adopting a resolution. The matter was brought before an emergency session of the General Assembly after efforts to arrange

[49] U.N. Doc. S/4023, June 11, 1958.

a "summit meeting" broke down. This time, unlike two years before, the United States and the Soviet Union were in opposite camps. The United States' contention that its action was necessary to meet the "indirect aggression" of the United Arab Republic was countered by the Soviet charge that the landing of armed forces constituted direct aggression and a threat to the peace. Neither side was able to mobilize sufficient support for the kind of resolution it wanted, and the Assembly finally adopted unanimously on August 22 proposal calling upon the Arab states to respect their obligations as members of the Arab League and authorizing the Secretary-General to make suitable arrangements by agreement with the interested parties to uphold the purposes and principles of the Charter and thereby facilitate the early withdrawal of foreign troops.[50] On September 29, the Secretary-General reported to the Assembly that he had worked out certain practical arrangements in consultation with the interested governments and that he had been informed by the governments of the United Kingdom and the United States that they intended to begin the complete withdrawal of their forces in the near future. Thus in this case as two years earlier the Assembly chose to achieve its ends by methods other than the use of collective measures.

A United Nations Force

The success of the United Nations in putting an end to hostilities in the Middle East and more particularly the role of the United Nations Emergency Force in accomplishing that result, revived interest in the possible creation of a permanent international police force which would be at the disposal of either the Council or the Assembly for purposes of keeping the peace. The idea of such a force is not new. Those who have advocated the idea in the past have been influenced by the analogy to the use of a police force in local communities to keep the peace, an analogy obviously far from complete. However, they have met with little success in getting their idea generally accepted and applied. At the time the League Covenant was being drafted, a French ministerial commission proposed a plan for an international force to be used to suppress aggression, but the idea was not acceptable to President Wilson and his advisors or to British leaders. In 1932, during the Geneva Disarmament Conference, the French proposed a plan for an international force to suppress aggression which would be part of a total scheme of

[50] General Assembly Resolution 1237 (ES-III), August 22, 1958. For report of the Secretary-General under this resolution, see U.N. Doc. A/3934/Rev. 1, Sept. 29, 1958.

disarmament, but the suggestion was coolly received. As we have seen, the Charter provided for the use of United Nations military forces on a national contingent basis to suppress breaches of the peace, but efforts to achieve agreement among the major powers on the principles governing the organization of this force were of no avail. In 1948, Secretary-General Lie proposed to the Assembly the creation of a United Nations Guard to assist United Nations missions in the field.[51] This force would consist of a nucleus of some 300 men individually recruited, and located and trained at headquarters, plus a volunteer reserve of some 500 men available on call. This proposal was more than the majority of the Assembly were prepared to accept, and, in the form finally approved in 1949,[52] provided for a United Nations Field Service of 300 men seconded by Member governments to provide certain technical services to field missions, plus a Field Service Panel of qualified persons who might be called to service by decision of the General Assembly or the Security Council. This hardly constituted a police force in the generally accepted sense of the term.

The United Nations force that went to the assistance of the Republic of Korea following the North Korean attack of June 25, 1950, was in the beginning exclusively a United States force and never comprised more than a relatively small number of men from other Members.[53] While it was constituted and functioned under Security Council resolutions, it was under United States command, was largely financed by the United States, and the United Nations exercised very limited control over its actual operations.[54] Furthermore, the national military contingents and other assistance were sent specifically to Korea for the purposes of repelling the North Korean armed attack and restoring international peace and security in that area. They were not available for comparable purposes in other areas, except by decision of the national governments concerned.

When the need of an international force to supervise the cease-fire

---

[51] U.N. Doc. A/565, *Annual Report of the Secretary-General on the Work of the Organization, 1 July 1947–30 June 1948*, pp. xvii–xviii.

[52] General Assembly Resolution 297 (IV), Nov. 22, 1949. See also, General Assembly, *Official Records, Fourth Session*, Suppl. No. 13, "Report of the Special Committee on a United Nations Guard," (Oct. 10, 1949).

[53] Numerically, the United States contributed 50.32 per cent of the ground forces, 85.89 per cent of the naval forces, and 93.38 per cent of the air force. For fuller details, see *United States Participation in the United Nations. Report of by the President to the Congress for the year 1951*, Dept. of State, Publ. 4583. (Washington: Government Printing Office, 1952), p. 288.

[54] See Leland M. Goodrich, *Korea; A Study of U.S. Policy in the United Nations* (New York: Council on Foreign Relations, 1956).

and withdrawal of forces in the Middle East was recognized in 1956, the Secretary-General was requested to prepare a plan.[55] He proposed a force that would be under United Nations command and direction, that would be composed of national contingents contributed by states that were not permanent members of the Security Council, and that would have the limited functions of checking and supervising the withdrawal of forces and of maintaining order in the areas separating the opposing forces. The force was not to be used to enforce withdrawal or for that matter to enforce any conduct by any Member against its will. The international character of the force was further emphasized by the provisions recommended by the Secretary-General and approved by the Assembly for its financing. Costs incident to the performance of the United Nations mission were in large part to be borne directly by the United Nations and apportioned among Members on the same basis as other United Nations expenses. But while the international character of the force was emphasized, its temporary character was also fully recognized. This was a force created to perform a particular function on recommendation of the Assembly and by agreement of the states directly concerned. Once this mission was performed, unless an additional mission were conferred upon it in the same way, the force would be disbanded.[56]

It was the temporary nature of the force, combined with the notable success of its operation, which prompted many to urge that the possibility of establishing such a force on a permanent basis be explored. There are, however, serious difficulties in the way of the establishment of a permanent international force that do not exist, or at least are not as serious, when it is a matter of creating a force for a special situation. First, there is the question of the functions to be performed. Is it to be limited to functions like those performed by UNEF, functions that in effect presuppose the consent of the interested parties, or is it to be a force which will be used to suppress threats to the peace and breaches of the peace by whomsoever committed? The creation of a force which would be powerful enough to deal with a situation of that kind is difficult to imagine at the present time. Then there is the question of the composition of such a force, whether it is to be composed of national contingents, thus making it clearly more dependent on national governments,

[55] See U.N. Doc. A/3302, Nov. 16, 1956.

[56] On UNEF, see Leland M. Goodrich and Gabriella E. Rosner, "The United Nations Emergency Force," *International Organization,* XI (1957), pp. 413–30; and *United Nations Emergency Force,* Report of the Secretary-General (A/3694, Oct. 9, 1957).

or whether it is to consist of individually recruited personnel pledged to serve the United Nations exclusively. Of course, the size of such a force would to a considerable extent be determined by the functions it is supposed to perform. But even if we presuppose a force of modest size—five to ten thousand men—there is the question of where it is going to be stationed. Then one has to consider questions of command arrangements, political direction, and the legal status of the force. And finally, how is the cost of the force to be financed? Any substantial addition to the assessment of Members to cover United Nations costs is likely to encounter strong opposition, as was evidenced by the reluctance of many Members to see the first ten million dollars of UNEF's cost covered in this way. The success of UNEF as a temporary operation combined with the serious problems that have to be resolved in establishing a permanent force suggest that the most that can be hoped for as a first step in that direction would be the establishment of a permanent command and headquarters with the bulk of the force contributed by Member governments when needed.[57]

It is quite clear that if a permanent international force is to be created in the near future it will be for a much more modest purpose than that for which the use of collective military measures was envisaged by the authors of the Charter. It will not in all likelihood be used for the purpose of deterring or suppressing a breach of the peace or act of aggression but rather as an aid to the responsible organs of the United Nations in their work of pacification. Instead of being used against the will of a state disturbing the peace for the purpose of restoring peace, it is more likely to be used on the basis of the consent of all interested parties to facilitate the termination of hostilities and the withdrawal of forces to which the states resorting to the use of armed force have, for different reasons, been willing to agree. Or perhaps, what is even more likely, the force will be used, again with the consent of the parties, to patrol a sensitive frontier in order to prevent incidents which may give rise to hostilities, or to police an area in which a plebiscite is to be held. In any case, in the words of Lester Pearson, the force will represent "an intermediate technique between merely passing reso-

[57] For a detailed study of problems and implications of a permanent international force, see William R. Frye, *A United Nations Peace Force* (New York: Oceana Publications, Inc. 1957). In his report on UNEF to the Thirteenth General Assembly, the Secretary-General concluded that agreement on general principles governing the establishment and operation of a United Nations force when needed was the maximum to be sought at this time. *United States Emergency Force. Summary Study of the Experience Derived from the Establishment and Operation of the Force.* U.N. Doc. A/3943, Oct. 9, 1958.

lutions and actual fighting," [58] and not a means of compelling disturbers of the peace to refrain from their unsocial action.

The U.N. as Keeper of the Peace: An Assessment

The role of the United Nations in keeping the peace is much less important today—and is likely to be so for some time—than it was initially intended to be. The principal reason for this has been the "cold war." As the result of the rapid deterioration in relations between the Soviet Union and the Western Powers after San Francisco, an agreed basis for peace by the conclusion of peace treaties with the defeated enemy powers was not achieved, and the major powers themselves were not willing to cooperate in maintaining the peace in the spirit which the Charter had envisaged. As a result, serious threats to international peace and security developed which the United Nations, already weakened by the failure of the permanent members of the Security Council to agree, was quite incapable of handling effectively. The result was that Members fell back on their reserved rights under Article 51 and 53 to conclude collective self-defense agreements, which did not differ in their basic features from the old treaties of alliance. It is on these arrangements, highly institutionalized in the case of NATO, that Members rely primarily for outside assistance in meeting any armed attack or threat thereof. Even when, as in the case of aggression against the Republic of Korea, collective military action is taken within the framework of the United Nations, these collective self-defense arrangements are likely to provide the hard core of joint military action.

In the light of experience to date and the probable course of future developments, the role of the United Nations in dealing with threats or acts of violence incidental to the "cold war" is likely to be limited to the exercise of psychological and political pressure, and to mediatory and restraining action. The Greek and Hungarian experiences were illustrative of the kind of political and psychological pressure that the United Nations can exercise, and the role it can play as a means of developing common attitudes and policies toward a particular threat to or disturbance of the peace. With respect to Korea, and more particularly the Chinese Communist intervention, the United Nations played an additional role of significance in that it supported the United States Administration in the face of strong counter pressures, in its desire to

[58] Lester B. Pearson, "Force for U.N.," *Foreign Affairs*, XXXIII, No. 3 (April 1957), p. 401.

keep a limited police action from spreading into a general war. Looking to the future, while we can expect Members to rely primarily on their own military forces and the military assistance available to them under collective self-defense arrangements in meeting any military threat or attack resulting from the "cold war," there are important functions which the United Nations can nevertheless perform—in developing and expressing commonly held views, in formulating common policies and courses of action, in supporting measures initially taken by parties to collective self-defense arrangements in meeting overt military attack, and in exercising a mediatory and restraining influence to prevent limited wars from developing into general wars.

But the "cold war" is not the only context within which the use or threat of force has occurred or is likely to occur in the future. Strong nationalist movements, in Asia and Africa in particular, and the desires of newly established states or nations aspiring to statehood to free themselves of colonial fetters have also produced situations of armed conflict. In dealing with such situations, the United Nations has demonstrated that it has an important role to play. To the extent that the permanent members of the Council have a common interest in preventing or terminating hostilities, the Security Council can be an effective instrument of United Nations action. If, however, Council action is prevented by the veto it becomes necessary to make use of the General Assembly. Furthermore, it may appear to the Asian and African Members, the likely initiators of U.N. action in cases of this kind, that the Assembly is the more promising forum because of the greater opportunities it offers for mobilizing opinion and achieving wide support on the part of governments for desired positions. Furthermore, the General Assembly has shown by its successful handling of the Middle East crisis that it can devise effective means for dealing with situations of great danger to the peace of the world.

But while the United Nations has made useful contributions to the keeping of a rather uneasy peace since the war, it is foolish to deny that its role must be a limited one so long as the "cold war" continues. Until the United States and the Soviet Union find the way to live together on terms of trust and cooperation, with the United Nations as a major instrument of that cooperation, peace and security are likely to be conditional more on what those two countries and their allies do than upon the debates and resolutions of the United Nations. This is not to deny that the United Nations will continue to have a role—and one of importance—in keeping the peace even between these two Goliaths, but its capacity to influence the situation is bound to seem somewhat inadequate in comparison with the power of these two Members to determine by their political actions whether the outcome shall be peace or war.

SUGGESTED READINGS

Atlantic Alliance: NATO's Role in the Free World. Report by a Study Group of the Royal Institute of International Affairs. London, 1952.

Claude, Inis, Jr. *Swords into Plowshares.* New York: Random House, Inc., 1956. Chap. 12.

Collective Defense in South East Asia. Report by a Study Group of the Royal Institute of International Affairs. London, 1956.

Frye, William R. *A United Nations Peace Force.* New York: Oceana Publications for Carnegie Endowment for International Peace, 1957.

Goodrich, Leland M., and Simons, Anne P. *The United Nations and the Maintenance of International Peace and Security.* Washington: The Brookings Institution, 1955. Part IV.

Goodrich, Leland M., and Rosner, Gabriella E. "The United Nations Emergency Force," *International Organization,* XI (1957), pp. 413–30.

Goodrich, Leland M. "Korea; Collective Measures Against Aggression," *International Conciliation,* No. 494 (October 1953), pp. 129–92.

Haas, Ernest B. "Types of Collective Security: An Examination of Operational Concepts," *American Political Science Review,* XLIX (1955), pp. 40–62.

Johnson, Howard C., and Niemeyer, Gerhart. "Collective Security: the Validity of an Ideal," *International Organization,* VIII (1954), pp. 19–35.

Kulski, W. W. "The Soviet System of Collective Security Compared with the Western System," *American Journal of International Law,* XLIX (1950), pp. 453–76.

Kirk, Grayson. "The Enforcement of Security," *Yale Law Review,* LV (1946), pp. 1081–96.

Ismay, Lord. *NATO: The First Five Years, 1949–1954.* Utrecht, 1955.

Martin, Andrew. *Collective Security, A Progress Report.* Paris: UNESCO, 1952.

Royal Institute of International Affairs. *International Sanctions.* London, 1938.

Thompson, Kenneth W. "Collective Security Reexamined," *American Political Science Review,* XLVII (1953), pp. 753–72.

U. S. Senate Committee on Foreign Relations, Subcommittee on the United Nations Charter. *Enforcement Action under the United*

Nations. Staff Study No. 7. Washington: Government Printing Office, 1955.

Wolfers, Arnold. "Collective Security and the War in Korea," *The Yale Review,* XLIII (1954), pp. 481–496.

Chapter IX

PEACEFUL SETTLEMENT AND ADJUSTMENT

FOR THE LAST century and a half, at least, efforts to achieve international peace have emphasized the need of acceptable methods for the peaceful settlement of disputes between nations. During the nineteenth century the emphasis was on arbitration. Then following the two Hague Conferences, judicial settlement was the favorite prescription of peace advocates. The League of Nations marked a substantial advance in the development and application of procedures of peaceful settlement and the United Nations is a continuation of the League approach.

As we have seen, the Charter stresses peaceful settlement as the complement to keeping the peace by collective measures. If peace is to be maintained, then disputes and differences must not lead to the use of force; they must be handled by peaceful procedures. But though governments have been willing to agree to this general proposition, they have in many instances shown a distinct reluctance to settle differences that arise between them by peaceful means. In this field the record of the United Nations has been disappointing.

The Problem of Peaceful Settlement

What is most discouraging to those who seek the substitution of methods of non-violence for methods of violence in the settlement of international differences is the lack of any positive correlation between the number of commitments that states enter into for the peaceful settlement of disputes and the actual use of the peaceful procedures for which provision is made. During the decade following the First

190

World War governments concluded an impressive number of bipartite and multipartite treaties for the peaceful settlement of international disputes,[1] but very little use was actually made of these agreements. Perhaps they had a useful psychological effect, but anyone taking them seriously as introducing a new era in international relations could only have been disappointed by the results.

Much of the thinking on the subject of peaceful settlement, especially by those whose approach is primarily legal, has been based on the assumption that international differences will respond to the same prescriptions that have proved effective for handling differences between individuals in a modern state. Such an approach fails to take adequately into account the weakness and embryonic development of international law and organization at the present time and the limited possibilities of development so long as prevalent national attitudes and value systems remain what they are.

If a dispute or situation involving a conflict of interests arises between two persons or groups of persons within a state, there are peaceful methods which are generally accepted and used for achieving a settlement or accommodation. If the dispute relates to legal rights and is not settled by direct talks between the parties or their representatives, either party can apply to the appropriate court for remedy, the other party must accept the court's jurisdiction, and the decision of the court is binding and can be enforced by appropriate means. If the dispute or situation arises from claims of a non-legal character, there are still recognized and reasonably effective means of achieving the necessary adjustment. One means is that of negotiation, as when a trade union and an employer negotiate a new labor contract defining future conditions of work. If the claim takes the form of a demand that the existing general law be changed, and is sufficiently important to call for legislative action, the adjustment or accommodation may take the form of a statute, which likewise is binding and can be enforced by appropriate means. In any case, whether the complaint is legal or political in nature, effective judicial, administrative and legislative methods are available for dealing with it. The state's authority and means of taking remedial action are usually adequate to preserve order and at the same time administer legal justice or introduce such changes in legal relations as may be necessary to keep the discontented from becoming so desperate as to challenge the existing order by force.

In international relations, the situation is quite different since we are dealing here with political units which themselves represent claims

[1] See Max Habicht, *Post-War Treaties for the Pacific Settlement of International Disputes* (Cambridge: Harvard University Press, 1931).

to supreme authority and since international agencies have not yet been developed which are capable of imposing their wills on member states. If disputes occur between states, they may, as in the case of disputes within the state, result from conflicting claims of legal right or from claims of a non-legal or political nature. Disputes of the first kind are usually called "legal disputes." [2] There has been general agreement in the past that these can most appropriately be submitted to arbitration or to courts for their final settlement.[3] Nevertheless, for such a dispute to be thus submitted it is necessary that the parties specifically agree to its submission by a written agreement concluded for the purpose, or to agree in advance that all disputes falling within certain defined categories shall be thus submitted. Even in this latter case, unless there is a permanent tribunal to which appeal can be made, a special agreement is necessary to establish the tribunal. Since submission to arbitration or judicial settlement requires the agreement of the parties, many disputes that can in principle be appropriately settled in that manner are not so dealt with, because one or more of the parties believes that its national interest will not be best served in this way. The stronger party may feel that it will gain more by negotiation than by a more objective procedure since negotiation will permit it to make use of its superior power. One party may find that domestic pressures prevent it from taking any step which appears to lessen its chances of winning its case. The party which is in possession of the territory or other object in controversy may prefer to sit tight. In any case, the "international community" does not have institutions or procedures at its disposal which enable it to enforce legal justice on the parties.

In the case of disputes or situations where one or more of the interested parties is advancing claims of a political nature, that is, is demanding something that the existing law does not give it and which involves some change of the existing legal order, the weakness of the "international community" is even more apparent. It is true, of course, that every international dispute can be "settled," in the sense that a decision can be given, on the basis of law.[4] Nevertheless, in these so-called "political disputes" or in those situations where demands are made that require for their satisfaction some change in the existing legal order, to say that international law can provide the terms of settlement

    [2] See Lincoln Bloomfield, "Law, Politics and International Disputes," *International Conciliation,* No. 516 (January 1958), pp. 260–77.
    [3] See, for example, Articles 38 of the 1907 Hague Convention for the Pacific Settlement of International Disputes, Article 13, paragraph 2 of the League Covenant, and Article 36 of the Statute of the International Court of Justice.
    [4] See Hans Kelsen, *Peace through Law* (Chapel Hill: University of North Carolina Press, 1944), p. 29.

or adjustment is stating a theoretical proposition that may be valid but does not help very much in providing a practical solution.

In the past, several methods of peaceful settlement have been proposed and utilized, particularly for dealing with these very difficult political disputes and situations. Of course negotiation between the parties is always the first recourse. Such negotiations may be carried on at various levels, through normal diplomatic channels, by foreign ministers or by heads of state. Good offices and mediation by a third party have long been recognized as appropriate procedures, and certainly since the beginning of this century, the offer of good offices or mediation has been recognized to be a friendly and proper action.[5] Since the Bryan treaties of 1913, conciliation has been increasingly recognized in principle as a method particularly appropriate for the settlement of political differences, though very little use has in fact been made of the various conciliation commissions which have since been established by treaty.[6] Under the Covenant, the members of the League recognized that the Council and Assembly could appropriately act as organs of mediation and conciliation; these organs, particularly the Council, were quite active in the interwar period in dealing with international disputes, chiefly those of a political nature. But neither Council nor Assembly had the authority to impose their views. In fact, we have not as yet succeeded in developing international organs with the authority to impose terms of adjustment, comparable to that vested in our domestic administrative and legislative organs.

Not only have political disputes and situations of conflict been most difficult to settle but they have also been the most dangerous ones in terms of their possible consequences. They generally involve conflicts of purpose and interest that are considered vital to the security and well-being of the parties concerned. They are the ones that can well lead to armed conflict if not peacefully settled or at least if some provisional accommodation of views—some temporary adjustment—is not reached. Very often the political dispute or situation of conflict is more fundamental than the actual controversy that initially commands attention. Thus the Wal Wal incident of 1934 between Italy and Ethiopia which resulted from conflicting territorial claims could easily have been settled by arbitration if it had not been for the fact that back of the Italian demands for reparation and recognition of legal territorial rights

[5] Technically good offices consists of the offer by a third party of its services in bringing the parties to a dispute together for negotiations, while the mediator goes one step further and makes substantive proposals which the parties may or may not accept.

[6] Conciliation involves inquiry plus mediation by agreement of the parties, usually with publication of the results of the effort.

was a desire to humiliate Ethiopia and bring parts of the country at least under effective Italian control for purposes of exploitation.

The combination of the difficulty of getting the parties to a political dispute or situation of conflict to agree to the terms of settlement and the danger of leaving such a matter unsettled has led in some instances to the assertion by the major powers of the right to formulate appropriate terms of settlement and to enforce them if necessary, in furtherance of their common interest in the maintenance of international peace and security. Thus, during the century between the Napoleonic Wars and the First World War the European Concert on occasion acted in this way, as when the major European powers intervened in the 1820's to give Greece its independence and put an end to the fighting. The major victors in the First World War laid down the terms of the new order in the peace treaties which they imposed on the defeated powers, incidentally settling a number of political controversies involving states other than the defeated enemy states. During the interwar period, the Conference of Ambassadors and the League Council dealt with varying degrees of success with a number of more or less serious political disputes and situations of conflict. In the drafting of the Charter, as we shall see, an attempt was made to establish an authority which would be able to deal with serious disputes and situations in such a way as to maintain international peace and security.

The Basic Assumptions of the Charter System

The authors of the Charter recognized the need of an effective system of peaceful settlement, but did not find in experience many sure guides to how such a system could be created. The institutions and procedures that had been developed in the course of the nineteenth century had many successes to their credit, but, nevertheless, they had been incapable of dealing effectively with the complex of conflicts and tensions which had produced the First World War. The League had been created hopefully, but from the beginning had been incapable of achieving the satisfactory settlement or adjustment of various disputes and situations, some of which led directly to the Second World War. It could not, for example, find and enforce a satisfactory settlement of the Polish-Lithuanian dispute over Vilna. The League was not even asked to consider Germany's demands on Czechoslovakia, and its efforts to improve German-Polish relations were limited to the interpretation and enforcement of treaty provisions which Germany basically challenged. In dealing with the Italian-Ethiopian dispute, the League

temporized and then its leading members acted half-heartedly in applying sanctions when Mussolini moved to satisfy his real ambitions by
force.[7] While the League Council and Assembly and the Permanent
Court of International Justice did deal successfully with a number of
disputes and situations that arose in the inter-War period, there was
little question that League organs and procedures failed, perhaps even
more than their nineteenth century counterparts, in dealing with those
disputes and situations most likely to lead to war. While the Permanent
Court gave thirty-two judgments in cases submitted to it, none of these
involved serious threats to the peace. In a sense these did not add up
to much of an achievement for peaceful settlement since the alternative
never was resort to war.

While the authors of the Charter did not have from the experience
of the past any sure guides to the construction of an effective peace
system, they nevertheless did find in this experience certain indications
of the necessary conditions of such a system and what were its essential
elements. Given the success of the Permanent Court in dealing with
legal disputes that were submitted to it, there was general agreement
that the new organization should have a Court as one of its principal
organs. Whether this should be a new Court similar to the old, or the
old Court somewhat made over was a matter of detail. It was also agreed
without difficulty that the organs and procedures of the new organization
should supplement and not take the place of the conventional and tested
methods of peaceful settlement such as negotiation and mediation
which had been in use for some time. If the new organization was to be
more successful than its predecessor, it was believed that something
must be done to strengthen its authority and thus increase the chances
that the recommendations and findings of its political organs would be
accepted and carried out by the parties. While it was unlikely that the
parties to political disputes would be willing to agree in advance to be
bound by the decisions of any international organ, it was thought possible so to strengthen the political authority and prestige of the mediatory
organ as to increase substantially the prospect that its proposals would
be accepted and carried out. In this connection, the experience of the
European Concert seemed relevant.

A major step in this direction was to give the Security Council the
power to order any collective measures necessary to the prevention or

[7] For details on various League efforts in connection with important political
disputes, see James T. Shotwell and Marina Salvin, *Lessons on Security and
Disarmament* (New York: King's Crown Press, 1949) and Frank P. Walters, *A
History of the League of Nations,* 2 vols. (New York: Oxford University Press,
1952).

suppression of any unlawful disturbance of the peace. Armed with this power, it was thought that the Security Council would be in a strong position to persuade parties to any dispute or threatening situation to accept its proposals for settlement or adjustment, even though these were strictly speaking only recommendations.

Furthermore, in order to strengthen the authority of the Council and, at the same time, make this increased authority acceptable to the major powers whose participation in the Organization was considered essential to its success, it was thought necessary to make these major powers permanent members of the Council and to require their concurrence for all decisions relating to peaceful settlement and enforcement action. Thus, the effectiveness of the Council was made conditional on the willingness of the major powers to work together.

At the time the Charter was written, it was not by any means certain that this cooperation would be forthcoming. Nevertheless, it was considered necessary for an effective system of peaceful settlement and adjustment. It was assumed that the major victors in the war then approaching its end would have an interest in cooperating to keep the peace after the destruction and suffering of the war. Furthermore, it was assumed that this interest would be the stronger because of the belief that having cooperated to win the war they would then cooperate to write the terms of the peace settlements and would consequently have a direct interest in preserving these against change by force. This common interest in keeping the peace being assumed, it was believed that the requirement of unanimity of the permanent members for non-procedural decisions of the Council would in fact contribute to agreement by making it clear to them that they would have to compromise and adjust their own differences in order to establish the common front which was necessary to keeping the peace. In retrospect it is clear that the authors of the Charter grossly exaggerated the dependence of the major powers on collaboration and underestimated their willingness to fall back on competitive policies if they were unable to get collaboration on their own terms.

But while the chief architects of the Charter placed the major emphasis on the concert of powers idea as an effective way of supplementing and strengthening the more conventional methods of peaceful settlement and adjustment, thought was also given to the role of a more general consensus representing the great majority of Members regardless of differences of military strength. As the result of the combined pressures of the smaller states and leaders of influential groups within some of the major powers,[8] steps were taken at San Francisco to strengthen considerably the role of the General Assembly, particularly

[8] For example, the leaders of the Republican Party in the United States.

in dealing with situations which, if allowed to develop, would impair friendly relations and in time endanger international peace and security. While there was no thought of making the General Assembly a world legislature, it was conceived as a world town-meeting which would through discussion and the adoption of resolutions recording wide areas of agreement, stimulate and promote desirable adjustments of conflicting national policies and attitudes.

The Elements of the System

The Charter system of peaceful settlement and adjustment consists of duties placed upon Members and of organs and procedures which are intended to aid Members in performing their duties and serving the general purposes of the Organization.

The Charter states that the first purpose of the United Nations is to maintain international peace and security, and to that end "to bring about by peaceful means, and in conformity with the principles of justice and international law, adjustment or settlement of international disputes or situations which might lead to a breach of the peace." [9] This must be regarded as a basic element of the Charter system, since it describes the common purpose of Members as well as of the principal organs.

The Charter places upon Members certain duties. They "shall settle their international disputes by peaceful means in such a manner that international peace and security, and justice, are not endangered." [10] More specifically

> *The parties to any dispute, the continuance of which is likely to endanger the maintenance of international peace and security, shall, first of all, seek a solution by negotiation, enquiry, mediation, conciliation, arbitration, judicial settlement, resort to regional agencies or arrangements, or other peaceful means of their own choice.* [11]

If they fail to settle it by these means, "they shall refer it to the Security Council." [12] If a dispute is submitted to the International Court of Justice, whether by specific agreement or in accordance with previous acceptance of the Court's compulsory jurisdiction, Member states that are parties undertake to comply with the decision of the Court. [13]

To facilitate the performance by Members of their duties under

[9] Article 1, par. 1.
[10] Article 2, par. 3.
[11] Article 33, par. 1.
[12] Article 37, par. 1,
[13] Article 94, par. 1,

the Charter and to further the general purpose of the Organization to achieve peaceful settlement or adjustment, the Security Council, the General Assembly, the Secretary-General, and the International Court of Justice are given certain responsibilities and powers.

The Security Council has the primary responsibility for the maintenance of peace and security.[14] It may investigate any dispute or situation brought to its attention to determine whether its continuance "is likely to endanger the maintenance of international peace and security," [15] and if it decides affirmatively, it may call upon the parties to settle the dispute by means of their own choice in accordance with their duty under Article 33, recommend appropriate procedures or methods of settlement or adjustment, or, if the parties have submitted the dispute after failing to settle it by means of their own choice, recommend terms of settlement.[16] The Council does not have the power under the Charter to take decisions with respect to the methods or terms of settlement which are legally binding upon the parties. This power is given only to the International Court of Justice.

Subject to the primary responsibility of the Security Council, the General Assembly may consider and make recommendations with respect to any dispute or situation brought to its attention. Though the clear assumption of the Charter is that disputes and situations of a serious nature will first be brought to the attention of the Security Council, the only specific limitations on the power of the General Assembly that do not apply to the Council are that the Assembly "shall" refer to the Security Council, either before or after discussion, any question on which action is necessary, and that while the Council is performing its functions with respect to a particular matter, the Assembly may not make a recommendation except at the Council's request.[17] The fact that the Assembly can take a decision by a two-thirds vote without any requirement of great-power concurrence means that the Assembly is more likely than the Council to take some decision regarding a dispute or situation that is properly before it. Both Assembly and Council, if they so desire, can ask the Court to give an advisory opinion on any legal question that may arise in connection with the consideration of a particular dispute or situation.

The Secretary-General is given the power by the Charter to bring to the attention of the Security Council any matter which in his opinion threatens the maintenance of international peace and security.[18] He has the same power with respect to the General Assembly under the Rules

---

[14] Article 24.
[15] Article 34.
[16] Article 33, 36, and 37.
[17] Article 11, par. 2 and Article 12, par. 1.
[18] Article 99.

of Procedure of that organ.[19] Any additional authority that he may have in dealing with disputes or situations flows by inference from his position as chief administrative officer of the Organization, or is given him by the agreement of the interested parties or decision of the Council or Assembly.

The International Court of Justice is the "principal judicial organ" of the United Nations [20] and by the express provision and clear intent of the Charter is the organ which is considered particularly appropriate for the settlement of legal disputes. Its jurisdiction comprises "all cases which the parties refer to it and all matters specially provided for in the Charter of the United Nations or in treaties and conventions in force." [21] If jurisdiction has been accepted in advance by the parties by formal declaration, and subject to the conditions of acceptance,[22] it has compulsory jurisdiction, without the requirement of a special agreement, over all legal disputes concerning:

(*a*) *the interpretation of a treaty;*
(*b*) *any question of international law;*
(*c*) *the existence of any fact which, if established, would constitute a breach of an international obligation;*
(*d*) *the nature or extent of the reparation to be made for the breach of an international obligation*

The Court also has compulsory jurisdiction under a number of international agreements other than the Charter. As has already been stated, it may also give advisory opinions, at the request of the General Assembly or the Security Council, on legal questions which are aspects of actual disputes or situations being considered by these organs. The decisions of the Court in cases submitted to it by the parties are binding. The opinions, of course, are advisory only, though they have great weight with the bodies which solicit them.

It is important to keep in mind that the United Nations system of peaceful settlement and adjustment is basically one that leaves a great

[19] Rule 13 of "Rules of Procedure of the General Assembly," U.N. Doc. A/3660, Sept. 6, 1957.
[20] Article 92.   [21] Article 36 of the Statute.
[22] Article 36 of the Statute. As of July 15, 1958, 36 states had accepted the compulsory jurisdiction of the Court by declarations under Article 36. Some of these declarations contained conditions of a highly restrictive nature as, for example, the declaration of the United States of August 14, 1946, which excluded from the Court's jurisdiction "disputes with regard to matters which are essentially within the jurisdiction of the United States of America as determined by the United States of America." See International Court of Justice, *Yearbook, 1957–1958,* pp. 38, 192–213.

deal of freedom of choice to the individual Members, and particularly the major powers. There is only one basic limitation placed upon Members—that they must use peaceful means to settle their international disputes and that they must refrain from the use of force in seeking to adjust their differences. They recognize that the United Nations—with its various organs and prescribed procedures—has as one of its principal purposes the peaceful settlement or adjustment of international disputes or situations. Nevertheless, they are left relatively free, in fact they are encouraged, to achieve this result "by means of their own choice," and recourse to the United Nations organs, far from being made mandatory, is definitely viewed as a last resort. Furthermore, the United Nations system was based on the assumption that the members of the wartime coalition, and above all the principal victors in the last War, would be able to agree among themselves on the terms of the peace settlements, thus providing the United Nations with a broad base of agreement among the major powers as a point of departure in the performance of its functions. We have seen how false this assumption proved to be.

The Submission of Disputes and Situations to the United Nations [23]

Both Members and non-Members may bring disputes and situations likely to lead to international friction or give rise to a dispute to the attention of the General Assembly or the Security Council. Except for the power which the Secretary-General has to bring matters to the attention of these organs, the power to initiate the consideration of disputes or situations is limited to states. Only states can bring disputes to the Court.

However, there is no obligation to submit any particular dispute or situation to any particular organ of the United Nations. Why, then, do states, especially Members, make the choices they do? Why do they bring some matters to the attention of the United Nations, while others which are equally resistant to solution by the parties by means of their own choice, remain unsettled and unsubmitted? Why do they submit some to the Security Council, some to the General Assembly, and others to the Court? It is clear that the decision to submit is a political decision, and that any state or group of states which decides to bring a matter before a United Nations organ does so because it hopes to gain some advantage for itself.

[23] For more detailed discussion, see Goodrich and Simons, *op. cit.*, Ch. 4,

The specific reasons for bringing particular disputes or situations to the attention of the United Nations and of particular organs are manifold. Rather than attempting to list these reasons, some examples from past experience will be given. It is quite clear that in each case submitted to the United Nations the initiating state has been guided primarily by a view of national interest. When, for example, the Iranian Government asked the Security Council to consider the alleged intervention of Soviet armed forces in the internal affairs of Iran in early 1946, it hoped to gain support for its position in current negotiations with Moscow over oil concessions in Iran's northern provinces. In other words the United Nations was asked by a small power to support it in dealing with a larger one. Also, quite clearly, the Russian and Ukrainian Governments asked the Council to consider the alleged interference of the United Kingdom in the internal affairs of Greece and Indonesia by the presence of British armed forces in these countries in retaliation for what was considered to be British prompting of the Iranian Government.

In December, 1946, the Greek Government was obviously motivated by a desire for outside assistance when it asked the Council to consider the support being given by its northern neighbors to guerrilla bands operating in its territory. Later in 1947, after the Security Council had been prevented by a Soviet veto from adopting proposals, introduced by Australia and the United States, based on the report of the Council's Committee of Investigation on the situation in Greece, the United States took the initiative in asking the General Assembly to consider the matter. The United States Government was at the time giving extensive military and economic support to Greece. Though United Nations action was clearly not essential to the success of the United States program of restraining Communism, the Administration in Washington nevertheless felt that its position in seeking to contain the expansion of Communist influence into Greece would be much stronger and less open to criticism as being self-seeking and imperialistic if it acted within a United Nations framework and in accordance with the terms of General Assembly resolutions.

As the "cold war" got underway in 1947, it increasingly determined the motivation of states, particularly the major powers, in bringing matters to the attention of the General Assembly and the Security Council. The United States Government asked the General Assembly to take up the question of Korean independence in September, 1947. It is highly doubtful that there was any expectation whatever that the Assembly would be able to recommend a plan acceptable to all the interested parties for giving Korea unity and independence. The United

States and the Soviet Union had failed to make any important progress toward agreement in two years of negotiation. Nevertheless, the United States saw in this course a means of marshalling additional strength to contain Communism, a result considered particularly necessary in view of the decision to withdraw United States forces from South Korea. Later, when the North Koreans attacked the Republic of Korea in June, 1950, the United States immediately asked the Security Council to take action. It was not that Washington felt that it was incapable of giving the necessary support alone—in fact it gave the great bulk of the assistance and could have given more if necessary. Nevertheless, the Truman Administration believed that the United States position before the world and particularly Asian public opinion would be much stronger if it acted in this way instead of proceeding independently with its own national forces in the exercise of the right of self-defense. Furthermore, and perhaps most important of all, Washington considered it desirable to demonstrate that "collective security" could be effective, that the United States was prepared to make it effective, and that the NATO members in Europe could therefore rest assured that in case of a Soviet attack in that part of the world the United States would not be found wanting.

Other examples of "cold war" motivation in submitting matters to the Security Council or the General Assembly may be cited. In March, 1948, the Chilean Government requested the Security Council to consider the alleged intervention of the Soviet Union in the internal affairs of Czechoslovakia. There was little possibility of any effective action being taken in the face of the Soviet veto, but in any case the true character of Soviet action would be publicized. In this instance it is interesting to note that the matter was brought before the Security Council instead of the Assembly, the reason being that the Council was so organized as to be able to meet on short notice while a special session of the Assembly would have involved considerable delay and might not have been agreed to by a majority of Members. Later, in 1949, the complaints against Hungary, Bulgaria, and Romania of alleged violation of human rights guaranteed by the terms of the peace treaties were submitted to the General Assembly. The absence of the veto did not assure effective action. Here again the purpose of the Bolivian and Australian Governments was to bring pressure to bear on the Communist governments, to embarrass them, and to win the propaganda war. There could have been little expectation that anything which the Assembly did would have any immediate effect on the policies and actions of the countries concerned.

Many of the disputes and situations submitted to the United

Nations have resulted from the drive for independence and equality on the part of Asian and African states and the desire of the Western powers to protect rights based on treaties or other legal acts. In most cases, the reason for submission by Asian and African Members has been to get United Nations support for demands for independence, support considered helpful in current negotiations or useful in giving moral encouragement to the independence movement. In some cases, the United Nations has been asked to take the burden from the shoulders of states that have assumed special responsibilities on their own accord. Thus, the United Kingdom initially submitted the Palestine question to the General Assembly after failing to find any solution which would be acceptable to Arabs and Jews. Likewise, the United States, unwilling to carry alone the responsibility of establishing Korea as an independent, united, and democratic state, asked the General Assembly to help in achieving a settlement.

In most cases where the demand for independence and equality has been made, the colonial power or the state possessing special privileges has been in the stronger legal position. It thus finds an interest in bringing the matter before the United Nations to obtain a settlement on the basis of law. The United Kingdom first submitted its oil dispute with Iran to the International Court of Justice and then asked the Security Council to consider Iran's failure to comply with the provisional order of the Court. Similarly, France and the United Kingdom in 1956 asked the Security Council to consider the Suez Canal question with a view to getting Egypt to comply with the terms of the 1888 Convention as interpreted by them.

In practically all instances, questions have not been submitted to the Security Council or the General Assembly by agreement of the interested parties. There have been a couple of exceptions. The question of the disposition of Italy's colonies was submitted to the General Assembly on the basis of an agreement between France, the United Kingdom, the United States, and the Soviet Union incorporated in the Treaty of Peace with Italy. It was agreed that if the four powers could not reach an accord on the matter within a year, the question should be submitted to the General Assembly for final decision. The peace treaty also provided that Trieste should be given an international status under Security Council guarantee, and thus the signatories agreed to certain decisions being taken by the Council.

Certainly not all disputes that the parties have been unable to settle by means of their own choice and not all situations likely to lead to international friction or to disputes have been submitted to United Nations organs. Only two questions relating to Germany have been considered by the United Nations—the Berlin blockade and the question of free elections. On neither side has there been a willingness to have the United Nations consider any important aspects of the German problem with a view to final settlement. Obviously, the major powers consider that this problem so directly concerns their major strategic interests that they are not willing to let other states less directly concerned participate in the final decision. Even when the United Nations was asked by the Western Powers to consider the Berlin blockade and the question of free elections, it was made clear that decisions regarding the future of Berlin and of Germany were reserved and that United Nations discussion and decision should be limited to fairly technical aspects of the larger problem.

There have been many seeming inconsistencies in the use made of the United Nations. While the situation in Indonesia resulting from the efforts of the Netherlands Government to re-establish its authority at the conclusion of the War was brought to the attention of the Security Council and considered at length by it, the situation in Indochina resulting from similar efforts on the part of the French to establish their authority in the face of native resistance was never brought before the United Nations, even by an Asian state. Again, while the United States submitted the Korean question to the Assembly, it first submitted, and then subsequently withdrew from consideration, the question of Formosa. Though the United States took the initiative in asking the Security Council to consider the Israeli, French, and British attacks on Egypt, the subsequent threat to the independence of Jordan was never brought before the United Nations and the United States acted unilaterally by a show of force to meet it. It thus seems clear that it is not the characteristics of particular disputes or situations which determine whether they shall be submitted to the United Nations, but rather the conclusions reached by governments as to whether on balance a national interest will be served thereby. By and large, major powers are not willing to submit questions to the United Nations where their important national interests are involved, unless they are quite confident that the advantage to be gained will directly outweigh possible disadvantages.

Submission of a dispute or situation to the United Nations requires a choice of organ. A variety of considerations, both legal and political, influence this decision. Since the Charter does attempt to differentiate the functions and powers of United Nations organs, Charter provisions, though as a rule very liberally interpreted, do influence to some extent the choice of organ. Thus, a dispute or situation which has already reached the point of actual violence is generally submitted to the

Security Council initially even though a veto is likely to be encountered, since the Charter not only gives the Council powers under such circumstances not enjoyed by the Assembly, but also requires the Assembly to refer to the Council any matter requiring enforcement action. Legal considerations are not usually decisive, however.

In most instances, the choice of organ is determined by what the initiating state wants or expects to achieve by submitting the question to the United Nations. If the time factor is important and the Assembly is not in session, a state is likely to bring its complaint to the Security Council, notwithstanding the possibility of veto, since the Council is so organized that it can meet on short notice. If this is not a decisive consideration, and if the purpose of bringing the matter to the United Nations is to score a propaganda advantage or get wider support for one's position, the General Assembly is likely to be the choice. In a good many cases, the exercise of the veto or the likelihood of the same is decisive. The likelihood of getting a favorable result is always an important consideration. Consequently in all cases involving claims of equality and national self-determination on the part of Asian and African peoples, the General Assembly is the forum that is generally favored, not only because it provides a better sounding-board but also because the Asian and African states and their friends are more likely to obtain the necessary majority there. If a state feels that it has a strong legal case, it is likely to favor submission to the Court.

Nature of United Nations Action [24]

Once a dispute or situation has been brought to the attention of a United Nations organ, the nature of the action which that organ takes is determined by a variety of considerations, including the functions and powers of the organ, its operating procedures, and the attitudes of its members.

If the dispute is submitted to the Court on the basis of agreement of the parties,[25] the Court, if it finds that it has jurisdiction, will give a judgment which is binding on the parties and which is a final determination of the case. The procedure by which this result is achieved is one which safeguards the rights and interests of the parties by ensuring them full and equal opportunity to present their views. The judgment is based

---

[24] For a more detailed discussion, see Goodrich and Simons, *op. cit.,* Parts II and III.

[25] Either agreement with respect to the specific dispute or earlier acceptance of the Court's compulsory jurisdiction.

on international law, unless the parties agree to have the Court decide *ex aequo et bono*. The qualifications of the judges and the independence of the Court of national control give assurance that the judgment will be fair and impartial. Nevertheless, states are not normally willing, as we have seen, to submit questions effecting their important national interests to court judgment because they insist on keeping fuller control of the ultimate terms of settlement than the judicial process permits. Consequently the disputes that are submitted to the Court are not generally those which effect important national interests, or which if unresolved would be likely to lead to hostilities.

In the case of the Security Council and the General Assembly, this power of final binding decision does not exist. These organs are more akin to permanent international conferences whose effectiveness in settling differences depends on the achievement of agreement among the interested parties. Neither the Security Council nor the General Assembly can tell parties or interested states what they must do. Each must achieve settlement by persuasion rather than by order. Being part of an organization based on the principle of sovereign equality, each must respect the right of every state to determine for itself what kind of settlement or adjustment it is prepared to accept. This fact does not mean, however, that the Council and the Assembly do not have special resources of persuasion at their disposal which can be skillfully used to produce the desired agreement.

According to the original theory of the Charter, the Security Council was to be the organ primarily responsible for dealing with disputes and situations the continuance of which was likely to endanger the peace. It was thought to have special qualifications for this task. It was small and compact, so organized as to be continuously available, and possessing the maximum of authority, of persuasive power, by virtue of the membership of the major powers and on the assumption of their agreement. The Council has not in fact, however, acquired this degree of authority because of the failure of the permanent members to agree.

So far as the General Assembly is concerned, its special resource is the fact that it represents the total membership of the Organization and its decisions reflect a large area of agreement among Member governments. While it does not have the power to order, any recommendation that it may make, particularly by a large majority, carries considerable moral influence. No state wants to be in the position of being out of line with the general consensus of the membership. Still, if in a particular dispute or situation, a state finds that a vital interest is at stake, it will be likely to stand by this national interest rather than yield to anything as amorphous as world opinion or the general consensus.

Since both the General Assembly and the Security Council lack authority to take legally binding decisions in the realm of peaceful settlement and thus must seek to achieve their objectives by persuasion, what these two organs actually do is usually determined by an estimate of the course of action which under all the circumstances is most likely to achieve the desired result. If the purpose of action is to get an immediate settlement or adjustment based on the consent of interested parties, the course followed will presumably be that which is most likely to identify and eliminate present differences and achieve an agreed settlement. If, on the other hand, the purpose of action is to gain a propaganda advantage in the "cold war" or build up pressure on one of the parties to accept a particular program, then the course followed will be that which at the same time serves the interests of the major proponents and is acceptable to an impressive majority.

When a dispute or situation is submitted to either the Security Council or the General Assembly the first question to be considered is whether the item shall be included on the agenda. Generally each organ has been very free in including on its agenda items submitted to it. The arguments advanced by members for not so doing have included the following: that the proposed course of action constitutes intervention in a matter essentially within the domestic jurisdiction of a state; that the matter is not of sufficient importance to warrant consideration by the United Nations organ; that action by the organ will not make any useful contribution to the settlement of the question; and that the parties have not yet exhausted methods of peaceful settlement of their own choice as required by Article 33 of the Charter. Few questions have been submitted to the Assembly or the Council by agreement of the interested parties and without any objection being raised to consideration.

Once the item has been included on the agenda of the Council or Assembly, the next step is customarily a full public presentation of the views of the parties to the dispute or the states directly interested. In the case of the Assembly, this normally takes place in one of the political committees though there may also be an extensive airing of views in the debate over inclusion of the item in the agenda. In this respect practice differs from that followed by the League Council or Assembly, which encouraged private talks before public debate. The advantage of the League practice [26] was that an effort was made to bring the parties together on an agreed settlement before they took

[26] A member of the organ was usually designated as *rapporteur* and explored with the parties privately the possibilities of settlement.

public positions from which it would be difficult to withdraw. Only rarely has any such course been followed in the United Nations. While there is always the possibility of confidential discussions outside the Council or Assembly chamber, the regular procedure of these organs does not encourage it. Furthermore the policy of discouraging states from bringing differences to the United Nations until all other means of settlement have been exhausted usually means that by the time the matter is considered by the Council or Assembly positions have become rigid and accommodation difficult.[27]

After the parties have presented their views, the Council or Assembly has a wide range of choices it can make with respect to the next and succeeding steps to be taken. It may decide that there are questions of fact or law which require clarification. If there is need of clarifying the facts, a committee of investigation may be established, as was done by the Security Council in dealing with the Greek complaint in 1946. This committee may also be authorized to conduct discussions with the parties and try to achieve some basis for a settlement. In this case it assumes mediatory functions. In case there is some legal issue that needs clarification, the Council or Assembly may ask the International Court of Justice to give an advisory opinion, as the Assembly did in dealing with the alleged violation of human rights and fundamental freedoms by Bulgaria, Hungary, and Romania.[28] Or the Council or Assembly may seek advice from other sources, such as the International Law Commission.

If the dispute or situation is of an especially serious nature, with the imminent threat of fighting or with hostilities actually taking place, it is usually considered desirable, before proceeding directly to efforts at peaceful settlement, to try to get the parties to agree to provisional measures which will prevent the further deterioration of relations and help create conditions more favorable to agreement. Thus in dealing with the situation in Indonesia in 1947 and again in 1948–49, the Security Council tried first of all to get the parties to agree to a cease-fire and a withdrawal of forces. Likewise in dealing with the Arab-Israeli conflict and the Indian-Pakistani dispute over Kashmir, the Council initially emphasized efforts to bring fighting to an end and the acceptance of arrangements which would provide some assurance that fighting would not be resumed. Usually for this purpose it has been found

[27] On timing, see Elmore Jackson, *Meeting of Minds* (New York: McGraw-Hill Book Company, Inc., 1952), pp. 137–46.

[28] The Permanent Court of International Justice was used more frequently for this purpose during the League period than the International Court of Justice has been since the United Nations began to function.

necessary to establish some subsidiary organ capable of conducting negotiations on the spot and exercising supervisory functions. Thus, in dealing with the Israeli-Arab conflict in Palestine in 1948 and 1949, the Security Council used the Mediator appointed by the Assembly to negotiate armistice agreements and then created the Truce Supervisory Organization to assist in seeing that the agreements were respected.[29] When Egyptian territory was invaded in 1956, first by Israeli forces and then by British and French forces, the General Assembly instructed the Secretary-General to use his efforts to obtain compliance by the parties with its resolutions and authorized the establishment of the United Nations Emergency Force to secure and supervise the cessation of hostilities.[30]

In dealing with the dispute or situation on its merits, the Council or Assembly has a wide range of possibilities from which to choose. It can call upon the parties to resume negotiations. It can offer its good offices, as the Council did in dealing with the Indonesian crisis in 1947. It can appoint a person to represent it in attempting to find a basis for a settlement as the Security Council has done in dealing with the Kashmir question. It can create a commission to exercise its functions of conciliation and to keep the parent organ informed of developments, as the Assembly did in dealing with the Greek and Palestine questions. It may find that the dispute is of a legal nature and should be settled by the Court. In that case, it can recommend to the parties that they submit their dispute to the Court, as the Council did in 1947 in dealing with the Corfu Channel dispute between Albania and the United Kingdom [31] over responsibility for damage to British warships from the explosion of mines.

Instead of establishing a subsidiary organ with extensive discretionary power to negotiate with the parties with a view to finding a settlement agreeable to them, the Council or the Assembly may itself prepare a detailed plan for the final settlement of the matter. This course has been followed by the Assembly in three notable instances. In dealing with the Palestine question, submitted by the United Kingdom, the Assembly drew up a detailed plan of settlement, involving political partition and economic union, and recommended its implementation.[32]

---

[29] On provisional measures, see Goodrich and Simons, Chap. XV and Eduardo Jiminez de Arechaga, *Voting and the Handling of Disputes in the Security Council* (New York: Carnegie Endowment, 1950). Ch. V.

[30] General Assembly Resolutions 998 (ES-1), 997 (ES-1), 999 (ES-1), and 1000 (ES-1).

[31] On possible courses of action open to Council and Assembly, see Goodrich and Simons, *op. cit.,* Chs. IX–XII.

[32] General Assembly Resolution 181 (II), Nov. 29, 1947.

The refusal of the Security Council to perform the role assigned to it was in part responsible for the failure of the plan to be carried out in full. When asked by the United States to consider the question of Korean independence, the General Assembly responded by proposing a plan for holding elections under United Nations observation and the forming of a national government.[33] This plan was never carried out in full because of the opposition of the Soviet Union which was in military occupation of the northern part of Korea. As has already been indicated, the Assembly was given the assignment, under the terms of the Italian peace treaty, of determining the final disposition of the Italian colonies if the Council of Foreign Ministers was unable to agree on a plan within a year. The Assembly adopted resolutions recommending a detailed plan which was fully implemented.[34] Generally speaking, the Council has limited itself to recommending methods of settlement, but on occasion it includes in its resolutions specific proposals of terms of settlement.

Once the Council or Assembly has made a recommendation, whether of method or of terms of settlement, the follow-up becomes of the greatest importance. It is for that reason that each organ has found it necessary repeatedly to create subsidiary organs to perform its functions, in part or in whole, and on the spot. In the case of the General Assembly, the very size of the body and the fact that it is only in session part of the time are additional reasons for the use of subsidiary organs.

Results Achieved

The record of the United Nations in the field of peaceful settlement has not for the most part been a particularly encouraging one. Generally speaking, the United Nations has been less successful than the League of Nations within a comparable period of time. The reasons for this are not too difficult to find. In the first place, the United Nations has not had the advantage of starting with an agreed peace settlement to which the principal members have been parties and which they have had an interest in implementing and maintaining against challenge by force. On the other hand, it must be admitted that the United Nations has had one advantage which the League did not have, namely, the inclusion as Members of all the major victor nations.

[33] General Assembly Resolution 112 (II), Nov. 14, 1947.
[34] General Assembly Resolution 289 (IV), Nov. 21, 1949, and 390 (V), Dec. 2, 1950.

But the real cause of the limited success of the United Nations has been the nature of the conflicts and tensions that have developed in the postwar world particularly among the major powers. Unlike the differences among the permanent members of the League Council during the years immediately following the First World War, the differences between the Soviet Union on the one hand and the Western Powers on the other have related to matters of ideology and basic national purpose and have been accompanied by profound distrust. The result has been failure to make those accommodations of conflicting policies and interests within the context of common purposes which are necessary if states are to act in concert. This failure of the major powers to agree has made the Security Council and the General Assembly less effective than they would otherwise have been in dealing with those conflicts and tensions resulting from the emergence of vigorous nationalist movements in Asia and Africa. With the United Nations organs unable to exercise their full authority and with the opposing parties unwilling to compromise, there has been a natural inclination to use these organs quite openly on occasion for achieving propaganda advantages rather than as means of achieving mutually acceptable accommodations of national policies and interests.

As has been suggested above, this tendency has been encouraged by voting practices and rules of procedure which make it possible for decisions to be taken by majority votes instead of general agreement. The result is that even though a resolution is only a recommendation and is not likely to be implemented except with the agreement of the parties directly involved, in the "cold war," as in the efforts to satisfy the nationalist aspirations of subject or recently subject peoples, a recommendation adopted by a substantial majority may be viewed as having important political value even if it is not implemented, or even if the desired course of action becomes more remote as a result of its adoption. Under these conditions, the goal of General Assembly action in particular is too frequently an impressive majority rather than an effective agreement.

Statistically the most successful of the organs of the United Nations has been the International Court of Justice.[35] The Court has given decisions on some dozen cases and with one exception its decisions have

[35] On the work of the Court, see Oliver J. Lissitzyn, *The International Court of Justice* (New York: Carnegie Endowment for International Peace, 1951), the I.C.J. Yearbooks, published annually, and the annual article by Manley O. Hudson in the January number of *American Journal of International Law* on the work of the Court.

been respected. It is significant, however, that the cases that have been decided by the Court have for the most part involved countries with a Western European orientation. Only one case has come to a final judgment in which states on opposite sides of the "iron curtain" have been involved, and in this case—the Corfu Channel dispute between Albania and the United Kingdom—the Court's judgment on the amount of damages has not been carried out. In the one case involving relations between a Western power and an Asian-African state, the Court decided that it did not have jurisdiction.[36]

The General Assembly and the Security Council have been less successful in getting disputes or situations peacefully settled or adjusted than in bringing fighting to an end and maintaining a tenuous condition of non-fighting. In dealing with the Kashmir question, for example, the Security Council was able to get the parties to agree to the cessation of hostilities, but has had no success in breaking down the hard core of disagreement separating India and Pakistan. Likewise, in dealing with the Palestine question, the Council, through the Acting Mediator (Ralph Bunche) was able to get the parties to agree to armistice agreements, and for a period of six or seven years, with the assistance of the Truce Supervisory Organization and the Mixed Armistice Commission, to achieve reasonable respect for them. In 1956, however, fighting broke out again on a large scale, with the added complication of British and French military intervention. Again the United Nations, this time through the General Assembly, succeeded in getting the parties to agree to the termination of hostilities and the withdrawal of forces. No progress has been made, however, toward getting an agreement on the basic political issues. Obviously, so long as the political differences remain unresolved the situation remains potentially explosive.

In only one of the initiatives that it has taken to achieve a peaceful settlement or adjustment, has the Council or Assembly been notably successful.[37] That was in dealing with the situation in Indonesia resulting from the attempt of the Dutch to re-establish their authority by force. The Security Council not only was able to bring hostilities to an end but also played an important role in bringing about an agreement between the Dutch and the Indonesians which provided the basis for the establishment of an independent Indonesian state. Neither Council nor

[36] There is pending before the Court a case between Portugal and India concerning right of passage over Indian territory. Portugal is the applicant.

[37] In settling the question of the future disposition of the Italian colonies, the General Assembly acted on the basis of an agreement of the states chiefly concerned.

Assembly has been able, however, to achieve a settlement of the more recent dispute between the Netherlands and Indonesia over West Irian (Dutch New Guinea). The Council and notably the Assembly have been called upon to perform roles somewhat similar to that in Indonesia in connection with the situations in Tunisia, Morocco, Cyprus, and Algeria. Tunisia and Morocco achieved independence by agreement with France and were subsequently admitted to United Nations membership. The United Nations contributed to this result by encouraging France to relax its controls and grant independence while holding out to Tunisian and Moroccan leaders the prospect of achieving their goals without resort to violence. In dealing with the questions of Algeria and Cyprus the United Nations has been less successful in promoting a peaceful accommodation.

One may say by way of general conclusion that where there has been a desire on the part of the interested parties to reach a settlement whether on a legal basis or by reasonable compromise, the United Nations through its appropriate organs has been able to contribute substantially to this result. Where opposing positions are rigidly adhered to, the United Nations has been able to do little to achieve any agreed settlement or adjustment. Its chief contribution, which is an important one, has been to achieve and maintain an uneasy truce, and to hold out to the aggrieved party the possibility that eventually satisfaction will be achieved without resort to force. In dealing with the aspirations of dependent peoples to control their own destinies, the United Nations has been able to make a valuable contribution by encouraging, on the one hand, constructive and forward looking solutions, and, on the other, by exercising restraint on those who may be inclined to press for extreme solutions by extreme methods. Perhaps the greatest contribution of the Organization to the work of peaceful settlement and adjustment is that it provides the means whereby disputes and situations can be considered outside the narrow context of the parties' conflicting interests and with adequate attention to the larger interest in international peace and security, human freedom, and the general welfare which the United Nations represents. The extent to which states take advantage of this opportunity and the measure of success that attends the use of United Nations procedures are bound to depend in the last analysis on the state of international relations and the policies and attitudes of individual Members. The United Nations does much to facilitate and encourage the peaceful accommodation of conflicting views and interests, but does not have the means to impose agreement or settlement if national attitudes are recalcitrant, uncooperative and distrustful.

SUGGESTED READINGS

Bloomfield, Lincoln. "Law, Politics and International Disputes," *International Conciliation,* No. 516 (January, 1958), pp. 260–77.

Claude, Inis, Jr. *Swords into Plowshares.* New York: Random House, Inc., 1056. Chap. 11.

Collins, J. Foster. "The United Nations and Indonesia," *International Conciliation,* No. 459 (March 1950), pp. 115–200.

Conwell-Evans, T. P. *The League Council in Action.* London: Oxford University Press, 1929.

Dunn, Frederick S. *Peaceful Change.* New York: Council on Foreign Relations, 1937.

Goodrich, Leland M. and Simons, Anne P. *The United Nations and the Maintenance of International Peace and Security.* Washington: The Brookings Institution, 1955. Parts 2 and 3.

Hoffmann, Stanley. "Sisyphus and the Avalanche: the United Nations, Egypt and Hungary," *International Organization,* XI (1957), pp. 446–69.

Hyde, James N. "Peaceful Settlement," *International Conciliation,* No. 444 (October 1948), pp. 531–74.

Jully, L. "Arbitration and Judicial Settlement; Recent Trends," *American Journal of International Law,* XLVIII (1954), pp. 380–407.

Kelsen, Hans. *Peace Through Law.* Chapel Hill: University of North Carolina Press, 1944.

Leonard, L. Larry. "The United Nations and Palestine," *International Conciliation,* No. 454 (October, 1949), pp. 607–786.

Lissitzyn, Oliver J. *The International Court of Justice.* New York: Carnegie Endowment for International Peace, 1951.

Rivlin, Benjamin. *The United Nations and the Italian Colonies.* New York: Carnegie Endowment for International Peace, 1950.

U.S. Senate Committee on Foreign Relations, Subcommittee on the United Nations Charter. *Pacific Settlement of Disputes in the United Nations.* Staff Study No. 5. Washington: Government Printing Office, 1954.

―――. *The International Court of Justice.* Staff Study No. 8. Washington: Government Printing Office, 1954.

Chapter X

THE ATOM AND
DISARMAMENT

THE WIDESPREAD belief that rivalry in national armaments is a cause of war, together with the economic burdens which increasingly expensive armaments impose, has resulted in repeated efforts to limit and reduce them by international agreement. There are those, however, who take the view that rivalry in armaments, even though a cause of war, is the product of more deep-seated conditions, and that until those conditions are remedied, there is little hope of achieving any agreed limitation. These two attitudes have been present in all discussions of disarmament.[1] The record of history would seem to suggest that those who believe armaments cannot be usefully treated as an independent cause of war have the better case. There remains the question, however, whether the revolutionary change in the nature of war as the result of recent technological developments has not presented us with a problem for the solution of which historical precedents have limited value.

The History of Disarmament Efforts

During the nineteenth century and down to the time of the First World War numerous efforts were made to achieve the limitation and reduction of national armaments by international agreement.[2] The Rush-Bagot agreement of 1817 between the United States and the United

[1] The word is used here to mean limitation and reduction by international agreement.

[2] Merze Tate, *The Disarmament Illusion* (New York: The Macmillan Company, 1942).

Kingdom limited naval armaments on the Great Lakes. Toward the end of the century, interest in disarmament was expressed by some European Governments. In 1899, the Russian Tsar invited twenty-seven other governments to a conference at The Hague, one of the chief items on the agenda of the conference being disarmament. However, it was not possible to reach any agreement, nor was it possible eight years later at the Second Hague Conference, called on the initiative of President Theodore Roosevelt. Still the idea did not die that rivalry in armaments was a cause of war and that disarmament was one of the promising roads to peace.

Those who were primarily responsible for writing the League of Nations Covenant accepted the view that armament rivalry was an important direct cause of war and that any organization with peace as its primary objective should try to bring about the reduction and limitation of national armaments. Article 8 of the Covenant emphasized this as one of the principal League approaches to the problem of peace. By its terms, members of the League recognized "that the maintenance of peace requires the reduction of national armaments to the lowest point consistent with national safety and the enforcement by common action of international obligations." "In order to render possible the initiation of a general limitation of the armaments of all nations," the Treaty of Versailles imposed drastic limitations on the armaments of defeated Germany.[3] Other peace treaties imposed comparable limitations on the armaments of Austria, Hungary, and Bulgaria. To assist in carrying out the Covenant provisions regarding disarmament, the League Council was made responsible for preparing proposals for the limitation of armaments to be submitted to members for their consideration and action.

In the League debates, there were two opposing views regarding the proper approach to the problem of disarmament, the "direct" and the "indirect." [4] It proved very difficult and in the end impossible to harmonize these views. Those who advocated the direct approach believed that rivalry in armaments was a direct cause of war and that, consequently, any agreement that would end or at least limit this rivalry would contribute to more friendly relations between nations and to improving the prospects of peace. They insisted that efforts to get agreement on the limitation and reduction of national armaments should not be made conditional on the more effective organization of international peace and security or the easing of international tensions and the settlement of differences. "The way to disarm is to disarm," was their slogan.

[3] See Introduction to Part V of the Treaty.
[4] See Salvador de Madariaga, *Disarmament* (New York: Coward-McCann, Inc., 1929) for an analysis of League discussions.

Among the nations which supported this approach in the inter-War period were the United States, the United Kingdom and the Dominions, the Soviet Union, and the Scandinavian countries.

Those who advocated the indirect approach argued that existing levels of national armaments were maintained because countries felt the need of them in order to provide for national security, and that until this need could be satisfied in some other way it was foolish to expect responsible statesmen to agree to limitation and reduction. This approach was taken particularly by France and by those continental European countries that had been victors in the First World War or that had bene-fitted from the territorial provisions of the peace treaties, and who feared that the defeated nations might become strong again and seek to recover their lost territories. The specific demand of the proponents of the indirect approach was that the existing system of collective security be strengthened as a condition of their accepting the reduction and limitation of their armaments. France, whose territory had been twice invaded by Germany within the memory of many living French-men, argued that it was necessary to maintain large armaments to pro-vide protection against a potentially stronger Germany and refused to agree to any reduction unless other states were prepared to give her firm guarantees that they would support her in case she was again the victim of aggression.

Beginning with the first session of the League Assembly, the merits of these two approaches were argued without any real and lasting agree-ment being reached. The nearest approach to agreement came in 1924 when the Assembly under the leadership of Ramsay MacDonald and Edouard Herriot approved the Geneva Protocol which sought to combine these two views under the formula of "arbitration, security, disarma-ment." Unfortunately this agreement was short-lived. A general election in the United Kingdom brought the Conservatives back into power, and the new Conservative Government would have nothing to do with the Protocol. All that was salvaged was the later agreement at Locarno to apply the principles of collective guarantee against aggression and peace-ful settlement to a limited area, the frontier between Germany on the one hand and France and Belgium on the other. This however was not enough to assure the success of the general disarmament effort. The Commission which was created to prepare a draft convention for the consideration of a general conference was unable to reach more than partial agreement, and the draft convention which it submitted with its report contained important and highly significant gaps.[5] When finally a

[5] League of Nations, *Documents of the Preparatory Commission*, Series X, pp. 562 *et seq.*

general disarmament conference was called in February, 1932, the world situation had deteriorated to such an extent that agreement on the limitation of armaments was completely out of the question.[6]

The only success in the inter-War period was achieved outside the League on the initiative of the United States. By the Washington Treaty of 1922 certain categories of the naval armaments of the major naval powers were limited and reduced, but this was only possible because of certain political agreements and understandings. Once these collapsed as the result of Japanese aggression against China in 1931 and the years following, the naval agreements became a threat to peace instead of a safeguard of peace.

The experience of the years immediately preceding the Second World War and of the War itself dampened considerably the enthusiasm of those who had believed in the direct approach to disarmament. It even raised doubts as to whether in the interest of peace, it was not perhaps more important to have enough armaments to keep the peace against a possible aggressor than to have a treaty limitation which might result in the peaceful nations being ill-prepared when the challenge of aggression came. The experience led many to believe that if the victors in the Second World War had been militarily prepared and had co-operated before as they did during the war, the whole costly struggle would have been avoided. Thus, it was thought desirable in organizing peace to be sure that the armaments necessary for keeping the peace were available and in the right hands. These views largely determined the Charter approach to the problem of disarmament.

Disarmament in the Charter

Unlike the Covenant, the Charter does not explicitly stress the limitation and reduction of armaments by international agreement as an independent and immediate approach to the goal of international peace and security, although it does recognize that the regulation of armaments is an important element in an effective system for maintaining peace and security. Article 1, in stating the purposes of the United Nations, makes no mention of disarmament. Rather, it stresses peaceful settlement and collective measures as the principal methods of maintaining international peace and security. Article 11 empowers the General Assembly to consider "the general principles of cooperation in the maintenance of international peace and security, including the principles governing disarmament and the regulation of armaments."

[6] For story of League disarmament efforts, see William E. Rappard, *The Quest for Peace* (Cambridge: Harvard University Press, 1940).

By the terms of Article 26, the Security Council is directed, ". . . in order to promote the establishment and maintenance of international peace and security with the least diversion for armaments of the world's human and economic resources," to formulate "plans . . . for the establishment of a system for the regulation of armaments."

The provisions of the Charter, taken together with the discussions that preceded its final adoption, suggest that the architects of the Charter did not look upon disarmament as a principal method of achieving peace and security but rather as a subsidiary one. What was believed to be important was that Members of the United Nations, and particularly the major powers, while pledged to settle their differences by peaceful means and to refrain from the use of force in any way inconsistent with the Charter, should have and be willing to use the armed forces and facilities that might be needed to put down aggression. Initially at least, Members would need to have additional forces of their own for any emergency that might arise. It was, however, recognized that these purely national armaments might become an economic burden that should be avoided. Furthermore, it was understood that the task of maintaining peace and security by collective measures would be simpler if national armaments were not allowed to remain or become too large. Nevertheless, the emphasis in the Charter was as much upon the desirability of a floor as upon the need of a ceiling for national armaments. It is in this sense that regulation is to be understood.

Furthermore, it was clearly intended that the regulation of national armaments should come after and not before the full implementation of the system of collective security. Only after military agreements had been concluded under Article 43 and the system of collective security was in good working order could it be determined what levels of national armaments were necessary to meet international obligations and to provide for emergency situations, and what levels constituted unnecessary diversions of personnel and resources from other more important peacetime uses. In other words, the Charter accepted the indirect approach and initially placed disarmament in a subordinate position. However, this was before the first atomic bombs were dropped on Hiroshima and Nagasaki.

The Impact of the Atomic Bomb and the Cold War

The explosion of the two atomic bombs in Japan in early August, 1945, not only was a decisive factor in inducing Japan to surrender but also produced widespread alarm, particularly in the United States, over the possible consequences of atomic warfare in the future. In announcing the explosion of the Hiroshima bomb, President Truman reminded the American public of the need of examining all "possible methods of protecting us and the rest of the world from the danger of sudden destruction."[7] The peril of the world was driven home by the President's statement that the bomb "had more power than 20,000 tons of TNT." In the United States it was recognized that while possession of the bomb provided a present advantage, it gave no assurance of future security. As scientists were agreed that sooner or later other countries would be able to develop it, no decision of the United States that it would not use the bomb again was sufficient to provide assurance against possible future use by another state. Some form of international control was required.

The bomb made its appearance at a time when the hopes that had been entertained regarding cooperation with the Soviet Union after the war were being dampened. The unyielding attitude of the Soviet Union on many important current questions such as Poland and the treatment of Germany and mountaing evidence of Soviet bad faith and expansionist purposes produced increasing skepticism in the United States regarding the possibility of effective cooperation with the Soviets. Possession of the bomb was recognized to be a powerful weapon in the hands of the United States that could be used to restore the balance of power which the United States had allowed to become dangerously tipped in Europe in the Soviet Union's favor following the end of hostilities. And yet the bomb was a wasting asset. Once the Soviet Union was able to develop a bomb of its own, the advantage of the United States would be greatly reduced, if not entirely lost.

Uncertainty as to how long it would take the Soviet Union to develop the bomb and awareness of the unimaginable consequences of atomic warfare led those who were responsible for United States policy to take the view that time was of the essence. The danger was thought to be so immediate and overwhelming as to justify, if not require, immediate consideration of the problem of international control of atomic energy apart from, and in advance of, that of the regulation of armaments in general. Thus it was the explosion of the bomb and the near-panic that resulted when responsible people in the United States began to reflect on the consequences of this act that led to placing one aspect of the problem of armaments regulation on the agenda of the first session of the General Assembly. It was not long before the debate had broadened out into other aspects of the disarmament problem and the

[7] *Documents on American Foreign Relations, 1945–1946* (Princeton: Princeton University Press for World Peace Foundation, 1948), p. 421.

United Nations found itself, in spite of the best efforts of its founders, right where the League had been.[8]

The decision to place the question on the agenda of the first session of the Assembly was a joint decision, taken by the Foreign Ministers of the United States, the United Kingdom and the Soviet Union at their Moscow meeting in December 1945. The United States had already reached agreement on November 15 with Canada and the United Kingdom, its partners in the development of the bomb. The proposal of these powers was that the Assembly should be asked to establish a commission consisting of the members of the Security Council and Canada which should make specific proposals

(*a*) *For extending between all nations the exchange of basic scientific information for peaceful ends,*

(*b*) *For control of atomic energy to the extent necessary to ensure its use only for peaceful purposes,*

(*c*) *For the elimination from national armaments of atomic weapons and of all other major weapons adaptable to mass destruction,*

(*d*) *For effective safeguards by way of inspection and other means to protect complying states against the hazards of violations and evasions.*[9]

This proposal with minor changes was accepted by the Soviet Union.[10] Why the Soviet Union was so agreeable to establishing the Commission and raised so many difficulties to block all agreement later is a difficult question to answer. Perhaps Stalin and his advisers underestimated the importance of the Commission, or possibly they foresaw the chance of gaining some propaganda advantages later by opening up the whole disarmament question. Or perhaps they simply reckoned that they stood to gain more than they could possibly lose by taking part in discussions the exact direction and substance of which were then unknown to them.

The Atomic Energy Commission was established by resolution of the General Assembly on January 24, 1946, and held its first meeting on June 14. Mr. Bernard Baruch, the United States Representative on the Commission, presented a carefully prepared proposal for interna-

---

[8] For a brief account of U.N. discussions and negotiations, see Goodrich and Simons, *op. cit.*, Part V; and United States Senate, 84th Cong., 2nd sess., Committee on Foreign Relations, Subcommittee on Disarmament, *Control and Reduction of Armaments: A Decade of Negotiations, 1945–1956*, Staff Study No. 3 (Washington: Government Printing Office, 1956).

[9] Department of State *Bulletin*, XIII (1945), p. 782.

[10] See James F. Byrnes, *Speaking Frankly* (New York: Harper & Brothers, Publishers, 1947), pp. 267–68.

tional control of atomic energy largely based on the recommendations contained in the Acheson-Lilienthal Report.[11] The proposal called for the establishment of an International Atomic Energy Authority which would be entrusted with: (1) managerial control or ownership of all atomic energy activities "potentially dangerous to world security"; (2) the power to control, inspect, or license all other atomic activities; (3) the duty of fostering the beneficial use of atomic energy; and (4) responsibility for research and development of an affirmative character. According to the Baruch proposal, once an adequate system of control was developed and put into effective operation: (1) the manufacture of atomic bombs should stop; (2) existing bombs should be disposed of; and (3) the proposed authority should be given possession of the full information necessary for the production of atomic energy. It was an essential part of the United States proposal that the plan should enter into effect by stages with the United States making information available and yielding control of activities to the extent necessary to complete each stage. Furthermore the United States was insistent on the establishment of a detailed system of inspection, the imposition of serious penalties for any violation of the control system, and the elimination of the veto in so far as the operation of the control system and the application of penalties were concerned.[12]

This proposal went much beyond what the Soviet Union was prepared to accept at the time. The Soviet counterproposals were comparatively simple in nature. They called for the conclusion of conventions prohibiting the production and employment of weapons based on the use of atomic energy, and the study of practical measures for the exchange of scientific information. It was quite clear from these proposals and from the further development of the Soviet position that the Soviet leaders were unwilling to accept any plan which would permit the United States to maintain at its discretion its current position of atomic superiority while preventing the Soviet Union from using all means at its disposal to achieve a status of equality in atomic weapons. The Soviet leaders undoubtedly also foresaw the possibility of using their proposal for outlawry advantageously in the propaganda war, since it might seem simpler and emotionally more appealing to people whose primary concern was fear of the consequences of the future use of atomic bombs.

In the course of Commission discussions, it soon became clear that

[11] U.S. Department of State, *A Report on the International Control of Atomic Energy,* Publ. 2498 (Washington: Government Printing Office, 1946).

[12] Atomic Energy Commission, *Official Records,* First Year, First Meeting (June 14, 1946), pp. 7–14.

the United States proposals were acceptable, at least in their broad out-lines, to all members of the Commission except the Soviet Union and Poland. It became clear that there were three principal points on which the United States and the Soviet Union took diametrically opposite positions. First, the Soviet Union firmly maintained that the manu-facture, possession, and use of atomic weapons should be prohibited without waiting for the establishment of an effective control system, while the United States insisted that the prohibition should not take effect until the control system was in operation and known to be effec-tive. Second, the Soviet Union insisted that the development of atomic energy should be left to each state and that subject to periodic inspec-tions by the proposed international authority, each state should assume responsibility for seeing that the prohibition was respected, while the United States insisted that development of atomic energy should be the exclusive responsibility of an International Atomic Development Authority, which would have powers of ownership, management, super-vision, leasing, licensing, and inspection. Third, the Soviet Union in-sisted that the international authority should be organized within the framework of the Security Council and that no enforcement action should be taken except by agreement of the permanent members, while the United States insisted that the provisions regarding penalties to be applied against violators of the proposed convention should not admit of the possibility of a "veto" by a non-complying state.

The Commission made some progress during 1946 in clarifying the technical aspects of the problem and the areas of agreement and dis-agreement. It made no real progress, however, in bridging or even nar-rowing the major differences between the United States and the Soviet Union. The Commission approved the unanimous conclusion of its Technical and Scientific Committee that effective control was tech-nologically possible; by implication it made it clear that the problem it had to deal with was basically a political one.[13]

Old Arguments in a New Setting

The effort, sponsored particularly by the United States, to achieve agreement on the international control of atomic energy without opening up the endless debate on disarmament, ended in complete deadlock. It became clear, if it was not already, that atomic weapons—which were the principal concern of the participants in the atomic discussions—

[13] See U.N. Atomic Energy Commission, *Official Records,* First Year, Special Supplement, "Report to the Security Council" (1946).

were primarily armaments, and only incidentally the most destructive force that the mind of man had yet devised. Viewing them as armaments, the chief power rivals were unwilling to relinquish any advantage with respect to possession or use which they might have or hope to gain, so long as they foresaw the possibility that they might need to make use of them in defense of an important national interest. Their destructiveness alone did not provide an acceptable reason for treating them differently from other armaments.

Since the United States had definitely achieved a propaganda advantage by submitting a plan of atomic energy control which not only provided effective guarantees against use for destructive purposes but also involved a voluntary relinquishment by the United States of the advantages of a monopoly position, though admittedly at a time of its own choosing, it was not surprising that the Soviet Union, when the Assembly met for the second part of its first session, should have sought to gain the diplomatic initiative by bringing forward a proposal which in turn would have wide popular appeal and support. Since it was not easy to outbid the United States in the atomic field alone, the Soviet Union turned its attention to the larger field of the limitation of armaments generally. Here it was at a great advantage over the Western powers, the United States in particular, since it was in the position to make more dramatic offers without serious embarassment if they were accepted. The withdrawal of United States armed forces after the war had left the defense of western Europe in a grave condition. Any proposal to reduce armed forces on a percentage base was certain to leave the Soviet Union relatively better off than the Western Powers because of its present superiority of forces and its more favorable geographical position.

When the General Assembly met for the second part of its first session in October 1946, it had before it a Soviet proposal recognizing the necessity of a general reduction of armaments and emphasizing the importance, as a primary objective, of the prohibition of the manufacture or use of atomic weapons. There ensued a wide-ranging discussion which was profoundly reminiscent of the League of Nations debates. To be sure, the specific issues had changed. Nevertheless, the basic approaches remained the same. On the one hand, the view of the Soviet Union was, in effect, that the way to peaceful and friendly relations was to prohibit atomic weapons and substantially to reduce other armaments of a more conventional nature. On the other hand the British and the Americans who had been the principal proponents of the "direct" approach during the period between the First and Second World Wars argued that before there could be any limitation or reduction there must be a foolproof control system which would protect complying states against the hazards of violation. Furthermore, with respect to armaments other than atomic, the argument was advanced, consistent with the premises of the Charter, that before there could be any limitation or reduction, the United Nations system of collective security must be implemented by making armed forces available to the Security Council, and some progress must be made in resolving major political problems, notably problems of the peace settlement.

While the debate in the General Assembly was free of much of the bitterness and vituperation which were to characterize future discussions in that organ, and the principal parties showed a superficial willingness to make concessions in the interest of agreement, the resolution adopted by the General Assembly on December 14 [14] did not in fact resolve any of the basic differences between the Soviet Union and the Western Powers. It consisted of a series of carefully formulated propositions which covered the underlying disagreements with the appearance of agreement. While recognizing that armaments should be regulated and reduced, and that atomic weapons should be prohibited, it also emphasized the importance of practical and effective safeguards and the need of strengthening the system of collective security. It gave no guidance to those who were dealing with the basic issues: How much? When? What form should the safeguards take?

The General Assembly debate and the resolution of December 14 marked the beginning of a new phase of the consideration of the disarmament problem. From this time on it seemed agreed that the control of atomic bombs was part of a larger problem of armament regulation, and that efforts to deal with one without dealing with the other were unrealistic and of no avail. For a time, on the insistence of the United States, an effort was made to keep the two discussions to some degree separate by continuing the Atomic Energy Commission with its original assignment, and by creating a special organ, the Commission for Conventional Armaments, to prepare proposals "for the general regulation and reduction of armaments and armed forces" and "for practical and effective safeguards," to the exclusion of matters within the competence of the Atomic Energy Commission.

This attempt at separate but parallel consideration continued into 1949 but ended in complete failure. The deadlock in the Atomic Energy Commission continued without any significant change. The Commission on Conventional Armaments was never able to get off the ground. A Western proposal for the collection, publication, and verification of information on military effectives and conventional armaments was

[14] General Assembly Resolution 41 (I).

treated by the Russians as a stall. By the summer of 1950, it was clear that efforts to achieve the regulation and reduction of armaments within the framework of the resolutions of the General Assembly had completely failed and held no promise for the future. Furthermore, the exploding of an atomic bomb by the Soviet Union in October, 1949, and the experience of the first months of the Korean conflict convinced the West, especially the United States, that the approach hitherto followed was no longer even in its own interest. It was clear that the United States no longer had a monopoly of atomic bombs, and that the advantage which it did possess was definitely a wasting asset. Furthermore, the Korean experience demonstrated that atomic weapons could not be used to advantage under all circumstances, and that in those situations where they were not used, superiority of conventional armaments conferred a real advantage. Thus, it became United States policy no longer to isolate the consideration of international control of atomic energy from the discussion of other aspects of the disarmament problems. This new approach had the further advantage of offering a broader front for the conduct of the cold war.

The United States took the initiative in asking the General Assembly in October, 1950, to combine the work of the two Commissions and henceforth to consider the problem of the regulation of armaments in all its aspects.[15] On January 11, 1952, the Sixth General Assembly adopted a resolution incorporating the new approach.[16] It affirmed its belief that a necessary condition of an effective collective security system was

> . . . the development by the United Nations of comprehensive and coordinated plans, under international control, for the regulation, limitation and balanced reduction of all armed forces and all armaments, for the elimination of all major weapons adaptable to mass destruction, and for the effective international control of atomic energy to ensure the prohibition of atomic weapons and the use of atomic energy for peaceful purposes only.

The Assembly established the Disarmament Commission "under the Security Council" with the same membership as the Atomic Energy Commission, to prepare proposals for carrying out these purposes.

In the debates in the General Assembly and in the subsequent discussions in the Commission, it was clear that the Soviet Union and the

[15] See address of President Truman to the General Assembly on October 24, 1950. U.N. General Assembly, *Official Records,* Fifth Session, 295th Plenary Meeting (Oct. 24, 1950), pp. 246–47.

[16] General Assembly Resolution 502 (VI), Jan. 11, 1952.

Western powers were still far apart on basic issues. On some questions which had long been under consideration, their positions had changed but generally speaking when one side adopted a position which was closer to that which had been maintained by the other, no significant narrowing of the gap resulted as the other by now had moved from its previous position or chose to emphasize even more the differences that remained. Thus, the Soviet Union now was prepared to have the decision prohibiting atomic weapons take effect simultaneously with a system of strict international control, but still insisted that the control system should not be of such a nature as "to interfere in the domestic affairs of states." The Western powers, however, insisted on a control system much more detailed and rigorous than the Soviet Union was prepared to accept, and continued to insist that the prohibition should not enter into force until the control system had proven to be effective. The Soviet Union was opposed to Western proposals for limitation of armaments at levels adequate for defense, but not for offense. Instead it proposed a one-third reduction of the armed forces and armaments of all the major powers within a year, without the guarantees with respect to compliance demanded by the West. It continued to oppose the disclosure of armament information by stages on the grounds that such a procedure would result in endless delay of reduction, and would mean the indefinite postponement of disclosure with respect to the most destructive weapons.

Efforts to Find a Fresh Approach

When the Eighth Assembly convened in September, 1953, the chances of some substantial progress in narrowing differences seemed more promising. Though the United States had exploded a thermonuclear bomb in November, 1952, the Soviet Union had announced in the following August that it had done the same, thus creating parity between the two superpowers in potentialities of destruction. Stalin had died in early March, 1953, and his successors appeared more conciliatory and desirous of some accommodation with the West. On July 27, the Korean armistice agreement had been signed. The tension between East and West seemed to have moderated to a considerable degree. After another extensive debate, more serious and less propagandistic than some of its predecessors, the Assembly, on November 28, by a unanimous vote with the Soviet bloc abstaining, adopted a resolution [17] "affirming the need of providing for:

[17] General Assembly Resolution 715 (VIII).

(*a*) *the regulation, limitation and balanced reduction of all armed forces and all armaments,*

(*b*) *The elimination and prohibition of atomic, hydrogen and other types of weapons of mass destruction,*

(*c*) *The effective international control of atomic energy to ensure the prohibition of atomic weapons and the use of atomic energy for peaceful purposes only,*

the whole programme to be carried out under effective international control and in such a way that no state would have cause to fear that its security was endangered." The Assembly requested the Disarmament Commission to continue its efforts and suggested that the Commission consider the desirability of establishing a subcommittee "consisting of the representatives of the Powers principally involved, which should seek in private an acceptable solution, and report to the Disarmament Commission as soon as possible. . . ." Implicit in this action was the belief that discussion in the Disarmament Commission and the Assembly had become so enmeshed with the seeking of propaganda advantage that it hindered the achievement of agreement.

Ten days later, in a speech before the General Assembly, President Eisenhower gave a new approach to the problem of international control of atomic energy by suggesting that there be established under the aegis of the United Nations an international atomic energy agency and that the governments in a position to do so make contributions from their stockpiles of normal uranium and fissionable materials for peaceful uses, thereby dedicating their strength "to serve the needs rather than the fears of mankind." [18] This proposal was intended to shift emphasis from the destructive to the constructive and peaceful uses of atomic energy. The Soviet Union indicated that it was willing to consider this proposal but that it did not alter its position on issues raised in the course of the disarmament debate.

From 1953 to 1957 the disarmament discussions were largely carried on within the subcommittee, envisaged by the General Assembly's November resolution, consisting of the United States, the Soviet Union, the United Kingdom, France and Canada, and at meetings of and by communication between the foreign ministers and heads of states. Old issues were rehashed and new ones explored. At times it seemed that progress was being made in narrowing the differences between the Soviet Union and the Western Powers to the point where some agreement on at least limited disarmament would be possible. Repeatedly however

[18] See below, pp. 234–235.

this appearance turned out to be an illusion because of some change in the negotiating position of one side or the other. By the end of 1957, the deadlock seemed more complete than ever.

The first hopeful development during the period was Soviet acceptance of a joint Anglo-French proposal of June 11, 1954,[19] as a basis for discussion. This proposal provided for a phased disarmament program after the constitution and functioning of an international control organ, the major phases being, first, the over-all limitation of military manpower and expenditures; second, the reduction by one-half of the agreed amounts of conventional armaments and armed forces followed by the prohibition of the manufacture of all kinds of atomic weapons; and third, the remaining reduction of conventional armaments and weapons followed by the total prohibition and elimination of all nuclear weapons and the conversion of existing stocks. Discussions in the Subcommittee developed compromise suggestions for reconciling the Soviet and Anglo-French positions. In March, 1955, the Anglo-French proposals were revised further and presented as a common position of the four Western powers.[20]

But already new developments were in progress which were to result in changed national positions, partly favorable, but as it appeared in the end, more unfavorable to agreement. Though during the early months of 1955 the Soviet leaders were emphasizing the merits of "peaceful coexistence," they made no attempt to conceal their displeasure over the admission of West Germany to full partnership in NATO, which took place on May 9. In March, 1955, the United States undertook a reappraisal of its disarmament policies in the light of general recognition that no method of inspection known to science could detect with any degree of certainty the existence of stockpiled atomic weapons.

On May 10, the Soviet Union submitted new proposals.[21] It accepted the Western position on the timing of the complete prohibition of atomic weapons and it abandoned its insistence on a one-third reduction of conventional armaments. It recognized possibilities of clandestine possession and manufacture of atomic weapons for a surprise attack, and the need of a permanent control organ to inspect and take positions to guard against such an attack. It insisted, however, on the liquidation of military, naval, and air bases in other states and by proposing to freeze armed forces and conventional armaments at the levels of December 31, 1954, it obviously sought to prevent a German

[19] U.N. Document DC/SC.1/10, June 11, 1954.
[20] U.N. Doc. DC/SC.1/15/Rev. 1, March 8, 1955.
[21] U.N. Doc. DC/SC.1/26/Rev. 2, pp. 9–22.

military contribution to NATO. The Soviet proposals also called for the inclusion of Communist China in any talks concerning the limitation of China's armaments.

At the Geneva Conference in July, President Eisenhower countered with his "open skies" and exchange-of-blueprints proposal.[22] This was presented as a step to build confidence between the two major rivals. It was addressed particularly to the problem of surprise attack which the United States policy makers had now come to believe was the principal danger to be guarded against. The "open skies" plan, as later elaborated on August 30,[23] provided for a stage-by-stage exchange of blueprints, inspection by permanent, on-the-spot observers, and iron-clad agreement under which each would submit to the other's unrestricted aerial reconnaissance. Subsequently on March 1, 1956, in a letter to Premier Bulganin, President Eisenhower stated that the United States would be prepared to work out "suitable and safeguarded arrangements so that future production of fissionable materials anywhere in the world would no longer be used to increase the stockpiles of atomic weapons." [24] The exchange of correspondence between President Eisenhower and Prime Minister Bulganin seemed for a time to indicate that their positions were becoming closer, but in May, Soviet spokesmen denounced the "open skies" proposal as in the interest of "intelligence services" and not likely to contribute to disarmament or mutual confidence.

In its tenth session, the General Assembly, over the objections of the members of the Soviet bloc, urged the Disarmament Commission's Subcommittee to continue negotiations and to give priority to confidence-building measures such as Eisenhower's "open skies" proposals and the Soviet proposal for ground inspection posts. It also suggested to the Subcommittee that it consider an Indian proposal for the suspension of nuclear test explosions.[25]

In the discussions in the Subcommittee in London from March 19 to May 4, 1956, there was a full presentation and discussion of the revised proposals of the two sides, and while some progress seemed to have been made in developing areas of agreement, their positions remained unreconciled. The Western Powers insisted on certain conditions: (1) Disarmament must proceed by stages, with progress from one stage to another depending upon the satisfactory completion of the preceding stage and upon the development of confidence through progress in the settlement of major political problems. (2) Under

[22] U.N. Doc. DC/SC.1/28.   [23] U.N. Doc. DC/SC.1/31.
[24] *The New York Times,* March 7, 1956.
[25] General Assembly Resolution 914 (X), Dec. 16, 1955.

proper safeguards provision must be made for stopping the build-up of stockpiles of nuclear weapons and devoting all future production to peaceful uses. (3) The program must provide for a strong central control organization with inspection rights, including aerial reconnaissance and for preliminary trial of inspection methods on a limited scale to test their effectiveness. (4) The program must provide for adequate safeguards if a major state fails to carry out its obligations.[26] The Soviet Union, on the other hand, indicated that it stood by its proposals of May 10, 1956. Since it had not been possible to reach agreement on nuclear disarmament, it proposed that agreement should be reached on the reduction of conventional armaments and the necessary controls, without such agreement being made conditional on an agreement for the prohibition of atomic weapons. It proposed that the limitation and reduction of conventional armaments should be applied to all countries, and that there should be created in Europe "a zone of limitation and inspection of armaments" composed of Germany and adjacent states, in which foreign troops would be limited and atomic weapons would be banned. Independent of agreement on disarmament, the Soviet Union proposed the discontinuance of hydrogen bomb tests and the banning of atomic weapons in Germany.[27]

The Disarmament Commission met in July, 1956, but was unable to resolve the issues that had prevented agreement in the Subcommittee. Nor was the General Assembly in its eleventh session any more successful. It adopted a resolution requesting the Disarmament Commission to convene the Subcommittee at an early date and recommending that these bodies consider various proposals that had been submitted and the views expressed in the Assembly discussions.[28]

When the Subcommittee again met in London in March, 1957, the talks took a new and encouraging turn when both sides agreed to discuss the problem of disarmament subject by subject rather than in terms of comprehensive plans. Suggestions that the use of nuclear weapons be partially restricted and that nuclear tests be temporarily prohibited were discussed. The Western Powers pressed for the Soviet views on a partial disarmament agreement. On April 30, the Soviet Union responded with proposals for partial disarmament covering both nuclear and conventional weapons. Three points in particular appeared to impress the Western Powers: (1) acceptance of broader zones of aerial inspection; (2) abandonment of the demand for the elimination of nuclear weapons; and (3) modification of measures for arms limita-

[26] See *United Nations Review*, Vol. 2, No. 12 (June 1956), p. 15.
[27] U.N. Document DC/83, Annex 5.
[28] General Assembly Resolution 1011 (XI), Feb. 14, 1957.

tion in Europe. The initial favorable reaction to Soviet proposals resulted in a re-examination of United States policy, culminating in decisions of the National Security Council on May 25, and consultations among NATO members, in order to get agreement on a joint Western proposal. In the meantime, the Soviet delegation, on June 14, proposed that a temporary suspension of tests be implemented separately for two or three years under international control.

On August 21, the United States, in agreement with its Western allies, informed the Subcommittee of its willingness to include the suspension of testing of atomic weapons as part of a first-step disarmament agreement, provided the Soviet Union agreed to a permanent cessation of production of fissionable materials for weapons purposes and the installation of an inspection system to insure performance within that period.[29] On August 29, the Western powers presented their complete partial disarmament plan.[30] The Western proposals were rejected by the Soviet delegation and the Subcommittee recessed on September 6.

While the Western plan made some concessions to the declared Soviet position, it contained certain provisions that were highly unpalatable to the U.S.S.R. It made the limitation and reduction of armed forces and armaments beyond the initial stage dependent on progress toward the solution of political questions; it tied the suspension of testing of atomic weapons to cessation of production of atomic materials for war purposes and an effective inspection system; it made no specific provision for the limitation of German armaments. And it specifically provided for the study of measures to control the sending of objects through outer space, at a time when the Soviet Union seemed confident of having achieved a leadership in that field which would counterbalance the leadership of the Western powers in capacity to deliver nuclear bombs by aircraft. Furthermore, the fact that the plan had been prepared after consultation among the NATO allies, including Western Germany, and had received their approval did not make it more palatable.

The abrupt termination of the discussions in the Subcommittee did not bode well for further discussions in the United Nations. When the General Assembly got around to its annual consideration of the disarmament question, it had before it a proposal of the Western Powers which carried approval of the position they had taken in their August 29 paper. After heated debate, centering particularly on Soviet insistence on an immediate end to the testing of nuclear weapons to be

[29] Department of State, *Bulletin,* XXXVII (1957), pp. 418–19.
[30] *Ibid.,* pp. 451–55.

followed by a general disarmament agreement, the Twelfth General Assembly approved the Western-sponsored proposal. By its resolution of November 14 it urged that the governments give priority to an agreement which, on its entry into force, would provide for the following:

(*a*) *The immediate suspension of testing of nuclear weapons with prompt installation of effective international control, including inspection posts . . . ;*

(*b*) *The cessation of the production of fissionable materials for weapons purposes . . . ;*

(*c*) *The reduction of stocks of nuclear weapons through a program of transfer . . . of fissionable material from weapons uses to nonweapons uses;*

(*d*) *The reduction of armed forces and armaments through adequate, safeguarded arrangements;*

(*e*) *The progressive establishment of open inspection with ground and aerial components to guard against the possibility of surprise attack;*

(*f*) *The joint study of an inspection system designed to ensure that the sending of objects through outer space shall be exclusively for peaceful and scientific purposes.*[31]

The resolution was opposed by the Soviet delegate who criticized it for failing to incorporate the Soviet Union's major suggestion, namely substantial reduction of armaments and armed forces and complete prohibition of atomic and hydrogen weapons. He repeated a number of Soviet proposals for minimum initial disarmament measures: (1) reduction of the armed forces of the U.S.S.R. and the U.S. to 1.7 million men each and of the United Kingdom and France to 650,000 men each; (2) agreement that states forego the use of nuclear and hydrogen weapons for two to three years, with all the necessary controls being instituted; and (3) reduction in the number of military bases in foreign countries and a reduction of Soviet, American, and French armed forces in Germany and in countries associated in NATO and the Warsaw Treaties.[32]

In the course of the Assembly debates, the delegate of the Soviet Union observed that "the history of the negotiations on disarmament in the Disarmament Commission and its Sub-Committee reveals the

[31] General Assembly Resolution 1148 (XII), Nov. 14, 1957.
[32] See General Assembly, *Official Records,* Twelfth Session, Plenary, 715th Meeting (Nov. 13, 1957).

complete bankruptcy of these bodies in their present form," [33] and announced that his country would no longer participate in the meetings of these organs as then constituted. According to the U.S.S.R., one of the basic reasons for the failure of the disarmament negotiations was that the great majority of United Nations Members were precluded from participation in them. It therefore proposed enlarging the Commission to include all Members of the United Nations. The Assembly, however, rejected this proposal. Instead, it passed a resolution [34] enlarging the Disarmament Commission by the addition of fourteen Member states, bringing membership in the Commission to twenty-five. During 1958–1959, Argentina, Australia, Belgium, Brazil, Burma, Czechoslovakia, Egypt, India, Italy, Mexico, Norway, Poland, Tunisia, and Yugoslavia were to be the new members. The Soviet Union found this compromise unacceptable and reaffirmed its intention no longer to participate in the work of the Commission.

As a result, discussion of the disarmament question at the twelfth session of the Assembly seemed to end in a discouraging impasse. No disarmament agreement had been concluded and differences between the Western powers and the U.S.S.R. had not been substantially narrowed. Future negotiations in the Disarmament Commission and its Sub-Committee appeared uncertain. Soviet appeals for a top-level meeting of heads of government of the major powers, outside of the United Nations, where disarmament might be discussed were received skeptically by the Western powers. The United States, in particular, maintained that such a meeting would not yield favorable results unless a minimum basis for discussion was agreed upon prior to a conference.

Atoms for Peace

The deadlock that had developed up to the end of 1953 over the international control of atomic weapons and the desire to introduce a fresh approach and a more hopeful and constructive note induced President Eisenhower in December of that year to present to the General Assembly his "atoms for peace" proposal.[35] In his address to the General Assembly President Eisenhower emphasized the importance of a more constructive and positive approach to the problem of atomic

[33] General Assembly, *Official Records,* Twelfth Session, Plenary, 718th Meeting (Nov. 19, 1957), p. 469.

[34] General Assembly Resolution 1150 (XII), Nov. 19, 1957.

[35] General Assembly, *Official Records,* Eighth Session, Plenary, 470th Meeting, (Dec. 8, 1953), pp. 450–52.

energy. In addition to seeking to reduce or prevent the use of atomic energy for military purposes, it was necessary to explore new ways of devoting the atom to peaceful uses. He specifically proposed that an International Atomic Energy Agency be created; that Governments "principally involved" make contributions from their stockpiles of normal uranium and fissionable materials to this Agency, that the Agency be made responsible for the impounding, storage, and protection of this material, and that the Agency devise methods whereby this fissionable material would be allocated to serve the peaceful pursuits of mankind. One purpose of the President's proposal was to "open up a new plan for peaceful discussion, and initiate at least a new approach to the many difficult problems that must be solved in both private and public conversation, if the world is to shake off the inertia imposed by fear, and is to make positive progress toward peace."

In the months following President Eisenhower's proposal, an eight-nation group, consisting of countries which had developed resources of nuclear raw materials or advanced atomic energy programs, prepared the first draft of a statute for the proposed agency.[36] At the ninth session of the General Assembly, in 1954, a resolution was unanimously adopted expressing the hope that such an agency would be established without delay and deciding that an international technical conference on the peaceful uses of atomic energy should be held under the auspices of the United Nations. This conference met in Geneva in August, 1955, and was a great success. Seventy-three states and eight specialized agencies were represented.[37]

In August, 1955, the draft statute was circulated to all members of the United Nations and the specialized agencies to get their views. The subject was again debated by the Tenth Assembly and a resolution endorsing the efforts of the negotiating group was unanimously adopted.[38] In response to the General Assembly's recommendation, the negotiating group was expanded to twelve nations, to include Brazil, Czechoslovakia, India, and the Soviet Union. The expanded group met in Washington in early 1956, and prepared a revised draft of the statute which was submitted in October to an international conference, consisting of all members of the United Nations and the specialized agencies. It was this conference which prepared and approved the Statute of the

[36] See Address by Secretary Dulles before the U.N. General Assembly on Sept. 23, 1954, Dept. of State, *Bulletin,* XXXI (1954), pp. 471–77.

[37] General Assembly, *Official Records,* Tenth Session, Annexes, Agenda Item 18 (1955); also, *Official Records,* First Committee, 757th–782nd Meetings (Oct. 7–Nov. 7, 1955).

[38] General Assembly Resolution 912 (X), Dec. 3, 1955.

International Atomic Energy Agency.[39] The Statute was signed on October 26 by the representatives of seventy governments, and entered into force on July 29, 1957.

The Statute provides for an International Atomic Energy Agency with a wide range of functions bearing on the peaceful use of atomic energy.[40] These functions include: the encouragement of research and the exchange of scientific information; the establishment and administration of safeguards to prevent misuse of atomic materials and to protect health; the maintenance or provision of necessary facilities, services, and equipment; and the establishment of controls over the use of such materials. The Agency is so constituted as to give the greater influence to those states which are sources of atomic materials or which have the most highly developed technology, the atomic "haves." Provision is made, however, for taking into account the interests of receiving nations, the "have nots." No obligation is placed upon members to contribute fissionable materials to the Agency, although such action is definitely encouraged. When such materials are contributed, the Agency has a responsibility for determining the conditions under which these materials are to be used by recipient states. In particular the Agency has the responsibility for determining standards which are to be applied to prevent diversion to military use and to safeguard health. The Agency is also authorized to establish a system of inspection and control.

Directing the Agency's affairs are a General Conference meeting in annual session and representing all members, and a Board of Governors consisting of "the five members most advanced in the technology of atomic energy" plus not more than twenty members chosen on the basis of criteria and by procedures set forth in the Statute. Thirteen members of the Board, including "the five members most advanced in the technology of atomic energy" were designated by the Agency's Preparatory Commission: Australia, Brazil, Canada, Czechoslovakia, France, India, Japan, Portugal, Sweden, the Union of South Africa, U.S.S.R., the United Kingdom, and the United States. At the first meeting of the General Conference which was held in Vienna, October 1–23, 1957, with fifty-four members represented, ten additional members of the Board of Governors—Argentina, Italy, Romania, Egypt, Pakistan, Indonesia, the Republic of Korea, Guatemala, Peru, and Turkey—were named. Sterling Cole of the United States was elected as the Agency's first Director-General. The Conference also approved

---

[39] For text, see Department of State, *Bulletin,* XII (1956), pp. 820–28.

[40] For an analysis of the provisions of the Statute, see Bernard G. Beckhoefer and Eric Stein, "Atoms for Peace: The New International Atomic Energy Agency," *Michigan Law Review,* LV, No. 6 (April, 1957), pp. 747–98.

basic arrangements for the effective functioning of the Agency, including the definition of the IAEA's relation to the United Nations, budget and financial provisions, staff regulations, preliminary outlines of programs, and the establishment of the permanent headquarters.

It is not expected that the Agency will supplant bilateral arrangements for making fissionable material available for peaceful uses. It is anticipated, however, that many states will prefer to receive grants from the Agency under its terms, rather than from single states under bilateral arrangements. Nor is it at all anticipated that the Agency will to any great extent prevent the use of fissionable material for military purposes. Members which are in the position to meet their own needs for fissionable material are free to use it for military purposes if they so desire. Nevertheless, the Agency is based on the hope that its successful operation will result in the increasing use of fissionable material for peaceful purposes, and that in the course of cooperating to this end, governments will become accustomed to Agency standards and methods for preventing military use and will subsequently be more willing to accept an international system of control and inspection which will apply to all fissionable material and will prevent further diversion of this important resource to military ends. Certainly, the disarmament negotiations to date and the policies being followed by the principal atomic powers in the Agency do not provide any ground for believing that this result will be achieved in the near future.

The United Nations and Disarmament: An Appraisal

The record of the United Nations in dealing with the disarmament problem, including the question of the international control of atomic energy, provides little encouragement for the "direct" approach to the problem. This experience would seem to confirm the lesson of earlier attempts, that until nations have made some progress in settling their other differences or have openly or tacitly agreed, with confidence in each other's good faith and intentions, to renounce the use of force in settling their differences, the chances of reaching an agreement on the limitation or reduction of armaments are very poor. Those who were responsible for writing the Charter seem to have accepted this lesson, and to have consigned disarmament to a subordinate position in constructing an effective system of international peace and security. They recognized that it was first necessary to provide dependable assurances that threats to the peace and breaches of the peace would be effectively dealt with by collective measures and that disputes and other conflict situations would be settled or adjusted by peaceful means before a general system of armament limitation and reduction would be possible.

Unfortunately, the atomic bomb and the "cold war" upset the Charter program. The first made it appear a matter of urgency to bring under control a particular weapon because of its destructiveness and the second made it impossible to keep the discussions within these narrow limits. And so we have witnessed the same exercises in seeming futility that characterized the discussions of the League of Nations, where from the beginning it was assumed that disarmament was one of the three major pillars of any peace structure.

As soon as the disarmament discussions got under way within the context of postwar international relations—the "cold war," divided Germany, Communist control of Eastern Europe, Communist aggression in Korea, confusion in the Middle East, opposing armed camps— it was clear that neither major power would agree to any terms that did not safeguard its strategic position. Every proposal, every position on a proposal made by another, was carefully calculated on the basis of how this would effect the security and power position of the state in question.

The situation is illustrated by an exchange which took place in the course of a hearing before the Subcommittee on Disarmament of the Senate Foreign Relations Committee on March 6, 1948. Senator Pastore, in questioning Mr. Libby of the Atomic Energy Commission, observed

> . . . *if you stop all production of fissionable material, and if you stopped all testing—let's assume that you could do it effectively, I am not getting into that at all, but let's assume that you could— wouldn't it be advantageous to us to enter into such an agreement if we were ahead? If we were ahead in our arsenal of bombs, nuclear and thermonuclear, as against the Russians, if you stalemated it now, wouldn't we be in a better position than they would?* [41]

If this is the kind of reasoning that is applied on both sides, if the questions that are asked are: "How will this proposal effect the relative strength of our country vis-a-vis its potential enemy? How will it affect its negotiating position in getting a major outstanding problem settled on advantageous terms?", it becomes obvious that unless some one makes a serious miscalculation, or unless there are compensating advantages offered in the form of greater security or the settlement of an outstanding

[41] *Control and Reduction of Armaments.* Hearing before a Subcommittee of the Committee on Foreign Relations, U.S. Senate, 85th Congress, 2nd session, part 15, March 6, 1958, pp. 1374–75.

political issue on favorable terms, a proposal for armament limitation which is favorable to one side is not likely to be acceptable to the other.

One should not, however, be wholly negative and pessimistic regarding the value of disarmament discussions and the possibility of getting some useful agreement. Past experience suggests that even countries that regard themselves as potential enemies may find that it is to their advantage to agree on some measures of limitation. If for example a particular method of warfare is widely regarded as inhumane and unnecessarily destructive and injurious in its effects, and if the military value of the method is open to some doubt, there may be a common interest in prohibiting it, as has happened in the past in the case of poisonous gas. And it is possible, now that the United States and the Soviet Union have entered into a period of atomic deadlock and would gain no relative advantage in adding to their present capacity to destroy each other, that they might be willing to agree to forego the cost of further additions to their stockpiles. There are obvious difficulties, however, in writing that kind of an agreement.

There is also the common interest which the two principal atomic powers have in preventing the membership in the club from becoming too large. Nevertheless, the fact that each depends on allies for support in meeting the threat of the other, makes it difficult for either to enter into this kind of an agreement. Thus, the United States, even though it recognizes the inconvenience, if not the danger of having atomic weapons in too many hands, is reluctant to deny to its friends the right to develop and test them.

The fact that disarmament discussions alone are not likely to be very productive does not mean that disarmament discussions when combined with the exploration of outstanding political differences may not result in progress both in limiting armaments and in improving political relations. Political differences between major powers do not have to be resolved before disarmament is possible, but at least some progress has to be made on the two fronts concurrently. Specific disarmament proposals may be very closely related to political issues, as for example the Soviet suggestion of a denuclearized zone in Central Europe and the German problem. Though the Western Powers have in their proposals placed greater specific emphasis on the settlement of political problems than the Soviet Union, the real difference has been regarding the terms of settlement. The Soviet Union wants Western acceptance of the *status quo* in Central Europe while the Western Powers want German unity on their terms and the liberalization of Eastern European regimes.

What then is the role of the United Nations? While the Security

Council and the General Assembly have definite responsibilities under the Charter for achieving the regulation of national armaments, it does not necessarily follow that the problem of disarmament with all its political involvements is one that should be handled wholly through United Nations procedures. The problem is so intimately intertwined with problems of great power relations and peace-making which the major victors in the Second World War have thus far been unable to resolve, that it would seem consistent with the general theory of the United Nations that these powers themselves must come to some agreements before the United Nations organs can discharge their responsibilities. Whether this can best be done through normal diplomatic channels, foreign ministers meetings or summit conferences is a matter of judgment. But in any case it would seem that unless the major powers are able to come to some agreement among themselves there is little hope that the United Nations will be able to break the disarmament deadlock.

SUGGESTED READINGS

Atomic Energy—Its International Implications. A Discussion by a Chatham House Study Group. London and New York: Royal Institute of International Affairs, 1948.

Beckhoefer, Bernard G. and Stein, Eric. "Atoms for Peace: the New International Atomic Energy Agency," *Michigan Law Review, LV* (1957), pp. 747–98.

Bernard, Stephen. "Some Political and Technical Implications of Disarmament," *World Politics,* VIII (1955), pp. 71–90.

Brodie, Bernard, ed. *The Absolute Weapon. Atomic Power and World Order.* New York: Harcourt Brace and Company, 1946.

Claude, Inis, Jr. *Swords into Plowshares.* New York: Random House, Inc., 1956. Chap. 13.

Goodrich, Leland M. and Simons, Anne P. *The United Nations and the Maintenance of International Peace and Security.* Washington: The Brookings Institution, 1955. Part V.

International Control of Atomic Energy: Growth of a Policy. Department of State Publication 2702. Washington: Government Printing Office, n.d. (1946?).

Kissinger, Henry A. *Nuclear Weapons and Foreign Policy.* New York: Harper & Brothers, Publishers, 1957.

Madariaga, Salvador de. *Disarmament.* New York: Coward-McCann, Inc., 1929.

Melman, Sepmour (ed.). *Inspection for Disarmament.* New York: Columbia University Press, 1958.

U.S. Senate Committee on Foreign Relations, Subcommittee on Disarmament. *Control and Reduction of Armaments: A Decade of Negotiations, 1945–1956.* Staff Study No. 3. Washington: Government Printing Office, 1956.

Chapter XI

THE PROTECTION OF
HUMAN RIGHTS

ONE OF THE major concerns of the United Nations [1] has been
to promote and encourage "respect for human rights and for fundamental freedoms for all without distinction as to race, sex, language or
religion." [2] This has distinguished it from the League of Nations which
preceded it, and generally from past efforts at international cooperation
to further international peace and promote human welfare. The Charter
reflects a new approach to human liberty and freedom born of the
experience of the Second World War and the years immediately preceding it, when flagrant violations of human rights and the denial of the
basic dignity of man were the hallmarks of regimes challenging and
violating international peace and security. This approach is a denial of
the proposition that the way in which a state treats its nationals is of no
concern to the outside world and therefore beyond the proper scope of
activity of international agencies.

Human Rights and the Charter

Under customary international law as it had developed and was
practiced before the establishment of the League of Nations, except as
some special provision had been made by an international agreement,
states were wholly free to determine the rights which their citizens
should enjoy within their territories, and how those rights should be
implemented. In some of the older democracies, the principle that the

[1] For a good review of United Nations activity, see James F. Green, *The
United Nations and Human Rights* (Washington: The Brookings Institution,
1956).
[2] Article I, par. 3 of the Charter.

242

individual had certain rights which his government must respect was fully accepted, and a body of domestic law had been developed by constitutional enactment, by legislation, and by decisions of the courts and administrative agencies for giving effect to this principle. In many instances the constitutions of these states contained formal enumerations of certain basic rights enjoyed by the individual, as for example the first ten amendments of the Constitution of the United States.

Notwithstanding, so far as international law was concerned, in each of these states the individual national had to look to the laws and governmental agencies of his state for protection and redress. If he felt that he had been denied a legal right, he could only appeal to the appropriate agencies—administrative or judicial—of his own government. If his appeal was denied there was nothing more that he could do about it. Nor would any foreign government normally have any interest in his case, or if it did, any legal basis for intervening in his behalf. Nor would any international agency be able to take up his claim.

If the person in question were the national of a foreign state, his situation would be different. In case he was denied the internationally accepted minimum of justice, his government could intervene, and if it was sufficiently influential, it might succeed in getting his claim respected or at least submitted to an international claims commission where the question whether he had been denied justice would be decided. It was only, then, in the case of the national of one country present in the territory of another that international law recognized an international standard of treatment for the individual, and in this situation whether the individual was actually accorded that treatment depended on whether his state decided to take the matter up diplomatically and whether its power and influence were sufficiently great to convince the other state that something should be done to give satisfaction to the claim.

At the conclusion of the First World War, an important step was taken in the direction of providing international protection for individuals in the enjoyment of rights against violation by their own governments. The qualified application of the principle of self-determination in the drawing of new state boundaries radically reduced the number and size of national minorities in Europe, but it by no means eliminated them. This would have been impossible without large-scale population transfers and exchanges. To improve the lot of the national minorities that remained, a number of states were required to accept special minority regimes, which guaranteed to individuals belonging to religious, linguistic or cultural minorities certain political and civil rights. The states which accepted such regimes were legally bound to carry out the terms. Furthermore the minority treaties or declarations required that these provisions be made part of the fundamental law of each state. Finally, in case of alleged violation, a procedure was provided by which appeal could be made to the League Council which was made responsible for seeing that rights conferred by the minority treaties and declarations were respected.[3]

While the special minority regimes did provide international protection for certain especially vulnerable groups which would have been left by customary international law completely at the mercy of the states in whose territory they found themselves, they did not prove to be very effective or satisfactory. For one thing they were basically discriminatory since they applied only to states that had been defeated in the war, that had come into existence by virtue of the peace treaties, or that had acquired additional territory as the result thereof. There were many states with national minorities that were not forced to accept special minority regimes. Furthermore the special protection for minorities as such had the effect of encouraging these groups to maintain their resistance to political integration and to remain discontented and rebellious minorities, lending encouragement to active irredentist movements in neighboring states. Also, it was clear, with the coming into power of the Nazis in Germany, that the minority treaties provided no adequate protection against the kind of racial intolerance and persecution that was characteristic of that regime.

The excesses of the Hitler regime in Germany, associated as they were not only with domestic cruelty and lawlessness but also with external aggression and ruthlessness, convinced many people that human rights and fundamental freedoms generally were matters with which the world must be concerned—if international peace, security, and justice were to be achieved. President Roosevelt expressed this point of view when, in his annual message to Congress on January 6, 1941, he said that ". . . in the future days, which we seek to make secure, we look forward to a world grounded upon four essential human freedoms . . . freedom of speech and expression . . . , freedom of every person to worship God in his own way . . . , freedom from want . . . , and freedom from fear." [4] These freedoms were given general endorsement in the Declaration by United Nations of January 1, 1942, and thus became war aims of the coalition of nations joined in war against the Axis powers.

[3] See P. de Azcarate, *League of Nations and National Minorities: An Experiment* (Washington: Carnegie Endowment for International Peace, 1945).

[4] For the text of the Roosevelt address to Congress, see *Documents on American Foreign Relations, 1940–1941* (Boston: World Peace Foundation, 1941), pp. 26–34.

It is significant that these freedoms went considerably beyond the traditional view of individual rights even as conceived within the context of national law. Though freedom of speech and freedom of religious worship were among the rights customarily guaranteed by law in Western democracies, freedom from fear and freedom from want were social objectives that required legislative and administrative action for their achievement. President Roosevelt in his message to Congress on January 11, 1944,[5] developed in greater detail what he had in mind and in so doing undertook an enumeration of social and economic rights which could only be implemented by legislative and administrative process over a period of considerable time. Included in his list were ". . . the right to a useful and remunerative job in the industries, or shops, or farms, or mines of the Nation . . . , the right to earn enough to provide adequate food and clothing and recreation . . . , the right to adequate medical care and the opportunity to achieve and enjoy good health . . . , and the right to adequate protection from the economic fears of old age, sickness, accident, and unemployment." President Roosevelt thus emphasized the need of being concerned in the making of the brave new world not only with traditional human rights but also with social and economic rights—human rights conceived in a much larger context than in the past.

In the preliminary discussions on the drafting of a Charter for a new international organization to take the place of the League, little attention was given to the matter of human rights. The Dumbarton Oaks Proposals contained only a brief reference to the promotion of human rights as one of the activities to be performed by the proposed General Assembly, and, under its authority, the Economic and Social Council. This was not surprising since under the impact of the war the major interest of officials in responsible positions was in winning the war and in creating an international organization which would be effective in maintaining international peace and security once the war was won. Naturally under these conditions the emphasis was on making international police action effective.

At the San Francisco Conference many delegations of participating states, as well as representatives of private organizations, argued for the inclusion of more detailed provisions regarding human rights. As a result of these pressures a number of amendments to the Dumbarton Oaks Proposals were adopted which had the common purpose of making more specific the responsibilities and powers of the Organization with respect to human rights and fundamental freedoms, and providing the necessary machinery for discharging these responsibilities. When finally approved, the Charter of the United Nations, in sharp contrast

[5] For the text, see House Doc. 377, 78th Congress (1944).

to the Covenant of the League of Nations, contained many specific provisions with respect to the obligations of Members, the responsibilities and powers of the Organization, and the machinery and procedures which were to be used in promoting respect for human rights and fundamental freedoms.

In the preamble to the Charter there is a re-affirmation of faith ". . . in fundamental human rights, in the dignity and worth of the human person, in the equal rights of men and women and of nations large and small." Article 1 declares one of the purposes of the Organization to be the achievement of ". . . international cooperation . . . in promoting and encouraging respect for human rights and for fundamental freedoms for all without distinction as to race, sex, language, or religion." Article 55 provides that ". . . the United Nations shall promote . . . universal respect for, and observance of, human rights and fundamental freedoms for all without distinction as to race, sex, language, or religion," and by the terms of Article 56, ". . . all Members pledge themselves to take joint and separate action in cooperation with the Organization . . ." for the achievement of this purpose, along with others set forth in Article 55.

By the terms of Article 13, the General Assembly ". . . shall initiate studies and make recommendations for the purpose of . . . assisting in the realization of human rights and fundamental freedoms for all without distinction as to race, sex, language, or religion." Article 62 authorizes the Economic and Social Council to ". . . make recommendations for the purpose of promoting respect for, and observance of, human rights and fundamental freedoms for all . . ." and Article 68 directs the Council to establish a commission ". . . for the promotion of human rights . . ." to assist it in the performance of its functions. Finally, under Article 76, one of the basic objectives of the trusteeship system is ". . . to encourage respect for human rights and for fundamental freedoms for all without distinction as to race, sex, language, or religion, and to encourage recognition of the interdependence of the peoples of the world."

It is to be noted, however, that nowhere in the Charter is the phrase "human rights and fundamental freedoms" defined. Some delegations at San Francisco desired such a definition but recognized that time did not permit attempting it. Furthermore, it is to be noted that while there are repetitive enumerations of United Nations purposes and functions, the key words are "promoting," "encouraging," and "assisting in the realization of," not "protecting," "safeguarding," and "guaranteeing."

The general philosophy of the authors of the Charter with respect

to the importance of the provision regarding human rights and fundamental freedoms was well stated in the report of the Secretary of State
to the President on the work of the San Francisco Conference. Com-
menting on the general significance of these provisions, he observed

> *Finally, no sure foundation of lasting peace and security can be
> laid which does not rest on the voluntary association of free
> peoples. Only so far as the rights and dignity of all men are
> respected and protected, only so far as men have free access to
> information, assurance of free speech and free assembly, freedom
> from discrimination on grounds of race, sex, language, or religion
> and other fundamental rights and freedoms, will men insist upon
> the right to live at peace, to compose such differences as they may
> have by peaceful methods, and to be guided by reason and good
> will rather than driven by prejudice and resentment.*[6]

The Universal Declaration of Human Rights

While the San Francisco Conference did not undertake to define
the human rights and fundamental freedoms respect for which was to
be promoted by the Organization, it tacitly recognized that this must be
one of the initial tasks of the United Nations. At its first session in
February 1946, the Economic and Social Council established the Commission on Human Rights, and decided that its work should be directed
towards submitting proposals and reports regarding:

(a) *an international bill of rights;*

(b) *international declarations or conventions on civil liberties,
the status of women, freedom of information, and similar matters;*

(c) *the protection of minorities;*

(d) *the prevention of discrimination on grounds of race, sex,
language or religion.*[7]

The Commission held its first session in January and February,
1947. A difference of opinion soon developed as to the exact nature
of the end product which should be prepared. The United States favored
a declaration that would set forth goals and aspirations rather than

[6] *Charter of the United Nations, Report to the President on the Results of the
San Francisco Conference by . . . the Secretary of State, June 26, 1945* (Department of State Publication 2349), p. 116.

[7] Economic and Social Council, *Official Records,* First Year, First Session
(1946), Annexes, p. 148.

legally binding commitments. This position was in part due to reluctance to embark upon the treaty process because of the requirement of Senate approval. The United Kingdom, on the other hand, was skeptical of the value of a declaration of general goals and preferred a treaty which would contain detailed and precise provisions and would legally bind all states accepting it. It was finally decided that both approaches should be adopted, and that two major documents should be prepared, one a declaration of general principles in the tradition of the French Declaration of the Rights of Man, and the other a covenant of binding obligations in the tradition of the English Bill of Rights.

In spite of obvious difficulties in the way of getting a general agreement on the definition of basic human rights and fundamental freedoms, the Commission was able within a comparatively short time to prepare a draft declaration of general principles. It had the benefit of various drafts prepared by Member States and the Secretariat, and the American Declaration of the Rights and Duties of Man adopted by the Bogotà Conference of American States in May, 1948.[8] The American Declaration was based on an earlier draft prepared by the Inter-American Juridical Committee at the request of the Mexico City Conference of early 1945. This Declaration had constituted the first intergovernmental statement of human rights in history.[9]

The task of the Commission in the preparation of the draft declaration was facilitated not only by the texts which were at its disposal but also by the fact that the purpose of the document was to define goals to be achieved and not legal obligations to be respected. Representatives of states with different cultural backgrounds, political and legal systems, and ideologies found it much easier to agree on general principles and goals which left considerable latitude of interpretation and application than upon binding commitments against which they must seriously and immediately measure their own national laws and practices. In fact, the Commission was able to finish its work by June 10, 1948. The draft was approved by the Economic and Social Council, and adopted by the General Assembly without a negative vote on December 10 of that year.[10]

The Declaration became operative upon approval by the General

[8] For the text, see *American Journal of International Law,* XLIII (1949), Suppl., pp. 133–39.

[9] For the text, see Ninth International Conference of American States, Bogotà, Columbia, March 30–May 2, 1948, *Final Act,* pp. 38–45.

[10] For the text, see U.N. General Assembly, *Official Records,* Third Session, First Part, "Resolutions," pp. 71–77.

Assembly. Since it was not a treaty and was not intended to impose legal obligations, it was not necessary to submit it to the Members for ratification in accordance with their various constitutional procedures. The opening paragraph of the Declaration clearly states the nature of the document and the purpose it was intended to serve. These are the words:

> *The General Assembly,*
>   *Proclaims this Universal Declaration of Human Rights as a common standard of achievement for all peoples and all nations, to the end that every individual and every organ of society, keeping this Declaration constantly in mind, shall strive by teaching and education to promote respect for these rights and freedoms and by progressive measures, national and international, to secure their universal and effective recognition and observance, both among the peoples of Member States themselves and among the peoples of territories under their jurisdiction.*

The Universal Declaration is all-inclusive in scope in the sense that it deals not only with civil and political rights, but with social and economic rights as well. Articles 1 and 2 are general in nature. They assert that ". . . all human beings are born free and equal in dignity and rights" and that everyone is entitled to ". . . all the rights and freedoms . . ." set forth in the Declaration, ". . . without distinction of any kind, such as race, color, sex, language, religion, political or other opinion, national or social origin, property, birth or other status." Furthermore, it is provided that no distinction is to be based on the international status of the country or territory to which the person belongs, thus making it clear that the Declaration applies to all non-self-governing territories.

Articles 2 to 21 inclusive deal with civil and political rights. The rights asserted are those that have been most widely recognized throughout the world, particularly in the countries of the West. Among the rights specified as belonging to every human being are the following: the right to life, liberty and security; the right to equal protection of the law; the right to a fair trial; the right to freedom of movement and residence within a country and to leave and return to it; the right to a nationality; the right to property; the right to freedom of thought, conscience and religion; the right to freedom of opinion and expression; the right to freedom of peaceful assembly and association; and the right to participate in the government of his country.

Articles 22 to 27 deal with social and economic rights. These are of a more novel nature, though they find precedents in the more recent national constitutions. They include the right to social security, the right to work under just and favorable conditions, the right to equal pay for equal work, the right to rest and leisure, the right to a standard of living adequate for health and well-being, the right to education and the right freely to participate in the cultural life of the community. Possibly the most novel provision of the Declaration is to be found in Article 28 which declares that ". . . everyone is entitled to a social and economic order in which the rights and freedoms set forth in this Declaration can be fully realized."

After the Assembly had adopted the Universal Declaration, the President (Evatt of Australia) declared that it had "the authority of the body of opinion of the United Nations as a whole, and millions of men, women and children all over the world, many miles from Paris and New York, will turn for help, guidance and inspiration to this document." [11] Undoubtedly the adoption of this Declaration without a dissenting vote was an impressive expression of a general consensus, and while the Declaration did not have the character of a treaty creating legal obligations for Members, it was bound to have a substantial influence on the subsequent discussions and decisions of the United Nations. It has been frequently referred to in resolutions of United Nations organs and its provisions have been many times invoked in United Nations discussions as defining the human rights and fundamental freedoms, respect for which it is the responsibility of the United Nations to promote. In a real sense, then, the hopes and fears that were expressed in the course of earlier discussions that the Declaration would have the effect of internationalizing, so to speak, questions which had hitherto been regarded as purely domestic, have been confirmed.

The Draft Covenants

Experience with the drafting of the Universal Declaration seemed to show that it was fairly easy to get nations to agree to a general declaration of human rights which would serve the purpose of a set of goals to be achieved by various means and a standard of achievement by which the progress of states might be measured. It was an entirely different matter to get Member states to agree to a treaty or treaties which would define these rights in legal language, impose upon the parties to them the obligation to conform, and provide means and procedures by which respect would be assured. Once the discussion started on the drafting of such a treaty, it was clear that the necessary consensus would not easily

[11] Quoted in U.N. Department of Social Affairs, *The Impact of the Universal Declaration of Human Rights.* Doc. ST/SOA/5/Rev. 1, June 29, 1953, p. 7.

be achieved if at all. Issues were raised which were not considered of particular importance so long as a declaration setting forth standards of achievement was being envisaged, but which became matters of deepest concern once the talk was of a legally binding treaty.

The first question to arise was whether there should be one or two treaties, or covenants as they came to be designated. The United States, the United Kingdom, and a number of other Western countries insisted that there should be a separate treaty for civil and political rights since these alone were capable of definition in legal terms and lent themselves to implementation by judicial procedures. Furthermore, the United States Government was concerned over the likelihood of Senate objection to a treaty guaranteeing economic and social rights and thought the chances of getting an agreement approved would be greater if it was limited to civil and political rights. These countries also pointed out that a treaty on economic and social rights would of necessity take the form of a commitment to legislative and administrative action and would therefore raise quite distinct problems of implementation. While strong objections were raised to separation, partly because of the fear that the likelihood of a covenant on economic and social rights would be jeopardized by it, the Assembly finally decided that there should be two covenants.

The attempt actually to define human rights and fundamental freedoms followed in general the pattern of the Universal Declaration though exact definition in treaty language proved difficult because of differences of cultural background, legal systems, ideology, and economic, social, and political conditions. In addition, some special difficulties were encountered. One of these related to the inclusion in each Covenant of a provision guaranteeing the right of self-determination. Although some Members argued strongly that this was not an individual right, and in any case should not be restricted, as was proposed, to non-self-governing territories, the majority of Members voted for its inclusion. This action alone constitutes a major obstacle to acceptance of the draft Covenants by a number of Western Members.

Another question on which there was strong disagreement related to inclusion of a provision in the draft Covenant on Civil and Political Rights requiring states to prohibit ". . . any advocacy of national, racial or religious hostility that constitutes an incitement to hatred and violence." The common law countries in particular objected to this provision because of the encouragement that it gave to censorship.

There was strong disagreement with regard to the scope of application of the Covenants. Generally speaking the Members with federal forms of government desired the inclusion of a clause taking account of the limited powers of the central government. It was argued that while the central government under a federal system was able to commit the state with respect to matters which lay within the federal competence, all it could be expected to do with respect to matters falling within the competence of the political subdivisions was to bring the provisions of the agreements to the attention of the appropriate constitutional authorities. Member states with centralized forms of government objected, however, that it would be unfair to subject some states to more extensive obligations than others, and in the end were victorious in their insistence that a clause be included providing that all provisions be extended to all parts of federal states without exception.

A closely related question was that of the extension of the provisions of the Covenant to non-self-governing territories. The Members administering such territories argued that they should be allowed some discretion in determining whether the provisions of the Covenant should be applied to these territories, but the view which finally prevailed allowed no exception to be made. This provision alone of the draft Covenants, rightly or wrongly, probably makes them unacceptable to some important Members of the United Nations.

With respect to the implementation of the proposed Covenants, a number of different views were expressed and proposals made. Three points of view in particular emerged in the course of discussions. One view, held by the United States, the United Kingdom, and a number of other states was that the implementation should be limited to the examination of complaints presented by states parties to the Covenants. A second view, supported particularly by Asian and Latin American Members, favored provision for petitions from individuals and non-governmental organizations. The Soviet Union was against specific provisions for implementation of any kind. The majority of Members, while believing that some provision for implementation was necessary, were unwilling to go beyond the use of inquiry and conciliation. The draft Covenant on Civil and Political Rights provides for the establishment of a Human Rights Committee to be composed of nine persons chosen by the International Court of Justice. If one party considers that another has violated any provision of the Covenant, the parties shall first negotiate, and if within six months the matter is not settled, either party may refer it to the Committee which is to investigate the facts, exercise its good offices, and report to the states concerned and to the Secretary-General for publication. A proposal of Australia that an International Court of Human Rights be established which might consider cases presented by states, individuals, or private organizations did not receive much support in the Commission. The Covenant on Economic, Social, and Cultural Rights provides for reports on progress made in achieving observance and for collaboration among the parties, the Economic and Social Council, and the specialized agencies in the preparation and consideration of these reports.

Though the Commission on Human Rights took the first steps in drafting a treaty on human rights even before the Assembly's approval of the Universal Declaration and concentrated its efforts on the task from 1949 on, the process has not yet been completed. The two draft Covenants on Civil and Political Rights and on Economic, Social, and Cultural Rights,[12] prepared by the Commission and transmitted to the General Assembly by the Economic and Social Council, have been discussed at great length but final Assembly action appears to be far distant. A decisive factor in the situation has been the reversal of United States policy, largely as the result of the opposition of many Senators to any treaty dealing with human rights. The present position of the United States appears to be that it will participate in discussions but will not be a party to any treaty or treaties.[13] This, taken together with the announced opposition of other important Members to specific provisions of the Covenants, gives a fairly strong indication that even though the draft Covenants are approved by the Assembly by the necessary majority votes, they are not likely to become operative, at least on a significant scale. In fact the past few years have witnessed a marked decline in interest in and enthusiasm for the Covenant method, and more attention to other approaches to the problem of assuring respect for human rights.

Other Ways of Fostering Respect

Even without the conclusion of international agreements defining the obligations of Members with respect to human rights and their implementation, there are many things which the United Nations has done and can do to further respect for human rights and fundamental freedoms. Even though the Charter is somewhat unclear with respect to the functions and powers of United Nations organs in taking remedial action with respect to actual complaints of violation, its provisions are sufficiently broad to permit the Organization to do a great variety of

[12] See U.N. Economic and Social Council, *Official Records,* Eighteenth Session, Suppl. No. 7, pp. 62–72.

[13] For the letter of April 3, 1953 from Secretary of State Dulles to Mrs. Oswald B. Lord, stating the new policy, and Mrs. Lord's statement before the Commission on Human Rights on April 8, see Department of State, *Bulletin,* XXVIII (1953), pp. 579–82.

things in addition to the drafting of covenants to further its objectives in this field.

One of the earliest and most clearly well-grounded activities of the United Nations was to compile and publish basic material about human rights in the *Yearbook on Human Rights,* the first issue of which was published in August, 1948. The volumes in this series contain constitutional and legislative texts on human rights, court decisions, laws and other texts dealing with human rights in non-self-governing and trust territories, provisions of international agreements and resolutions of international agencies on human rights, and accounts of the activities of the United Nations in the field. These volumes are invaluable for reference purposes, and provide the data upon which sound policy decisions, whether by international agencies or by national governments must be based.

While the United Nations cannot dictate to individual states the courses which they are to follow with respect to human rights, it can give its assistance to any state desiring and requesting it in the development of legal provisions and administrative and judicial practices. The United Nations technical assistance programs have directly or indirectly done much to improve the situation in many countries with respect to human rights. This contribution has taken a variety of forms, including assistance in the drafting of legal codes, in developing administrative procedures, and in creating conditions of well-being which assure the enjoyment of better standards of living and create an environment more favorable to the enjoyment of civil and political rights. When the United States Government revised its attitude toward adherence to covenants on human rights, its representative on the Commission on Human Rights proposed as an alternative that more attention should be given to technical assistance as an approach to the problem.

Less ambitious than the drafting of a comprehensive covenant or covenants covering the whole field of human rights is the study of special aspects of the problem and the drafting of appropriate proposals for dealing with them. A number of these special aspects have thus been taken up by the United Nations with varying degrees of success. A great deal of time and energy was devoted during the early years of the United Nations to the question of freedom of information. In one of its early resolutions, the General Assembly characterized freedom of information as "a fundamental human right" and "the touchstone of all freedoms to which the United Nations is consecrated." [14] Efforts however to draft a convention on freedom of information which would be

[14] General Assembly Resolution 59 (I), Dec. 14, 1946.

generally acceptable to Members were unsuccessful. The specific issue on which necessary agreement could not be reached was the extent to which this freedom should be subject to limitation in the interest of accuracy, fair play, and good international relations. The United States insisted on virtually unrestricted freedom of the press which most other Members were not willing to accept.[15]

The United Nations has given a great deal of attention to the prevention of discrimination and the protection of minority groups. At its first session in January-February, 1947, the Commission on Human Rights decided to create a Subcommission on Prevention of Discrimination and Protection of Minorities. The prevention of discrimination and the protection of minorities are in effect two aspects of the same problem. Members of minority groups that seek full acceptance and equal right of participation desire to be protected against discrimination; those that desire to retain their cultural identity while enjoying political and civil rights emphasize minority protection. Much of the discussion that has taken place in the Subcommission, the Commission on Human Rights, the Economic and Social Council, and the Assembly has been concerned with definition and program. Achievement to date has been largely limited to the clarification of issues. There has been a general unwillingness in the postwar period to revert to the earlier League approach to the minority problem.

One of the most publicized achievements of the United Nations in dealing with specific aspects of human rights has been the conclusion of a genocide convention. In its first session in 1946, the General Assembly adopted a resolution condemning genocide "as a crime under international law." [16] In this resolution the Assembly declared genocide to be

> *a denial of the right of existence of entire human groups, as homicide is the denial of the right to live of individual human beings; such denial of the right of existence shocks the conscience of mankind, results in great losses to humanity in the form of cultural and other contributions represented by these human groups, and is contrary to moral law and to the spirit and aims of the United Nations.*

Subsequently, on December 8, 1948, the General Assembly approved a Convention on the Prevention and Punishment of the Crime of

---

[15] See Carroll Binder, "Freedom of Information and the United Nations," *International Organization*, VI (1952), pp. 210–26.

[16] General Assembly Resolution 96 (I), Dec. 11, 1946.

Genocide without a dissenting vote. The convention, after reaffirming the Assembly's declaration that genocide was a crime under international law, defined genocide as meaning

> *any of the following acts committed with intent to destroy, in whole or in part, a national, ethnical, racial or religious group, as such:*
> *(a) Killing members of the group;*
> *(b) Causing serious bodily or mental harm to members of the group;*
> *(c) Deliberately inflicting on the group conditions of life calculated to bring about its physical destruction in whole or in part;*
> *(d) Imposing measures intended to prevent births within the group;*
> *(e) Forcibly transferring children of the group to another group.*[17]

The Convention came into force on January 12, 1951. At the end of 1951, fifty states had deposited their ratifications, many, however, with reservations which raised questions regarding the exact nature of their commitments.[18] The Convention has not been ratified by two major powers—the United Kingdom and the United States. It is too early to judge the effectiveness of the Convention in restraining excesses such as were practiced by the Nazis in Germany before and during the Second World War.

Another aspect of human rights with which the United Nations has shown continuing concern is the question of equal rights for women. Largely as the result of the pressure of organized women, the Economic and Social Council established and has since maintained a separate Commission on the Status of Women. The activities of the United Nations with respect to the rights of women have covered a wide range. The Organization has been concerned with securing the same political rights for women as for men, equal economic opportunity, equal educational opportunities, the right of married women to retain their nationality, and an improved status in private law. To achieve these objectives, the appropriate organs of the United Nations have made full use of their armory of techniques and procedures. Studies have been initiated, facts have been reported, hortatory resolutions have been adopted, conventions have been drafted, and technical assistance programs have been utilized. The results are difficult to evaluate, but

[17] General Assembly Resolution 266 A (III), Dec. 9, 1948.

[18] For the Court's opinion on interpretation of these reservations, see *Reservations to the Convention on Genocide, Advisory Opinion: I.C.J. Reports 1951,* p. 15.

probably add up to some real progress in improving the conditions of women in many countries.

In addition to being called upon to deal with particular aspects of the general problem of human rights, the United Nations in a number of instances has been asked to consider allegations of the denial of human rights under particular circumstances. This has raised a serious question of competence, since the Charter provisions do not make it at all clear what positive steps, if any, the organs of the United Nations can take to secure respect for particular human rights in concrete situations. As we have seen, the Charter declares that one of the purposes of the Organization is ". . . to achieve international cooperation . . . in promoting and encouraging respect for human rights and for fundamental freedoms," authorizes the General Assembly to ". . . make recommendations for the purpose of . . . assisting in the realization of human rights and fundamental freedoms," and requires the United Nations to ". . . promote . . . universal respect for, and observance of, human rights and fundamental freedoms."

On the other hand, by the terms of Article 2, paragraph 7, the United Nations may not ". . . intervene in matters which are essentially within the domestic jurisdiction of any state." [19] Since the Charter does not say what are the human rights which are to be respected and observed, and since Members have not been able to agree on any supplemental treaty defining these rights and requiring parties to respect them, the argument has been made with some justification that no Member can be rightly accused under the Charter of having violated any international obligation to respect any specific human right, nor can any action of specific disapproval or condemnation be taken by any organ without violating the domestic jurisdiction provision of the Charter. This generally has been the position of Members that have been charged with violating specific human rights, and while organs of the United Nations, particularly the General Assembly, have not been sufficiently impressed by the argument to refrain from discussion and the adoption of resolutions, often of a condemnatory nature, it cannot be said that United Nations action has been particularly effective.

In 1946, the Indian Government requested the General Assembly to consider the alleged violations by the South African Government of the basic human rights of persons of Indian origin. The South African Government argued that the Assembly had no competence in the matter since the treatment of its own nationals was a domestic matter, unless it could be shown that some international agreement to which it

---

[19] For further discussion of this limitation, see above, pp. 74–79.

was a party specifically required it to respect the human right in question. The Indian Government did not rely wholly on Charter provisions since it contended that the Capetown Agreement of 1927 (renewed in 1932) which defined the status of Indians in South Africa had also been violated. The General Assembly never explicitly decided the question of competence but then and later it undertook to discuss the question and adopt resolutions urging settlement of the matter in accordance with Charter principles. What the General Assembly did resulted in no improvement in the treatment of the people in question. The attitude of the Government of South Africa progressively became more non-cooperative.

In 1952, a related matter, the treatment of racial minorities by the Government of the Union of South Africa under its policy of racial segregation (*apartheid*) was brought to the attention of the Assembly. The Assembly set up a commission to study the situation and enunciated certain principles for the guidance of multiracial states. When the Commission reported that the *apartheid* legislation and regulations were incompatible with the provisions of the Charter and the Universal Declaration,[20] the Assembly took note of the report, asked the Commission to continue its study of the situation and to suggest measures of alleviation, and invited the South African Government to cooperate with the Commission.[21] The South African Government refused to cooperate and maintained its policy intact. When the Assembly later considered the matter in its tenth session, though failing to continue the Commission, it repeated its early views regarding South African racial legislation. Though the Assembly in dealing with this particular situation was able to proceed on the basis of a strong majority consensus, its action has been ineffective in altering South African policy.

In the case of the alleged violation of human rights by Hungary, Bulgaria, and Romania, the General Assembly was in a stronger legal position, in a sense, since the peace treaties had contained express provisions obligating these states to respect basic human rights and fundamental freedoms. Since negotiations were under way between the parties to the treaties when the matter was first brought to the Assembly's attention, the Assembly initially limited itself to expressing deep concern and drawing the attention of the states to their obligations under the treaties. Later when negotiations for settlement in accordance with treaty procedures broke down, the Assembly again considered the

[20] See U.N. General Assembly, *Official Records,* Eighth Session, Suppl. No. 16 (Doc. A/2505).

[21] General Assembly Resolution 721 (VIII), Dec. 8, 1953.

matter and adopted a resolution condemning the three governments for their refusal to fulfill their treaty obligations.[22] In this case, the Assembly publicized the facts of the situation and gave support to the position of the Western Powers but was unable to do anything immediately to achieve greater respect for the rights in question.

The General Assembly has been asked to consider cases where the Soviet Union has been accused of practicing forced labor, wrongfully detaining prisoners of war, preventing Soviet brides from leaving the country, and imposing arbitrary personal restraints. In some instances resolutions adopted by the General Assembly have been followed in time by remedial action by the Soviet Government. One cannot however establish with any certainty a cause and effect relationship. All of these complaints have of course afforded the opportunity for condemning Soviet Communism and have in some instances invoked retaliatory accusations.

Conclusions

It is difficult to evaluate the work of the United Nations in promoting respect for, and observance of, human rights. Quite clearly, the Universal Declaration of Human Rights has served a useful purpose to the extent that it has provided goals of achievement and standards against which we can measure the progress of various states. Efforts to achieve a legal formulation of these rights and to put back of them the sanctions and means of enforcement appropriate to laws have completely failed. Clearly, social, political, and legal developments in the various countries of the world are as yet too uneven and diverse to permit the degree of uniformity and standardization that a legal approach requires. In time, it may be possible to get this kind of agreement and to use the method of international law and law enforcement to maintain a minimum standard of respect for human rights by all governments throughout the world.

For the time being and for the foreseeable future, the role of the United Nations in promoting respect for human rights will need to be a more limited one. Certainly, as we have already seen, the establishment of goals, of objectives to be achieved by a variety of means, is desirable. Furthermore, the United Nations will no doubt continue to perform a useful service by assembling and making available accurate and complete information regarding the status of human rights in the

[22] General Assembly Resolution 385 (V), Nov. 3, 1950.

different countries of the world. Assistance can also be rendered the less developed countries, under various assistance programs, in improving laws and administrative practices, and in creating conditions favorable to the fuller enjoyment of all human rights, social, economic, and cultural, as well as civil and political. In giving this assistance the specialized agencies as well as the United Nations have important contributions to make. In fact, in some instances, as in the case of the Expanded Program of Technical Assistance an important responsibility of the United Nations may be that of coordination.

It is not at all clear how effective the United Nations can be in dealing with specific complaints of violation. First, there is the strong legal argument to be overcome that since the Charter does not commit Members to respect defined rights and freedoms, there is no basis for saying that a Member has violated a particular right until it has expressly agreed to respect it. The Universal Declaration, it can be argued, does not serve that purpose since it defines future goals and not present commitments. Even if this argument is not accepted, as the General Assembly has quite consistently been unwilling to do, there is not much that the General Assembly can do to impose its view on a recalcitrant state, or to induce such a state to alter its policy. The Assembly's powers are limited to publicizing the facts, and developing a consensus through appropriate resolutions. Its authority is essentially moral, and unless the government whose conduct is under criticism is sufficiently desirous of being favorably judged to alter its course even in the face of strong domestic considerations and some loss of face, there is not much that the United Nations as such can do about it. The situation is not likely to be one that can convincingly be found to constitute a threat to international peace. It may of course happen that the position of the accused is sufficiently vulnerable to permit effective pressures to be exercised by one or more Members, but there are usually certain risks and inconveniences involved in this kind of private pressure.

General Assembly resolutions and debates, admittedly, may be ineffective in dealing with a particular complaint or series of complaints. Indeed, they may add tension to a situation, not ease it. Nevertheless they may be a necessary step in the development of a general consensus regarding what constitute fundamental human rights and freedoms and what attitudes should be taken regarding their violation, and in preparing the way for a more effective system of observance and compliance at a later date. It is necessary that the question of human rights be treated as a political problem before it is ready for handling as a legal problem.

SUGGESTED READINGS

Binder, Carroll. "Freedom of Information and the United Nations," *International Organization,* VI (1952), pp. 210–26.

Corbett, P. E. *The Individual and World Society.* Princeton: University Center for Research on World Political Institutions, 1953.

Eagleton, Clyde. "Excesses of Self-Determination," *Foreign Affairs,* XXXI (1953), pp. 592–604.

Green, James F. *The United Nations and Human Rights.* Washington: The Brookings Institution, 1956. Also in Asher and Associates, *The United Nations and Promotion of the General Welfare,* Washington: The Brookings Institution, 1957, Part 3.

Lauterpacht, H. *International Law and Human Rights.* New York: Frederick A. Praeger, Inc., 1950.

Neal, Marian. "The United Nations and Human Rights," *International Conciliation,* No. 489 (March 1953), pp. 113–74.

Robinson, Nehemiah. *Universal Declaration of Human Rights: Its Origin, Significance and Interpretation.* New York: Institute of Jewish Affairs, 1950.

Sorensen, Max. "Federal States and the International Protection of Human Rights," *American Journal of International Law,* XLVI (1952), pp. 195–218.

———. "The Quest for Equality," *International Conciliation,* No. 507 (March 1956), pp. 291–349.

United Nations, Department of Social Affairs. *The Impact of the Universal Declaration of Human Rights.* Doc. ST/SOA/5/Rev. 1, June 29, 1953.

United Nations Educational, Scientific and Cultural Organization, ed. *Human Rights, Comments and Interpretations: A Symposium.* Paris: UNESCO, 1949.

U.S. Senate Committee on Foreign Relations, Subcommittee on the United Nations Charter. *Human Rights, Domestic Jurisdiction and the United Nations Charter.* Staff Study No. 11. Washington: Government Printing Office, 1955.

Chapter XII

THE PROMOTION OF ECONOMIC AND SOCIAL WELFARE

ONE OF THE principal purposes of the United Nations, as defined in Article 1 of the Charter, is to ". . . achieve international cooperation in solving international problems of an economic, social, cultural, or humanitarian character." Furthermore, the Charter does not stop with this statement of general purpose but proceeds to devote two whole chapters and a number of scattered provisions to the further elaboration of this purpose and to defining the mechanism and procedures by which it is to be achieved. Article 55 relates this explicitly to the primary purpose of the Organization, the maintenance of international peace and security, in the following words:

> *With a view to the creation of conditions of stability and well-being which are necessary for peaceful and friendly relations among nations based on respect for the principle of equal rights and self-determination of peoples, the United Nations shall promote:*
> *a) higher standards of living, full employment, and conditions of economic and social progress and development;*
> *b) solutions of international economic, social, health, and related problems; and international cultural and educational cooperation;*

The United Nations Approach

Though the U.N. Charter places unprecedented emphasis on the importance of economic and social cooperation, organized international cooperation for economic and social purposes considerably antedates

262

efforts by similar means to achieve peace and security. The first permanent international organizations, going back about a century—the International Telegraphic Union and the Universal Postal Union—were established to facilitate communication between peoples of different countries. Before the League of Nations was established, permanent international institutions had been set up to further international cooperation in the fields of public health, agriculture, labor and transportation.[1] During the First World War, the Allied and Associated Powers found that it was necessary to establish permanent organs of cooperation to deal with such matters as the allocation of shipping, and the most effective utilization of available supplies of foodstuffs, raw materials, and munitions.[2] Had this cooperation continued after the armistice in dealing with problems of economic rehabilitation and reconstruction, the world economy would probably have developed on a much sounder basis.

The Covenant of the League of Nations did not explicitly stress international cooperation in dealing with economic and social problems as one of the major activities of the organization. A phrase in the Preamble and two articles dealing with "social and other activities" and "international bureaus" were the extent of the Covenant's direct concern, apart from provisions relating to the mandates system. A major criticism that can be made of the authors of the Covenant was that they did not adequately appreciate the importance of this part of the League's work. Their emphasis was too heavily on the political, on matters more directly relating to international peace and security. Nevertheless, in actual practice, the League was able, on the basis of scant Covenant provisions, to develop an impressive machinery, a varied set of procedures, and a substantial record of achievement in furthering economic and social welfare.[3] In fact, when the League was approaching the end of its political effectiveness, the value of its economic and social work was so widely recognized that an attempt was made—which proved to be too late—to reorganize the League as an organization for the promotion of economic and social cooperation. It was thought that it might continue to do its useful work in this field even though for all practical purposes the League had ceased to function as an organization to keep the peace.

[1] See Paul S. Reinsch, *International Public Unions* (Boston: World Peace Foundation, 1916).

[2] See J .A. Salter, *Allied Shipping Control, an Experiment in International Administration* (New York: Oxford University Press, 1921).

[3] See League of Nations Secretariat, *Ten Years of World Cooperation* (Geneva, 1930), and Walters, *op. cit.*

In fact many of the activities of the League of a non-political nature were continued during the war. Particularly in the economic and social field, the actual development of the League system in practice, and the ideas that were being considered before the outbreak of war deeply influenced the architects of the United Nations system. It was a natural development that the provisions of the Charter should accord great importance to the economic and social responsibilities of the new Organization. The Soviet Union was not at all enthusiastic about placing these added responsibilities on the United Nations, since it was principally interested in the peace and security objective and furthermore was understandably not sympathetic with a proposal whose aim was to destroy the validity of Marxian ideology. Nevertheless, even the Soviet Union bowed to the insistence of the Western democracies that economic and social well-being be included among the major objectives of the United Nations.

Factors Conditioning the United Nations System

While international cooperation in the economic and social fields has been of long standing, governments have been extremely cautious in committing themselves to specific purposes and policies and to the creation of machinery and procedures of cooperation. One of the principal reasons for this has been the fact that governments have generally been particularly jealous of their powers in dealing with matters affecting directly the welfare of their citizens. Only when the necessity of some qualification of national sovereignty to meet an immediately pressing need is obvious, has there been a willingness to assume international commitments and to establish international organs with defined functions and powers. Furthermore, those states with federal forms of governments, such as the United States, have often been cautious or even negative in their attitude toward international cooperation in this field because of possible encroachment on the reserved powers of the constituent states or provinces.

At the time the Charter was drafted the atmosphere of public opinion and government policy in the principal democracies was extremely favorable to international cooperation for welfare purposes.[4] The War was still going on and the people of most countries had become familiar with a large and expanding role for government in meeting common social and economic needs. Furthermore, the War had been

[4] See, for example, J. B. Condliffe and A. Stevenson, *The Common Interest in International Economic Organization* (Montreal: I.L.O., 1944).

preceded by only a short time by a world-wide depression which had required the active intervention of government to meet pressing social and economic necessities. Also, the War had necessitated cooperation on an unprecedented scale between belligerent countries to meet their needs for munitions, raw materials, food and shipping; and its disrupting effects on national economies and the destruction wrought had convinced peoples and governments that the cooperation which had been made necessary by it could not be suddenly ended, as had happened after the First World War, without suicidal consequences.

Early in the War, the United States Government emphasized the need of cooperation among the Allies in dealing with common economic problems. The need of a cooperative approach to postwar economic problems was stressed by Under-Secretary of State Welles in a speech which he delivered at the University of Toronto in February 1943.[5] He strongly advocated conferences and consultations with a view to reaching agreement on policies and institutional arrangements for promoting the common economic welfare of the nations united in the war. Clearly, such cooperation in dealing with pressing economic problems was viewed as preparing the way for the permanent political cooperation to maintain international peace and security which was considered necessary in the postwar period.

The pattern of postwar cooperation in dealing with economic and social problems was only in part determined by the San Francisco Conference. At the time the Charter of the United Nations was being put into final form, specialized intergovernmental agencies were already in operation, or in the process of being established under the pressure of present or widely anticipated need. The Universal Postal Union had been functioning since 1874; the International Telecommunications Union since 1934, when it was established as the result of uniting the International Telegraph Union(1865) and the International Radio Telegraph Union(1903). The International Meteorological Organization, established in 1878, was to be reorganized in 1947 by intergovernmental agreement as the World Meteorological Organization. The International Labour Organization, established at the end of the First World War to further social justice by improving the conditions of labor, was actively functioning, though the circumstances of the War had forced the transfer of its headquarters from Geneva to Montreal.

To assist in the work of relief and rehabilitation in the areas which had been liberated, the United Nations Relief and Rehabilitation Administration had been established in 1943 and was hard at work when the San Francisco Conference was in session. Also, in 1943, a United

[5] Department of State, *Bulletin,* VIII (1943), p. 179.

Nations Conference on Food and Agriculture had met at Hot Springs, Virginia and had taken the first step toward the establishment of the United Nations Food and Agriculture Organization. Its purposes were to raise nutritional levels, to improve the efficiency of agricultural production, and to better the conditions of rural populations. This became an operating agency in October, 1945. In July, 1944, at the Bretton Woods Conference, the Articles of Agreement of the International Monetary Fund and the International Bank for Reconstruction and Development were signed after extensive preliminary negotiations between the United States and the United Kingdom. These agencies were to assist in stabilizing national currencies and to provide financial aid in economic reconstruction and development. Later, in November and December, another United Nations conference, meeting in Chicago, drafted the constitution of an international organization to assist in the development of safe and efficient international civil aviation (the International Civil Aviation Organization). Plans were well under way for the establishment of an international organization to further educational, scientific and cultural cooperation, though the Conference which drafted the Constitution of the United Nations Educational, Scientific, and Cultural Organization did not meet until November 1, 1945, over four months after the Charter of the United Nations was signed at San Francisco.

With these various agencies already in existence or in process of being established, with national governments committed to them and to the piecemeal, functional approach which they represented, and with powerful pressure groups in many instances insisting on the autonomy of agencies in which they were specially interested, those who were engaged in writing the Charter at San Francisco were not free to determine the future pattern of international organization for economic and social cooperations, either on the basis of what was ideally desirable or as if they were writing the basic constitution of world cooperation on a clean slate. They had to accommodate their thinking and adapt the results of their deliberations to the facts of international life, and these dictated a decentralized system with great variety of structure, power, and procedures, and with the newly created general international organization playing an important role, but not a controlling one.

The Scope and Mechanism of Cooperation

While the authors of the Charter found it necessary to recognize that intergovernmental action in the economic and social field would not be limited to the United Nations, they were nevertheless in agreement that the new Organization should have important and comprehensive responsibilities. In principle, the scope of the United Nations' work was to be as broad as the area of international concern. Lest the words of the Dumbarton Oaks Proposals permit a too narrow interpretation of the scope of the Organization's responsibilities, delegations at San Francisco, under pressure from private groups, insisted on a more detailed description of fields which were to be the concern of the United Nations than was included in the Proposals. While it was assumed that the specific actions to be taken by the Organization might vary, depending upon what had already been done, what agencies were already in existence or functioning, and what specific type of activity seemed most appropriate to the given situation, there was no inclination to accept any qualification in principle of its broad responsibility for promoting international cooperation in economic, social, cultural, educational, health, and related fields.

Not only did the Charter, as written, define the scope of responsibility in broad terms, but it also committed the Organization and its Members to some fairly specific objectives and principles of policy. It directed that the United Nations should promote "higher standards of living, full employment, and conditions of economic and social progress and development." [6] It thus made clear that the Organization was not to play a passive role with respect to matters which laissez faire economic doctrine had considered outside the realm of direct state responsibility. Rather, it accepted as guiding principles of international economic and social policy the basic premises of the New Deal in the United States and of social democracy everywhere. While the Charter did not attempt to prescribe the specific means by which its social and economic goals were to be achieved, it did make it clear that the Members of the United Nations were to "take joint and separate action in cooperation with the Organization" to achieve the purposes set forth in the Charter.[7] This could only be interpreted as requiring at least that Members show good faith and seriousness of purpose. International cooperation for economic and social well-being was to be something more than a formality in the postwar world.

While the Charter places primary responsibility for the maintenance of international peace and security on the Security Council—a responsibility which, as we have seen, the Council has not been able to discharge effectively and which the General Assembly has in fact largely assumed—the Charter is equally explicit in making the General Assembly the central organ for discharging the Organization's responsibilities

[6] Article 55.   [7] Article 56.

in the field of economic and social cooperation. In part, this was a concession to the smaller states who had reluctantly accepted the special role of the Security Council and the major powers in matters of peace and security. More fundamentally, however, this was recognition of the fact that in an area where all states were more or less directly concerned and where it was not proposed, in any case, to give the Organization coercive powers, it was fitting and proper that the General Assembly should have the major role. It was in dealing with questions in the area of economic and social cooperation that the Assembly could most fittingly perform the functions of a "town meeting of the world."

To understand and to evaluate fairly the work of the United Nations in the economic and social field, it is first necessary to recognize the nature and limits of what the General Assembly and other United Nations organs may and can do. Here it is especially important to realize that neither the Assembly, nor the Economic and Social Council which functions under its authority, has the power to take decisions with respect to matters of substance within the economic and social field that are binding upon Member states, least of all upon the citizens of those states. The powers of legislation and taxation which have in the past been the peculiar prerogatives of states in dealing with economic and social problems still remain so vested. No United Nations organ has these powers.

All that the Assembly can do is initiate studies, discuss, make recommendations, set up programs, and call upon Members to give them their support. All the specific powers which the Charter confers upon the Assembly fall into one or more of these categories. Thus it may discuss any question within the scope of the Charter and make recommendations to Members.[8] It may initiate studies and make recommendations to promote international cooperation in the economic, social, cultural, educational, and health fields.[9] It may recommend measures for the peaceful adjustment of any situation likely to impair the general welfare.[10] It approves the budget of the United Nations.[11] This gives it the power to determine how much money may be spent, but does not give any guarantee that the money will be available if governments are not willing or able to make their assigned contributions. It examines the budgets of the specialized agencies but can only make recommendations with respect to them. It may make recommendations for the coordination of the policies and activities of the specialized agencies,[12] and initiate negotiations among states for the creation of new ones.[13]

While the Charter places primary responsibility in the economic

[8] Article 10.   [9] Article 13.   [10] Article 14.
[11] Article 17.   [12] Article 58.   [13] Article 59.

and social field on the General Assembly, it was clear to those who wrote the Charter that the Assembly would not be so constituted or capable of functioning as to do all that needed to be done. Being a large and cumbersome body and normally meeting only once a year for a limited period of time it would be in need of the help of other organs in preparing its work and in seeing to it that its decisions had some influence on the course of events. Under the League Covenant, the Council, which was primarily a political organ, had important responsibilities in connection with the initiation of measures in the economic and socal field and the implementing of decisions. As we have seen, there was growing sentiment toward the end of the League's active existence that this arrangement was not satisfactory. Those who were responsible for writing the Charter had little difficulty in deciding that a separate council should be established to perform the quasi-executive functions which the League Council had performed. Thus, the Economic and Social Council became one of the principal organs of the United Nations, though in reality it is little more than a subsidiary organ of the General Assembly.

The Economic and Social Council is composed of eighteen members elected by the General Assembly. The Charter contains no provisions assuring membership in the Council to any state or group of states. Though a proposal was made at San Francisco which would assure the states of chief industrial importance of membership it did not receive sufficient support to be adopted. In practice, however, the permanent members of the Security Council have been elected to membership and consistently re-elected when their terms have expired. But while the Council has generally reflected in its membership the economic inequalities of states, it has not in actual practice achieved the role of executive organ in its relations with the General Assembly. The fact that the Charter places the Council under the authority of the Assembly should not necessarily be decisive on this point. It does not prevent the Council from achieving a position of leadership on the basis of the prestige and authority of its members and the exigencies of the situation, but that it has not done.

The Council's independent Charter powers are sufficiently impressive. It ". . . may make or initiate studies and reports with respect to international economic, social, cultural, educational, health and related matters and may make recommendations with respect to such matters to the General Assembly, to the Members of the United Nations, and to the specialized agencies concerned." [14] It may prepare draft conventions for submission to the Assembly and may call interna-

[14] Article 62, par. 1.

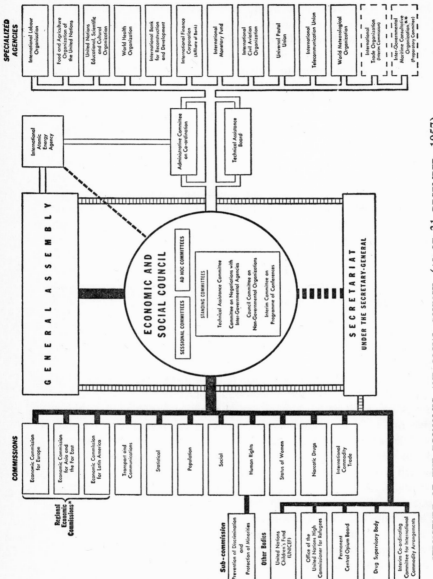

STRUCTURE OF THE ECONOMIC AND SOCIAL COUNCIL (AS OF 31 DECEMBER, 1957)

* The Economic Commission for Africa was established on April 29, 1958.

** Expected to become specialized agency with approval of agreement by IMCO Conference early in 1959.

tional conferences with respect to matters within its competence.[15] It may enter into agreements with specialized agencies defining their relations to the United Nations, subject to approval by the Assembly, and it may coordinate the activities of the specialized agencies through consultations with and recommendations to such agencies and through recommendations to the Assembly and Members of the United Nations.[16] It may take steps to obtain regular reports from the specialized agencies, and may communicate its observations on these reports to the Assembly.[17] It may perform such functions as fall within its competence in connection with carrying out the recommendations of the Assembly.

But while these powers appear adequate to permit the Council to assume an important role in United Nations activity, in practice the Council has not been a very effective organ and has been overshadowed by the Assembly. Paradoxically this has in large measure been due to its composition. The facts that the chief industrial states have been for all practical purposes permanent members of the Council and that the more advanced states, economically and politically, have had representation in the Council out of proportion to their actual numbers in the Organization, have made the Council a more cautious and conservative body than the Assembly, particularly in questions of human rights, economic development, and assistance to underdeveloped states which have been the major economic and social issues before the United Nations. Consequently those states interested in having the United Nations take positive action on these issues have found it to their advantage to appeal from the Council to the Assembly and to reopen and fully discuss questions which the Council has already considered, sometimes as though the Council had never given any time and thought to them.

If the Council, composed of representatives of governments without technical proficiency in the large number and great variety of questions which come before it, is to perform its function as an executive organ effectively, it needs a great deal of expert technical assistance. To provide this assistance, the Charter not only states generally that subsidiary organs may be created, but also specifically directs the Council to set up ". . . commissions in economic and social fields—and for the promotion of human rights, and such other commissions as may be required for the performance of its duties." [18] Acting under this provision of the Charter, the Council has established a number of functional commissions such as the Transport and Communications Commission, the Statistical Commission, the Social Commission, and the Commission on Narcotic Drugs. The Dumbarton Oaks Proposals envisaged that the

[15] Article 62, pars. 3 and 4. [16] Article 63.
[17] Article 64. [18] Article 68.

commissions should be composed of experts chosen on the basis of personal qualification who would be in the position to provide the best technical advice. But at San Francisco, this requirement was dropped, and in practice the view has come to prevail that these commissions should be composed of Member states whose governments in turn appoint the individuals who serve. These individuals may or may not be experts in their fields and in most cases they act under government instructions. As a consequence, even in the functional commissions which, if the League precedent were followed would provide the objective technical assistance which is needed in dealing with complicated economic and social problems, there has been a definite tendency for the political factor to intrude and become dominant. One result has been that a heavy responsibility has been placed on the Secretariat, though this load has been somewhat lessened by the Council's practice of setting up *ad hoc* committees of experts.[19]

In addition to the functional commissions, the Economic and Social Council has established four regional economic commissions to assist it in the performance of its functions. The creation of these commissions was not foreseen at the San Francisco Conference. The General Assembly, in its first session, urged the establishment of regional economic commissions for Europe and for Asia and the Far East "in order to give effective aid to the countries devastated by war." [20] This the Council did on March 28, 1947. On February 25, 1948, the Council established an Economic Commission for Latin America and on April 9, 1958 it established an Economic Commission for Africa. These commissions undertake research and advise the Council on problems of a regional nature and make direct recommendations to member governments, governments admitted in an advisory capacity, and specialized agencies on matters falling within their competence. They are composed of countries within the areas and of certain other countries with special interests. Countries not Members of the United Nations may be members of these commissions or have advisory or consultative status. These commissions have proved to be among the most successful of the United Nations' organs in promoting constructive co-operation in the economic field. Being close to the problems of their respective areas, they have been responsive to them and have on the whole dealt with them to the satisfaction of both the countries of the region and outside Members. Furthermore they have stimulated the spirit of self-help in meeting regional problems.[21]

[19] For criticism of the United Nations practice, see A. Loveday, "An Unfortunate Decision," *International Organization,* I (1947), pp. 279–90.
[20] General Assembly Resolution 46 (I), Dec. 11, 1946.
[21] See Robert E. Asher and Associates, *The United Nations and Promotion*

Any description of the United Nations mechanism for cooperation in promoting human welfare would of course be incomplete without some indication of the role of the specialized agencies. As we have seen, the Charter recognizes that much of the work of international cooperation in this field will be carried out by inter-governmental organizations set up by agreement of the governments concerned, with or without United Nations initiative. These organizations fall into a variety of categories. Some are purely temporary, as was the United Nations Relief and Rehabilitation Administration (UNRRA), set up at the conclusion of the war to meet a passing need of great urgency. Others are regional in character, being limited in their membership and the scope of their operations to particular areas, as for example the Organization of European Economic Cooperation (OEEC) and the economic agencies of the Organization of American States (OAS). Still others are global in membership and in the scope of their activities, and are also regarded as permanent, but nevertheless deal with fairly narrow technical matters such as the International Bureau of Weights and Measures or the International Union for the Protection of Industrial Property. Finally there are those agencies ". . . established by intergovernmental agreement and having wide international responsibilities . . ." in economic and social fields, such as the International Labour Organization (ILO) and the Food and Agriculture Organization (FAO) which have important duties in large areas of the United Nations' fields of concern. These, the Charter envisages, should be brought into a defined relation with the United Nations by the conclusion of special agreements, and when this is done, the agency in question becomes a specialized agency in the language of the Charter.

As of the present, twelve intergovernmental agencies have been established to discharge responsibilities of varying degrees of importance and comprehensiveness in the field of economic and social cooperation, and have become specialized agencies by being brought into relation with the United Nations by the conclusion of agreements.[22] These include the following:

1. *The International Labour Organization* (ILO). This organization was established at the end of the First World War to improve conditions of labor throughout the world on the assumption that social

---

of General Welfare (Washington: The Brookings Institution, 1957), pp. 50–53; David Wightman, *Economic Cooperation in Europe* (London: Stevens & Son, 1956); and C. Hart Schaaf, "The United Nations Economic Commission for Asia and the Far East," *International Organization,* VII (1953), pp. 463–81.

[22] For the constitutions of these organizations and the agreements that have been concluded, see Amos J. Peaslee, *International Governmental Organizations: Constitutional Documents* (The Hague, Nijhoff, 1956), 2 vols., and *Yearbook of the United Nations,* published annually by the United Nations Secretariat.

justice is a necessary condition of international peace. It continued to function during World War II, moving its headquarters temporarily from Geneva to Montreal, Canada. With the establishment of the United Nations, it revised its constitution to achieve greater autonomy and concluded an agreement with the United Nations by which it became one of the first of the family of specialized agencies. Its constitution provides for the direct representation of national employer and worker organizations, as well as governments, and gives to these representatives individual votes. Furthermore, in the drafting of labor conventions, the ILO has developed procedures which constitute a considerable advance over conventional treaty-making methods in the evolution of what might be called an international legislative process.[23]

2. *The Food and Agriculture Organization of the United Nations* (FAO). This organization was established during the Second World War for the purpose of raising nutritional levels and improving the efficiency of the production and distribution of food and agricultural products. The structure of the organization is conventional in nature and its powers are limited pretty much to research, publication, discussion, and recommendation. It has succeeded to the functions and assets of the International Institute of Agriculture, and like it, has its seat in Rome.

3. *The United Nations Educational, Scientific, and Cultural Organization* (UNESCO). This organization is based on the assumptions ". . . that since wars begin in the minds of men, it is in the minds of men that the defenses of peace must be constructed . . . , that ignorance of each other's ways and lives . . ." has been a common cause of distrust leading to war, and that peace must be founded ". . . upon the intellectual and moral solidarity of mankind." Its purposes and functions are to advance and diffuse knowledge and understanding. In addition to establishing the usual organs of cooperation, the Constitution provides for National Commissions to act in an advisory capacity. The headquarters of the organization are in Paris.

4. *The International Civil Aviation Organization* (ICAO). This organization was established under a convention concluded in Chicago in December, 1944, for the purpose of insuring "the safe and orderly growth of international civil aviation." The convention superseded the Paris Convention of 1919 which established the International Commission for Air Navigation. A major function of the organization is to adopt international standards and recommend practices for furthering the safety of international air transportation, and in this connection, the organization has developed significant methods of international rule-making. Its headquarters are in Montreal.

[23] For further elaboration of this point, see below, pp. 282–284.

5. *The International Bank for Reconstruction and Development* (Bank). The Bank is one of the organizations established under the 1944 Bretton Woods agreements. The purpose of the Bank is to provide funds by direct loan or by guaranteeing private loans for the reconstruction of devastated areas and for the development of "productive facilities and resources in less developed countries." A unique feature of the Bank is the provision contained in its Articles of Agreement for weighted voting in meetings of the Board of Governors and Executive Directors in order to give to the major contributors of funds a proportionate influence over policy. Its headquarters are in Washington.

6. *The International Finance Corporation* (IFC). This agency was established in 1956 as an affiliate of the Bank to encourage the growth of productive private enterprise, particularly in the less developed areas. It may invest in productive private undertakings in areas where sufficient private capital is not available on reasonable terms. Its organization and membership are the same as the Bank's and its headquarters are in Washington.

7. *The International Monetary Fund* (Fund). Like the Bank, the Fund was set up under the provisions of the Bretton Woods agreements. Its principal purposes are to promote international monetary cooperation, to facilitate expansion and growth of international trade, and to "promote exchange stability." It seeks to achieve its purposes through the establishment of par values of national currencies, the acceptance by members of certain restrictions upon their right to modify the value of their currencies, and the use of a fund to support weak currencies. The organization and voting procedures of the Fund are similar to those of the Bank. It has its headquarters in Washington.

8. *The World Health Organization* (WHO). This organization was set up as the result of United Nations initiative. Its constitution was drafted by an International Health Conference meeting in New York during June and July, 1946. It became the successor to the health activities of the League of Nations and the International Office of Public Hygiene in Paris. The objective of the organization is "the attainment by all peoples of the highest possible level of health," defined as "a state of complete physical, mental and social well being." It has a wide variety of functions, including the encouraging of research, the distribution of information, the rendering of technical assistance, and the establishment of international standards. Its headquarters are in Geneva.

9. *The Universal Postal Union* (UPU). The Union was first established in 1874 under the terms of a Postal Convention signed at Berne, Switzerland. It was one of the first of the international public unions of the pre-1914 period. The present constitution was signed at

Brussels on July 11, 1952, and contains some significant changes of earlier arrangements to conform to the specialized agency pattern. Its purpose is to provide for more efficient international postal service. The headquarters are at Berne, Switzerland.

10. *The International Telecommunications Union* (ITU). This organization dates from 1932 when by a convention drafted at Madrid the International Telegraphic Convention was combined with the Radio-telegraph Convention, and the International Telegraph Union became the International Telecommunications Union. The International Tele-graph Union, first established in 1865, had been restricted to telegraphic communication. The primary purpose of the ITU is to further the improvement and efficient use of telecommunication services of all kinds. The headquarters are at Geneva.

11. *The World Meteorological Organization* (WMO). This agency is the successor to the International Meteorological Organization, established in 1878. Its convention was drafted in 1947, and entered into force in 1950. Its main purposes are to provide for more efficient meteorological services, better weather information, and "the uniform publication of observations and statistics." The headquarters are at Lausanne, Switzerland.

12. *The Inter-Governmental Maritime Consultative Organization* (IMCO). This is the latest of the specialized agencies to come into being. A Provisional Maritime Consultative Council was established in 1946, and on the initiative of the United Nations a draft convention for IMCO was drawn up, but this did not enter into force until 1957, due to delays in ratification. Of all the specialized agencies, it has the smallest number of members, in part because of the specialized nature of its work. The purpose of IMCO is to promote the more efficient and safe operation of maritime transport. The headquarters are at London.

For all practical purposes, the International Atomic Energy Agency (IAEA) [24] is a specialized agency. Though it has concluded an agreement with the United Nations defining its relation to that Organization, and though it has most of the attributes of a specialized agency, including the right under the terms of the agreement with the United Nations to ask the International Court of Justice for an advisory opinion, it is not officially considered to be a specialized agency. Its anomalous status was the result of a compromise between the views of those desiring full autonomy for the agency and those wishing to have it brought under the control of the United Nations.

Though initially there were wide variations in the membership of the United Nations and the specialized agencies, these variations have

[24] See above, pp. 234–237.

been greatly reduced, particularly as the result of the decision of the Communist countries to increase their participation. At the present time, the membership of the UPU, the ITU and the WMO is more extensive than that of the UN, while that of FAO, IFC, the Bank, the Fund and IMCO, is in varying degrees more restricted. Nor do numbers tell the whole story, since some states such as the Federal Republic of Germany, the Republic of Korea, Viet-Nam, and Switzerland are members of specialized agencies without being Members of the United Nations.[25] Perhaps even more significant than differences of membership, from the point of view of the structure of power and influence in the agencies, are the differences in the composition, powers and voting procedures of agency organs as compared with those of the United Nations. An example is the provision for weighted voting in the governing bodies of the Bank and the Fund.

The agreements which have been concluded between the agencies and the United Nations vary somewhat in their terms but, in general, and with few exceptions, they do not substantially restrict the independence of the various specialized agencies. They provide for the exchange of information, reciprocal rights of representation at meetings, cooperation in developing uniform personnel practices and statistical methods, submission of reports, consideration of recommendations, and, in general, cooperation with a view to better coordination of policies and activities. They are, however, agreements between equals and are to be viewed as instruments of, or laying the basis for, inter-agency cooperation, and in no sense as means of subordinating the agencies to United Nations direction and control. As we shall see shortly, the most impressive example of cooperation in practice has been afforded by the Expanded Program of Technical Assistance.[26]

This brief survey of the mechanism of international cooperation in the economic and social field should not be ended without a brief mention of the role of non-governmental organizations in the United Nations.[27] Non-governmental organizations have for a long time played an important role in international life. Even though not formally recognized in the League Covenant, they exercised an important influence on League activities. At San Francisco, the United States Government accorded a consultative status to representatives of national non-govern-

---

[25] See chart showing membership as of Dec. 31, 1957, pp. 94–95.

[26] On problem of coordination see Robert E. Asher and Associates, *The United Nations and Promotion of the General Welfare* (Washington: The Brookings Institution, 1957), Ch. III.

[27] See Carnegie Endowment for International Peace, *Consultation between the United Nations and Non-Governmental Organizations,* United Nations Series 3 (New York, 1949).

mental organizations and they had a significant influence in the drafting of the economic and social provisions of the Charter. One Charter provision that undoubtedly resulted largely from this experience was Article 71 which provides that the Economic and Social Council ". . . may make suitable arrangements for consultation with non-governmental organizations which are concerned with matters within its competence." Under arrangements that have been developed, designated non-governmental organizations, primarily those that are international in their structure, are given the opportunity to present their views to the Council on matters with respect to which they have special competence. The conditions under which this opportunity is afforded are closely defined.

Methods of Promoting Economic and Social Welfare

Since the United Nations is not equipped with the normal powers of national governments, it is forced to rely primarily on methods of information and persuasion to achieve its purposes. Having to deal directly with national governments, its methods are directed toward influencing the policies and activities of these governments. Only exceptionally is it able to undertake operations permitting it to deal directly with the individuals who are in need of assistance or guidance or whose conduct needs to be controlled, and then only with the consent of the governments of those states within whose jurisdiction the individuals happen to be. We cannot, then, expect the United Nations to use the methods with which we are familiar when problems are being handled by state authorities, nor can we fairly use the same standards in judging the United Nations' performance that we are accustomed to use in judging the work of national or local governments.

Generally speaking, the methods that are available to the United Nations and to the specialized agencies in the promotion of human welfare are the following: (1) The assembling and publication of information and analyses, and the preparation of analytical studies of economic and social problems; (2) the illumination of issues, the presentation of various points of view, the narrowing of areas of disagreement and the development of areas of agreement through discussions initiated by the appropriate organs; (3) the use of international conventions and other forms of written international agreement, and of resolutions, recommendations, and declarations to establish international standards of conduct which governments are urged to respect regardless of the degree of legal commitment; and (4) the development of operational activities and action programs which either directly or taken in cooperation with the programs of the national governments will help to achieve specific human welfare objectives.[28]

The statistical work of the United Nations has been of outstanding importance. It has benefited greatly from the pioneer work done by the League of Nations and other international organizations in earlier times and from the achievements of non-governmental organizations in this field. By virtue of the nearly universal character of its membership and the willingness and even eagerness, in most instances, of Member governments to cooperate, the United Nations has been able to extend the geographical coverage of reliable statistical data.[29] Unfortunately, the Soviet Union and the other Communist-controlled countries have not been too cooperative in providing statistical data, and this fact has accounted for large gaps in the Organization's coverage. Furthermore, some of the newer underdeveloped countries have not been in the position to provide the kind of statistical information which United Nations agencies have needed. In addition to expanding the geographical coverage of available statistics, the United Nations has also done a great deal to extend reliable statistical coverage to new substantive areas.

In addition to extending statistical coverage, the United Nations has made a substantial contribution to increasing the comparability of statistical data. This of course, is of the greatest importance if available statistical data from other countries is to be used as a basis for developing sound policies and programs in any one country or for arriving at sound conclusions as to how international economic and social problems should be handled. A concrete example of one of the contributions that the United Nations has made in this respect is the establishment of the *Standard International Trade Classification*.[30] This provides governments with a guide which they can follow in preparing foreign trade statistics. It will permit students of international trade problems and others concerned with policy in this area to make comparisons, knowing that the things they compare are in fact comparable. At the end of 1954, it has been estimated that 90 per cent of the statistics of international trade transactions were covered by this classification.

Perhaps the most spectacular and currently best publicized activity

[28] See Asher and Associates, *op. cit.*, Ch. IV.

[29] Examples of invaluable statistical publications are the *Statistical Yearbook*, the *Demographic Yearbook*, and the *Monthly Bulletin of Statistics*.

[30] U.N. Statistical Office, *Commodity Indexes for the Standard International Trade Classification*, Statistical Papers Series M, No. 10 (April, 1953).

of the United Nations in the statistical field is the assistance rendered to underdeveloped countries both in developing their own official statistical procedures and in training personnel in the best statistical methods. Between 1948 and 1954, the United Nations and the specialized agencies provided 143 consultants and advisors to forty-three countries under the technical assistance program. Even more basic has been the establishment of educational and training programs which have made possible the training of native personnel so that each underdeveloped country may in time be able to stand on its own feet.

While statistical data constitute necessary raw material for the student and the policy maker, before these data can provide useful guidance in the formulation of national policy or the solution of international problems, they must be analysed, various hypotheses must be tested, and sound conclusions must be drawn. The work of the United Nations and the specialized agencies in this respect has also been of great value. Most of this has been done by the experts in the United Nations Secretariat and the secretariats of the specialized agencies. However, the United Nations has also drawn on outside experts, either as consultants or as members of *ad hoc* committees, for assistance in preparing analyses and reports. The results of these studies, whether emanating from Secretariat personnel, from outside experts, or from political organs of the United Nations, aided in varying degrees by Secretariat personnel, are usually made public and are generally available to governments and scholars. They thus can serve as a common aid to governments in formulating policy, and do undoubtedly have an important, though statistically unmeasurable, influence on government policies with respect to the matters in question. Among the more important studies and surveys prepared and published by the United Nations are the *World Economic Report* and the *Preliminary Report on the World Social Situation.*

One weakness of secretarial studies and surveys is that while they may be factually complete and comprehensive, they tend to be restrained in respect to analysis and conclusions. Since members of the Secretariats, whether of the United Nations or the specialized agencies, feel inhibited from engaging in political controversy and do not feel that they can wisely push their views much beyond what appears to be the general consensus, studies and surveys prepared and published under the official auspices of the United Nations or the specialized agencies are not generally characterized by the vigor and independence of thought which are to be found in the better private studies.

While in the long run the United Nations may make its major

contribution to the solution of economic and social problems by the assembly and publication of factual information and by the initiation and publication of surveys and analytical studies, the attention of the general public is more likely to be attracted by the public debates which take place in the organs of the United Nations and the specialized agencies and the resolutions that are adopted by them. These undoubtedly serve the useful purpose of drawing attention to important questions, giving national governments the opportunity to present their views, helping to clarify issues, and assisting in developing wider agreement on critical issues. However, their importance and their contribution to the actual achievement of useful results are likely to be over emphasized. Certainly their constructive value cannot be measured by the amount of space that has to be given to them in United Nations publications or even by the attention which is given them in the popular press.

In fact, public debate sometimes does more to delay effective intergovernmental cooperation than to advance it. While this is particularly true of public debate on political issues with which we are not particularly concerned at this point, it is also true of many of the public discussions on issues in the field of economic and social cooperation. There is always the temptation to say things for their effect on domestic constituencies or for their propaganda effect, without too much regard to whether they will contribute to eventual agreement, or in some cases, without too much desire to contribute to such agreement. Many, if not most, of the speeches of delegates of the Communist-controlled states on economic and social issues have had as their real purpose to discredit Western capitalism and democracy. That, of course, is not surprising since Communists can hardly be expected willingly to contribute to the strengthening of an economic and social system which they strongly oppose and which they are convinced must give way to a socialist order.

The opportunities afforded for public debate are very wide indeed. Under the Charter, the General Assembly can discuss and make recommendations with respect to any matter within the scope of the Charter. Since this includes the provisions relating to purposes and principles it is obvious that this gives the Assembly a very free hand. While it is true that the Assembly and the Economic and Social Council, like the other organs of the United Nations, are subject to the limitation that they cannot intervene in any matter essentially within the domestic jurisdiction of a state, this limitation, as we have seen, has been interpreted very narrowly. For one thing, it does not exclude the possibility of discussion of any topic since discussion as such is not regarded as intervention under the Charter. Consequently, any member can request the General Assembly to consider any question it pleases, and so long as procedural requirements are adhered to, it can be assured at least of a debate on whether the item should be included in the agenda. Furthermore, the general debate on the Secretary-General's Report gives every Member government the opportunity to raise those issues which are of particular concern to itself and to make public observations upon them.

Generally, though not always, the purpose of discussion in the General Assembly and the Economic and Social Council, is to come to some conclusion, immediately or eventually. This conclusion is registered in the form of a resolution which, in so far as it deals with substantive matters, is a recommendation addressed to Members or to the specialized agencies. Though such a resolution may be adopted by the necessary majority, it does not impose upon Members any legal obligations to take action. Thus, it is not a legislative action. Any Member that dissents is free to continue its dissent. Consequently, the possibility of taking substantive decisions by less than a unanimous vote—thought by many to be a great advance of United Nations procedure—does not eliminate the desirability, in fact the necessity, of achieving a more substantial consensus, particularly on the part of states whose active cooperation is required for the implementation of the resolution, if any positive result is to be achieved. Thus, for instance, the General Assembly may adopt by the requisite vote a resolution calling upon members to make funds available to underdeveloped states for financing non-self-liquidating projects such as public roads and school buildings. If, however, the United States does not give its support to the resolution, it is likely to prove of little avail since United States financial assistance would be necessary for carrying out such a program.

While resolutions are not, strictly speaking, binding upon members, they do have their effects, even though adopted in the face of vigorous opposition by important states. They do represent a measure of agreement among Members, a consensus, the significance of which is determined as much by the quality of the states which support them as by the number. Since they do represent the opinion of a substantial part of the international community, even those Members which are in the minority, important though they may be, are not particularly happy over the situation. Their policy and conduct are likely to be affected to some extent by their desire to be in harmony with the predominant opinion of the United Nations.

While the United Nations organs do not have the power to create new international legal obligations for Members, the General Assembly and the Economic and Social Council, acting under its authority, may prepare draft conventions and submit them to Members for their ratification, or organize international conferences for that purpose. The same may be done by the specialized agencies. The United Nations has not used this method very frequently but has found it a useful method of dealing with problems which lend themselves particularly to the legal approach. Thus the United Nations approved and submitted to its Members and other states for ratification a draft convention on genocide and the draft constitution of the World Health Organization. Of the specialized agencies, the ILO has made most frequent use of the convention technique. Under its constitution, the International Labor Conference may adopt conventions by a two-thirds vote and submit them to member states for their approval, each member being obligated to bring the convention to the attention of the appropriate constitutional authorties. By the end of 1954, the ILO had approved and submitted to its members 103 conventions covering various aspects of labor conditions. Since the Second World War, however, this method has been less commonly used, in part because the possibilities of fruitful use have been less apparent than formerly and also because the special problems of underdeveloped territories have commanded increasing attention during this period.

While the international agreement or convention is a useful tool in the armory of methods available to the United Nations for achieving its economic and social purposes, it has proven to have certain serious shortcomings in actual practice. First, it is not applicable to many situations of increasingly frequent occurrence or if applicable, is capable of providing only a small part of the remedial action required. It may be necessary to provide the legal basis for the necessary international action, but it does not by itself provide an assurance that the action will be taken. In those cases where it appears necessary to alter the policies and conduct of states, to induce them to refrain from certain conduct, and to pursue other lines of policy and action, the imposition of legal duties alone may not be enough. This may be due to the weakness and inadequacy of international enforcement machinery, or it may be because some states are not yet able because of their limited economic, social, and political development, to conform to the standards prescribed. But defective as may be the means of enforcing international conventions, they still can have considerable authority due to the desire of states not to appear as violators of the law. This accounts in part for another weakness of the convention method. In order to avoid being placed in the position of violators of the law, states commonly insist on so defining their obligations as to give them a great deal of freedom of action. Furthermore, even if a convention is approved by the General Assembly or by a conference specially called for the purpose, there is no assurance that the record of ratification will be good. One of the major problems that the ILO has had to face has been the reluctance of members to ratify conventions, once they have been approved by the Conference.

Still, notwithstanding its defects, the convention method has been highly useful in dealing with many international problems in the economic and social fields. Even where enforcement is difficult and ratifications are few, conventions help to establish standards which influence state policies and conduct. They provide standards of future achievement even though they may be higher than the level of acceptable present achievement. In some cases, particularly where effective methods of enforcement are available, they provide the essential legal basis for effective international action. Conventions regarding the traffic in and use of narcotics are a case in point, as are the constitution and regulations of the World Health Organization. Where the benefits derived from uniformity are obviously greater than any advantages to be derived from non-conformity, the convention method can be clearly effective.

Finally, the United Nations may seek to achieve its economic and social purposes by initiating and carrying out, with the consent and cooperation of states concerned, programs of assistance involving actual field operations. These may take a wide variety of forms. On the one hand, there is the assistance given to a particular country on its request in dealing with an emergency situation, in developing its administrative procedures, in improving its health or educational facilities, or in meeting any other need peculiar to the country in question. Such assistance may also be generalized in a program that is made available to all states desiring to benefit from it, as in the case of the Expanded Program of Technical Assistance.[31] Then there is the possibility of an action program to meet some broad social need which more often then not is temporary in character and which may or may not be limited to one country. Falling in this category are the program for the relief of refugees, the program providing special assistance to children (UNICEF), the Palestine relief and works program, and the program of relief and reconstruction in Korea. The International Bank for Reconstruction and Development is primarily operational in the sense that its activities take the form of loans which it makes on the basis of

[31] See Walter R. Sharp, *International Technical Assistance* (Chicago: Public Administration Service, 1952).

agreement with the state directly concerned. The stress in the postwar period on the need of bringing so-called underdeveloped countries more nearly to the level of economic and social development reached by the more developed countries of western Europe and North America has created an atmosphere particularly favorable to the use of action programs and has involved the United Nations and the specialized agencies more and more in operations of an administrative nature.

Summary and Evaluation

In summarizing and evaluating the work of the United Nations in the economic, social, and cultural fields, it is important to bear in mind that the United Nations and the specialized agencies represent only a part of the total governmental approach to the solution of problems in this area. To take the case of the United States, the Member with the highest per capita wealth and therefore capable of making the major contribution to the work of the Organization, only a relatively small proportion of its total effort and expenditure of funds for dealing with international economic and social problems and for improving cultural relations with other countries is channeled through the United Nations and the specialized agencies. A much larger part is dispensed under bilateral arrangements or under multilateral arrangements such as were developed in the administration of the Marshall Plan, which have no organic connection with the United Nations or the specialized agencies. The reasons for this disproportionate division are to be found in considerations of national policy since it is the Member governments in the last analysis which determine what the scope of United Nations activity is to be. This being the case, a first question to be considered in any evaluation of United Nations activity is what advantages from a strictly national point of view do Members receive or hope to secure from acting through the United Nations rather than independently of it or outside it.

The advantages of the United Nations approach to the Members themselves are numerous and are well illustrated by the experience of the Organization to date. Where the problem to be dealt with is recognized as being global in scope, the United Nations or a specialized agency is an appropriate and available means by which international cooperation of the necessary geographic extent can be quickly and most easily organized. Thus, the United Nations and its specialized agencies have been generally and readily accepted as the appropriate and most effective agencies for dealing with such matters as the control of traffic in narcotics and other harmful drugs, the control of communicable diseases, the provision of satisfactory international postal and telegraphic services, and the assurance of maximum safety and efficiency in international civil aviation. No government would seriously propose to take such matters out of the hands of the United Nations and its specialized agencies and transfer them to regional agencies or agencies established under purely bilateral arrangements. With the developments of modern science and technology, the area of global international concern is steadily expanding and the advantages to be gained through the global approach are increasing.

Another advantage that the United Nations and its specialized agencies offer is that they are able to mobilize the skills and resources of a great number of nations for dealing with international problems. Perhaps the best example of this is the contribution that the United Nations and the specialized agencies have been able to make in the field of technical assistance. Under the Expanded Program of Technical Assistance, the skills and resources of a large number of countries are available and can be utilized in providing the assistance that under-developed countries sorely need in order to improve their health and educational facilities, their agricultural methods, their methods of land utilization, their communication and transportation facilities, and their financial and administrative procedures. While a few countries such as the United States are able to provide most of the skills and resources that are needed, and in any case make the major contribution under the United Nations program, even the United States finds difficulty in providing some of the highly specialized skills that are needed in dealing with the problems of new states in Asia and Africa. Furthermore, the experts which the more advanced Western countries are able to provide are not always the best equipped from the point of view of cultural background and understanding to work under the special conditions which prevail in the more backward countries of greatest need. There is also the point to be emphasized that persons from small countries of equal or even somewhat inferior technical skill may be better equipped to deal with the problems of other small countries than persons from the larger countries that are accustomed to think in larger terms, both programmatic and budgetary. The United Nations and the specialized agencies, therefore, provide the means by which all countries, great and small, industrially developed and industrially backward, with all their cultural diversities, may best make their particular contribution to the achievement of common goals. The use of the United Nations does not of course exclude the possibility of combining resources on a more limited basis for meeting certain more narrowly defined needs such as the economic reconstruction of western Europe or the development of the economic strength and stability of countries that are of particular concern to the Western democracies in their struggle with Communism.

Another important advantage that members derive from channeling their policies and activities through the United Nations is that thereby they acquire greater international influence and prestige for themselves and counter in advance some of the objections and criticisms that might be directed against independent national action. For instance, if the United States had limited its foreign aid to such assistance as it might render unilaterally or under arrangements concluded bilaterally with recipient countries, often in unequal bargaining positions, it would have been widely accused of economic imperialism, and many countries would have refused to receive its assistance. To the extent that it has participated in cooperative programs of assistance, it provides some assurance that its great economic power will not be abused and that the aid rendered will be administered as much in the interest of the recipient country as of the giver. The support given to the Expanded Program of Technical Assistance testifies to the advantage which the more advanced Members of the United Nations and the specialized agencies see in using this cooperative device. It is of course a fact that for a variety of reasons, states in the position to give aid to other states do insist on exercising direct control over a substantial part of such aid and the terms on which it is rendered through bilateral arrangements, but it is significant that these governments, including the Soviet Union, see the advantage of using the United Nations approach as well.

The advantage of having national policies framed within a United Nations context and of being able to defend and justify national actions within that context has been accentuated by the diplomatic and propaganda necessities of the "cold war." The economic and social purposes and principles set forth in the Charter are values to which all Members are pledged, Communist and non-Communist alike. While the Communist countries may have accepted these values with some misgivings, perhaps with tongue in cheek, and certainly in many instances with special meanings, they cannot appear publicly to disown them. Consequently they, as well as the non-Communist Members, must make it appear that their policies and acts are in accord with these values and are intended to further these purposes. It thus becomes advantageous to any Member that is actively engaged in the "cold war" to appeal to the United Nations, to propose action through the Organization, and to use the United Nations as a world forum wherein it can make its own case in terms of United Nations purposes and principles. While some idealists may find this a cheap and improper advantage to seek, it is, nevertheless, a use rival factions commonly make of the machinery of government. It is a part of the contest for control of the instruments of power, and part of the process by which policies and programs are in the end formulated and put into effect.

What in fact have the United Nations and the specialized agencies been able to achieve in the promotion of human welfare? What have they accomplished that could not have been done equally well by other means, i.e., by other means than a global organization with general responsibilities? Of course, it is difficult, if not impossible, to measure in quantitative terms what the United Nations has accomplished in the promotion of general welfare. It is not fair, for example, to judge the relative importance of the Expanded Program of Technical Assistance in comparison with national programs solely by the amount of money spent or the number of persons employed. Nor for that matter is there any quantitative measure of the extent of some of the positive achievements of the United Nations, in view of their somewhat intangible character.

There is general agreement, however, that the achievements of the United Nations have been substantial. To a large extent, these achievements have been in dealing with problems of a technical and non-political character, or in dealing with situations where concerted efforts have been needed to meet great suffering, or in meeting urgent demands for aid in achieving a minimum standard of living.

In the technical field, the United Nations and the specialized agencies have successfully initiated or carried on the work of improving international communication and transportation facilities, of improving health facilities and conditions, and of combatting social evils such as traffic in narcotic drugs. These activities have concerned all peoples and for the most part have been generally supported without regard to ideological frontiers. They fall in the tradition of the nineteenth century international technical cooperation through public international unions and of much of the economic and social work of the League.

The United Nations has rendered an important service in helping to provide for refugees who have been driven from their homes by war, revolution, and natural disaster. Unfortunately, the refugee problem has taken on political overtones due to the relatively large numbers of these refugees that have left their homes to escape from Communism. The uncooperative attitude of the Communist Members of the Organization has not, however, prevented the United Nations and its agencies from performing a useful service in assisting these refugees to resettle and become useful members of new communities.[32]

[32] See John G. Stoessinger, *The Refugee and the World Community* (Minneapolis: University of Minnesota Press, 1956).

The Second World War not only produced the refugee problem but also catastrophic economic destruction and dislocation. The restoration of disrupted economies has required collective action on the part of the more fortunately situated states. In the wake of the advancing Allied armies, the United Nations Relief and Rehabilitation Administration—never technically a part of the United Nations system—undertook the combined task of providing relief and immediate economic assistance to the devastated areas. Emerging "cold war" tensions brought the work of this organization to an end, thus terminating the one ambitious effort to meet the relief and rehabilitation needs of devastated and dislocated areas by a wide cooperative effort, including Communist and non-Communist countries. Following the termination of UNRRA in 1946, efforts in the field of relief, rehabilitation, and reconstruction came to be carried on primarily by United Nations agencies in which the Communist countries did not participate, or under arrangements such as the European Recovery Program which were organized and carried out entirely outside the framework of the United Nations. One important exception was the Economic Commission for Europe which proved to be an instrumentality of considerable value in the work of European economic recovery in which both Communist and non-Communist countries participated.[33] A striking and more recent example of what the United Nations can do in remedying a particular economic dislocation was given by the action of the United Nations on the initiative of the Secretary-General in clearing the Suez Canal for traffic after it had been blocked during the Anglo-French attack on Egypt in October-November 1956.

Generally speaking, the United Nations has not lived up to the level of accomplishment set by the Charter in the field of general economic cooperation to maintain economic stability and prosperity. As we have seen, the economic assistance programs that were necessary to get Europe on the road to economic health were organized and administered outside the United Nations. The effort to establish an International Trade Organization with important responsibilities in the fields of commercial policy, commodity policy, and trade competition failed. The General Agreements on Tariffs and Trade (GATT), negotiated independently of the United Nations, represents about all that has been salvaged from the ambitious International Trade Organization project. European countries have developed special interest in projects for European economic cooperation such as the European Payments Union, the European Coal and Steel Community, the European Common Market, and the European Atomic Energy Community, while Asian, African, and Latin American countries have been primarily

[33] See David Wightman, *Economic Cooperation in Europe.*

interested in the more rapid development of their underdeveloped economies. Notwithstanding, the United Nations has performed useful work by carrying out valuable studies, making available statistical and other information and analyses of world economic conditions, and assisting through discussions at the technical and political levels in the clarification of issues and the establishment of standards of achievement.

Probably the greatest achievement of the United Nations—and its greatest advance over previous cooperative efforts—has been in calling attention to the special needs of underdeveloped areas, in stimulating programs of assistance, and in actually organizing programs such as the Expanded Program of Technical Assistance which has placed at the disposal of underdeveloped countries various forms of technical aid without the political conditions that are sometimes attached by donor states and without the risks that weaker countries have in the past run in accepting aid from more advanced and stronger countries. United Nations aid to underdeveloped countries has been given not only through technical assistance programs but also through loans by the World Bank, and now by assistance from the International Finance Corporation, and the Special Projects Fund set up under the terms of the General Assembly's resolution of December 14, 1957,[34] as an expansion of the technical assistance and development activities of the United Nations. The emphasis on this part of the United Nations work has been due not alone to the existence of the need but also to the competition of the Communist and the free worlds for the favor of underdeveloped countries. While the United Nations commends itself more particularly to representatives of the free world as the instrument by which such aid can be given, even the Communist members are forced to admit the strength of the appeal of United Nations assistance.

In the economic and social fields, the United Nations and its specialized agencies are engaged in part in meeting needs that have long existed but under conditions of our modern technological society exist in even greater degree today. In meeting these needs the United Nations and the specialized agencies are indispensable. But perhaps even more important are the services they render in meeting needs that only in part are the result of modern technological developments and the growth of economic interdependence, needs that have emerged primarily from the intellectual awakening of the peoples of the backward areas of the world. These peoples, or at least their leaders, are no longer willing to accept the conditions of hunger, pestilence, and misery which in the past have been their lot. Nor are they willing any longer to put their trust in the carriers of the "White Man's Burden." They

[34] General Assembly Resolution 1219 (XII).

demand assistance in improving their lot but not on imperialist terms. This is the need which the United Nations and the specialized agencies are peculiarly equipped to meet and this is the great service which the United Nations is in course of performing. How well it assists in meeting the rising economic and social expectations of the peoples of the under-developed areas of the world may well determine the future course of history.

SUGGESTED READINGS

Asher, Robert E. and Associates. *The United Nations and Promotion of the General Welfare.* Washington: The Brookings Institution, 1957.

Asher, Robert E. "Economic Cooperation under U.N. Auspices," *International Organization,* Summer, 1958.

Carnegie Endowment for International Peace. *Coordination of Economic and Social Activities.* New York, 1948.

Cheever, D. S., and Haviland, H. F., Jr. *Organizing for Peace: International Organization in World Affairs.* Boston: Houghton Mifflin Company, 1954.

Claude, Inis, Jr. *Swords into Plowshares.* New York: Random House, Inc., 1956. Chap. 16.

Dunn, Frederick S. *War and the Minds of Men.* New York: Harper & Brothers, Publishers, 1950.

Higgins, Benjamin and Malenbaum, Wilfred. "Financing Economic Development," *International Conciliation,* No. 502 (March, 1955), pp. 275—339.

Jenks, C. Wilfred. "Co-ordination in International Organization: An Introductory Survey," *British Yearbook of International Law,* XXVIII (1951), pp. 29–89.

Matecki, B. E. "Establishment of the International Finance Corporation; A Case Study," *International Organization,* X (1956), pp. 261–75.

Mitrany, David A. *A Working Peace System.* London: National Peace Council, 1946.

Niebuhr, Reinhold. "The Theory and Practice of UNESCO," *International Organization,* IV (1950), pp. 3–11.

Rees, Elfan. "The Refugee and the United Nations," *International Conciliation,* No. 492 (June, 1953), pp. 267–313.

Sharp, Walter R. *International Technical Assistance: Programs and Organization.* Chicago: Public Administration Service, 1952.

U.S. Senate Committee on Foreign Relations, Subcommittee on the United Nations Charter. *The United Nations and the Specialized*

Agencies. Staff Study No. 10. Washington: Government Printing Office, 1955.

Vernon, Raymond. "Organizing for World Trade," *International Conciliation,* No. 505 (November, 1955), pp. 163–222.

Wightman, David. *Economic Cooperation in Europe.* London: Stevens and Son, 1956.

Chapter XIII

HELPING DEPENDENT PEOPLES

LESS THAN a half-century separates the year in which Rudyard Kipling wrote "The White Man's Burden," and the date of the signing of the Charter of the United Nations, and yet the attitudes expressed with respect to non-self-governing territories seem to be centuries apart. Kipling gave expression to sentiments of racial superiority and paternalistic altruism and asserted the special God-given responsibility of the white peoples to govern and educate the colored peoples of Asia and Africa. The Charter emphasizes the equality of peoples and their equal claims to self-determination and full economic, social, and political development under the guarantee of a world organization in which all peoples participate. Recognizing that many peoples in the world are not in control of their own destinies and are still at primitive levels of development, the Charter asserts the special responsibility of the United Nations to see that proper assistance is given in order that the natives of dependent and under-developed territories may experience some of the advantages of more developed societies.

Imperialism and the League Mandate System

Modern imperialism—the control by the economically and politically more advanced states over areas inhabited by peoples of a different culture—reached its height in the closing years of the nineteenth century. It was the product of forces that were released by the Industrial Revolution and the rise of nationalism. Though vast colonial empires had been created in the seventeenth and eighteenth centuries, it was in the latter quarter of the nineteenth century that the forces of modern industrialism, finance capitalism, and nationalism combined to bring about the extension of control by the more advanced states over vast areas of Asia, Africa, Central America, and the Pacific.

At the very time that imperialism was at its height, however, voices of criticism were being raised. Of these the most penetrating and influential was that of J. A. Hobson in his study of imperialism, first published in London in 1902.[1] Hobson, though providing the basis for later Communist doctrine, did not accept the inevitability of imperialism and its evils, and did believe that by constructive social policy these evils could be avoided. The evils which he stressed were principally: (1) exploitation of the native populations by the colonial powers; and (2) disregard of the interests of other states and peoples, resulting in international tension and war.

It was largely to meet the indictment of imperialism, as formulated by Hobson and other writers, that proposals were advanced at the time of the elaboration of the League Covenant to place certain dependent territories under an international mandate system.[2] As the result of President Wilson's insistence, and in the face of strong opposition from some of the would-be beneficiaries from an old-style division of the colonial spoils, certain territories which were ceded by the defeated Central Powers to the victorious Principal Allied and Associated Powers were placed under a League mandate system, intended to provide international guarantees that in certain dependent areas administered by more advanced states the interests of the native peoples and of other states would not be disregarded. It was also believed that these guarantees would contribute to the alleviation of international tensions and the avoidance of future international conflict.

A major defect of the League mandates system, as experience was to show, was that it applied to only a part, and a relatively small part, of the areas under colonial rule. It applied to those territories formerly parts of the German and Ottoman Empires which were ceded to the victor nations but obviously these were not the only territories ". . . inhabited by peoples not yet able to stand by themselves under the strenuous conditions of the modern world."[3] For these other more numerous and more important areas—the colonial possessions of the United Kingdom, the United States, France, Japan, Italy, Belgium, the Netherlands, Spain, and Portugal—the Covenant only provided that

[1] J. A. Hobson, *Imperialism, A Study* (London: George Allen & Unwin, Ltd., 1902).

[2] Notably by General Jan Smuts in his *League of Nations: A Practical Suggestion* (New York: The Nation Press, 1919).

[3] Article 22 of the Covenant.

members ". . . undertake to secure just treatment of the native inhabitants." [4] There was no attempt to define "just treatment" and no provision for international supervision or guarantees of any kind.

Under the League mandates system, the mandated territories were placed under the administration of more advanced states, generally the states that would have annexed them outright if former practices had been followed. While the mandatory power was made responsible for administering the territory, it was required to do this subject to certain international obligations imposed by the Covenant and the mandate agreement. These obligations, varying with the category into which the mandate fell,[5] were: to assist the territory to achieve full independence (Class A); to guarantee to the native peoples certain minimum rights and to protect them against specific abuses and evils (Classes A, B and C); and to secure equal opportunities for the trade and commerce of all nations (Classes A and B.) The League Council was made responsible for supervising the administration of mandated territories. The mandated powers were required to make annual reports on the administration of the territories under their tutelage and the Permanent Mandates Commission, composed of persons appointed by the Council on the basis of qualification by training and experience, was authorized to examine these reports, and advised the Council on the discharge of its responsibilities. While the Covenant established the principle of international accountability for the administration of those territories placed under mandate, it did not provide an effective method of getting the information that was needed for the exercise of League supervision, nor did it provide the means of enforcing League standards in case of violation. The Permanent Mandates Commission could not conduct inquiries on the spot to check on the accuracy of the reports of the mandatory powers. The Council, in addition to being a political body and therefore subject to the influence of political considerations, did not have the power to take effective enforcement action against any state failing to discharge its responsibilities as a mandatory power. Such sanctions as existed were purely moral.[6]

The Mandates system came in for a great deal of criticism, partly because of the weakness of its provisions for guaranteeing international

[4] Article 23 (b) of the Covenant.

[5] Class A: Palestine (U.K.), Syria and the Lebanon (France), and Iraq (U.K.); Class B: Tanganyika (U.K.), Togoland (U.K.), Togoland (France), Ruanda Urundi (Belgium), Cameroons (U.K.), Cameroons (France); Class C: Western Samoa (New Zealand), Nauru (U.K., N.Z., and Australia), New Guinea (Australia), and the North Pacific Islands (Japan).

[6] On the working of the League Mandates System, see Quincy Wright, *Mandates under the League of Nations* (Chicago: University of Chicago Press, 1930).

accountability, and partly because of its discriminatory character. It was viewed by many as being little more than an attempt to give added respectability to old-fashioned colonialism. A more judicious view would seem to be that while failing to live up to the expectations of its more idealistic proponents, it did achieve substantial benefits both in the quality of administration of dependent territories and in changing prevailing attitudes and expectations regarding the treatment of dependent peoples. One mandated territory (Iraq) was brought to independence during the League period, and Syria and Lebanon were in the threshold of independence when the Second World War broke out. There is evidence that standards of administration in dependent territories generally were favorably affected by League practices. Certainly the League mandate system gave encouragement and support to those who, more conscious of the evils of colonialism than of its benefits, were working for its termination and for the realization by dependent peoples of the benefits of self-government.

The Second World War and the Concept of Trusteeship

With the outbreak of the Second World War, the problem of dependent peoples was presented in a different and more urgent context. The unexpected ease with which Japan conquered Western colonial possessions in Asia and the Pacific area, in contrast to the resistance of the Philippine people to whom independence had been promised, and the need of the Allies for the cooperation of Asian peoples if Japanese military aggression was to be defeated, convinced many, in the United States especially, that the age of colonialism was past and that new assurances must be given to the dependent peoples of Asia. In particular it was felt that they should be given firm assurances that within measurable time they would have the opportunities and advantages of self-government. This feeling was particularly strong in the United States Government where from the beginning of the war responsible officials, from the President down, were convinced that colonialism was dead and that at the conclusion of the war some comprehensive system of international trusteeship must be established.

A major obstacle to the development of an agreed Allied position during the War was the reluctance of Prime Minister Churchill to accept any position which implied a weakening of the British Empire. His attitude was dramatically expressed when he said that he had not ". . . become the King's First Minister in order to preside over the liquidation of the British Empire." [7] In the Atlantic Charter, Roosevelt and Churchill had asserted ". . . the right of all peoples to choose the form of government under which they will live." This was interpreted by Churchill, however, as not applying to colonial peoples, though Roosevelt never accepted this view.

During the War a great deal of time and thought was given in the Department of State to the preparation of proposals for an expanded system of trusteeship which would apply to all dependent areas, and not just those which had been under League mandate or which might be detached from the defeated Axis powers. This was in line with views strongly held by President Roosevelt and Secretary of State Hull.[8] Article 12 of the Draft Constitution of International Organization, prepared in the Department of State under the date of July 14, 1943, opened with the following paragraph which was indicative of Administration thinking:

> *1. To those non-self-governing territories which are inhabited by peoples not yet able to stand by themselves, the principle of trusteeship shall be applied in their governance in accordance with which the welfare of the inhabitants and the general interest of other peoples shall be assured under the authority and supervision of the International Organization.*[9]

In spite of the initiative that the Department had taken in preparing comprehensive proposals for an expanded trusteeship system after the war, the proposals that the Department submitted to the other Dumbarton Oaks conferees in the summer of 1944 contained nothing on the subject of trusteeship due to a disagreement that had arisen between the Department of State and the War and Navy Departments over the application of the trusteeship principle to Japanese-owned or -mandated islands in the Pacific. Since this interdepartmental difference was not resolved by the time of the Dumbarton Oaks Conversations, the Dumbarton Oaks Proposals had nothing to say on the subject of trusteeship. This was one of the gaps left to be filled by later negotiations.

At the Yalta Conference in February, 1945, Churchill, Roosevelt, and Stalin agreed that the five nations that were to have permanent seats on the Security Council should consult prior to the conference to draft Charter proposals relating to the establishment of a trusteeship

---

[7] *The London Times,* Nov. 11, 1942.

[8] See Cordell Hull, *The Memoirs of Cordell Hull* (New York: The Macmillan Company, 1948), Vol. II, pp. 1234–38.

[9] *Postwar Foreign Policy Preparation, 1939–1945.* Department of State Publ. 3580 (Washington, 1949), p. 481.

system. It was also agreed that trusteeship would ". . . only apply to (a) existing mandates of the League of Nations; (b) territories detached from the enemy as the result of the present war; (c) any other territory which might voluntarily be placed under trusteeship." [10]

When the San Francisco Conference met, the Sponsoring Powers and France had not as yet consulted on the trusteeship question. As a result, their consultations occurred simultaneously with the consideration of the matter by the technical committee of the Conference (Committee II/4) and in the drafting of the Charter provisions on non-self-governing territories, advance agreement of the major powers did not have the same degree of decisive influence that it had with respect to other provisions of the Charter. Furthermore, as the result of the inter-departmental disagreement in Washington, the United States initiative lost much of its momentum, and at San Francisco the actual plan adopted owed as much, if not more, to the initiatives of other participants. In particular, though the United States had earlier been the advocate of a comprehensive declaration of principles, at San Francisco this approach seems to have been overlooked in the United States proposals; it was the United Kingdom and Australia that took the lead in proposing what subsequently became Chapter XI of the Charter. It was never made clear, however, whether all the proponents of this Declaration regarded it as having the same legal effect as other provisions, since the original United Kingdom proposal was that it should be an annex to the Charter.[11]

With respect to the trusteeship provisions of the Charter, the United States proposals, particularly those providing for a Trusteeship Council with substantial powers, were generally accepted. Nevertheless, the strong initiative which the United States had earlier taken as an advocate of trusteeship was considerably dulled by the concern which the United States delegation now had to show for the protection of American strategic interests in the Pacific area. Instead of appearing as the uninhibited leader of the attack on old-style colonialism, the United States found itself in the unfortunate position of having to defend one of the traditional interests of colonial powers, the interest in national security, against proposals intended to give greater recognition and protection to the special interests of native peoples.

But while the United States found it necessary for reasons of

[10] U.S. Dept. of State, "The Conferences of Malta and Yalta, 1945," *Foreign Relations of the United States* (Washington: Government Printing Office, 1955), p. 977.

[11] See Geoffrey L. Goodwin, *Britain and the United Nations* (New York: Manhattan Publishing Company, 1957), pp. 352–53.

national security to take a position somewhat less advanced than the earlier position of advocacy of an international trusteeship for all dependent territories which had been favored by many people in the Administration and outside, the debates at San Francisco and the provisions of the Charter as finally written made it clear that colonialism as it had been practiced in the nineteenth century and the first decade of the twentieth was in retreat. While some of the major powers, because of their particular responsibilities and interests, might be forced to adopt conservative and cautious attitudes, the War itself had so discredited colonialism as to make it no longer defensible in traditional terms. If so-called advanced nations were to continue to justify their rule of dependent areas, it could only be done as the performance of an international responsibility and with some assurance other than that provided by the good faith of the administering state that the welfare of the native peoples would be given first consideration.

The Charter and Dependent Peoples

The Charter of the United Nations represents a considerable advance over the Covenant of the League of Nations in its provisions for the protection and advancement of dependent peoples. It would be a mistake to say that in all respects it is an improvement. While this is a matter of subjective judgment, there are certainly good reasons for believing that in some respects, as for example the provisions governing the composition of the Trusteeship Council, the Charter is not an improvement. But if we accept the premise that the international community is rightfully concerned with the manner in which non-self-governing peoples are governed, and that this justifies international accountability for the administration of non-self-governing territories, the Charter goes considerably further than the Covenant in providing the legal basis and the practical means for making this concern effective.

In the first place, the Charter defines the purposes of the United Nations and the responsibilities of its principal organs in such broad and generous terms as to bring particular aspects of the administration of dependent territories within its sphere of concern and to provide the basis for appropriate action by these organs. The first purpose of the Organization is declared to be the maintenance of international peace and security, and consequently the United Nations may concern itself with any situation which constitutes a threat to that peace and may take such action as the Charter authorizes. More specifically, it is a declared purpose of the Organization ". . . to develop friendly relations among nations based on respect for the principle of equal rights and self-determination of peoples, and to take other appropriate measures to strengthen universal peace." [12] Still more specifically, the General Assembly ". . . may recommend measures for the peaceful adjustment of any situation, regardless of origin, which it deems likely to impair the general welfare or friendly relations among nations, including situations resulting from a violation of the provisions of the present Charter setting forth the Purposes and Principles of the United Nations." [13] Even making allowance for the limitation imposed by the provisions of Article 2(7) for safeguarding domestic jurisdiction, these and other provisions of the Charter provide a broad and flexible basis for United Nations consideration of any situation involving a non-self-governing territory endangering international peace and friendly relations among nations.

Three out of nineteen chapters of the Charter are explicitly concerned with the welfare and advancement of non-self-governing peoples. One of the major advances of the Charter over all earlier international arrangements is the Declaration Regarding Non-Self-Governing Territories contained in Chapter XI. As we have seen, the original United Kingdom proposal was that this should be an annex to the Chapter, but in the course of its consideration at San Francisco it was agreed to include the Declaration in the body of the document. There have been some efforts to give the Declaration the character of a unilateral statement of policy, distinguishing it from other provisions of the Charter from the point of view of legal commitment. In spite of some statements made and some decisions that were taken in the course of the San Francisco Conference, notably the decision not to include at the end of the introductory paragraph of Article 73 the word "undertake," it is difficult to see how any reasonable interpretation of the Chapter would permit obligations under it to be regarded as any less binding than those of other Chapters of the Charter. This then represents the acceptance by all Members administering non-self-governing territories of certain specific international commitments as to the purposes and substance of their policies and actions.

According to Article 73 of the Charter (the first of two articles constituting Chapter XI),

Members of the United Nations which have or assume responsibilities for the administration of territories whose peoples have not

[12] Article 2, par. 2. The phrase "based on respect for the principle of equal rights and self-determination of peoples" was inserted at San Francisco on the proposal of the Soviet Union without there being apparently any general agreement as to its meaning.

[13] Article 14.

> *yet attained a full measure of self-government recognize the principle that the interests of the inhabitants of these territories are paramount, and accept as a sacred trust the obligation to promote to the utmost, within the system of international peace and security established by the present Charter, the well-being of the inhabitants of these territories.*

In the discharge of these responsibilities, Members accept the obligation (a) to ensure "the political, economic, social, and educational advancement" of these peoples, "their just treatment, and their protection against abuses"; (b) "to develop self-government" and assist in the progressive development of free political institutions; (c) "to further international peace and security"; (d) "to promote constructive measures of development," to encourage research and to cooperate with each other and with specialized international bodies in the practical achievement of the above social, economic and scientific purposes; and

> *(e) to transmit regularly to the Secretary-General for information purposes, subject to such limitation as security and constitutional considerations may require, statistical and other information of a technical nature relating to economic, social and educational conditions in the territories for which they are respectively responsible other than [territories under trusteeship].*

It is particularly to be noted that the obligation which Members assume with respect to the non-self-governing territories that they administer is "to develop self-government" and that "independence" does not appear as a purpose. It was explained, however, by the United Kingdom representative at the Conference that independence was one form of self-government though not necessarily the only one. It is also to be noted that the obligation under paragraph (e) to transmit information "of a technical nature" does not extend to information with respect to political conditions though at one stage in the drafting of the article, the word "political" did appear. Finally it is to be particularly noted that Article 73 does not contain any provision expressly giving to an established organ of the United Nations any supervisory power or function.

Article 74, the other part of the Declaration, contains a rather weak and meaningless statement to the effect that Members also agree that their policies with respect to non-self-governing territories, ". . . no less than in respect of their metropolitan areas, must be based on the principle of good neighborliness, due account being taken of the interests and well-being of the rest of the world, in social, economic, and commercial matters."

The trusteeship provisions contained in Chapters XII and XIII of the Charter, together with the provisions of the trusteeship agreements, go considerably beyond the Declaration in defining the specific obligations of Members and particularly in providing machinery and procedures of international supervision. However, these provisions are made applicable only to those areas falling within any of three enumerated categories that are placed under trusteeship by trusteeship agreements concluded between the "states directly concerned" and approved by the General Assembly. The three categories are

(a) *territories now held under mandate;*

(b) *territories which may be detached from enemy states as a result of the Second World War; and*

(c) *territories voluntarily placed under the system by states responsible for their administration.*[14]

In practice, a comparatively small part of the total area and population of non-self-governing territories has been brought under the trusteeship system. Furthermore, this must have been the result foreseen by those who were primarily responsible for writing the Charter provisions since only in the case of Southwest Africa has it been claimed that the reasonable expectations of the authors have been disappointed.

The basic objectives of the trusteeship system are stated in Article 76. They go somewhat beyond the objectives set forth in the Declaration, particularly in respect to the political objective and the treatment to be accorded other Members. The listed objectives include: (a) the furtherance of international peace and security; (b) the promotion of the political, economic, social and educational advancement of the inhabitants and "their progressive development towards self-government or independence"; (c) the encouragement of respect for human rights and fundamental freedoms and of recognition of the interdependence of peoples; and (d) the assurance of equal treatment in social, economic, commercial and legal matters for all Members and their nationals. The duties of administering states, as well as the extent of their authority are spelled out in greater detail in the trust agreements that have been concluded and approved by the General Assembly for each territory.[15]

A trusteeship agreement may designate a particular area or areas as strategic. For areas so designated, the functions of the United Nations

[14] Article 77.

[15] See, for example, the Trusteeship Agreement for the Territory of Tanganyika as approved by the General Assembly on December 13, 1946. U.N. Doc. T/Agreement 2, June 9, 1947.

are exercised by the Security Council instead of the General Assembly. The Charter does provide, however, that the basic objectives of the trusteeship system shall apply to strategic areas so designated, and that the Security Council, in discharging its responsibilities, shall avail itself of the assistance of the Trusteeship Council when performing functions relating to political, economic, social, and educational matters.[16]

As indicated above, the supervisory functions of the United Nations with respect to trust territories other than strategic areas are performed by the General Assembly, assisted by the Trusteeship Council, an organ composed of a limited number of administering and non-administering states [17] and operating under its authority. This represents a marked contrast to the League mandate system where this authority was vested in the Council acting with the advice and assistance of the Permanent Mandates Commission, composed of persons chosen for their individual competence. This of course means that ultimate authority under the trusteeship system is vested in the representative organ, instead of the organ whose composition is based on recognition of the greater responsibilities of the major powers for keeping peace. It also means that the organ which is supposed to give assistance to the Assembly is itself a political organ, though so composed as to give equal voting power to the administering and non-administering members.

In addition to locating the authority for supervision differently than did the Covenant in the case of the mandates system, the Charter defines this authority somewhat more liberally. For example, in addition to specifying that "the General Assembly and, under its authority, the Trusteeship Council," may consider reports by the administering authority, it also states that they may ". . . accept petitions and examine them in consultation with the administering authority . . . , provide for periodic visits to the respective trust territories," and ". . . take these and other actions in conformity with the terms of the trusteeship agreements." [18] The Trusteeship Council is directed to formulate a questionnaire upon the basis of which each administering authority is required to make an annual report.

The United Nations in Action

The functioning of the United Nations as an organization for the advancement of non-self-governing peoples has been deeply influenced

[16] Article 83.

[17] For composition of the Trusteeship Council, see above, pp. 112–113, 116–117.

[18] Article 87.

by the "cold war" and by the emergence of nationalism in Asia and Africa as a powerful force in the post-War world.[19] The latter has taken the form primarily of a revolt against colonialism and a demand for a fuller share of the good things of life for hitherto subject peoples. In the context of the "cold war" and as the result of the relative increase in the numerical strength of Asian and African members, this force has achieved great influence in the United Nations, particularly in the General Assembly. While the Asian and African Members, greatly increased in number and relative importance as the result of the breaking of the membership deadlock in 1955, have not joined forces on all issues before the United Nations, they have generally acted together, and have received support from such opposite sources as the Latin American Members and the Soviet bloc, on issues involving the economic, social, and political advancement of non-self-governing territories and their ultimate achievement of self-government or independence.

The activity of the United Nations in the advancement of dependent peoples has not been limited by any means to action under Chapters XI, XII, and XIII of the Charter. In the discharge of its responsibilities for the maintenance of international peace and security and the development of friendly relations among nations, the United Nations has had occasion to deal with a number of situations where the right of native peoples to determine their own future has been involved. Thus, in the Indonesian case, the Security Council was called upon to deal with a situation resulting from the efforts of the Netherlands Government to put down by force an independence movement which had already been accorded a degree of recognition. As we have seen, the Security Council made a substantial contribution to the achievement of Indonesian independence. In submitting the Palestine question to the General Assembly in 1947, the United Kingdom Government asked that organ to find a solution which would permit the termination of the mandate and the achievement of independence. The Assembly's recommendation provided for political division into two independent states and economic union. This recommendation was never fully implemented but this, and subsequent action by the Assembly and the Security Council, undoubtedly did contribute to the creation of an independent state of Israel. In connection with Korea, the General Assembly was asked to find a way by which Korea would achieve unity and independence. The plan proposed was not accepted by the Soviet Union and was carried out in South Korea only. Nevertheless, United Nations action did contribute to the establishment of the Republic of Korea in the south.

More recently, the United Nations has been asked to consider

[19] See above, pp. 54–56.

situations in Tunisia, Morocco, and Algeria where there have been strong independence movements. Here the role of the United Nations has been less easy to evaluate. On the one hand, it would appear that General Assembly action or threat of action may well have been an important influence inducing France to agree to independence for Tunisia and Morocco. In the case of Algeria, there is no evidence that the United Nations has had any influence, except possibly to exacerbate feelings on both sides. In the Algerian case in particular, the role of the United Nations has been complicated by the fact that some of its Members seek to use the affair to weaken and discredit France and the West, while others are reluctant to do anything which will seriously weaken and antagonize France even though they may have reservations on the validity of France's position. In the case of Cyprus, the General Assembly has also been asked to deal with a very touchy problem, the handling of which has been complicated by "cold war" maneuvering and the defense interests of NATO.

While the principle of self-determination has been invoked in many of the above cases, it has received full and extended consideration during the drafting of the covenants on human rights. In the course of these discussions, the leading proponents of the cause of self-government, including independence, for dependent peoples have had the opportunity to press their claim for the explicit recognition of the principle of self-determination which, if accepted, would greatly strengthen their case for granting independence immediately or at an early date to specific territories. As we have seen,[20] the colonial powers, with considerable support from other Members, have strongly opposed the inclusion of a self-determination article in the Covenants and have indicated their unwillingness to accept the Covenants with such an article included. There is some question whether or not the cause of political advancement for dependent peoples has been helped by this debate and by other seemingly irresponsible invocations of the principle.[21]

Many of the activities of the United Nations in the broad field of economic and social cooperation have contributed to the welfare and development of the non-self-governing territories. Though the colonial governments have in some instances shown an unfortunate reluctance to take advantage of this assistance, there is no question that their dependent peoples have benefited greatly from much that the United Nations and the specialized agencies have done. This has been true particularly of the work of the regional commissions of ECOSOC, especially

[20] See above, p. 251.
[21] See Clyde Eagleton, "Excesses of Self-Determination," *Foreign Affairs,* XXXI, No. 4 (July 1953), pp. 592–604.

the Economic Commission for Asia and the Far East, the technical assistance program, the malaria control program of the World Health Organization, and the surveys and loan operations of the World Bank. Particularly in respect to economic and social development, it is important to call attention not only to what the United Nations has done under its general programs but also to what has been achieved under bilateral programs, and under regional arrangements such as the Colombo Plan for Cooperative Economic Development in South and Southeast Asia, which, while not part of the United Nations effort, have the same general purposes in view.[22]

The General Assembly and the Declaration

We have seen that Chapter XI of the Charter represented a new departure in the carrying out of the idea of international accountability, and that its inclusion in the Charter left unanswered important questions regarding its exact meaning and significance. It is therefore not surprising that the activity of the United Nations under this Declaration has raised some highly contentious issues and produced on the part of some Members of the Organization some highly forceful reactions. In fact it has been with respect to what the United Nations can and should do under the terms of this Declaration that the division within the membership of the Organization between the Afro-Asian bloc, supported by some Latin American Members and the Communist Members, and the Western colonial powers and their friends, has been most pronounced.

Though the Declaration defines the duties of Members administering non-self-governing territories, it does not expressly provide for any form of supervision or control by organs of the United Nations. Though administering states are required to transmit certain kinds of information to the Secretariat regularly "for information purposes," there is no suggestion in the Declaration that this information is to be used in any way to provide the basis for some form of international supervision.

The issue was raised at the first session of the General Assembly in 1946. It was strongly contended that the General Assembly had no authority under the Charter to consider this information, to set up special machinery for its study, or to make any recommendations to Members regarding the discharge of their responsibilities under the

[22] For fuller discussion, see Robert E. Asher and Associates, *The United Nations and Promotion of the General Welfare* (Washington: The Brookings Institution, 1957), esp. Ch. XX.

Declaration. Such action, it was argued, would violate the domestic jurisdiction principle of the Charter and in any case would be unwise. In support of the view that the General Assembly should take action along these lines, it was pointed out that under Article 10 of the Charter the General Assembly ". . . may discuss any questions or any matters within the scope of the present Charter . . . ," and may make recommendations to Members. Certainly the provisions of Chapter XI were within the "scope" of the Charter.

After a heated debate, the Assembly finally adopted a resolution [23] which requested the Secretary-General to summarize, analyze, and classify the information submitted under Article 73(e) and to report to the General Assembly. It also set up an *ad hoc* committee to examine the Secretary-General's report and make recommendations to the Assembly regarding procedures to be followed. In spite of strong opposition by the colonial powers, the General Assembly has never relinquished the authority which it thus asserted in its first session. The issues of the composition, functions and powers of the committee have been repeatedly argued. Up to the present, out of deference to the attitudes of the colonial powers, the committee has not been placed on a permanent basis.[24] It consists of an equal number of administering and nonadministering members. Due to the fact, however, that Belgium has refused to participate in the work of the committee, its active membership is somewhat unbalanced.

From the beginning, the General Assembly has been concerned with the determination of what territories are non-self-governing. The Charter does not specify who is to make this determination nor does it indicate in any detail the considerations that are to be taken into account in determining whether the people of a particular territory have "attained a full measure of self-government." Obviously an administering state which resents the degree of supervision which the General Assembly has attempted to impose might be tempted to avoid this unwanted interference by claiming that a particular territory had achieved "a full measure of self-government" even though the facts might not support this contention. In its first session, the General Assembly adopted a resolution listing as non-self-governing territories the seventy-four territories concerning which eight Members had transmitted information.[25] Thus the Assembly initially accepted determination by the administering states.

Subsequently, however, the Assembly took the view that while the

---

[23] General Assembly Resolution 66 (I), Dec. 14, 1946.

[24] Its present title is Committee on Information from Non-Self-Governing Territories.

[25] See General Assembly Resolution 66 (I), Dec. 14, 1946.

administering state might make the initial determination whether or not a territory was non-self-governing, once that state had determined a territory to be non-self-governing by accepting the obligation to transmit information, it could not by itself decide that the territory had become fully self-governing and cease to transmit information. In other words, the Assembly insisted on the right to take this decision. This right it has exercised in a number of instances.[26] Furthermore, the Assembly has given a great deal of attention to the listing of factors to be taken into account in determining whether a particular territory has ceased to be non-self-governing. In 1953, the General Assembly adopted a resolution listing factors that might be used as a guide in making the determination.[27] These factors, thirty-four in number, were divided into: (1) those indicative of independence; (2) those indicative of separate systems of self-government; and (3) those indicative of free association of the territory on an equal basis with the metropolitan or other country.

The debates of the General Assembly, both on factors to be taken into account in determining whether full self-government had been achieved, and on the question whether particular territories had achieved it, showed the complexity of the problem and the limitations of Assembly action. If an administering state takes the position that a particular territory is self-governing and ceases to transmit information on it, there is little that the Assembly can do except exercise moral suasion. Furthermore the Assembly and its subsidiary organs have limited means of establishing the facts since they do not have the authority to send visiting missions into the territory. To a large extent the effectiveness of the United Nations depends on the voluntary cooperation of the administering states and a condition of that cooperation may well be the adoption of a reasonable and conciliatory attitude by the Assembly. This is illustrated by the decision of the General Assembly to accept the United States' determination that Puerto Rico had become fully self-governing even though serious doubts were expressed by some non-Communist members of the Assembly.[28]

Generally speaking, the efforts of the General Assembly, under the stimulus of the anti-colonial bloc, have been directed to strengthening the system of international accountability under Chapter XI, both by expanding and making more precise the duties of administering states and by increasing the scope and effectiveness of General Assembly

[26] Greenland, Indonesia, Puerto Rico, Surinam and the Dutch Antilles, the Gold Coast, Tunis, and Morocco.

[27] General Assembly Resolution 742 (VIII), Nov. 27, 1953.

[28] For a more complete discussion of the determination of non-self-governing territories, see Asher and Associates, *op. cit.,* pp. 888–915.

supervision. Thus, one of the issues with which the Assembly has been very much concerned is the kind of information to be transmitted under Article 73(e). There is in the article no specific requirement that political information be transmitted. The administering state, however, is obligated to assist the people of the non-self-governing territory ". . . in the progressive development of their free political institutions." It has been argued that if the Assembly is to evaluate the extent to which this duty is being performed, the administering state should make available information regarding political development and more particularly the extent to which natives are trained for and used in administrative positions. Some administering states transmit this kind of information on a voluntary basis. The Assembly has never taken the position that administering states are obligated to submit political information, but it has encouraged them to do so and has included items relating to political development in the "Standard Form" for the guidance of Members in transmitting information under Article 73(e). The Form indicates, however, that the transmitting of such information is optional.

Furthermore, the General Assembly has considered a number of proposals to associate natives of non-self-governing territories more closely with its work of supervision. A proposal that the General Assembly convene a conference of representatives of non-self-governing peoples was defeated, largely because of the opposition of administering states. The eighth session of the Assembly invited administering Members to attach to their delegations qualified indigenous representatives from more advanced territories. In 1955, the Assembly turned down an Indian proposal that representatives of territorial governments be admitted as observers by the Committee on Information, with the consent of the administering states. Generally speaking, the persistent effort in the Assembly on the part of the anti-colonial bloc has been to assimilate the system of accountability under Chapter XI to the trusteeship system, thus achieving by a process of indirection what appears to have been the purpose of the Department of State experts in 1942 and 1943. Since that time, the official attitude of the United States has become much more sympathetic toward the point of view of the colonial powers.

While it has been quite widely accepted that the General Assembly may consider the information transmitted by the administering states and make recommendations to Members with respect to matters covered by Chapter XI, it is also generally agreed that the Assembly should not direct its criticisms or recommendations to a particular administering state as it has done under the trusteeship system. While its recommendations assume a fairly concrete form, they are general in the sense that they are directed to all similarly situated. The Assembly has adopted the practice of devoting its attention each year to some major aspect of colonial administration. Its resolutions have reflected its functional specialization. Thus, the Assembly has adopted recommendations that equal treatment in education be given to all inhabitants; that technical training of dependent peoples should be emphasized and that the administering states should cooperate with the specialized agencies to that end; and that increased technical aid should be provided. In 1955, the General Assembly decided to sponsor a review of progress achieved in non-self-governing territories since the creation of the United Nations in order to evaluate the extent to which these areas were advancing towards the fulfillment of Charter goals.

Any evaluation of what the United Nations has been able to achieve under Chapter XI is bound to be most difficult. There is little concrete evidence to warrant the conclusion that by its efforts or as the result of the incorporation of the Declaration in the Charter the peoples of non-self-governing territories are any further along the road of economic, social, and political progress than they would have been if the Charter did not exist. Probably no administering state would admit that its policies have been more enlightened or that it has given more support and encouragement to the aspirations of dependent peoples as the result of United Nations prodding than it would have done if left to its own devices. And yet there is some reason to believe that widespread interest in the development of dependent territories, the desire of colonial powers to have their policies and actions understood and approved, and above all, the rapid progress that has been made since the war in transforming dependent areas into self-governing political units are not wholly unrelated to the fact that Chapter XI is in the Charter and that the General Assembly has been a jealous guardian of the standards of conduct there set forth, always ready to prod the administering states to greater achievement rather than be satisfied with less.

The United Nations and Trusteeship

In comparison with what the early planners in the Department of State envisaged, the United Nations trusteeship system is a modest operation. Even in comparison with the League mandates system, it does not impress one as being particularly revolutionary. And if we think of its potentialities in comparison with those of the system of accountability under Chapter XI, we must admit that they are limited indeed, unless of course the states now administering non-self-governing territories generally choose to place them under trusteeship. There has been no indication of that. Paradoxically, the more successful the trusteeship system is in fulfilling its present commitments, the sooner it will cease to exist, unless, of course, its scope is greatly extended in the meantime.

The trusteeship system was slow in getting started because its existence depended on the conclusion of trusteeship agreements and their approval by the General Assembly, or, in the case of strategic areas, by the Security Council. Until the agreements were in force, there were no territories under trusteeship, and furthermore, in view of the provisions governing the composition of the Trusteeship Council, no possibility of organizing the Council. There was considerable delay in the conclusion of agreements. This resulted, in part, from the slowness of governments in deciding to place mandated territories under trusteeship, and on what terms, though only the Union of South Africa in the end refused. More importantly, it was due to the unfortunate phrasing of Article 79 which provided that the trusteeship agreements should be initially concluded by "the states directly concerned." The Charter did not explain what criteria were to be applied in determining these states and there was no general agreement among Members of the United Nations. The result was that this particular requirement was in the end by-passed. Each agreement was drawn up by the state in control of the territory, after consultation with such other states as it might choose, and then became effective when approved by the General Assembly and ratified by the submitting state.

Up to the present time, eleven territories have been placed under trusteeship. Ten of these were former mandated territories, and one (Somaliland) was detached from Italy by the terms of the Italian peace treaty and placed under trusteeship by an Assembly resolution which the parties to the Italian peace treaty had agreed in advance to accept. The territories that have thus been placed under trusteeship are:

Territory	Administering Authority	Former Status
Cameroons (British)	United Kingdom	League Mandate (B)
Togoland (British)	United Kingdom	League Mandate (B)
Tanganyika	United Kingdom	League Mandate (B)
Cameroons (French)	France	League Mandate (B)
Togoland (French)	France	League Mandate (B)
Ruanda Urundi	Belgium	League Mandate (B)
Nauru	Australia [29]	League Mandate (C)
New Guinea	Australia	League Mandate (C)
Western Samoa	New Zealand	League Mandate (C)
North Pacific Islands	United States	League Mandate (C) (administered by Japan)
Somaliland	Italy	Italian colony

[29] On behalf of Australia, New Zealand, and the United Kingdom.

Except for the class A mandated territories which had either achieved independence or at the time the Charter was written were considered ready for it, Southwest Africa is the only former mandated territory that has not been placed under trusteeship. The Union of South Africa has consistently refused to be moved from its position that the territory should be integrated into the Union and that in so doing it was violating no international obligation. Though the legal right of the Union Government not to place the territory under trusteeship has been admitted by most of the other Members, the General Assembly has insisted, with the backing of the International Court of Justice,[30] that the Union is under international responsibilities for the administration of the territory and that it is the Assembly, as the successor to the League Council, that is responsible for seeing that those responsibilities are discharged. The Union, however, has shown no willingness to accept this view or to cooperate with the General Assembly in its efforts to exercise this function through a special committee on South-West Africa.[31]

In actual operation, the trusteeship system has developed elements of strength and weakness which make its evaluation difficult in terms either of comparison with the League mandates system or of achievement of its declared purposes. First, it is quite clear that the emphasis upon positive, constructive action both in the general purposes of trusteeship and in the specific commitments assumed by administering authorities has helped to speed up the economic, social, and political development of trust territories, and by the example set, has probably helped to accelerate this development in all non-self-governing territories. Today, it is generally taken for granted that the trust territories will sooner or later achieve full independence or self-government, and in most cases sooner rather than later. That was not the expectation with respect to all mandated territories under the League. One trust territory—British Togoland—has already achieved independence, in union with the Gold Coast, as the state of Ghana. Somaliland is due to achieve independence in 1960. Other African Territories will in all likelihood achieve independence or self-government within a larger framework. Some of these results no doubt would have been achieved under the more liberal postwar policies of colonial powers, especially the United Kingdom, even if the trusteeship system had not been established, but it is not easy to believe that the existence of formal commitments and machinery and procedures of international supervision have not made a difference.

[30] I.C.J. "International Status of South-West Africa," Advisory Opinion, July 11, 1950. *I.C.J. Reports, 1950,* p. 19.

[31] See Asher and Associates, *op. cit.,* pp. 941–44.

The procedures that have been developed under the trusteeship system for giving interested parties the opportunity to present complaints and for establishing the facts regarding the administration of trust territories have marked a considerable improvement over League procedures and have provided the basis for more effective international supervision. The annual reports by the administering authorities and their examination by the Trusteeship Council ". . . constitute the backbone of the system of international supervision." [32] The reports are prepared on the basis of a detailed questionnaire prepared by the Council. The adequacy of the questionnaire has been a subject of frequent discussion and particularly the need of variations to take account of particular situations. When the report of an administering authority is being examined, a representative of the authority is present to answer questions and give supplementary information.

Under the trusteeship system, the right of petition is widely accorded and exercised with the result that a major problem facing the Trusteeship Council has been the screening of petitions to prevent abuse and misuse of the Council's time. Petitions are presented not only to the General Assembly and the Trusteeship Council, but also to the visiting missions, and not only in writing but also orally. A major departure from League practice has been to allow the petition to come to the United Nations organ directly without the requirement that it be first submitted to the administering authority.

The greatest improvement in trusteeship arrangements for hearing grievances and establishing the facts is the provision for visiting missions—now organized on the basis of one visit to each territory every three years—which makes it possible for the General Assembly and the Trusteeship Council to get firsthand information. While the visiting missions that have been organized and sent to trust territories have not been uniformly successful in achieving their purpose, they provide the Assembly and Council with an invaluable means of independent intelligence, as well as also serving an important educational function for Secretariat staff and members of the Council.

While the United Nations procedures for airing complaints and clarifying the facts have been reasonably successful and have marked a degree of improvement over League procedures, the organization of supervisory authority has not been equally successful. Vesting responsibility for the performance of United Nations functions in all trust territories, except strategic areas, in the General Assembly, assisted by the Trusteeship Council, was intended to strengthen the Organization's authority, as indeed it has. The General Assembly, composed as it is

[32] *Ibid.*, p. 946.

of a majority of states with anti-imperialistic leanings, has proven to be a vigorous defender of the rights of dependent peoples and an alert critic of the conduct of colonial powers. It was hoped to keep the Assembly under restraint by having initial responsibility assumed by the Trusteeship Council and by giving that organ the status of a principal organ of the United Nations; that hope has only in part been realized. What has actually happened in practice is that the General Assembly has more often than not proceeded as though the matter were initially being considered by it and has not treated the Council's recommendations as having great weight and therefore entitled in most cases to acceptance without serious question.

One reason for the relative ineffectiveness of the Trusteeship Council, and probably the most important one, has been its essentially political character. An important reason for the considerable influence and prestige of the Permanent Mandates Commission of the League of Nations was the fact that it was composed of recognized experts on colonial problems whose opinions on the questions that came before them were entitled to great weight. The Trusteeship Council, on the other hand, is a political body. Its members are Members of the United Nations, and the individuals who attend meetings of the Council are appointed by and receive their instructions from governments. While they may be qualified experts in their own right, they are nevertheless recognized as representatives of their respective governments. This being the case, the Trusteeship Council suffers in competition with the General Assembly. Since the Council, like the Assembly, is a political organ with no convincing claim to expert status, Members who desire the United Nations to exert strong pressure on the administering authorities to speed up the development of trust territories or show more consideration for the rights and interests of the native peoples, naturally prefer to utilize the Assembly where their numbers are likely to assure a favorable result instead of the Trusteeship Council where there is a built-in equality of strength. Whereas in the Council it is necessary to win the support of at least one administering member, in the Assembly no such action is necessary.

A weakness which the United Nations trusteeship system shares with the League mandate system is that even if it is plainly established that the administering authority has failed to discharge its responsibilities and has in fact clearly disregarded the terms of the Charter and the trusteeship agreement, there is no clearly effective action that the United Nations organ can take. If the conduct of the administering state is of such extreme nature as to constitute a threat to or a breach of international peace and security, the Security Council, of course, can take appropriate action if the necessary agreement of its permanent members is forthcoming. But short of that, the General Assembly can only recommend and its recommendations carry only such weight as the states to which they are directed choose to attach to them. Since most Members of the United Nations do take their responsibilities seriously and do not like to be in the position of having their actions widely condemned, the amount of influence which recommendations adopted by substantial majorities have is not likely to be inconsequential. But it is probably true that this influence can be dissipated by the irresponsible and immoderate use of the Assembly's powers, and more particularly by the use of the Assembly's powers to serve extraneous purposes, such as some advantage in the "cold war."

General Conclusions

The change that has taken place in the generally prevailing attitudes toward colonialism and its future is one of the significant phenomena of our times. Before the Second World War there was widespread criticism of colonialism and support for the principle of trusteeship, but, generally speaking, colonial powers were still hopeful that by adopting more enlightened policies they could continue to maintain their special positions in their colonies for a long time to come. While the mandate system had been accepted on a limited basis, it had involved no real commitment to ultimate self-government or independence for any territory other than those under Class A mandates.

The Second World War and the years following have witnessed a remarkable change. Colonial powers are now everywhere on the defensive. The United States and the United Kingdom have definitely committed themselves to self-government or independence for their dependent territories, though in some instances their practice has lagged behind their professions. Other colonial powers have been compelled by circumstances beyond their control to relinquish their authority. Though many dependencies because of their size, their scattered location, and limited resources may never become independent, self-government within a larger framework of association is for them now generally recognized to be an attainable goal, as witness the recently organized British West Indian Federation.

The United Nations has been a very important factor in the development of these attitudes. It has played an important part in the process of translating dependence into independence or self-government, and it can play a more important role in the future if it is not too greatly handicapped by extraneous pressures, impatience, and distrust. While the organization and procedures for the discharge of its responsibilities can without doubt be improved, the extent of its success will be more dependent upon the state of international relations and national attitudes than upon machinery.

It is unfortunate that during the past decade issues involving the future of dependent peoples have become enmeshed in the strategies and rivalries of the "cold war." The fact that the Soviet Union and the other Communist countries have been so ready to rally to the support of the Asian and African peoples in their demands for independence has not increased the willingness of the Western colonial powers to accept United Nations supervision or grant native demands. With some justification they and their friends have felt that the real purpose of Communist action at least is to weaken the position of the West. The tendency of the dependent peoples, once independent, to espouse "neutralism" and even to appear to balance the scales in Communism's favor has not made it easier for the Western powers to grant demands for independence.

It is also unfortunate that pressures to relinquish control of dependent territories have coincided with the relative decline of the colonial powers in national power and prestige. France is a striking example. France emerged from the Second World War with hurt pride, lack of self-confidence, and a great loss of power, and consequently, has found it extremely difficult to make those adjustments in its relations with dependencies which suggest further loss of power and prestige as traditionally interpreted.

It is not surprising that the Asian and African states that have recently acquired independence or freed themselves from special forms of foreign control should, against the background of their previous experience, tend to exaggerate the present danger of Western imperialism to them and sometimes adopt attitudes which seem from the Western point of view unreasonable and even hostile. Unfortunately, this tendency to take extreme and even belligerent positions, and to press their views in the United Nations organs in an uncompromising manner has not been well suited to win the cooperation of the colonial powers and their friends.

While there is little prospect at present that the tensions of the "cold war" will be substantially reduced in the near future, this need not prevent interested states from recognizing that the United Nations can be a most useful instrument for achieving the economic, social, and political development of dependent territories and for guiding the native inhabitants to self-government or independence. It would appear to be much to the advantage of the dependent peoples and those states which sincerely make the cause of these peoples their own that the United Nations should increasingly become the effective means by which this development is encouraged and guided. If the United Nations is to be this means, it is necessary that understanding should be shown on all sides, that the colonial powers recognize the legitimate interest of other nations in the nature and speed of development and the appropriateness of United Nations assistance, and that the Members that are inclined to be critical of colonialism recognize the present responsibilities of the administering states and press their views and proposals with understanding of practical difficulties and the need of proceeding on the basis of consent. It must also be recognized that the achievement of the goal of independence or self-government is not sufficient by itself. This suggests that the United Nations has new and in some respects more difficult tasks to perform in helping to create those conditions—political, economic, social, and educational—which are the necessary foundations of stable and responsible government. Even when the task of helping a politically dependent people to become self-governing has been completed, that of helping a politically independent people that is still very much dependent on the rest of the world remains.

SUGGESTED READINGS

Asher, Robert E. and Associates. *The United Nations and Promotion of the General Welfare*. Washington: The Brookings Institution, 1957. Part IV.

Claude, Inis, Jr. *Swords into Plowshares*. New York: Random House, Inc., 1956. Chap. 15.

Finkelstein, Lawrence S. "Colonial Activities," in L. Larry Leonard, *International Organization,* New York: McGraw-Hill, Book Company, 1951, pp. 477–533.

———. *Somaliland Under Italian Administration: A Case Study in United Nations Trusteeship*. New York: Woodrow Wilson Foundation, 1955.

Fox, Annette Baker. "International Organization for Colonial Development," *World Politics,* III (1951), pp. 340–68.

Haas, Ernest B. "The Reconciliation of Conflicting Colonial Policy Aims: Acceptance of the League of Nations Mandate System," *International Organization,* VI (1952), pp. 521–36.

————. "The Attempt to Terminate Colonialism: Acceptance of the United Nations Trusteeship System," *International Organization,* VII (1953), pp. 1–21.

Hall, Duncan H. *Mandates, Dependencies and Trusteeship.* Washington: Carnegie Endowment for International Peace, 1948.

Murray, James N., Jr. *The United Nations Trusteeship System.* Urbana: University of Illinois Press, 1957.

Rivlin, Benjamin. "Self-Determination and Dependent Areas," *International Conciliation,* No. 501 (January 1955), pp. 195–271.

Toussaint, Charmian Edwards. *The Trusteeship System of the United Nations.* New York: Frederick A. Praeger Inc., 1956.

U.S. Senate Committee on Foreign Relations, Subcommittee on the United Nations Charter. *The United Nations and Dependent Territories.* Staff Study No. 9. Washington: Government Printing Office, 1955.

Wright, Quincy. *Mandates under the League of Nations.* Chicago: Chicago University Press, 1930.

Chapter XIV

FACING THE FUTURE

THE UNITED NATIONS was originally created in order to achieve certain agreed purposes. It was never looked upon by its architects as an end in itself. But there was in the minds of all an element of doubt, since clearly the degree of its success would be largely dependent upon the policies and attitudes of its Members. The Organization has been in existence for over a dozen years. Therefore there is some basis for a judgment as to the extent to which it has succeeded in achieving its goals. We are in the position where we can form tentative conclusions at least regarding the reasons for its not achieving more than it has, and what can be done to improve its future prospects. We are in a better position than we were in 1945 to decide whether the United Nations road is one we should continue to travel, or whether it is a dead end, offering for the long-run only occasions for additional frustrations and disappointments.

The Initial Hopes

At the time of the San Francisco Conference when the Charter of the United Nations was written and signed by the delegations of fifty states there were high hopes, if not real expectations, that this would provide the basis for the better world which President Roosevelt had pictured in his wartime addresses. More specifically, it was hoped that the major allies in the war that was then approaching its victorious conclusion would be able to agree on the terms of a fair and just peace settlement. Such a settlement would, on the one hand, contain provisions which would give the victor nations assurance that they would not again be the victims of fascist aggression. On the other hand, it would give the peoples of the liberated countries the opportunity to determine their own future in accordance with democratic principles.

319

It was hoped that the conclusion of such a peace settlement would provide the basis for cooperation between the major victor nations— the permanent members of the Security Council—in the keeping of the peace. Just as it was hoped that these states, after the ordeal through which they had passed, would find that it was in their interest to co-operate to make a peace which would eliminate the specific dangers they had faced, so it was hoped that once they had made the peace, they would recognize a common interest in maintaining it against any efforts to destroy it by force. To have cherished such hope may have been excessively optimistic considering the experience of the past but nevertheless, it was the premise upon which the peace and security provisions of the Charter were based.

There was also a widely-held hope at San Francisco, particularly among those groups which had been the victims of racial and religious persecution, that the United Nations would take effective action to achieve respect for basic human rights and fundamental freedoms. The world had been shocked by the Nazi treatment of racial, religious, and national minority groups before and during the war. Such brutality came to be associated with international aggression. Consequently it was believed that if individuals and minority groups could be protected in the enjoyment of human rights, the cause of international peace and security would be that much more secure.

Those who wrote the Charter, particularly the representatives of non-Communist states, looked to the United Nations to help deal with complex international economic and social problems which would exist in any case but would become more urgent and difficult as the result of the dislocations of the war. The experience of the Great Depression of the 'thirties was not forgotten; the lesson of that depression was that it not only created poverty, suffering, and malnutrition, but that it also resulted in political instability and, worst of all, fascism and aggression. The hope that the United Nations would help to achieve economic development, full employment, and general well-being was therefore closely associated with the quest for international peace and security.

Finally there was the hope, held particularly by those who saw the evils and perils of colonialism, that the United Nations would assume a special responsibility in connection with the administration of non-self-governing territories, and that with its help and guidance, peoples who had been subject to the rule of other peoples, and who had been treated as unable "to stand by themselves under the strenuous conditions of the modern world" would be able to achieve self-government or independence, and would no longer be denied the right to stand on their own feet and to assume responsibility for helping themselves.

The Record

What has the United Nations actually done to justify these initial hopes? The world which we know today certainly falls short of the hopes and expectations of those who took the lead in drafting the Charter. While there is no satisfactory method of statistically measuring the extent of this shortcoming, most observers would agree that the gap is considerable. Let us briefly look at the record.

Many of the problems which one would have expected the peace treaties at the end of the war to settle remain unresolved. This is not to suggest that peace treaties necessarily settle problems in the sense of providing lasting solutions satisfactory to everybody. Nevertheless, for the time being they do provide arrangements to be lived with which have a formal legal validity. The relations of the former allies with Italy have been settled and placed on a generally acceptable basis. Not so, however, their relations with Germany and Japan. Even the first step toward an agreed German peace settlement has not been taken; Germany remains divided and no government for the whole of Germany exists. Likewise, there is no one agreed peace treaty between Japan and her former enemies. The United States and most of the other states at war with Japan have concluded a treaty of peace, but the Soviet Union was not a party to it. Instead it has concluded a separate treaty. The fate of parts of Japan's prewar empire, especially Korea and Formosa, has not been determined by agreement of all the states concerned. While peace treaties have been concluded with the former enemy states of Eastern Europe, the Soviet Union and the Western Powers have been in disagreement over the execution of their terms, and the status of liberated areas has been a matter of serious discord.

Without agreement on the basic features of a peace settlement, it is not surprising that the Soviet Union and the major Western Powers have pulled apart on other issues as well. Especially is this so if we take into account the ideological differences separating the two camps, the mutual distrust and fear going back to the Bolshevik Revolution, and the traditional inability of major allies to preserve their cooperation—and in this case the cooperation between the Soviet Union and the West had been limited—after victory has been won. Without agreement on the terms of peace and with mounting mutual distrust and fear, that measure of cooperation upon which the Charter system for the maintenance of peace and security in the postwar period was premised proved impossible of achievement.

In those instances where the major powers, and particularly the United States and the Soviet Union, have had a common interest in preventing or putting an end to hostilities, the United Nations has been able to take decisions and achieve a considerable measure of success in keeping or restoring peace. In those instances where the vital interests of the two super-powers have been in sharp opposition, the results have been much less satisfactory. The right of veto in the Security Council has usually prevented action there. The General Assembly, limited to discussion and recommendation, is not well suited in any case to react quickly and decisively by collective measures to a major threat to the peace. Efforts to equip it and use it for that purpose have not thus far had very reassuring results.

Recent events have shown, however, that though the Assembly is not likely to be effective in taking collective enforcement measures to deal with a threat to the peace, it can perform a very important pacifying function. It provides the means by which the uncommitted states and those not directly involved in the situation may most effectively mediate and it constitutes a world forum in which the common desire to avoid a general war can find expression and acceptable arrangements can be developed to that end. In a world teetering on the edge of atomic self-destruction, stop-gap arrangements that keep violence within manageable limits are no mean achievement.

Though the United Nations has achieved a considerable measure of success in preventing hostilities or ending them once they have begun, its record as the settler or adjuster of disputes and controversies has been considerably less satisfying. Less use has been made of the International Court of Justice for the settlement of legal disputes than was made of the Permanent Court of International Justice during a comparable period. Neither the Council nor the Assembly has been particularly successful in achieving the settlement of the disputes and controversies that have agitated international relations in the postwar period. Only in the case of Indonesia has the Security Council made an important contribution to the settlement of a troublesome question. The Assembly has been used more commonly by one side or the other to build up support for its point of view and to appeal to world opinion than to achieve an acceptable accommodation of conflicting views. In the one case where it has made proposals for the settlement of an important question that have been accepted, the disposition of the Italian colonies, the interested parties agreed in advance to consider the Assembly's recommendations as binding.

"Cold war" issues have been largely resistant to United Nations suggestions and recommendations for their settlement. United Nations organs have had somewhat more success in dealing with questions involving the nationalist aspirations of the peoples of Asia and Africa. Often these have become involved in the "cold war" struggle, and, however, the mistrust and fears incident to this struggle have prevented the major powers from joint action in support of agreed terms of settlement. Furthermore, the Western colonial powers have been strongly resistant to United Nations consideration of questions involving claims to independence or self-government for their dependencies on the ground that these relate to matters essentially within their domestic jurisdiction. Of late, there have been encouraging signs that the Secretary-General may be able to obtain constructive results as mediator in disputes that have not yielded to other United Nations methods.

Thus far the United Nations has not been able to achieve the regulation of national armaments because of the unresolved differences between the Soviet Union and the Western Powers. Though the Charter did not make disarmament a primary purpose of the Organization, as did the Covenant of the League, it did emphasize the need of placing specific national armed forces and facilities at the disposal of the Security Council to enable it effectively to discharge its "primary responsibility," and it did emphasize the importance of achieving by agreement ". . . the least diversion for armaments of the world's human and economic resources." These goals the United Nations has not been able to achieve, even in the face of the common danger from thermonuclear war.

To provide greater assurance of their national security, in case of a threat to or breach of the peace, particularly an attack encouraged, supported, or carried out by a major power, Members of the United Nations have turned to the use of the right of individual or collective self-defense, reserved under Article 51 of the Charter. In the exercise of this right various collective self-defense arrangements have been concluded, of which NATO is an outstanding example. These may provide the parties to them with an increased sense of security and may help to achieve an uneasy peace based on an essentially unstable equilibrium of forces, but they give no reliable assurance for the long run, any more than the treaties of alliance of the past, that the declared purpose of the United Nations—the maintenance of international peace and security—will be achieved.

The United Nations has been very active in the field of human rights. Probably its major achievement has been the adoption of the Universal Declaration of Human Rights, proclaimed to be a ". . . common standard of achievement for all peoples and all nations." As such it is a document of great value, and it provides a standard by which to measure the acts and accomplishments of peoples and governments, even though in a strictly legal sense it is not binding. While the attempt to draft and put into force covenants of human rights has thus far proven unsuccessful, and may well be considered a premature, if not misguided effort, the discussions that have taken place in connection with these and other attempts to define individual liberties and human freedoms have served the useful purposes of clarifying the complexities of the problem and clearing the ground for those efforts that are likely to be most rewarding. It cannot be denied that in many countries, including some that are popularly regarded as being on the side of freedom, the state of individual liberties is far from satisfactory. The world has a long distance to go before the standards of the Universal Declaration will be universally respected. But the United Nations is making an important contribution to that result by keeping an internationally accepted standard ever before the eyes of peoples and governments and by alerting those who are sensitive, to the need of remedial action in specific situations.

In promoting economic and social cooperation the United Nations has been engaged in a wide range and great variety of activities, some carried out directly, some through its family of specialized agencies. It is difficult to generalize regarding the Organization's accomplishments and at the same time be meaningful. Considering the limitations under which the United Nations has been forced to work—the limited powers of its organs and the sensitivity of governments to outside intervention in many matters within this field, not to mention the unfavorable world political situation—the accomplishments of the Organization have been substantial and encouraging. It has assisted in carrying out emergency tasks such as the relief of Arab refugees in Palestine and the relief and resettlement of refugees uprooted by the War. It has organized and administered a most successful program for the feeding of undernourished children. It has provided indispensable assistance in combating certain communicable diseases, such as malaria, and in improving national public health services. It has organized and administered the Expanded Program of Technical Assistance which has made available to underdeveloped countries on acceptable terms technical assistance which they need for their social, economic, and political development. It has given sympathetic consideration to the needs of underdeveloped countries for funds to assist them in their economic development and has helped to make these funds available in growing amounts and on increasingly favorable terms. It has been active and successful in encouraging the use of atomic energy for peaceful purposes and in breaking down the walls of secrecy that have hampered the efforts of scientists throughout the world.

With respect to non-self-governing territories, the United Nations has established more firmly than ever before the principle of the international accountability of the administering state. Furthermore, by its action in the discharge of its responsibility both for the maintenance of international peace and security and the development of friendly relations and for seeing to it that administering states perform their Charter duties, the United Nations has played an important part in transforming non-self-governing territories into self-governing or independent ones. The increase in the number of independent states since the war has been in large measure due to the influence of United Nations standards and actions. Some people would not view this as an unmixed blessing. However, so long as peoples have the desire to be independent and free of foreign rule, it is not consistent with the principles of democracy or the purposes to which the Members of the United Nations have subscribed, to deny this opportunity except on the clearest grounds of incompetence. The United Nations has provided the means whereby peoples who continue to need help after achieving independence can receive that assistance on terms more consistent with their pride and desire for equality than those inherent in colonial rule. Undoubtedly one of the major achievements of the United Nations has been its role in assisting non-self-governing peoples in their transition to independence, and in providing assistance to them in their efforts to satisfy rising economic and social expectations.

Why More Has Not Been Done

Granting that the record of United Nations achievement has been substantial, one cannot deny that in many respects it has been inadequate to the needs of today. In a world faced with the possibility of self-extermination by the devices of destruction which science has placed in our hands, it would seem that we can ill afford the risks of continued armament rivalry, and of conflicts and tensions which may at any time break out into open violence. When scientists tell us of the wonderful possibilities of the use of atomic energy for peaceful purposes, it would seem shortsighted and indeed stupid to continue to place the major emphasis on the use of atomic energy for destructive purposes, and to starve, or at least support in a niggardly fashion, those efforts directed toward using this new source of energy to make man's future more promising rather than more uncertain. At a time when we have developed the capacity to produce all that is needed to meet the minimum food, clothing, and shelter needs of the people of the world, it seems fantastic that millions should still be denied the bare essentials of life. Why has not the United Nations been more effective in meeting the great needs of the world today, granted that what is needed is only in part within the range of the efforts of an international organization? The answer is certainly not an easy one.

It must be admitted, as the world federalists have not tired of pointing out, that the United Nations suffers from an inherent weakness, its lack of authority. Since it is an organization of sovereign states, it can only do what its Members are willing to support. It has no independent authority to pass laws, to levy taxes, and to enforce its will by force if necessary. Nevertheless, this lack of power cannot be accepted as a decisive factor in the situation unless we are prepared to resign ourselves for the foreseeable future to the continuation, if not the progressive aggravation, of the present condition of fear and uncertainty. The plain fact is that the world is not ready for world government today. World government requires the existence of a world community— a sense of social solidarity on the part of peoples of the world and their governments. Such a sense of solidarity does not exist today. If it did, even a loose form of organization like the United Nations would work much better than it does. Good machinery is important, but it does not explain the difference between success and failure in the present world situation. In fact it is quite possible that a loose form of organization like the United Nations is better suited to the needs of the world at its present stage of development than what the world federalists propose.

Undoubtedly an important cause of the limited success of the United Nations has been the persistent strength of nationalism. In the West, there have been some evidences of a weakening of nationalism and of the recognition of the needs of integrating national states into larger functional units, such as the European Coal and Steel Community and the European Atomic Energy Community. Nevertheless, we find in the West that nationalism still remains a powerful sentiment, as witness the reluctance of France to loosen its control over its colonial empire, the unwillingness of the Western colonial powers to accept United Nations oversight of the administration of their colonies, and the sensitivity of the United States to any infringement of its domestic jurisdiction.

While there are evidences of the sublimation of nationalist attitudes in the West, the Asian and African continents are experiencing a nationalist awakening similar to what happened in Europe in the nineteenth century. The newly independent countries of these continents and those peoples not yet independent are extremely jealous of their national independence and aspirations and resent any limitation of them. Similar sentiments exist in Latin America. Fortunately, these more recent manifestations of nationalism are directed less against action by an international organization such as the United Nations than against interference by other more powerful and economically more advanced national states. However, in many instances Asian-African nationalism has been an obstacle to United Nations action, either directly by opposing such action, as in the case of Iran's resistance to United Nations consideration of its oil dispute with the United Kingdom, or indirectly by provoking Western resistance by its extreme demands.

Another important cause of United Nations weakness is Communism. Unlike nationalism, Communism offers as part of its basic ideology the promise of an integrated world community, but the goal to be achieved and the path to it are not those of the Charter. While the Soviet Union, the chief Communist Member of the United Nations, was one of the original sponsors of the Organization and professes full and explicit acceptance of its principles and purposes, it is obvious that its interpretation of these purposes and principles and its interest in the Organization differ fundamentally from those of the leading Western democracies. While attaching some value to the Organization as a means of providing for its security and furthering its political interests in the "cold war," the Soviet Union understandably has not supported those activities which are primarily concerned with making Western capitalist economies function more effectively. While it has given its support to United Nations actions likely to further the independence of non-self-governing people and thereby weaken Western colonialism, it has fairly consistently opposed any United Nations policy or program which would restrict state sovereignty in the common interest. Because of the basic incompatibility of its ideology with many of the basic assumptions of the Charter, Communism may be regarded as a greater cause of United Nations weakness than even nationalism in its most extreme form. In the case of nationalism, there is considerable evidence that it can by a process of sublimation become the basis of a healthy internationalism. It is too early to be sure that even with its commitment to "peaceful coexistence," Communism is prepared to make the necessary concessions.

In addition to being handicapped by these two powerful ideologies representative of widespread individual and group attitudes, the United

Nations has suffered, and has been seriously restricted in its activities, by the state of international relations that has prevailed since the war. In part, these relations have been the result of ideological conflicts; in part they have resulted from War and its aftermath and the struggle of peoples for security in the face of growing insecurity. Revolutionary technological developments, especially in the utilization of atomic energy, have played an important part. The total result, however, has been unfavorable to the success of an organization whose success was premised on trust, mutual confidence, and the willingness of the major powers to cooperate as equals.

If we consider calmly and objectively the difficulties that the United Nations has had to contend with, we should be impressed by the fact that it has actually achieved so much, and not surprised that it has accomplished so little. It has certainly been called upon to discharge its responsibilities under most unfavorable conditions.

The U.N. and the Future

Faced with these difficulties, the United Nations looks to an uncertain future. And yet it is one of the hopeful elements in a world situation that is full of peril. What can be done to make the United Nations more effective in fulfilling its purposes? What role can we envisage for the United Nations in the years ahead?

Though the Charter provided for its amendment and, more specifically, made provision for a review conference at the end of ten years,[1] it is generally agreed that the future of the Organization is not dependent upon any extensive Charter revision. While a good case can be made for amendment of the Charter provisions relating to such matters as the composition and voting procedure of the Security Council and the powers and voting procedure of the General Assembly, it is hard to see how such amendments are to be consummated in the present state of international relations. Furthermore, if there is an improvement in relations between the major powers which would permit the changes to be made, they would probably no longer be necessary. Formal amendment, except on relatively inconsequential points, appears to be out of the question, for the time being.

The United Nations has shown a remarkable capacity for development within the limits of the existing Charter. There is no reason to believe that the possibilities of further development have been exhausted. The General Assembly has taken over a substantial part of the Security

[1] Articles 108 and 109.

Council's responsibilities for the maintenance of international peace and security. It has taken important steps to equip itself to discharge these responsibilities. There is nothing in the Charter to prevent it from going even further in organizing itself to perform these duties. Of course it would require Charter amendment to give it the power to do some of the things that the Security Council can do, such as order enforcement measures, but it is doubtful if the Assembly should be given such powers in any case. Nor have the Charter limits of what the General Assembly might do in encouraging self-government for non-self-governing territories or in developing programs of economic and social development for underdeveloped territories been reached. Certainly, the International Court of Justice can become more effective in the settling of disputes and furthering the development of international law without any amendment of the Charter.

What is necessary is that Member states adopt different attitudes toward the use of the Organization and develop more constructive policies with respect to the extent and manner of its use. This need not involve on the part of any state the sacrifice of a national interest to the achievement of some United Nations purpose. After all, that is too much to expect in a world of nation states. It simply means that Member states should, consistent with their Charter obligations and a long-range view of the interests of their peoples, recognize the fact of their common concerns and work together in good faith to do those things which working independently they cannot do, or do as well. In a recent address, Secretary-General Dag Hammarskjöld quoted from a memorandum prepared by Mr. Eyre Crowe for the British Foreign Office in 1907, advising that Britain's best safeguard for the future would be a national policy that is

> *so directed as to harmonize with the general desires and ideals common to all mankind, and more particularly that . . . is closely identified with the primary and vital interests of a majority, or as many as possible of the other nations.*[2]

As the Secretary-General pointed out, this is a policy and a principle which it is wise for all nations to follow, and is the policy and the principle upon which the United Nations is based.

One of the purposes, and in a real sense, the basic purpose of the United Nations is ". . . to be a center for harmonizing the actions of nations in the attainment . . ." of common ends.[3] In a sense this means that the United Nations serves as a neutral meeting ground where con-

[2] *United Nations Review,* IV, No. 11 (May 1958), p. 10.
[3] Article 1, par. 4.

flicting interests can be adjusted and suggests that one of the principal functions of the Organization is to serve as a conference table where the opposing parties can get together and adjust their differences. This is an important function and serves to define what is undoubtedly an important role of the United Nations in the major conflicts of our time. Furthermore, it is a function which the Secretary-General and his principal assistants, and the officers of the principal political organs are in a particularly favorable position to perform. Nevertheless, the United Nations cannot be satisfied with a role which is basically neutral as to values. It must seek to preserve the peace by harmonizing the policies and actions of states, but always on terms which will represent progress toward the achievement of those values for which the United Nations stands. These constitute the life blood of the Organization and unless it is loyal to them, and continuously seeks to bring their fulfillment nearer by its actions, it loses its vital force and becomes a piece of lifeless machinery that can easily and properly be dispensed with once it has served or failed to serve its utilitarian purpose.

It is by its devotion to the values set forth in the Charter, by its skill in keeping them before the eyes of peoples and of governments as standards of achievement, and by its eventual success in getting them transformed into national policies and actions that the United Nations will in the end justify itself. By so doing it will contribute to laying the foundations for a real world community capable of developing institutions appropriate to its needs and expressing its unity. Before that goal can be reached, however, much hard work must be done in blunting the sharp edges of conflict, in preserving an uneasy peace, and in developing those areas of cooperation which become feasible under the circumstances of the time. Again quoting the late Secretary-General Hammarskjöld:

> We should recognize the United Nations for what it is—an admittedly imperfect but indispensable instrument of nations in working for a peaceful evolution toward a more just and secure world order. At this stage of human history, world organization has become necessary. The forces at work have also set the limits within which the power of world organization can develop at each step and beyond which progress, when the balance of forces so permits, will be possible only by processes of organic growth in the system of custom and law prevailing in the society of nations.[4]

[4] *United Nations Review,* IV, No. 11 (May 1958), p. 7.

SUGGESTED READINGS

Claude, Inis, Jr. *Swords into Plowshares*. New York: Random House, Inc., 1956. Chaps. 14, 17 and 18.

Dawson, Kenneth H. "The United Nations in a Disunited World," *World Politics,* VI (1954), pp. 209–35.

Eichelberger, Clark M. *UN: The First Ten Years*. New York: Harper & Brothers, Publishers, 1955.

Evatt, Herbert V. *The Task of Nations*. New York: Duell, Sloan & Pearce, Inc., 1949.

Feller, A. H. *United Nations and World Community*. Boston: Little, Brown and Company, 1952.

Finklestein, Lawrence S. "Reviewing the United Nations Charter," *International Organization,* IX (1955), pp. 213–31.

Hoffman, Stanley. "The Role of International Organization: Limits and Responsibilities," *International Organization,* X (1956), pp. 357–72.

Mangone, Gerard J. *The Idea and Practice of World Government*. New York: Columbia University Press, 1951.

Review of the United Nations Charter. Final Report of the Sub-Committee on the United Nations Charter of the Committee on Foreign Relations, U.S. Senate, 84th Cong. 2nd Sess. Report No. 1797. Washington: Government Printing Office, 1956.

Schuman, Frederick L. *The Commonwealth of Man*. New York: Alfred A. Knopf, Inc., 1952.

Strengthening the United Nations. Report of the Commission to Study the Organization of Peace. New York, 1957.

Wilcox, Francis O. and Marcy, Carl M. *Proposals for Changes in the United Nations*. Washington: The Brookings Institution, 1955.

A NOTE ON AIDS
TO STUDY

THE UNITED NATIONS OFFICE (formerly Department) of Public Information has prepared and published a number of useful aids to understanding of the Organization. Primarily intended for the general public are *How to Find Out About the United Nations* (2nd rev. ed., May, 1958) and *Basic Facts about the United Nations* (Fourteenth ed., July, 1958). *Everyman's United Nations* (Fifth ed., 1956) is a useful reference book on the structure, functions and work of the United Nations and the specialized agencies during the ten-year period ending December 31, 1955. The Office publishes an annual *Yearbook of the United Nations* which gives comprehensive and detailed information on the structure and working of the Organization and the specialized agencies, with summaries of action taken on various questions, texts of important resolutions, and references to key documents. The *Yearbook* is an invaluable reference book. The Office also publishes a monthly journal, the *United Nations Review* (formerly the *United Nations Bulletin,* appearing semi-monthly) which contains summaries of particular activities of the United Nations and semi-popular articles on the work of the Organization and its related agencies in different fields.

To contribute to knowledge and understanding of how the Charter of the United Nations has been applied in practice, the Secretariat has prepared and published the *Repertory of Practice of United Nations Organs,* 5 vols. (New York, 1955) and Supplement No. 1, 2 vols. (New York, 1958). As a guide to United Nations documentation, the Headquarters Library publishes monthly the *United Nations Documents Index* which lists the documents and publications of the United Nations and the specialized agencies received during each month. It has also

332

published *A Bibliography of the Charter of the United Nations* (1955) which lists books, pamphlets and articles on the Charter and its origins appearing during the period 1941–54 inclusive.

Two periodicals, privately published, deserve notice because of their special value to anyone interested in the United Nations. These are *International Organization,* published quarterly by the World Peace Foundation in Boston, and *International Conciliation,* published five times a year by the Carnegie Endowment for International Peace in New York. The first contains scholarly articles, factual summaries of the activities of international agencies, and a select bibliography. The latter presents factual statements and analyses of problems in the field of international organization. Its annual number on issues before the current General Assembly is invaluable to an appreciation of the work of that organ.

Appendix A

THE COVENANT OF THE LEAGUE OF NATIONS[1]

With Amendments in Force January 1, 1945

THE HIGH CONTRACTING PARTIES,

In order to promote international cooperation and to achieve international peace and security

by the acceptance of obligations not to resort to war,

by the prescription of open, just and honorable relations between nations,

by the firm establishment of the understandings of international law as the actual rule of conduct among Governments, and

by the maintenance of justice and a scrupulous respect for all treaty obligations in the dealings of organized peoples with one another,

Agree to this Covenant of the League of Nations.

ARTICLE 1. MEMBERSHIP AND WITHDRAWAL

1. The original Members of the League of Nations shall be those of the Signatories which are named in the Annex to this Covenant and also such of those other States named in the Annex as shall accede without reservation to this Covenant. Such accessions shall be effected by a declaration deposited with the Secretariat within two months of the coming into force of the Covenant. Notice thereof shall be sent to all other Members of the League.

[1] Entered into force on January 10, 1920. Subsequent amendments are indicated by italics or footnotes.

335

2. Any fully self-governing State, Dominion or Colony not named in the Annex may become a Member of the League if its admission is agreed to by two-thirds of the Assembly, provided that it shall give effective guaranties of its sincere intention to observe its international obligations, and shall accept such regulations as may be prescribed by the League in regard to its military, naval and air forces and armaments.

3. Any Member of the League may, after two years' notice of its intention so to do, withdraw from the League, provided that all its international obligations and all its obligations under this Covenant shall have been fulfilled at the time of its withdrawal.

ARTICLE 2.   EXECUTIVE ORGANS

The action of the League under this Covenant shall be effected through the instrumentality of an Assembly and of a Council, with a permanent Secretariat.

ARTICLE 3.   ASSEMBLY

1. The Assembly shall consist of representatives of the Members of the League.

2. The Assembly shall meet at stated intervals and from time to time, as occasion may require, at the Seat of the League or at such other place as may be decided upon.

3. The Assembly may deal at its meetings with any matter within the sphere of action of the League or affecting the peace of the world.

4. At meetings of the Assembly each Member of the League shall have one vote and may have not more than three Representatives.

ARTICLE 4.   COUNCIL

1. The Council shall consist of representatives of the Principal Allied and Associated Powers [United States of America, the British Empire, France, Italy and Japan], together with Representatives of four other Members of the League. These four Members of the League shall be selected by the Assembly from time to time in its discretion. Until the appointment of the Representatives of the four Members of the League first selected by the Assembly, Representatives of Belgium, Brazil, Greece and Spain shall be Members of the Council.

2. With the approval of the majority of the Assembly, the Council may name additional Members of the League, whose Representatives shall always be Members of the Council; the Council with like ap-

proval may increase the number of Members of the League to be selected by the Assembly for representation on the Council.

2. *bis. The Assembly shall fix by a two-thirds' majority the rules dealing with the election of the non-permanent Members of the Council, and particularly such regulations as relate to their term of office and the conditions of re-eligibility.*

3. The Council shall meet from time to time as occasion may require, and at least once a year, at the Seat of the League, or at such other place as may be decided upon.

4. The Council may deal at its meetings with any matter within the sphere of action of the League or affecting the peace of the world.

5. Any Member of the League not represented on the Council shall be invited to send a Representative to sit as a member at any meeting of the Council during the consideration of matters specially affecting the interests of that Member of the League.

6. At meetings of the Council, each Member of the League represented on the Council shall have one vote, and may have not more than one Representative.

ARTICLE 5. VOTING AND PROCEDURE

1. Except where otherwise expressly provided in this Covenant or by the terms of the present Treaty, decisions at any meeting of the Assembly or of the Council shall require the agreement of all the Members of the League represented at the meeting.

2. All matters of procedure at meetings of the Assembly or of the Council, including the appointment of Committees to investigate particular matters, shall be regulated by the Assembly or by the Council and may be decided by a majority of the Members of the League represented at the meeting.

3. The first meeting of the Assembly and the first meeting of the Council shall be summoned by the President of the United States of America.

ARTICLE 6. SECRETARIAT AND EXPENSES

1. The permanent Secretariat shall be established at the Seat of the League. The Secretariat shall comprise a Secretary-General and such secretaries and staff as may be required.

2. The first Secretary-General shall be the person named in the Annex; thereafter the Secretary-General shall be appointed by the Council with the approval of the majority of the Assembly.

3. The secretaries and the staff of the Secretariat shall be appointed by the Secretary-General with the approval of the Council.

4. The Secretary-General shall act in that capacity at all meetings of the Assembly and of the Council.

5. *The expenses of the League shall be borne by the Members of the League in the proportion decided by the Assembly.*

ARTICLE 7.   SEAT, QUALIFICATIONS OF OFFICIALS, IMMUNITIES

1. The Seat of the League is established at Geneva.

2. The Council may at any time decide that the Seat of the League shall be established elsewhere.

3. All positions under or in connection with the League, including the Secretariat, shall be open equally to men and women.

4. Representatives of the Members of the League and officials of the League when engaged on the business of the League shall enjoy diplomatic privileges and immunities.

5. The buildings and other property occupied by the League or its officials or by Representatives attending its meetings shall be inviolable.

ARTICLE 8.   REDUCTION OF ARMAMENTS

1. The Members of the League recognize that the maintenance of peace requires the reduction of national armaments to the lowest point consistent with national safety and the enforcement by common action of international obligations.

2. The Council, taking account of the geographical situation and circumstances of each State, shall formulate plans for such reduction for the consideration and action of the several Governments.

3. Such plans shall be subject to reconsideration and revision at least every 10 years.

4. After these plans shall have been adopted by the several Governments, the limits of armaments therein fixed shall not be exceeded without the concurrence of the Council.

5. The Members of the League agree that the manufacture by private enterprise of munitions and implements of war is open to grave objections. The Council shall advise how the evil effects attendant upon such manufacture can be prevented, due regard being had to the necessities of those Members of the League which are not able to manufacture the munitions and implements of war necessary for their safety.

6. The Members of the League undertake to interchange full and

frank information as to the scale of their armaments, their military, naval and air programs and the condition of such of their industries as are adaptable to warlike purposes.

ARTICLE 9. PERMANENT MILITARY, NAVAL AND AIR COMMISSION

A permanent Commission shall be constituted to advise the Council on the execution of the provisions of Articles 1 and 8 and on military, naval and air questions generally.

ARTICLE 10. GUARANTIES AGAINST AGGRESSION

The Members of the League undertake to respect and preserve as against external aggression the territorial integrity and existing political independence of all Members of the League. In case of any such aggression or in case of any threat or danger of such aggression the Council shall advise upon the means by which this obligation shall be fulfilled.

ARTICLE 11. ACTION IN CASE OF WAR OR THREAT OF WAR

1. Any war or threat of war, whether immediately affecting any of the Members of the League or not, is hereby declared a matter of concern to the whole League, and the League shall take any action that may be deemed wise and effectual to safeguard the peace of nations. In case any such emergency should arise the Secretary-General shall on the request of any Member of the League forthwith summon a meeting of the Council.

2. It is also declared to be the friendly right of each Member of the League to bring to the attention of the Assembly or of the Council any circumstance whatever affecting international relations which threatens to disturb international peace or the good understanding between nations upon which peace depends.

ARTICLE 12. DISPUTES TO BE SUBMITTED FOR SETTLEMENT

1. The Members of the League agree that, if there should arise between them any dispute likely to lead to a rupture, they will submit the matter either to arbitration *or judicial settlement* or to inquiry by the Council, and they agree in no case to resort to war until three months

after the award by the arbitrators *or the judicial decision,* or the report by the Council.

2. In any case under this Article the award of the arbitrators *or the judicial decision* shall be made within a reasonable time, and the report of the Council shall be made within six months after the submission of the dispute.

ARTICLE 13.   ARBITRATION OR JUDICIAL SETTLEMENT

1. The Members of the League agree that, whenever any dispute shall arise between them which they recognize to be suitable for submission to arbitration *or judicial settlement,* and which can not be satisfactorily settled by diplomacy, they will submit the whole subject-matter to arbitration *or judicial settlement.*

2. Disputes as to the interpretation of a treaty, as to any question of international law, as to the existence of any fact which, if established, would constitute a breach of any international obligation, or as to the extent and nature of the reparation to be made for any such breach, are declared to be among those which are generally suitable for submission to arbitration *or judicial settlement.*

3. *For the consideration of any such dispute, the court to which the case is referred shall be the Permanent Court of International Justice, established in accordance with Article 14, or any tribunal agreed on by the parties to the dispute or stipulated in any convention existing between them.*

4. The Members of the League agree that they will carry out in full good faith any award *or decision* that may be rendered, and that they will not resort to war against a Member of the League which complies therewith. In the event of any failure to carry out such an award *or decision,* the Council shall propose what steps should be taken to give effect thereto.

ARTICLE 14.   PERMANENT COURT OF INTERNATIONAL JUSTICE

The Council shall formulate and submit to the Members of the League for adoption plans for the establishment of a Permanent Court of International Justice. The Court shall be competent to hear and determine any dispute of an international character which the parties thereto submit to it. The Court may also give an advisory opinion upon any dispute or question referred to it by the Council or by the Assembly.

ARTICLE 15.   DISPUTES NOT SUBMITTED TO ARBITRATION OR JUDICIAL SETTLEMENT

1. If there should arise between Members of the League any dispute likely to lead to a rupture, which is not submitted to arbitration *or judicial settlement* in accordance with Article 13, the Members of the League agree that they will submit the matter to the Council. Any party to the dispute may effect such submission by giving notice of the existence of the dispute to the Secretary-General, who will make all necessary arrangements for a full investigation and consideration thereof.

2. For this purpose the parties to the dispute will communicate to the Secretary-General, as promptly as possible, statements of their case with all the relevant facts and papers, and the Council may forthwith direct the publication thereof.

3. The Council shall endeavor to effect a settlement of the dispute, and, if such efforts are successful, a statement shall be made public giving such facts and explanations regarding the dispute and the terms of settlement thereof as the Council may deem appropriate.

4. If the dispute is not thus settled, the Council either unanimously or by a majority vote shall make and publish a report containing a statement of the facts of the dispute and the recommendations which are deemed just and proper in regard thereto.

5. Any member of the League represented on the Council may make public a statement of the facts of the dispute and of its conclusions regarding the same.

6. If a report by the Council is unanimously agreed to by the Members thereof other than the Representatives of one or more of the parties to the dispute, the Members of the League agree that they will not go to war with any party to the dispute which complies with the recommendations of the report.

7. If the Council fails to reach a report which is unanimously agreed to by the members thereof, other than the Representatives of one or more of the parties to the dispute, the Members of the League reserve to themselves the right to take such action as they shall consider necessary for the maintenance of right and justice.

8. If the dispute between the parties is claimed by one of them, and is found by the Council, to arise out of a matter which by international law is solely within the domestic jurisdiction of that party, the Council shall so report, and shall make no recommendation as to its settlement.

9. The Council may in any case under this Article refer the dispute to the Assembly. The dispute shall be so referred at the request of either party to the dispute, provided that such request be made within 14 days after the submission of the dispute to the Council.

10. In any case referred to the Assembly, all the provisions of this Article and of Article 12 relating to the action and powers of the Council shall apply to the action and powers of the Assembly, provided that a report made by the Assembly, if concurred in by the Representatives of those Members of the League represented on the Council and of a majority of the other Members of the League, exclusive in each case of the Representatives of the parties to the dispute, shall have the same force as a report by the Council concurred in by all the members thereof other than the Representatives of one or more of the parties to the dispute.

ARTICLE 16.   SANCTIONS OF PACIFIC SETTLEMENT

1. Should any Member of the League resort to war in disregard of its covenants under Articles 12, 13, or 15, it shall *ipso facto* be deemed to have committed an act of war against all other Members of the League, which hereby undertake immediately to subject it to the severance of all trade or financial relations, the prohibition of all intercourse between their nationals and the nationals of the covenant-breaking State, and the prevention of all financial, commercial or personal intercourse between the nationals of the covenant-breaking State and the nationals of any other State, whether a Member of the League or not.

2. It shall be the duty of the Council in such case to recommend to the several Governments concerned what effective military, naval or air force the Members of the League shall severally contribute to the armed forces to be used to protect the covenants of the League.

3. The Members of the League agree, further, that they will mutually support one another in the financial and economic measures which are taken under this Article, in order to minimize the loss and inconvenience resulting from the above measures, and that they will mutually support one another in resisting any special measures aimed at one of their number by the covenant-breaking State, and that they will take the necessary steps to afford passage through their territory to the forces of any of the Members of the League which are cooperating to protect the covenants of the League.

4. Any Member of the League which has violated any covenant of the League may be declared to be no longer a Member of the League by

a vote of the Council concurred in by the Representatives of all the other Members of the League represented thereon.

ARTICLE 17. DISPUTES INVOLVING NON-MEMBERS

1. In the event of a dispute between a Member of the League and a State which is not a Member of the League, or between States not Members of the League, the State or States not Members of the League shall be invited to accept the obligations of membership in the League for the purposes of such dispute, upon such conditions as the Council may deem just. If such invitation is accepted, the provisions of Articles 12 to 16, inclusive, shall be applied with such modifications as may be deemed necessary by the Council.

2. Upon such invitation being given, the Council shall immediately institute an inquiry into the circumstances of the dispute and recommend such action as may seem best and most effectual in the circumstances.

3. If a State so invited shall refuse to accept the obligations of membership in the League for the purposes of such dispute, and shall resort to war against a Member of the League, the provisions of Article 16 shall be applicable as against the State taking such action.

4. If both parties to the dispute when so invited refuse to accept the obligations of Membership in the League for the purposes of such dispute, the Council may take such measures and make such recommendations as will prevent hostilities and will result in the settlement of the dispute.

ARTICLE 18. REGISTRATION AND PUBLICATION OF TREATIES

Every treaty or international engagement entered into hereafter by any Member of the League shall be forthwith registered with the Secretariat and shall as soon as possible be published by it. No such treaty or international engagement shall be binding until so registered.

ARTICLE 19. REVIEW OF TREATIES

The Assembly may from time to time advise the reconsideration by Members of the League of treaties which have become inapplicable, and the consideration of international conditions whose continuance might endanger the peace of the world.

ARTICLE 20.   ABROGATION OF INCONSISTENT OBLIGATIONS

1. The Members of the League severally agree that this Covenant is accepted as abrogating all obligations or understandings *inter se* which are inconsistent with the terms thereof, and solemnly undertake that they will not hereafter enter into any engagements inconsistent with the terms thereof.

2. In case any Member of the League shall, before becoming a Member of the League, have undertaken any obligations inconsistent with the terms of this Covenant, it shall be the duty of such Member to take immediate steps to procure its release from such obligations.

ARTICLE 21.   ENGAGEMENTS THAT REMAIN VALID

Nothing in this Covenant shall be deemed to affect the validity of international engagements, such as treaties of arbitration or regional understandings like the Monroe doctrine, for securing the maintenance of peace.

ARTICLE 22.   MANDATORY SYSTEM

1. To those colonies and territories which as a consequence of the late war have ceased to be under the sovereignty of the States which formerly governed them and which are inhabited by peoples not yet able to stand by themselves under the strenuous conditions of the modern world, there should be applied the principle that the well-being and development of such peoples form a sacred trust of civilization and that securities for the performance of this trust should be embodied in this Covenant.

2. The best method of giving practical effect to this principle is that the tutelage of such peoples should be intrusted to advanced nations who by reason of their resources, their experience or their geographical position can best undertake this responsibility, and who are willing to accept it, and that this tutelage should be exercised by them as Mandatories on behalf of the League.

3. The character of the mandate must differ according to the stage of the development of the people, the geographical situation of the territory, its economic conditions and other similar circumstances.

4. Certain communities formerly belonging to the Turkish Empire

have reached a stage of development where their existence as independent nations can be provisionally recognized subject to the rendering of administrative advice and assistance by a Mandatory until such time as they are able to stand alone. The wishes of these communities must be a principal consideration in the selection of the Mandatory.

5. Other peoples, especially those of Central Africa, are at such a stage that the Mandatory must be responsible for the administration of the territory under conditions which will guarantee freedom of conscience and religion, subject only to the maintenance of public order and morals, the prohibition of abuses such as the slave trade, the arms traffic and the liquor traffic, and the prevention of the establishment of fortifications or military and naval bases and of military training of the natives for other than police purposes and the defense of territory, and will also secure equal opportunities for the trade and commerce of other Members of the League.

6. There are territories, such as Southwest Africa and certain of the South Pacific islands, which, owing to the sparseness of their population, or their small size, or their remoteness from the centers of civilization, or their geographical contiguity to the territory of the Mandatory, and other circumstances, can be best administered under the laws of the Mandatory as integral portions of its territory, subject to the safeguards above mentioned in the interests of the indigenous population.

7. In every case of mandate, the Mandatory shall render to the Council an annual report in reference to the territory committed to its charge.

8. The degree of authority, control or administration to be exercised by the Mandatory shall, if not previously agreed upon by the Members of the League, be explicitly defined in each case by the Council.

9. A permanent Commission shall be constituted to receive and examine the annual reports of the Mandatories and to advise the Council on all matters relating to the observance of the mandates.

ARTICLE 23. SOCIAL AND OTHER ACTIVITIES

Subject to and in accordance with the provisions of international conventions existing or hereafter to be agreed upon, the Members of the League:

(*a*) will endeavor to secure and maintain fair and humane conditions of labor for men, women and children, both in their own countries and in all countries to which their commercial and industrial relations extend, and for that purpose will establish and maintain the necessary international organizations;

(*b*) undertake to secure just treatment of the native inhabitants of territories under their control;

(*c*) will intrust the League with the general supervision over the execution of agreements with regard to traffic in women and children, and the traffic in opium and other dangerous drugs;

(*d*) will intrust the League with the general supervision of the trade in arms and ammunition with the countries in which the control of this traffic is necessary in the common interest;

(*e*) will make provision to secure and maintain freedom of communications and of transit and equitable treatment for the commerce of all Members of the League. In this connection, the special necessities of the regions devastated during the war of 1914–1918 shall be borne in mind;

(*f*) will endeavor to take steps in matters of international concern for the prevention and control of disease.

ARTICLE 24.   INTERNATIONAL BUREAUS

1. There shall be placed under the direction of the League all international bureaus already established by general treaties if the parties to such treaties consent. All such international bureaus and all commissions for the regulation of matters of international interest hereafter constituted shall be placed under the direction of the League.

2. In all matters of international interest which are regulated by general conventions but which are not placed under the control of international bureaus or commissions, the Secretariat of the League shall, subject to the consent of the Council and if desired by the parties, collect and distribute all relevant information and shall render any other assistance which may be necessary or desirable.

3. The Council may include as part of the expenses of the Secretariat the expenses of any bureau or commission which is placed under the direction of the League.

ARTICLE 25.   PROMOTION OF RED CROSS AND HEALTH

The Members of the League agree to encourage and promote the establishment and cooperation of duly authorized voluntary national Red Cross organizations having as purposes the improvement of health, the prevention of disease and the mitigation of suffering throughout the world.

ARTICLE 26. AMENDMENTS

1. Amendments to this Covenant will take effect when ratified by the Members of the League whose Representatives compose the Council and by a majority of the Members of the League whose Representatives compose the Assembly.

2. No such amendment shall bind any Member of the League which signifies its dissent therefrom, but in that case it shall cease to be a Member of the League.

Annex

I. ORIGINAL MEMBERS OF THE LEAGUE OF NATIONS, SIGNATORIES OF THE TREATY OF PEACE

*United States of America	Haiti
Belgium	*Hedjaz
Bolivia	Honduras
Brazil	Italy
British Empire	Japan
Canada	Liberia
Australia	Nicaragua
South Africa	Panama
New Zealand	Peru
India	Poland
China	Portugal
Cuba	Romania
†Ecuador	Serb-Croat-Slovene State [Yugoslavia]
France	Siam
Greece	Czechoslovakia
Guatemala	Uruguay

* Never accepted membership by ratification of treaty of peace.

† Did not accept membership by ratification of treaty of peace, but was admitted in 1934.

STATES INVITED TO ACCEDE TO THE COVENANT

Argentine Republic	Denmark
Chile	Netherlands
Colombia	Norway

Paraguay
Persia [now Iran]
Salvador
Spain

Sweden
Switzerland
Venezuela

II. FIRST SECRETARY-GENERAL OF THE LEAGUE OF NATIONS THE HONORABLE SIR JAMES ERIC DRUMMOND, K.C.M.G., C.B.

Appendix B

CHARTER OF THE
UNITED NATIONS

We the peoples of the United Nations determined

to save succeeding generations from the scourge of war, which twice in
our lifetime has brought untold sorrow to mankind, and

to reaffirm faith in fundamental human rights, in the dignity and worth
of the human person, in the equal rights of men and women and of
nations large and small, and

to establish conditions under which justice and respect for the obligations arising from treaties and other sources of international law
can be maintained, and

to promote social progress and better standards of life in larger freedom,

and for these ends

to practice tolerance and live together in peace with one another as good
neighbors, and

to unite our strength to maintain international peace and security, and

to ensure, by the acceptance of principles and the institution of methods,
that armed force shall not be used, save in the common interest, and

to employ international machinery for the promotion of the economic
and social advancement of all peoples,

have resolved to combine our efforts
to accomplish these aims.

Accordingly, our respective Governments, through representatives assembled in the city of San Francisco, who have exhibited their full

powers found to be in good and due form, have agreed to the present Charter of the United Nations and do hereby establish an international organization to be known as the United Nations.

Chapter I.   Purposes and Principles

ARTICLE 1

The Purposes of the United Nations are:

1. To maintain international peace and security, and to that end: to take effective collective measures for the prevention and removal of threats to the peace, and for the suppression of acts of aggression or other breaches of the peace, and to bring about by peaceful means, and in conformity with the principles of justice and international law, adjustment or settlement of international disputes or situations which might lead to a breach of the peace;

2. To develop friendly relations among nations based on respect for the principle of equal rights and self-determination of peoples, and to take other appropriate measures to strengthen universal peace;

3. To achieve international cooperation in solving international problems of an economic, social, cultural, or humanitarian character, and in promoting and encouraging respect for human rights and for fundamental freedoms for all without distinction as to race, sex, language, or religion; and

4. To be a center for harmonizing the actions of nations in the attainment of these common ends.

ARTICLE 2

The Organization and its Members, in pursuit of the Purposes stated in Article 1, shall act in accordance with the following Principles.

1. The Organization is based on the principle of the sovereign equality of all its Members.

2. All Members, in order to ensure to all of them the rights and benefits resulting from membership, shall fulfil in good faith the obligations assumed by them in accordance with the present Charter.

3. All Members shall settle their international disputes by peaceful means in such a manner that international peace and security, and justice, are not endangered.

4. All Members shall refrain in their international relations from the threat or use of force against the territorial integrity or political inde-

pendence of any state, or in any other manner inconsistent with the Purposes of the United Nations.

5. All Members shall give the United Nations every assistance in any action it takes in accordance with the present Charter, and shall refrain from giving assistance to any state against which the United Nations is taking preventive or enforcement action.

6. The Organization shall ensure that states which are not Members of the United Nations act in accordance with these Principles so far as may be necessary for the maintenance of international peace and security.

7. Nothing contained in the present Charter shall authorize the United Nations to intervene in matters which are essentially within the domestic jurisdiction of any state or shall require the Members to submit such matters to settlement under the present Charter; but this principle shall not prejudice the application of enforcement measures under Chapter VII.

Chapter II.   Membership

ARTICLE 3

The original Members of the United Nations shall be the states which, having participated in the United Nations Conference on International Organization at San Francisco, or having previously signed the Declaration by United Nations of January 1, 1942, sign the present Charter and ratify it in accordance with Article 110.

ARTICLE 4

1. Membership in the United Nations is open to all other peace-loving states which accept the obligations contained in the present Charter and, in the judgment of the Organization, are able and willing to carry out these obligations.

2. The admission of any such state to membership in the United Nations will be effected by a decision of the General Assembly upon the recommendation of the Security Council.

ARTICLE 5

A Member of the United Nations against which preventive or enforcement action has been taken by the Security Council may be suspended from the exercise of the rights and privileges of membership by the General Assembly upon the recommendation of the Security Council. The exercise of these rights and privileges may be restored by the Security Council.

ARTICLE 6

A Member of the United Nations which has persistently violated the Principles contained in the present Charter may be expelled from the Organization by the General Assembly upon the recommendation of the Security Council.

Chapter III.   Organs

ARTICLE 7

-1. There are established as the principal organs of the United Nations: a General Assembly, a Security Council, an Economic and Social Council, a Trusteeship Council, an International Court of Justice, and a Secretariat.

2. Such subsidiary organs as may be found necessary may be established in accordance with the present Charter.

ARTICLE 8

. The United Nations shall place no restrictions on the eligibility of men and women to participate in any capacity and under conditions of equality in its principal and subsidiary organs.

Chapter IV.   The General Assembly

COMPOSITION

ARTICLE 9

1. The General Assembly shall consist of all the Members of the United Nations.

2. Each Member shall have not more than five representatives in the General Assembly.

FUNCTIONS AND POWERS

ARTICLE 10

The General Assembly may discuss any questions or any matters within the scope of the present Charter or relating to the powers and functions of any organs provided for in the present Charter, and, except as provided in Article 12, may make recommendations to the Members of the United Nations or to the Security Council or to both on any such questions or matters.

ARTICLE 11

1. The General Assembly may consider the general principles of cooperation in the maintenance of international peace and security, including the principles governing disarmament and the regulation of armaments, and may make recommendations with regard to such principles to the Members or to the Security Council or to both.

2. The General Assembly may discuss any questions relating to the maintenance of international peace and security brought before it by any Member of the United Nations, or by the Security Council, or by a state which is not a Member of the United Nations in accordance with Article 35, paragraph 2, and, except as provided in Article 12, may make recommendations with regard to any such questions to the state or states concerned or to the Security Council or to both. Any such question on which action is necessary shall be referred to the Security Council by the General Assembly either before or after discussion.

3. The General Assembly may call the attention of the Security Council to situations which are likely to endanger international peace and security.

4. The powers of the General Assembly set forth in this Article shall not limit the general scope of Article 10.

ARTICLE 12

1. While the Security Council is exercising in respect of any dispute or situation the functions assigned to it in the present Charter, the General Assembly shall not make any recommendation with regard to that dispute or situation unless the Security Council so requests.

2. The Secretary-General, with the consent of the Security Council, shall notify the General Assembly at each session of any matters relative

to the maintenance of international peace and security which are being dealt with by the Security Council and shall similarly notify the General Assembly, or the Members of the United Nations if the General Assembly is not in session, immediately the Security Council ceases to deal with such matters.

ARTICLE 13

1. The General Assembly shall initiate studies and make recommendations for the purpose of:

a. promoting international cooperation in the political field and encouraging the progressive development of international law and its codification;

b. promoting international cooperation in the economic, social, cultural, educational, and health fields, and assisting in the realization of human rights and fundamental freedoms for all without distinction as to race, sex, language, or religion.

2. The further responsibilities, functions, and powers of the General Assembly with respect to matters mentioned in paragraph 1 (b) above are set forth in Chapters IX and X.

ARTICLE 14

Subject to the provisions of Article 12, the General Assembly may recommend measures for the peaceful adjustment of any situation, regardless of origin, which it deems likely to impair the general welfare or friendly relations among nations, including situations resulting from a violation of the provisions of the present Charter setting forth the Purposes and Principles of the United Nations.

ARTICLE 15

1. The General Assembly shall receive and consider annual and special reports from the Security Council; these reports shall include an account of the measures that the Security Council has decided upon or taken to maintain international peace and security.

2. The General Assembly shall receive and consider reports from the other organs of the United Nations.

ARTICLE 16

The General Assembly shall perform such functions with respect to the international trusteeship system as are assigned to it under Chapters XII and XIII, including the approval of the trusteeship agreements for areas not designated as strategic.

ARTICLE 17

1. The General Assembly shall consider and approve the budget of the Organization.

2. The expenses of the Organization shall be borne by the Members as apportioned by the General Assembly.

3. The General Assembly shall consider and approve any financial and budgetary arrangements with specialized agencies referred to in Article 57 and shall examine the administrative budgets of such specialized agencies with a view to making recommendations to the agencies concerned.

VOTING

ARTICLE 18

1. Each member of the General Assembly shall have one vote.

2. Decisions of the General Assembly on important questions shall be made by a two-thirds majority of the members present and voting. These questions shall include: recommendations with respect to the maintenance of international peace and security, the election of the non-permanent members of the Security Council, the election of the members of the Economic and Social Council, the election of members of the Trusteeship Council in accordance with paragraph 1 (c) of Article 86, the admission of new Members to the United Nations, the suspension of the rights and privileges of membership, the expulsion of Members, questions relating to the operation of the trusteeship system, and budgetary questions.

3. Decisions on other questions, including the determination of additional categories of questions to be decided by a two-thirds majority, shall be made by a majority of the members present and voting.

ARTICLE 19

A Member of the United Nations which is in arrears in the payment of its financial contributions to the Organization shall have no vote in the General Assembly if the amount of its arrears equals or exceeds the amount of the contributions due from it for the preceding two full years. The General Assembly may, nevertheless, permit such a Member to vote if it is satisfied that the failure to pay is due to conditions beyond the control of the Member.

PROCEDURE

ARTICLE 20

The General Assembly shall meet in regular annual sessions and in such special sessions as occasion may require. Special sessions shall be convoked by the Secretary-General at the request of the Security Council or of a majority of the Members of the United Nations.

ARTICLE 21

The General Assembly shall adopt its own rules of procedure. It shall elect its President for each session.

ARTICLE 22

The General Assembly may establish such subsidiary organs as it deems necessary for the performance of its functions.

Chapter V.   The Security Council

COMPOSITION

ARTICLE 23

1. The Security Council shall consist of eleven Members of the United Nations. The Republic of China, France, the Union of Soviet Socialist Republics, the United Kingdom of Great Britain and Northern Ireland, and the United States of America shall be permanent members of the Security Council. The General Assembly shall elect six other Members of the United Nations to be non-permanent members of the Security Council, due regard being specially paid, in the first instance to the contribution of Members of the United Nations to the maintenance of international peace and security and to the other purposes of the Organization, and also to equitable geographical distribution.

2. The non-permanent members of the Security Council shall be elected for a term of two years. In the first election of the non-permanent members, however, three shall be chosen for a term of one year. A retiring member shall not be eligible for immediate re-election.

3. Each member of the Security Council shall have one representative.

FUNCTIONS AND POWERS

ARTICLE 24

1. In order to ensure prompt and effective action by the United Nations, its Members confer on the Security Council primary responsibility for the maintenance of international peace and security, and agree that in carrying out its duties under this responsibility the Security Council acts on their behalf.

2. In discharging these duties the Security Council shall act in accordance with the Purposes and Principles of the United Nations. The specific powers granted to the Security Council for the discharge of these duties are laid down in Chapters VI, VII, VIII, and XII.

3. The Security Council shall submit annual and, when necessary, special reports to the General Assembly for its consideration.

ARTICLE 25

The Members of the United Nations agree to accept and carry out the decisions of the Security Council in accordance with the present Charter.

ARTICLE 26

In order to promote the establishment and maintenance of international peace and security with the least diversion for armaments of the world's human and economic resources, the Security Council shall be responsible for formulating, with the assistance of the Military Staff Committee referred to in Article 47, plans to be submitted to the Members of the United Nations for the establishment of a system for the regulation for armaments.

VOTING

ARTICLE 27

1. Each member of the Security Council shall have one vote.

2. Decisions of the Security Council on procedural matters shall be made by an affirmative vote of seven members.

3. Decisions of the Security Council on all other matters shall be

made by an affirmative vote of seven members including the concurring votes of the permanent members; provided that, in decisions under Chapter VI, and under paragraph 3 of Article 52, a party to a dispute shall abstain from voting.

PROCEDURE

ARTICLE 28

1. The Security Council shall be so organized as to be able to function continuously. Each member of the Security Council shall for this purpose be represented at all times at the seat of the Organization.

2. The Security Council shall hold periodic meetings at which each of its members may, if it so desires, be represented by a member of the government or by some other specially designated representative.

3. The Security Council may hold meetings at such places other than the seat of the Organization as in its judgment will best facilitate its work.

ARTICLE 29

The Security Council may establish such subsidiary organs as it deems necessary for the performance of its functions.

ARTICLE 30

The Security Council shall adopt its own rules of procedure, including the method of selecting its President.

ARTICLE 31

Any Member of the United Nations which is not a member of the Security Council may participate, without vote, in the discussion of any question brought before the Security Council whenever the latter considers that the interests of that Member are specially affected.

ARTICLE 32

Any Member of the United Nations which is not a member of the Security Council or any state which is not a Member of the United Nations, if it is a party to a dispute under consideration by the Security Council, shall be invited to participate, without vote, in the discussion relating to the dispute. The Security Council shall lay down such conditions as it deems just for the participation of a state which is not a Member of the United Nations.

Chapter VI. Pacific Settlement of Disputes

ARTICLE 33

1. The parties to any dispute, the continuance of which is likely to endanger the maintenance of international peace and security, shall, first of all, seek a solution by negotiation, enquiry, mediation, conciliation, arbitration, judicial settlement, resort to regional agencies or arrangements, or other peaceful means of their own choice.

2. The Security Council shall, when it deems necessary, call upon the parties to settle their dispute by such means.

ARTICLE 34

The Security Council may investigate any dispute, or any situation which might lead to international friction or give rise to a dispute, in order to determine whether the continuance of the dispute or situation is likely to endanger the maintenance of international peace and security.

ARTICLE 35

1. Any Member of the United Nations may bring any dispute, or any situation of the nature referred to in Article 34, to the attention of the Security Council or of the General Assembly.

2. A state which is not a Member of the United Nations may bring to the attention of the Security Council or of the General Assembly any dispute to which it is a party if it accepts in advance, for the purposes of the dispute, the obligations of pacific settlement provided in the present Charter.

3. The proceedings of the General Assembly in respect of matters brought to its attention under this Article will be subject to the provisions of Articles 11 and 12.

ARTICLE 36

1. The Security Council may, at any stage of a dispute of the nature referred to in Article 33 or of a situation of like nature, recommend appropriate procedures or methods of adjustment.

2. The Security Council should take into consideration any procedures for the settlement of the dispute which have already been adopted by the parties.

3. In making recommendations under this Article the Security Council should also take into consideration that legal disputes should as a general rule be referred by the parties to the International Court of Justice in accordance with the provisions of the Satute of the Court.

ARTICLE 37

1. Should the parties to a dispute of the nature referred to in Article 33 fail to settle it by the means indicated in that Article, they shall refer it to the Security Council.

2. If the Security Council deems that the continuance of the dispute is in fact likely to endanger the maintenance of international peace and security, it shall decide whether to take action under Article 36 or to recommend such terms of settlement as it may consider appropriate.

ARTICLE 38

Without prejudice to the provisions of Articles 33 to 37, the Security Council may, if all the parties to any dispute so request, make recommendations to the parties with a view to a pacific settlement of the dispute.

Chapter VII.   Action With Respect to Threats to the Peace, Breaches of the Peace, and Acts of Aggression

ARTICLE 39

The Security Council shall determine the existence of any threat to the peace, breach of the peace, or act of aggression and shall make recommendations, or decide what measures shall be taken in accordance with Articles 41 and 42, to maintain or restore international peace and security.

ARTICLE 40

In order to prevent an aggravation of the situation, the Security Council may, before making the recommendations or deciding upon the measures provided for in Article 39, call upon the parties concerned to comply with such provisional measures as it deems necessary or desirable. Such provisional measures shall be without prejudice to the rights, claims, or position of the parties concerned. The Security Council shall duly take account of failure to comply with such provisional measures.

ARTICLE 41

The Security Council may decide what measures not involving the use of armed force are to be employed to give effect to its decisions, and it may call upon the Members of the United Nations to apply such measures. These may include complete or partial interruption of economic relations and of rail, sea, air, postal, telegraphic, radio, and other means of communication, and the severance of diplomatic relations.

ARTICLE 42

Should the Security Council consider that measures provided for in Article 41 would be inadequate or have proved to be inadequate, it may take such action by air, sea, or land forces as may be necessary to maintain or restore international peace and security. Such action may include demonstrations, blockade, and other operations by air, sea, or land forces of Members of the United Nations.

ARTICLE 43

1. All Members of the United Nations, in order to contribute to the maintenance of international peace and security, undertake to make available to the Security Council, on its call and in accordance with a special agreement or agreements, armed forces, assistance, and facilities, including rights of passage, necessary for the purpose of maintaining international peace and security.

2. Such agreement or agreements shall govern the numbers and types of forces, their degree of readiness and general location, and the nature of the facilities and assistance to be provided.

3. The agreement or agreements shall be negotiated as soon as possible on the initiative of the Security Council. They shall be concluded between the Security Council and Members or between the Security Council and groups of Members and shall be subject to ratification by the signatory states in accordance with their respective constitutional processes.

ARTICLE 44

When the Security Council has decided to use force it shall, before calling upon a Member not represented on it to provide armed forces in fulfillment of the obligations assumed under Article 43, invite that Member, if the Member so desires, to participate in the decisions of the Security Council concerning the employment of contingents of that Member's armed forces.

ARTICLE 45

In order to enable the United Nations to take urgent military measures, Members shall hold immediately available national air-force contingents for combined international enforcement action. The strength and degree of readiness of these contingents and plans for their combined action shall be determined, within the limits laid down in the special agreement or agreements referred to in Article 43, by the Security Council with the assistance of the Military Staff Committee.

ARTICLE 46

Plans for the application of armed force shall be made by the Security Council with the assistance of the Military Staff Committee.

ARTICLE 47

1. There shall be established a Military Staff Committee to advise and assist the Security Council on all questions relating to the Security Council's military requirements for the maintenance of international peace and security, the employment and command of forces placed at its disposal, the regulation of armaments, and possible disarmament.

2. The Military Staff Committee shall consist of the Chiefs of Staff of the permanent members of the Security Council or their representatives. Any Member of the United Nations not permanently represented on the Committee shall be invited by the Committee to be associated with it when the efficient discharge of the Committee's responsibilities requires the participation of that Member in its work.

3. The Military Staff Committee shall be responsible under the Security Council for the strategic direction of any armed forces placed

at the disposal of the Security Council. Questions relating to the command of such forces shall be worked out subsequently.

4. The Military Staff Committee, with the authorization of the Security Council and after consultation with appropriate regional agencies, may establish regional subcommittees.

ARTICLE 48

1. The action required to carry out the decisions of the Security Council for the maintenance of international peace and security shall be taken by all the Members of the United Nations or by some of them, as the Security Council may determine.

2. Such decisions shall be carried out by the Members of the United Nations directly and through their action in the appropriate international agencies of which they are members.

ARTICLE 49

The Members of the United Nations shall join in affording mutual assistance in carrying out the measures decided upon by the Security Council.

ARTICLE 50

If preventive or enforcement measures against any state are taken by the Security Council, any other state, whether a Member of the United Nations or not, which finds itself confronted with special economic problems arising from the carrying out of those measures shall have the right to consult the Security Council with regard to a solution of those problems.

ARTICLE 51

Nothing in the present Charter shall impair the inherent right of individual or collective self-defense if an armed attack occurs against a Member of the United Nations, until the Security Council has taken the measures necessary to maintain international peace and security. Measures taken by Members in the exercise of this right of self-defense shall be immediately reported to the Security Council and shall not in any way affect the authority and responsibility of the Security Council under the present Charter to take at any time such action as it deems necessary in order to maintain or restore international peace and security.

Chapter VIII. Regional Arrangements

ARTICLE 52

1. Nothing in the present Charter precludes the existence of regional arrangements or agencies for dealing with such matters relating to the maintenance of international peace and security as are appropriate for regional action, provided that such arrangements or agencies and their activities are consistent with the Purposes and Principles of the United Nations.

2. The Members of the United Nations entering into such arrangements or constituting such agencies shall make every effort to achieve pacific settlement of local disputes through such regional arrangements or by such regional agencies before referring them to the Security Council.

3. The Security Council shall encourage the development of pacific settlement of local disputes through such regional arrangements or by such regional agencies either on the initiative of the states concerned or by reference from the Security Council.

4. This Article in no way impairs the application of Articles 34 and 35.

ARTICLE 53

1. The Security Council shall, where appropriate, utilize such regional arrangements or agencies for enforcement action under its authority. But no enforcement action shall be taken under regional arrangements or by regional agencies without the authorization of the Security Council, with the exception of measures against any enemy state, as defined in paragraph 2 of this Article, provided for pursuant to Article 107 or in regional arrangements directed against renewal of aggressive policy on the part of any such state, until such time as the Organization may, on request of the Governments concerned, be charged with the responsibility for preventing further aggression by such a state.

2. The term enemy state as used in paragraph 1 of this Article applies to any state which during the Second World War has been an enemy of any signatory of the present Charter.

ARTICLE 54

The Security Council shall at all times be kept fully informed of activities undertaken or in contemplation under regional arrangements or by regional agencies for the maintenance of international peace and security.

Chapter IX. International Economic and Social Cooperation

ARTICLE 55

With a view to the creation of conditions of stability and well-being which are necessary for peaceful and friendly relations among nations based on respect for the principle of equal rights and self-determination of peoples, the United Nations shall promote:

a. higher standards of living, full employment, and conditions of economic and social progress and development;

b. solutions of international economic, social, health, and related problems; and international cultural and educational cooperation; and

c. universal respect for, and observance of, human rights and fundamental freedoms for all without distinction as to race, sex, language, or religion.

ARTICLE 56

All Members pledge themselves to take joint and separate action in cooperation with the Organization for the achievement of the purposes set forth in Article 55.

ARTICLE 57

1. The various specialized agencies, established by intergovernmental agreement and having wide international responsibilities, as defined in their basic instruments, in economic, social, cultural, educational, health, and related fields, shall be brought into relationship with the United Nations in accordance with the provisions of Article 63.

2. Such agencies thus brought into relationship with the United Nations are hereinafter referred to as specialized agencies.

ARTICLE 58

The Organization shall make recommendations for the coordination of the policies and activities of the specialized agencies.

ARTICLE 59

The Organization shall, where appropriate, initiate negotiations among the states concerned for the creation of any new specialized agencies required for the accomplishment of the purposes set forth in Article 55.

ARTICLE 60

Responsibility for the discharge of the functions of the Organization set forth in this Chapter shall be vested in the General Assembly and, under the authority of the General Assembly, in the Economic and Social Council, which shall have for this purpose the powers set forth in Chapter X.

Chapter X. The Economic and Social Council

COMPOSITION

ARTICLE 61

1. The Economic and Social Council shall consist of eighteen Members of the United Nations elected by the General Assembly.

2. Subject to the provisions of paragraph 3, six members of the Economic and Social Council shall be elected each year for a term of three years. A retiring member shall be eligible for immediate re-election.

3. At the first election, eighteen members of the Economic and Social Council shall be chosen. The term of office of six members so chosen shall expire at the end of one year, and of six other members at the end of two years, in accordance with arrangements made by the General Assembly.

4. Each member of the Economic and Social Council shall have one representative.

FUNCTIONS AND POWERS

ARTICLE 62

1. The Economic and Social Council may make or initiate studies and reports with respect to international economic, social, cultural, educational, health, and related matters and may make recommendations with respect to any such matters to the General Assembly, to the Members of the United Nations, and to the specialized agencies concerned.

2. It may make recommendations for the purpose of promoting respect for, and observance of, human rights and fundamental freedoms for all.

3. It may prepare draft conventions for submission to the General Assembly, with respect to matters falling within its competence.

4. It may call, in accordance with the rules prescribed by the United Nations, international conferences on matters falling within its competence.

ARTICLE 63

1. The Economic and Social Council may enter into agreements with any of the agencies referred to in Article 57, defining the terms on which the agency concerned shall be brought into relationship with the United Nations. Such agreements shall be subject to approval by the General Assembly.

2. It may coordinate the activities of the specialized agencies through consultation with and recommendations to such agencies and through recommendations to the General Assembly and to the Members of the United Nations.

ARTICLE 64

1. The Economic and Social Council may take appropriate steps to obtain regular reports from the specialized agencies. It may make arrangements with the Members of the United Nations and with the specialized agencies to obtain reports on the steps taken to give effect to its own recommendations and to recommendations on matters falling within its competence made by the General Assembly.

2. It may communicate its observations on these reports to the General Assembly.

ARTICLE 65

The Economic and Social Council may furnish information to the Security Council and shall assist the Security Council upon its request.

ARTICLE 66

1. The Economic and Social Council shall perform such functions as fall within its competence in connection with the carrying out of the recommendations of the General Assembly.

2. It may, with the approval of the General Assembly, perform services at the request of Members of the United Nations and at the request of specialized agencies.

3. It shall perform such other functions as are specified elsewhere in the present Charter or as may be assigned to it by the General Assembly.

VOTING

ARTICLE 67

1. Each member of the Economic and Social Council shall have one vote.

2. Decisions of the Economic and Social Council shall be made by a majority of the members present and voting.

PROCEDURE

ARTICLE 68

The Economic and Social Council shall set up commissions in economic and social fields and for the promotion of human rights, and such other commissions as may be required for the performance of its functions.

ARTICLE 69

The Economic and Social Council shall invite any Member of the United Nations to participate, without vote, in its deliberations on any matter of particular concern to that Member.

ARTICLE 70

The Economic and Social Council may make arrangements for representatives of the specialized agencies to participate, without vote, in its deliberations and in those of the commissions established by it, and for its representatives to participate in the deliberations of the specialized agencies.

ARTICLE 71

The Economic and Social Council may make suitable arrangements for consultation with non-governmental organizations which are concerned with matters within its competence. Such arrangements may be made with international organizations and, where appropriate, with national organizations after consultation with the Member of the United Nations concerned.

ARTICLE 72

1. The Economic and Social Council shall adopt its own rules of procedure, including the method of selecting its President.

2. The Economic and Social Council shall meet as required in accordance with its rules, which shall include provision for the convening of meetings on the request of a majority of its members.

Chapter XI. Declaration Regarding Non-Self-Governing Territories

ARTICLE 73

Members of the United Nations which have or assume responsibilities for the administration of territories whose peoples have not yet attained a full measure of self-government recognize the principle that the interests of the inhabitants of these territories are paramount, and accept as a sacred trust the obligation to promote to the utmost, within the system of international peace and security established by the present Charter, the well-being of the inhabitants of these territories, and, to this end:

a. to ensure, with due respect for the culture of the peoples concerned, their political, economic, social, and educational advancement, their just treatment, and their protection against abuses;

b. to develop self-government, to take due account of the political aspirations of the peoples, and to assist them in the progressive development of their free political institutions, according to the particular circumstances of each territory and its peoples and their varying stages of advancement;

c. to further international peace and security;

d. to promote constructive measures of development, to encourage research, and to cooperate with one another and, when and where appropriate, with specialized international bodies with a view to the practical achievement of the social, economic, and scientific purposes set forth in this Article; and

e. to transmit regularly to the Secretary-General for information purposes, subject to such limitation as security and constitutional considerations may require, statistical and other information of a technical nature relating to economic, social, and educational conditions in the territories for which they are respectively responsible other than those territories to which Chapters XII and XIII apply.

ARTICLE 74

Members of the United Nations also agree that their policy in respect of the territories to which this Chapter applies, no less than in respect of their metropolitan areas, must be based on the general principle of good-neighborliness, due account being taken of the interests and well-being of the rest of the world, in social, economic, and commercial matters.

Chapter XII. International Trusteeship System

ARTICLE 75

The United Nations shall establish under its authority an international trusteeship system for the administration and supervision of such territories as may be placed thereunder by subsequent individual agreements. These territories are hereinafter referred to as trust territories.

ARTICLE 76

The basic objectives of the trusteeship system, in accordance with the Purposes of the United Nations laid down in Article 1 of the present Charter, shall be:

a. to further international peace and security;

b. to promote the political, economic, social, and educational advancement of the inhabitants of the trust territories, and their progressive development towards self-government or independence as may be appropriate to the particular circumstances of each territory and its peoples and the freely expressed wishes of the peoples concerned, and as may be provided by the terms of each trusteeship agreement;

c. to encourage respect for human rights and for fundamental freedoms for all without distinction as to race, sex, language, or religion, and to encourage recognition of the interdependence of the peoples of the world; and

d. to ensure equal treatment in social, economic, and commercial matters for all Members of the United Nations and their nationals, and also equal treatment for the latter in the administration of justice, without prejudice to the attainment of the foregoing objectives and subject to the provisions of Article 80.

ARTICLE 77

1. The trusteeship system shall apply to such territories in the following categories as may be placed thereunder by means of trusteeship agreements:

a. territories now held under mandate;

b. territories which may be detached from enemy states as a result of the Second World War; and

c. territories voluntarily placed under the system by states responsible for their administration.

2. It will be a matter for subsequent agreement as to which territories in the foregoing categories will be brought under the trusteeship system and upon what terms.

ARTICLE 78

The trusteeship system shall not apply to territories which have become Members of the United Nations, relationship among which shall be based on respect for the principle of sovereign equality.

ARTICLE 79

The terms of trusteeship for each territory to be placed under the trusteeship system, including any alteration or amendment, shall be agreed upon by the states directly concerned, including the mandatory power in the case of territories held under mandate by a Member of the United Nations, and shall be approved as provided for in Articles 83 and 85.

ARTICLE 80

1. Except as may be agreed upon in individual trusteeship agreements, made under Articles 77, 79, and 81, placing each territory under the trusteeship system, and until such agreements have been concluded, nothing in this Chapter shall be construed in or of itself to alter in any manner the rights whatsoever of any states or any peoples or the terms of existing international instruments to which Members of the United Nations may respectively be parties.

2. Paragraph 1 of this Article shall not be interpreted as giving grounds for delay or postponement of the negotiation and conclusion of agreements for placing mandated and other territories under the trusteeship system as provided for in Article 77.

ARTICLE 81

The trusteeship agreement shall in each case include the terms under which the trust territory will be administered and designate the authority which will exercise the administration of the trust territory. Such authority, hereinafter called the administering authority, may be one or more states or the Organization itself.

ARTICLE 82

There may be designated, in any trusteeship agreement, a strategic area or areas which may include part or all of the trust territory to which the agreement applies, without prejudice to any special agreement or agreements made under Article 43.

ARTICLE 83

1. All functions of the United Nations relating to strategic areas, including the approval of the terms of the trusteeship agreements and of

their alteration or amendment, shall be exercised by the Security Council.

2. The basic objectives set forth in Article 76 shall be applicable to the people of each strategic area.

3. The Security Council shall, subject to the provisions of the trusteeship agreements and without prejudice to security considerations, avail itself of the assistance of the Trusteeship Council to perform those functions of the United Nations under the trusteeship system relating to political, economic, social, and educational matters in the strategic areas.

ARTICLE 84

It shall be the duty of the administering authority to ensure that the trust territory shall play its part in the maintenance of international peace and security. To this end the administering authority may make use of volunteer forces, facilities, and assistance from the trust territory in carrying out the obligations towards the Security Council undertaken in this regard by the administering authority, as well as for local defense and the maintenance of law and order within the trust territory.

ARTICLE 85

1. The functions of the United Nations with regard to trusteeship agreements for all areas not designated as strategic, including the approval of the terms of the trusteeship agreements and of their alteration or amendment, shall be exercised by the General Assembly.

2. The Trusteeship Council, operating under the authority of the General Assembly, shall assist the General Assembly in carrying out these functions.

Chapter XIII. The Trusteeship Council

COMPOSITION

ARTICLE 86

1. The Trusteeship Council shall consist of the following Members of the United Nations:

a. those Members administering trust territories;

b. such of those Members mentioned by name in Article 23 as are not administering trust territories; and

c. as many other Members elected for three-year terms by the General Assembly as may be necessary to ensure that the total number of members of the Trusteeship Council is equally divided between those Members of the United Nations which administer trust territories and those which do not.

2. Each member of the Trusteeship Council shall designate one specially qualified person to represent it therein.

FUNCTIONS AND POWERS

ARTICLE 87

The General Assembly and, under its authority, the Trusteeship Council, in carrying out their functions, may:

a. consider reports submitted by the administering authority;

b. accept petitions and examine them in consultation with the administering authority;

c. provide for periodic visits to the respective trust territories at times agreed upon with the administering authority; and

d. take these and other actions in conformity with the terms of the trusteeship agreements.

ARTICLE 88

The Trusteeship Council shall formulate a questionnaire on the political, economic, social, and educational advancement of the inhabitants of each trust territory, and the administering authority for each trust territory within the competence of the General Assembly shall make an annual report to the General Assembly upon the basis of such questionnaire.

VOTING

ARTICLE 89

1. Each member of the Trusteeship Council shall have one vote.

2. Decisions of the Trusteeship Council shall be made by a majority of the members present and voting.

PROCEDURE

ARTICLE 90

1. The Trusteeship Council shall adopt its own rules of procedure, including the method of selecting its President.

2. The Trusteeship Council shall meet as required in accordance with its rules, which shall include provision for the convening of meetings on the request of a majority of its members.

ARTICLE 91

The Trusteeship Council shall, when appropriate, avail itself of the assistance of the Economic and Social Council and of the specialized agencies in regard to matters with which they are respectively concerned.

Chapter XIV.   The International Court of Justice

ARTICLE 92

The International Court of Justice shall be the principal judicial organ of the United Nations. It shall function in accordance with the annexed Statute, which is based upon the Statute of the Permanent Court of International Justice and forms an integral part of the present Charter.

ARTICLE 93

1. All Members of the United Nations are *ipso facto* parties to the Statute of the International Court of Justice.

2. A state which is not a Member of the United Nations may become a party to the Statute of the International Court of Justice on conditions to be determined in each case by the General Assembly upon the recommendation of the Security Council.

ARTICLE 94

1. Each Member of the United Nations undertakes to comply with the decision of the International Court of Justice in any case to which it is a party.

2. If any party to a case fails to perform the obligations incumbent upon it under a judgment rendered by the Court, the other party may have recourse to the Security Council, which may, if it deems necessary, make recommendations or decide upon measures to be taken to give effect to the judgment.

ARTICLE 95

Nothing in the present Charter shall prevent Members of the United Nations from entrusting the solution of their differences to other tribunals by virtue of agreements already in existence or which may be concluded in the future.

ARTICLE 96

1. The General Assembly or the Security Council may request the International Court of Justice to give an advisory opinion on any legal question.

2. Other organs of the United Nations and specialized agencies, which may at any time be so authorized by the General Assembly, may also request advisory opinions of the Court on legal questions arising within the scope of their activities.

Chapter XV.   The Secretariat

ARTICLE 97

The Secretariat shall comprise a Secretary-General and such staff as the Organization may require. The Secretary-General shall be appointed by the General Assembly upon the recommendation of the Security Council. He shall be the chief administrative officer of the Organization.

ARTICLE 98

The Secretary-General shall act in that capacity in all meetings of the .General Assembly, of the Security Council, of the Economic and Social Council, and of the Trusteeship Council, and shall perform such other functions as are entrusted to him by these organs. The Secretary-General shall make an annual report to the General Assembly on the work of the Organization.

ARTICLE 99

The Secretary-General may bring to the attention of the Security Council any matter which in his opinion may threaten the maintenance of international peace and security.

ARTICLE 100

1. In the performance of their duties the Secretary-General and the staff shall not seek or receive instructions from any government or from any other authority external to the Organization. They shall refrain from any action which might reflect on their position as international officials responsible only to the Organization.

2. Each Member of the United Nations undertakes to respect the exclusively international character of the responsibilities of the Secretary-General and the staff and not to seek to influence them in the discharge of their responsibilities.

ARTICLE 101

1. The staff shall be appointed by the Secretary-General under regulations established by the General Assembly.

2. Appropriate staffs shall be permanently assigned to the Economic and Social Council, the Trusteeship Council, and, as required, to other organs of the United Nations. These staffs shall form a part of the Secretariat.

3. The paramount consideration in the employment of the staff and in the determination of the conditions of service shall be the necessity of securing the highest standards of efficiency, competence, and integrity. Due regard shall be paid to the importance of recruiting the staff on as wide a geographical basis as possible.

Chapter XVI. Miscellaneous Provisions

ARTICLE 102

1. Every treaty and every international agreement entered into by any Member of the United Nations after the present Charter comes into force shall as soon as possible be registered with the Secretariat and published by it.

2. No party to any such treaty or international agreement which has not been registered in accordance with the provisions of paragraph 1 of this Article may invoke that treaty or agreement before any organ of the United Nations.

ARTICLE 103

In the event of a conflict between the obligations of the Members of the United Nations under the present Charter and their obligations under any other international agreement, their obligations under the present Charter shall prevail.

ARTICLE 104

The Organization shall enjoy in the territory of each of its Members such legal capacity as may be necessary for the exercise of its functions and the fulfillment of its purposes.

ARTICLE 105

1. The Organization shall enjoy in the territory of each of its Members such privileges and immunities as are necessary for the fulfillment of its purposes.

2. Representatives of the Members of the United Nations and officials of the Organization shall similarly enjoy such privileges and immunities as are necessary for the independent exercise of their functions in connection with the Organization.

3. The General Assembly may make recommendations with a view to determining the details of the application of paragraphs 1 and 2 of this Article or may propose conventions to the Members of the United Nations for this purpose.

Chapter XVII. Transitional Security Arrangements

ARTICLE 106

Pending the coming into force of such special agreements referred to in Article 43 as in the opinion of the Security Council enable it to begin the exercise of its responsibilities under Article 42, the parties to the Four-Nation Declaration, signed at Moscow, October 30, 1943, and France, shall, in accordance with the provisions of paragraph 5 of that Declaration, consult with one another and as occasion requires with other Members of the United Nations with a view to such joint action on behalf of the Organization as may be necessary for the purpose of maintaining international peace and security.

ARTICLE 107

Nothing in the present Charter shall invalidate or preclude action, in relation to any state which during the Second World War has been an enemy of any signatory to the present Charter, taken or authorized as a result of that war by the Governments having responsibility for such action.

Chapter XVIII. Amendments

ARTICLE 108

Amendments to the present Charter shall come into force for all Members of the United Nations when they have been adopted by a vote of two thirds of the members of the General Assembly and ratified in accordance with their respective constitutional processes by two thirds of the Members of the United Nations, including all the permanent members of the Security Council.

ARTICLE 109

1. A General Conference of the Members of the United Nations for the purpose of reviewing the present Charter may be held at a date and place to be fixed by a two-thirds vote of the members of the General Assembly and by a vote of any seven members of the Security Council. Each Member of the United Nations shall have one vote in the conference.

2. Any alteration of the present Charter recommended by a two-thirds vote of the conference shall take effect when ratified in accordance with their respective constitutional processes by two thirds of the Members of the United Nations including all the permanent members of the Security Council.

3. If such a conference has not been held before the tenth annual session of the General Assembly following the coming into force of the

present Charter, the proposal to call such a conference shall be placed on the agenda of that session of the General Assembly, and the conference shall be held if so decided by a majority vote of the members of the General Assembly and by a vote of any seven members of the Security Council.

Chapter XIX. Ratification and Signature

ARTICLE 110

1. The present Charter shall be ratified by the signatory states in accordance with their respective constitutional processes.

2. The ratifications shall be deposited with the Government of the United States of America, which shall notify all the signatory states of each deposit as well as the Secretary-General of the Organization when he has been appointed.

3. The present Charter shall come into force upon the deposit of ratifications by the Republic of China, France, the Union of Soviet Socialist Republics, the United Kingdom of Great Britain and Northern Ireland, and the United States of America, and by a majority of the other signatory states. A protocol of the ratifications deposited shall thereupon be drawn up by the Government of the United States of America which shall communicate copies thereof to all the signatory states.

4. The states signatory to the present Charter which ratify it after it has come into force will become original Members of the United Nations on the date of the deposit of their respective ratifications.

ARTICLE 111

The present Charter, of which the Chinese, French, Russian, English, and Spanish texts are equally authentic, shall remain deposited in the archives of the Government of the United States of America. Duly certified copies thereof shall be transmitted by that Government to the Governments of the other signatory states.

IN FAITH WHEREOF the representatives of the Governments of the United Nations have signed the present Charter.

DONE at the city of San Francisco the twenty-sixth day of June, one thousand nine hundred and forty-five.

Appendix C

STATUTE OF THE INTERNATIONAL COURT OF JUSTICE

ARTICLE 1

The International Court of Justice established by the Charter of the United Nations as the principal judicial organ of the United Nations shall be constituted and shall function in accordance with the provisions of the present Statute.

Chapter I. Organization of the Court

ARTICLE 2

The Court shall be composed of a body of independent judges, elected regardless of their nationality from among persons of high moral character, who possess the qualifications required in their respective countries for appointment to the highest judicial offices, or are jurisconsults of recognized competence in international law.

ARTICLE 3

1. The Court shall consist of fifteen members, no two of whom may be nationals of the same state.
2. A person who for the purposes of membership in the Court could be regarded as a national of more than one state shall be deemed to be a national of the one in which he ordinarily exercises civil and political rights.

ARTICLE 4

1. The members of the Court shall be elected by the General Assembly and by the Security Council from a list of persons nominated by the national groups in the Permanent Court of Arbitration, in accordance with the following provisions.

2. In the case of Members of the United Nations not represented in the Permanent Court of Arbitration, candidates shall be nominated by national groups appointed for this purpose by their governments under the same conditions as those prescribed for members of the Permanent Court of Arbitration by Article 44 of the Convention of The Hague of 1907 for the pacific settlement of international disputes.

3. The conditions under which a state which is a party to the present Statute but is not a Member of the United Nations may participate in electing the members of the Court shall, in the absence of a special agreement, be laid down by the General Assembly upon recommendation of the Security Council.

ARTICLE 5

1. At least three months before the date of the election, the Secretary-General of the United Nations shall address a written request to the members of the Permanent Court of Arbitration belonging to the states which are parties to the present Statute, and to the members of the national groups appointed under Article 4, paragraph 2, inviting them to undertake, within a given time, by national groups, the nomination of persons in a position to accept the duties of a member of the Court.

2. No group may nominate more than four persons, not more than two of whom shall be of their own nationality. In no case may the number of candidates nominated by a group be more than double the number of seats to be filled.

ARTICLE 6

Before making these nominations, each national group is recommended to consult its highest court of justice, its legal faculties and schools of law, and its national academies and national sections of international academies devoted to the study of law.

ARTICLE 7

1. The Secretary-General shall prepare a list in alphabetical order of all the persons thus nominated. Save as provided in Article 12, paragraph 2, these shall be the only persons eligible.

2. The Secretary-General shall submit this list to the General Assembly and to the Security Council.

ARTICLE 8

The General Assembly and the Security Council shall proceed independently of one another to elect the members of the Court.

ARTICLE 9

At every election, the electors shall bear in mind not only that the persons to be elected should individually possess the qualifications required, but also that in the body as a whole the representation of the main forms of civilization and of the principal legal systems of the world should be assured.

ARTICLE 10

1. Those candidates who obtain an absolute majority of votes in the General Assembly and in the Security Council shall be considered as elected.

2. Any vote of the Security Council, whether for the election of judges or for the appointment of members of the conference envisaged in Article 12, shall be taken without any distinction between permanent and non-permanent members of the Security Council.

3. In the event of more than one national of the same state obtaining an absolute majority of the votes both of the General Assembly and of the Security Council, the eldest of these only shall be considered as elected.

ARTICLE 11

If, after the first meeting held for the purpose of the election, one or more seats remain to be filled, a second and, if necessary, a third meeting shall take place.

ARTICLE 12

1. If, after the third meeting, one or more seats still remain un-filled, a joint conference consisting of six members, three appointed by the General Assembly and three by the Security Council, may be formed at any time at the request of either the General Assembly or the Security Council, for the purpose of choosing by the vote of an absolute majority one name for each seat still vacant, to submit to the General Assembly and the Security Council for their respective acceptance.

2. If the joint conference is unanimously agreed upon any person who fulfils the required conditions, he may be included in its list, even though he was not included in the list of nominations referred to in Article 7.

3. If the joint conference is satisfied that it will not be successful in procuring an election, those members of the Court who have already been elected shall, within a period to be fixed by the Security Council, proceed to fill the vacant seats by selection from among those candidates who have obtained votes either in the General Assembly or in the Security Council.

4. In the event of an equality of votes among the judges, the eldest judge shall have a casting vote.

ARTICLE 13

1. The members of the Court shall be elected for nine years and may be re-elected; provided, however, that of the judges elected at the first election, the terms of five judges shall expire at the end of three years and the terms of five more judges shall expire at the end of six years.

2. The judges whose terms are to expire at the end of the above-mentioned initial periods of three and six years shall be chosen by lot to be drawn by the Secretary-General immediately after the first election has been completed.

3. The members of the Court shall continue to discharge their duties until their places have been filled. Though replaced, they shall finish any cases which they may have begun.

4. In the case of the resignation of a member of the Court, the resignation shall be addressed to the President of the Court for transmission to the Secretary-General. This last notification makes the place vacant.

ARTICLE 14

Vacancies shall be filled by the same method as that laid down for the first election, subject to the following provision: the Secretary-General shall, within one month of the occurrence of the vacancy, proceed to issue the invitations provided for in Article 5, and the date of the election shall be fixed by the Security Council.

ARTICLE 15

A member of the Court elected to replace a member whose term of office has not expired shall hold office for the remainder of his predecessor's term.

ARTICLE 16

1. No member of the Court may exercise any political or administrative function, or engage in any other occupation of a professional nature.

2. Any doubt on this point shall be settled by the decision of the Court.

ARTICLE 17

1. No member of the Court may act as agent, counsel, or advocate in any case.

2. No member may participate in the decision of any case in which he has previously taken part as agent, counsel, or advocate for one of the parties, or as a member of a national or international court, or of a commission of enquiry, or in any other capacity.

3. Any doubt on this point shall be settled by the decision of the Court.

ARTICLE 18

1. No member of the Court can be dismissed unless, in the unanimous opinion of the other members, he has ceased to fulfil the required conditions.

2. Formal notification thereof shall be made to the Secretary-General by the Registrar.

3. This notification makes the place vacant.

ARTICLE 19

The members of the Court, when engaged on the business of the Court, shall enjoy diplomatic privileges and immunities.

ARTICLE 20

Every member of the Court shall, before taking up his duties, make a solemn declaration in open court that he will exercise his powers impartially and conscientiously.

ARTICLE 21

1. The Court shall elect its President and Vice-President for three years; they may be re-elected.
2. The Court shall appoint its Registrar and may provide for the appointment of such other officers as may be necessary.

ARTICLE 22

1. The seat of the Court shall be established at The Hague. This, however, shall not prevent the Court from sitting and exercising its functions elsewhere whenever the Court considers it desirable.
2. The President and the Registrar shall reside at the seat of the Court.

ARTICLE 23

1. The Court shall remain permanently in session, except during the judicial vacations, the dates and duration of which shall be fixed by the Court.
2. Members of the Court are entitled to periodic leave, the dates and duration of which shall be fixed by the Court, having in mind the distance between The Hague and the home of each judge.
3. Members of the Court shall be bound, unless they are on leave or prevented from attending by illness or other serious reasons duly explained to the President, to hold themselves permanently at the disposal of the Court.

ARTICLE 24

1. If, for some special reason, a member of the Court considers that he should not take part in the decision of a particular case, he shall so inform the President.

2. If the President considers that for some special reason one of the members of the Court should not sit in a particular case, he shall give him notice accordingly.

3. If in any such case the member of the Court and the President disagree, the matter shall be settled by the decision of the Court.

ARTICLE 25

1. The full Court shall sit except when it is expressly provided otherwise in the present Statute.

2. Subject to the condition that the number of judges available to constitute the Court is not thereby reduced below eleven, the Rules of the Court may provide for allowing one or more judges, according to circumstances and in rotation, to be dispensed from sitting.

3. A quorum of nine judges shall suffice to constitute the Court.

ARTICLE 26

1. The Court may from time to time form one or more chambers, composed of three or more judges as the Court may determine, for dealing with particular categories of cases; for example, labor cases and cases relating to transit and communications.

2. The Court may at any time form a chamber for dealing with a particular case. The number of judges to constitute such a chamber shall be determined by the Court with the approval of the parties.

3. Cases shall be heard and determined by the chambers provided for in this Article if the parties so request.

ARTICLE 27

A judgment given by any of the chambers provided for in Articles 26 and 29 shall be considered as rendered by the Court.

ARTICLE 28

The chambers provided for in Articles 26 and 29, may, with the consent of the parties, sit and exercise their functions elsewhere than at The Hague.

ARTICLE 29

With a view to the speedy despatch of business, the Court shall form annually a chamber composed of five judges which, at the request of the parties, may hear and determine cases by summary procedure. In addition, two judges shall be selected for the purpose of replacing judges who find it impossible to sit.

ARTICLE 30

1. The Court shall frame rules for carrying out its functions. In particular, it shall lay down rules of procedure.

2. The Rules of the Court may provide for assessors to sit with the Court or with any of its chambers, without the right to vote.

ARTICLE 31

1. Judges of the nationality of each of the parties shall retain their right to sit in the case before the Court.

2. If the Court includes upon the Bench a judge of the nationality of one of the parties, any other party may choose a person to sit as judge. Such person shall be chosen preferably from among those persons who have been nominated as candidates as provided in Articles 4 and 5.

3. If the Court includes upon the Bench no judge of the nationality of the parties, each of these parties may proceed to choose a judge as provided in paragraph 2 of this Article.

4. The provisions of this Article shall apply to the case of Articles 26 and 29. In such cases, the President shall request one or, if necessary, two of the members of the Court forming the chamber to give place to the members of the Court of the nationality of the parties concerned, and, failing such, or if they are unable to be present, to the judges specially chosen by the parties.

5. Should there be several parties in the same interest, they shall, for the purpose of the preceding provisions, be reckoned as one party

only. Any doubt upon this point shall be settled by the decision of the Court.

6. Judges chosen as laid down in paragraphs 2, 3, and 4 of this Article shall fulfil the conditions required by Articles 2, 17 (paragraph 2), 20, and 24 of the present Statute. They shall take part in the decision on terms of complete equality with their colleagues.

ARTICLE 32

1. Each member of the Court shall receive an annual salary.
2. The President shall receive a special annual allowance.
3. The Vice-President shall receive a special allowance for every day on which he acts as President.
4. The judges chosen under Article 31, other than members of the Court, shall receive compensation for each day on which they exercise their functions.
5. These salaries, allowances, and compensations shall be fixed by the General Assembly. They may not be decreased during the term of office.
6. The salary of the Registrar shall be fixed by the General Assembly on the proposal of the Court.
7. Regulations made by the General Assembly shall fix the conditions under which retirement pensions may be given to members of the Court and to the Registrar, and the conditions under which members of the Court and the Registrar shall have their traveling expenses refunded.
8. The above salaries, allowances, and compensation shall be free of all taxation.

ARTICLE 33

The expenses of the Court shall be borne by the United Nations in such a manner as shall be decided by the General Assembly.

Chapter II.   Competence of the Court

ARTICLE 34

1. Only states may be parties in cases before the Court.
2. The Court, subject to and in conformity with its Rules, may request of public international organizations information relevant to cases

before it, and shall receive such information presented by such organizations on their own initiative.

3. Whenever the construction of the constituent instrument of a public international organization or of an international convention adopted thereunder is in question in a case before the Court, the Registrar shall so notify the public international organization concerned and shall communicate to it copies of all the written proceedings.

ARTICLE 35

1. The Court shall be open to the states parties to the present Statute.

2. The conditions under which the Court shall be open to other states shall, subject to the special provisions contained in treaties in force, be laid down by the Security Council, but in no case shall such conditions place the parties in a position of inequality before the Court.

3. When a state which is not a Member of the United Nations is a party to a case, the Court shall fix the amount which that party is to contribute towards the expenses of the Court. This provision shall not apply if such state is bearing a share of the expenses of the Court.

ARTICLE 36

1. The jurisdiction of the Court comprises all cases which the parties refer to it and all matters specially provided for in the Charter of the United Nations or in treaties and conventions in force.

2. The states parties to the present Statute may at any time declare that they recognize as compulsory *ipso facto* and without special agreement, in relation to any other state accepting the same obligation, the jurisdiction of the Court in all legal disputes concerning:

  a. the interpretation of a treaty;

  b. any question of international law;

  c. the existence of any fact which, if established, would constitute a breach of an international obligation;

  d. the nature or extent of the reparation to be made for the breach of an international obligation.

3. The declarations referred to above may be made unconditionally or on condition of reciprocity on the part of several or certain states, or for a certain time.

4. Such declarations shall be deposited with the Secretary-General of the United Nations, who shall transmit copies thereof to the parties to the Statute and to the Registrar of the Court.

5. Declarations made under Article 36 of the Statute of the Permanent Court of International Justice and which are still in force shall be deemed, as between the parties to the present Statute, to be acceptances of the compulsory jurisdiction of the International Court of Justice for the period which they still have to run and in accordance with their terms.

6. In the event of a dispute as to whether the Court has jurisdiction, the matter shall be settled by the decision of the Court.

ARTICLE 37

Whenever a treaty or convention in force provides for reference of a matter to a tribunal to have been instituted by the League of Nations, or to the Permanent Court of International Justice, the matter shall, as between the parties to the present Statute, be referred to the International Court of Justice.

ARTICLE 38

1. The Court, whose function is to decide in accordance with international law such disputes as are submitted to it, shall apply:

a. international conventions, whether general or particular, establishing rules expressly recognized by the contesting states;

b. international custom, as evidence of a general practice accepted as law;

c. the general principles of law recognized by civilized nations;

d. subject to the provisions of Article 59, judicial decisions and the teachings of the most highly qualified publicists of the various nations, as subsidiary means for the determination of rules of law.

2. This provision shall not prejudice the power of the Court to decide a case *ex aequo et bono,* if the parties agree thereto.

Chapter III. Procedure

ARTICLE 39

1. The official languages of the Court shall be French and English. If the parties agree that the case shall be conducted in French, the judgment shall be delivered in French. If the parties agree that the case shall be conducted in English, the judgment shall be delivered in English.

2. In the absence of an agreement as to which language shall be

employed, each party may, in the pleadings, use the language which it prefers; the decision of the Court shall be given in French and English. In this case the Court shall at the same time determine which of the two texts shall be considered as authoritative.

3. The Court shall, at the request of any party, authorize a language other than French or English to be used by that party.

ARTICLE 40

1. Cases are brought before the Court, as the case may be, either by the notification of the special agreement or by a written application addressed to the Registrar. In either case the subject of the dispute and the parties shall be indicated.

2. The Registrar shall forthwith communicate the application to all concerned.

3. He shall also notify the Members of the United Nations through the Secretary-General, and also any other states entitled to appear before the Court.

ARTICLE 41

1. The Court shall have the power to indicate, if it considers that circumstances so require, any provisional measures which ought to be taken to preserve the respective rights of either party.

2. Pending the final decision, notice of the measures suggested shall forthwith be given to the parties and to the Security Council.

ARTICLE 42

1. The parties shall be represented by agents.

2. They may have the assistance of counsel or advocates before the Court.

3. The agents, counsel, and advocates of parties before the Court shall enjoy the privileges and immunities necessary to the independent exercise of their duties.

ARTICLE 43

1. The procedure shall consist of two parts: written and oral.

2. The written proceedings shall consist of the communication to the Court and to the parties of memorials, counter-memorials and, if necessary, replies; also all papers and documents in support.

3. These communications shall be made through the Registrar, in the order and within the time fixed by the Court.

4. A certified copy of every document produced by one party shall be communicated to the other party.

5. The oral proceedings shall consist of the hearing by the Court of witnesses, experts, agents, counsel, and advocates.

ARTICLE 44

1. For the service of all notices upon persons other than the agents, counsel, and advocates, the Court shall apply direct to the government of the state upon whose territory the notice has to be served.

2. The same provision shall apply whenever steps are to be taken to procure evidence on the spot.

ARTICLE 45

The hearing shall be under the control of the President or, if he is unable to preside, of the Vice-President; if neither is able to preside, the senior judge present shall preside.

ARTICLE 46

The hearing in Court shall be public, unless the Court shall decide otherwise, or unless the parties demand that the public be not admitted.

ARTICLE 47

1. Minutes shall be made at each hearing and signed by the Registrar and the President.

2. These minutes alone shall be authentic.

ARTICLE 48

The Court shall make orders for the conduct of the case, shall decide the form and time in which each party must conclude its arguments, and make all arrangements connected with the taking of evidence.

ARTICLE 49

The Court may, even before the hearing begins, call upon the agents to produce any document or to supply any explanations. Formal note shall be taken of any refusal.

ARTICLE 50

The Court may, at any time, entrust any individual, body, bureau, commission, or other organization that it may select, with the task of carrying out an enquiry or giving an expert opinion.

ARTICLE 51

During the hearing any relevant questions are to be put to the witnesses and experts under the conditions laid down by the Court in the rules of procedure referred to in Article 30.

ARTICLE 52

After the Court has received the proofs and evidence within the time specified for the purpose, it may refuse to accept any further oral or written evidence that one party may desire to present unless the other side consents.

ARTICLE 53

1. Whenever one of the parties does not appear before the Court, or fails to defend its case, the other party may call upon the Court to decide in favor of its claim.

2. The Court must, before doing so, satisfy itself, not only that it has jurisdiction in accordance with Articles 36 and 37, but also that the claim is well founded in fact and law.

ARTICLE 54

1. When, subject to the control of the Court, the agents, counsel, and advocates have completed their presentation of the case, the President shall declare the hearing closed.

2. The Court shall withdraw to consider the judgment.

3. The deliberations of the Court shall take place in private and remain secret.

ARTICLE 55

1. All questions shall be decided by a majority of the judges present.

2. In the event of an equality of votes, the President or the judge who acts in his place shall have a casting vote.

ARTICLE 56

1. The judgment shall state the reasons on which it is based.
2. It shall contain the names of the judges who have taken part in the decision.

ARTICLE 57

If the judgment does not represent in whole or in part the unanimous opinion of the judges, any judge shall be entitled to deliver a separate opinion.

ARTICLE 58

The judgment shall be signed by the President and by the Registrar. It shall be read in open court, due notice having been given to the agents.

ARTICLE 59

The decision of the Court has no binding force except between the parties and in respect of that particular case.

ARTICLE 60

The judgment is final and without appeal. In the event of dispute as to the meaning or scope of the judgment, the Court shall construe it upon the request of any party.

ARTICLE 61

1. An application for revision of a judgment may be made only when it is based upon the discovery of some fact of such a nature as to be a decisive factor, which fact was, when the judgment was given, unknown to the Court and also to the party claiming revision, always provided that such ignorance was not due to negligence.
2. The proceedings for revision shall be opened by a judgment of the Court expressly recording the existence of the new fact, recognizing

that it has such a character as to lay the case open to revision, and declaring the application admissible on this ground.

3. The Court may require previous compliance with the terms of the judgment before it admits proceedings in revision.

4. The application for revision must be made at latest within six months of the discovery of the new fact.

5. No application for revision may be made after the lapse of ten years from the date of the judgment.

ARTICLE 62

1. Should a state consider that it has an interest of a legal nature which may be affected by the decision in the case, it may submit a request to the Court to be permitted to intervene.

2. It shall be for the Court to decide upon this request.

ARTICLE 63

1. Whenever the construction of a convention to which states other than those concerned in the case are parties is in question, the Registrar shall notify all such states forthwith.

2. Every state so notified has the right to intervene in the proceedings; but if it uses this right, the construction given by the judgment will be equally binding upon it.

ARTICLE 64

Unless otherwise decided by the Court, each party shall bear its own costs.

Chapter IV.   Advisory Opinions

ARTICLE 65

1. The Court may give an advisory opinion on any legal question at the request of whatever body may be authorized by or in accordance with the Charter of the United Nations to make such a request.

2. Questions upon which the advisory opinion of the Court is asked shall be laid before the Court by means of a written request containing

an exact statement of the question upon which an opinion is required, and accompanied by all documents likely to throw light upon the question.

ARTICLE 66

1. The Registrar shall forthwith give notice of the request for an advisory opinion to all states entitled to appear before the Court.

2. The Registrar shall also, by means of a special and direct communication, notify any state entitled to appear before the Court or international organization considered by the Court, or, should it not be sitting, by the President, as likely to be able to furnish information on the question, that the Court will be prepared to receive, within a time limit to be fixed by the President, written statements, or to hear, at a public sitting to be held for the purpose, oral statements relating to the question.

3. Should any such state entitled to appear before the Court have failed to receive the special communication referred to in paragraph 2 of this Article, such state may express a desire to submit a written statement or to be heard; and the Court will decide.

4. States and organizations having presented written or oral statements or both shall be permitted to comment on the statements made by other states or organizations in the form, to the extent, and within the time limits which the Court, or, should it not be sitting, the President, shall decide in each particular case. Accordingly, the Registrar shall in due time communicate any such written statements to states and organizations having submitted similar statements.

ARTICLE 67

The Court shall deliver its advisory opinions in open court, notice having been given to the Secretary-General and to the representatives of Members of the United Nations, of other states and of international organizations immediately concerned.

ARTICLE 68

In the exercise of its advisory functions the Court shall further be guided by the provisions of the present Statute which apply in contentious cases to the extent to which it recognizes them to be applicable.

Chapter V.   Amendment

ARTICLE 69

Amendments to the present Statute shall be effected by the same procedure as is provided by the Charter of the United Nations for amendments to that Charter, subject however to any provisions which the General Assembly upon recommendation of the Security Council may adopt concerning the participation of states which are parties to the present Statute but are not Members of the United Nations.

ARTICLE 70

The Court shall have power to propose such amendments to the present Statute as it may deem necessary, through written communications to the Secretary-General, for consideration in conformity with the provisions of Article 69.

INDEX

399